WOMEN ON THE DEFENSIVE

Living through

Conservative Times

WOMEN on the DEFENSIVE

Sylvia Bashevkin

The University of Chicago Press

Chicago & London

SYLVIA BASHEVKIN is professor of political science at the University of Toronto. She is the author of *Toeing the Lines: Women and Party Politics in English Canada* and *True Patriot Love: The Politics of Canadian Nationalism* and the editor of *Canadian Political Behaviour* and *Women and Politics in Western Europe.*

The University of Chicago Press, Chicago 60637
The University of Chicago Press, Ltd., London
© 1998 by Sylvia Bashevkin
All rights reserved. Published 1998
Printed in the United States of America
07 06 05 04 03 02 01 00 99 98   1 2 3 4 5
ISBN: 0–226-03883–1 (cloth)
ISBN: 0–226-03885–8 (paper)

Library of Congress Cataloging-in-Publication Data
Bashevkin, Sylvia B.
     Women on the defensive : living through conservative times /
Sylvia Bashevkin.
          p.   cm.
     Includes bibliographical references and index.
     ISBN 0-226-03883-1 (cloth : alk. paper). — ISBN 0-226-03885-8
(pbk. : alk. paper)
     1. Women's rights—History—20th century—Cross-cultural studies.
     2. Women in politics—History—20th century—Cross-cultural studies.
     3. Feminism—History—20th century—Cross-cultural studies.
     I. Title.
     HQ1236.B27   1998
     305.42′09′04—dc21   97-35168
                                                              CIP

⊗ The paper used in this publication meets the minimum requirements of the American National Standard for Information Sciences— Permanence of Paper for Printed Library Materials, ANSI Z39.48–1992.

Contents

Acknowledgments

Let me begin where most authors end, by thanking my husband and daughters for their good humor and encouragement. Together, they ensured that I got out enough to experience what life was like under new conservative leaders in Canada, the United States, and Great Britain. I credit much of the vigor of this manuscript to their sustained faith in the project and to their infectious high spirits.

The broad outlines of what became *Women on the Defensive* appeared in four scholarly journal articles, published in *International Political Science Review* (July 1994), *Canadian Journal of Political Science* (December 1994 and June 1996), and *Comparative Political Studies* (January 1996). The text of this book is up-to-date through the middle of 1997, and all monetary amounts are reported in the currency of the respective country.

I am grateful to the anonymous readers who assessed both the journal articles and this longer manuscript and to Maureen Baker, R. J. Benewick, William Berman, Stephen Clarkson, Martin Durham, Beth Fischer, Vivien Hart, Judith Adler Hellman, Joni Lovenduski, Tanya Melich, Donald J. Savoie, Ronnee Schreiber, Suzanne Staggenborg, Maren Stein, Gladys Symons, Annis May Timpson, and Lisa Young for their helpful comments. Colleagues at Simon Fraser University, the University of British Columbia, the University of California at Irvine, Georgetown University, the University of New Brunswick at St. John, the University of Toronto Faculty of Law, the 1993 American Political Science Association meetings, the 1994 Société québécoise de science politique conference, and the 1994 Canadian Political Science Association meetings all helped to sharpen the arguments presented here, as did participants in the Feminist Legal Analysis section of the Ontario Bar Association.

The field research for this study was supported by the Social Sciences and Humanities Research Council of Canada, and a teaching leave was provided by the Connaught Research Fund at the University of Toronto. I am extremely grateful to both organizations for their support. Many research assistants helped to keep the project moving, and I want to thank Sian Evans in London; Rebecca Leitman and Christy Chandler in Washington, D.C.; and Lisa Young, Jocelyne Praud, Karen Jones, Cheryl Collier, Vito Ciraco, Louise Ferrie-Blecher, Julie Bernier, Karen Murray, and Yan Peng in Toronto.

Many thanks to Eleanor Dennison, Hyla Levy, and Marian Reed of the University of Toronto for their help in preparing the manuscript and to Laura Larson for her copyediting at the final stage. I particularly appreciate the insightful guidance offered by John Tryneski, senior editor at the University of Chicago Press, who remained ever mindful of the author's own voice.

My most humbling debt in this project is to the more than one hundred activists and experts who shared their views of what happened during conservative times. In Britain, the United States, and Canada, these respondents granted time for interviews and ongoing access to a wealth of primary materials. As promised, I have tried to protect their anonymity each step of the way. To each and every interviewee, my deepest thanks.

All errors of fact and judgment remain mine alone.

Introduction

On the edge of the public gardens in what was once a thriving industrial city, gangs of young people gather day and night around a large
statue. They wear torn clothes, heavy boots, and thick metallic studs
all over. Many look thin and drawn. None appears to work in the common sense of the word. The youths are watched from a distance by
police and private security guards, who cluster around the doors of
department stores, electronics outlets, and jewelry shops.

Hordes of women shoppers are also out, searching for end-of-
summer bargains. They step carefully around cardboard platforms and
sleeping bags belonging to older homeless people, who curl along the
edges of Market Street. Like the shoppers, the shy lap dogs leashed to
the sleepers keep a wary eye on the youths, who from time to time
tease their fierce fighting dogs.

Nearly all of the shoppers look better nourished than the youths and
the homeless. They seem to have money to spend, places to live, a
sense of security. Yet, on closer look, tension and more are apparent
on these women's faces. Taut jaws, deep lines, and the not so occasional black eye stand out. Their children are edgy, agitated, sometimes bruised. Kids are tired of shopping, mothers are tired of being
patient, and everyone is trying to navigate an uneasy truce among the
gangs, the sleepers, and the police.

The city is Manchester, and the statue is a graffiti-covered Queen
Victoria. Critics of British conservatism say this same scene appears
virtually everywhere, except in a few affluent pockets of the urban
Southeast. In trendy parts of London, they argue, rising property values and a well-dressed middle class mask the rot at the core of British
society since 1979. Conservatives hardly agree. In their view, home-

lessness, unemployment, and other problems were created by a failure to be economically competitive and personally responsible. There was no choice but to build on the ruins left by previous governments.

Six months later, the large Toronto concert hall is sold out, full of affluent, middle-aged women who watch a fashion show and gourmet cooking demonstration before the main event. On an extremely cold night even by Canadian standards, the lobby is a sea of fur coats, coiffed heads, and glittering accessories. The main speaker is introduced by a conservative journalist who blasts government spending, socialism, and high public deficits. She urges tonight's guest to come out of retirement to govern Canada, now afflicted with the dreaded "British disease."

The audience is primed for the main attraction, who appears on stage in high black pumps and a bright red suit. Margaret Thatcher proceeds to wow the audience with her interpretive history of the twentieth century. The struggle between communism and individual freedom, between fascism and the Allies, between big government and personal choice are pivots as she hammers home the free market theology that is her trademark.

During the question-and-answer session, one woman asks about the need for some state activities, to provide for public education and health care. Thatcher replies that current tax rates are simply not sustainable; she claims that private investment and economic growth only occur in low-tax, free market environments. The audience erupts in thunderous, sustained cheering. The evening concludes with yet more animated applause and, in most of the hall, a standing ovation.

One month later during lunch hour on a hot day in Washington, D.C., a woman calls out, "Sign the petition. Fight pornography and violence against women." She is standing at a busy corner beside a small table, dressed completely in black. Her arms hold a large sign and a huge *Hustler* magazine cover. Throngs of well-dressed women pass by every minute, as do nearly as many well-dressed men. Women walking by smile at the sign. It says, PORNOGRAPHY VIOLATES WOMEN. FEMINISTS FIGHTING PORNOGRAPHY.

The voice yells, "I want your signatures, not your smiles. Don't call us when you get raped." "What a bitch," one woman mutters. "She's totally cracked," another remarks. Men glance up at the poster, giggle, and keep on walking. After a short time, the woman folds up her stand and disappears into the crowd.

Whatever happened to the vibrant social movements of the 1960s and 1970s? Were they swallowed up in the greedy good times of the 1980s? Did the lean, mean 1990s spell final disaster, as more and more people adopted a "me first" approach to life?

Social scientists write about cycles of protest, the peaks and valleys marking the high and low points of group activity.[1] It is not surprising that they tend to focus on the heights—the energetic periods when soaring involvement stimulates fresh ideas and new claims for public awareness and response. Far less research examines the valleys, the periods after movements establish themselves, when progress may be slower and opposition greater than during earlier times.

This book presents the first comparative view of a very significant valley for modern feminism. Only four years after the United Nations declared 1975 the International Year of the Woman, Margaret Thatcher became prime minister of Britain. Thatcher's Conservative regime was committed to reducing the size of government, including its welfare state dimension. Along with John Major, her successor as party leader, she emphasized individual initiative and personal responsibility as the keys to Britain's future. Thatcher's impatience with groups and the basic idea of collective action was never ambiguous. In fact, she insisted there was no such thing as society, only individuals and families.[2] Thatcher directly challenged the power of trade unions and questioned what the women's movement had ever done for her.[3] Clearly, that movement faced a formidable challenge during more than seventeen years of Conservative rule following 1979.

The ideas associated with the neoconservative revolution or Thatcherism in Britain also gained currency across the Atlantic. In 1980, Ronald Reagan became president of the United States and was succeeded in 1988 by his vice president, George Bush. Together, Reagan and Bush held office for twelve years. Both of these Republicans admired Thatcher's philosophy of small government and individual responsibility, themes they embellished with an emphasis on "family values" and social conservatism. Not only did Reagan and Bush seek to restrict an already limited U.S. welfare state—when compared with its Western industrial counterparts—but also they sought to advance an agenda on abortion and employment issues that was directly at odds with that of the American women's movement.

In 1984, Canadians elected a Conservative government led by Brian Mulroney. During his nine years as prime minister, Mulroney selectively adapted themes from Thatcher and Reagan for a Canadian audience. Less government, more open trading patterns, and a shift of power away from the federal level were hallmarks of his Conservative platform. Each position clashed with women's movement views, particularly in English Canada, where Mulroney's policies on free trade and the constitution were bitterly contested.

Like Thatcher and Reagan, Mulroney had begun life as an outsider. Raised in a small mining settlement in northern Quebec, he had an early upbringing as modest as that of Thatcher (who grew up over the family grocery store in Grantham) and Reagan (who spent his youth in the economically depressed towns of the American Midwest). All three grew up far from their nation's capital, instilled with a fervent sense of individual initiative and a belief that, left to their own devices, local people could and would take care of each other. They also viewed government as an onerous burden, a heavy weight that Reagan later described in his autobiography as "the silent form of socialism."[4] This enemy had created too much public bureaucracy, government regulation, taxes, and welfare dependence. Their common prescription for the ailment was equally clear: lower taxes, reduced government spending, deregulation, and an emphasis on individual, voluntary effort.

Beyond their ideas, Thatcher, Reagan, and Mulroney shared a fiercely partisan view of politics. Each was committed to defeating not just Labour, Democratic, and Liberal incumbents but also the interventionist policies these parties had pursued. All three leaders seemed to enjoy power and its varied trappings, seeing themselves as beacons of light for individual freedom on the world stage. Thatcher and Mulroney worked to bring their countries closer to the United States, a nation they both deeply admired, just as they worked to build close personal relationships with Ronald Reagan. In later years when they were all out of office and Reagan was in poor health, Thatcher celebrated her seventieth birthday at a massive gala for more than six hundred guests in Washington, D.C. Brian Mulroney and Nancy Reagan were featured speakers, paying warm tribute to the evening's honoree.[5] The Anglo-American triumvirate, in short, formed an exclusive mutual admiration society, one that had its bases in shared experiences, visions, and friendships.

Feminist organizations in Britain, the United States, and Canada faced off against this cozy trio during the conservative years. They were on the defensive—facing political leaders and a public mood that wanted government to do less, not more; that wanted people to make responsible choices individually, not present radical demands collectively. In a defensive situation, groups have all they can do to hold on to what they won before things changed, let alone to move forward beyond that point. Although the movements women organized and the leaders people elected did vary, the grounds for conflict were clear. In each case, tough times had replaced better ones. Women's groups were forced to reassess, to reevaluate, to deal with what Susan Faludi termed the politics of "backlash."[6]

This study extends Faludi's account in arguing that the new conservative challenge was far more than a strictly American phenomenon. The chapters that follow demonstrate how organized feminism in all three countries faced a shared political threat, a common wall of opposition that varied in its appearance and could be scaled or otherwise breached in differing ways. What happened after 1979, we maintain, is an international story that hinges on a basic shift on both sides of the Atlantic. From this perspective, the Thatcher-Reagan-Mulroney years were an age of not just economic but also political globalization. Conservative forces were ascendant in more than one context, squeezing out alternative points of view across national boundaries. Trade unions, moderate and left political parties, environmental groups, and civil rights organizations all found themselves on the defensive along with women's groups, marginalized by a dominant belief system that ceded little room to competing outlooks.

Feminism, defined here as the organized pursuit of women's social, political, and economic equality, developed in the late nineteenth century as part of a broadly progressive challenge to the status quo. Both early activism in the suffrage period and following and also what became modern feminism in the late 1960s and following were predicated on a positive role for government. *Intervention, regulation,* and *bureaucracy* were far from dirty words in the lexicon of twentieth-century women's movements, because achievements like pure food and drug or equal pay laws were grounded in these very concepts.

By way of contrast, the new or neoconservatism of Margaret Thatcher, Ronald Reagan, and Brian Mulroney explicitly rejected the baggage of positive government. These leaders embraced an individualist, pro-market creed that elevated personal responsibility far above any notion of the state's role. Each adopted tough-minded and often punitive language in dealing with advocates of an older, pro-community perspective, whether these critics were inside or outside their own parties. Margaret Thatcher, for example, spoke in scornful terms of the compromising "wets" in the British Conservative party as well as the "moaning minnies" outside it who kept talking about unemployment rates.[7]

By refusing to view governments as responsible for their citizens and seeing individuals as responsible only for themselves, conservatives after 1979 effected a major realignment of political ideas. Conservatism no longer elevated the traditions and values of a broadly defined social unit. Instead, it was a libertarian-style defense of the right of achieving individuals to earn more, spend more, consume more, and pay less to support those who did not achieve in material terms. This ethos, however, was tempered in all three cases and especially in the United States by a social conservatism that said women's choices would not be their own, particularly on the issue of abortion. In this respect, the pure libertarian achiever of the neoconservatives remained an entrepreneurial man, just as he was in the age of Adam Smith.

Placing the spotlight on materially successful individuals meant conservatives of the Thatcher, Reagan, and Mulroney variety gave short shrift to everyone else. A person who upheld the pro-market doctrine was described early on by Margaret Thatcher as "one of us," a phrase that clearly cast others as unwelcome outsiders.[8] Political critics and social protesters were in the latter category, alongside welfare recipients, minority group activists, and others who did not embrace the new conservative message on individual achievement. Divisions between insiders and outsiders, rich and poor, blacks and whites, men and women, widened as a result of both the discourse and actions of conservative governments. This social polarization represents what American political scientist Joel Krieger calls the "de-integrative" face of the new conservatism.[9] It became a slow but steady fragmentation, eroding any sense of shared identity that transcended individuals. Not surprisingly, what disappeared was the same social outlook that new conservatives sought to deny at the level of ideas.

How British, American, and Canadian women's movements managed in tough times is the subject of this book. Using a wide variety of sources including public debates and interviews with more than a hundred activists in the three countries, *Women on the Defensive* presents the first comprehensive account of what happened in the conservative era. The story reveals both setbacks and persistence, a mixture of difficult losses as well as some progress despite right-of-center leaders. In each case, women's groups managed to challenge crucial parts of the conservative agenda. Marches, demonstrations, lobbies, and media campaigns all helped to focus critical attention on each regime. But even though they survived Thatcher, Reagan, Mulroney, and their successors, feminists were clearly placed on the defensive by these leaders. And like any defensive struggle, this one entailed serious costs.

First, many participants were exhausted, burned out by the experience of organizing in hard times. The strong individualism of the period made it difficult to attract new activists. This swing away from collective values opened up space for opponents to argue that women were already equal, that equality was a luxury in tough times, or that protesters were by nature whiners and bleeding hearts who could never be satisfied. Faced with these charges, groups in each country tried to shift gears but not always in a unified way. Differences between moderate and militant ways of coping with the conservative challenge became evident in all three countries. Second, the fact that governments switched their priorities and reduced spending in such areas as housing, pensions, and welfare made life worse for significant numbers of women—particularly single mothers and the elderly. Poverty and economic insecurity tend to put a damper on political involvement and remain negative, depressing issues on their own. In simple terms, movement organizations often found it difficult to respond to the rush of bad news. Much of what conservative governments did to cut programs happened quickly, secretively, and in such a convoluted way that groups had trouble explaining just how harsh these measures really were. Finally, we need to emphasize that some women benefited from the economic growth and conservative policies of the 1980s and following. Equipped with advanced education and, in growing numbers of cases, professional degrees, affluent "women in suits" commanded good jobs, decent salaries, and unprecedented social prestige. What they held in common with impoverished teenage mothers or widowed pensioners was, over time, less and less apparent.

Women on the Defensive begins at the level of ideas, where the collision between conservatism and feminism had its bases. Chapter 1 argues that leading women's groups endorsed government intervention in the economy and greater spending on social welfare programs, while they rejected private, individual answers to public problems. Conventional patterns of order, hierarchy, and decision making—including in the family—were directly challenged. By way of contrast, leading conservatives after 1979 wanted to scale back the size and scope of government. Freeing business from the yoke of state regulation and privatizing what had been public sector activities would get government off people's backs and allow individuals to take responsibility for their own lives. In the United States in particular, prominent conservatives embraced the same traditional social values endorsed by the Catholic Church and by Protestant fundamentalist and evangelical denominations.

How did this collision of ideas play out politically? Chapter 2 examines policy battles between women's groups and conservatives, comparing developments before versus after the elections of Thatcher, Reagan, and Mulroney. The record of what national legislatures and courts decided *before* these leaders came to power shows considerable momentum for groups in the United States, the United Kingdom, and the Canadian Parliament—momentum that was later stopped and virtually reversed in the first two cases. In Britain and the United States, movement claims fared demonstrably worse after conservative political executives came to power—and they did worse over time in the shift from Thatcher to Major, and especially from Reagan to Bush. In Canada, court and legislative decisions were more pro-feminist during the Mulroney years than earlier, since constitutional equality rights came into force in 1985. Yet other bitter conflicts divided Canadian Conservatives and women's groups.

How else did conservative elites affect women's lives? Chapter 3 examines the "money crunch," the pattern of policy changes that reduced public spending and government regulation in many areas. Because large numbers of women in all three countries were clients as well as employees of state programs, the question of how conservatives influenced work, welfare, taxation, and so on, is crucial. In general, eligibility rules for social welfare programs were tightened, and, in both North American cases, responsibility was devolved from federal governments to lower levels. Conservatives also attempted to cut off the flow of funds to groups and programs that opposed these directions. The language conservatives used to isolate and marginalize their critics grew more harsh, more polarizing over time. Overall, the money crunch not only impoverished many women in the general public, but it also led to a fraying of the broader social fabric that had been woven since the era of the Great Depression.

Chapter 4 turns to the informal side of the story. More than a hundred movement activists in the three countries were questioned about their experiences in tough times. Many shared a common sense of not being listened to and feeling like outsiders once conservatives won power. In comparative terms, their reflections reveal how activists in North America could exploit multiple cracks in federal systems, whereas British movement groups tried to move forward using levers that were available through the European Community. Five women from each country reflect on what transpired. Their comments reveal the day-to-day story of life on the defensive: trying to hold on to previous gains, maintain public credibility, reverse new proposals from the right, and, at the same time, offer something positive to retain and attract supporters. They describe how sustained conflict between conservatives and feminists unfolded, including in Canada and Britain where the formal record was more favorable than that in the United States.

Tough times strained cohesion among women in all three countries. Chapter 5 shows how internal splits opened up in the years after 1979, in part because conservative leaders relied on a divide-and-conquer approach. British Tories could point to the towering presence of Margaret Thatcher as proof that no ambitious woman needed a movement in order to succeed. The growth of organized antifeminism on the American right allowed the Reagan and Bush administrations to claim they were helping women, while they actively blocked what feminists saw as progress. Canadian Conservatives were able to divide feminists internally, often using prominent politicians like Justice Minister Kim Campbell to drive the wedge. Although these splits did not destroy women's movements, they cut women off from each other and cast doubt on efforts to represent them as a coherent interest.

Were circumstances different after these conservatives lost power? Chapter 6 assesses developments beginning with the 1992 defeat of George Bush and the election of a Democrat, Bill Clinton, as U.S. president. In 1993, Canadian Liberals led by Jean Chrétien returned to power, and, in 1997, the British Labour party led by Tony Blair won its first general election in nearly twenty years. Each change was greeted enthusiastically by many movement activists, who believed they were at last emerging from a long, dark period. Yet new leaders seemed reluctant to serve as close allies, as all three established a clear distance from women's groups. The ideas of conservative individualism remained powerful in that leaders like Clinton, Chrétien, and Blair were loath to expand either public spending or government intervention.

The options available to new political executives were limited by the fiscal situations they inherited. Both Clinton and Chrétien faced a veritable mountain of debt upon assuming power—to the point that extensive government borrowing under Reagan, Bush, and Mulroney belied their fiscal responsibility rhetoric. Moreover, once Republicans won control of the U.S. Senate and House of Representatives in 1994, social conservatives became ever more outspoken critics of women's movement claims. In Canada, the Chrétien government embarked on a massive program of spending cuts that dwarfed earlier efforts during the Mulroney years.

For students of public policy, this analysis sheds light on a number of core themes in the comparative literature. On the question of federal versus unitary state structures, materials presented in chapters 2 and following reveal that feminist groups were *not* weakest in Canada, the most decentralized of the three cases under consideration. Beginning with the classic work of David Truman in the early 1950s, political scientists have hypothesized that federal systems of dividing power between national and subnational levels of government tend to weaken societal interests. Groups, according to this perspective, organize themselves in a way that mirrors the larger federal arrangement; because interests are thus fragmented and decentralized, their internal unity is compromised—along with their effectiveness.[10]

Truman's approach suggests organizations working in a unitary system like the British one would be advantaged, because their target audience remains centralized in one identifiable location, Westminster. Interests operating in this environment would not be forced to spread out geographically to pressure multiple sources of subnational power and could concentrate resources on a single national target. Both North American systems considered in this study are federal ones, with Canada considerably larger in territory, more sparsely settled, and more decentralized in jurisdictional terms than the United States. If the three cases are arrayed along a spectrum, therefore, from most to least centralized, their order would be Britain, then the United States, and finally Canada.

The argument that centralized state structures translate into advantageous conditions for women's groups, however, is not sustained by the results of this study. British feminism of the 1970s and 1980s was in many respects a radical, grassroots phenomenon; as activists describe in their own words in chapter 4, groups that did pursue legislative and judicial change seemed more distant from the corridors of power than their North American counterparts. The fact that feminist campaigns to change British employment law, for example, often implicated institutions of the European Union (notably the European Court of Justice) underlines their very limited clout among domestic elites during the Thatcher years. Conversely, Truman's view would predict the ability neither of American feminists to move forward a broad policy agenda at the national and state levels through the 1970s nor of Canadian organizations to gain important advances at federal and provincial levels through the Mulroney years. Contrary to views of the unitary state as an advantage, therefore, federal arrangements with their multiple access points appeared to assist feminist interests, because decision makers in North America could not exert "a reliable power of veto" over group claims as they could in Britain.[11]

More important, this study challenges key assumptions about the success of organized interests in congressional versus parliamentary systems. A series of institutional arguments, advanced primarily by researchers based in the United States, maintains that groups with a diffuse base of support (including environmental and feminist organizations) are better off in the American context with its separation of powers at the national level, weak patterns of party discipline, and multiple points of access. This same literature points to disadvantages facing groups in parliamentary systems, in which powerful political executives in a majority government situation have little reason to compromise with external interests.[12]

A similar line of argument appears in the comparative literature on women and politics, in which an opportunity structures approach has been used to explain the conditions under which feminists were or, alternatively, were not effective policy players. One of the best-known statements of this view appeared in Joyce Gelb's *Feminism and Politics,* a 1989 study of groups in the United States, Great Britain, and Sweden. Gelb portrays women's movements that remain "separate from" partisan and trade union organizations as more likely to exert "political impact" than those that enter coalitions with other interests.[13] Her view suggests movements outside the American congressional system cannot be as influential as organized feminism in the United States, because the former tend to be less independent or autonomous than the latter. Parallel with a larger institutional literature, Gelb's position indicates parliamentary structures are by definition less congenial to women's movement claims than U.S.-style congressional ones.

This line of argument generates predictions that are directly at odds with the evidence presented in this book. If applied to the fate of women's movement claims after conservative leaders won office, Gelb's approach would expect feminism in the United States to lose less ground, or hold up far better, than its Canadian or British counterparts—a pattern that contradicts the findings of this study. From a Canadian perspective, the lack of constitutionally entrenched equality rights in the United States and the long absence (until early 1993) of national parental leave provisions render suspect the use of an American standard with respect to movement success.

At a conceptual level, this study suggests researchers turn away from assumptions about the inherent advantages of congressional systems and autonomous feminist groups. It focuses instead on the challenges facing movement activists and their allies in conservative times and on the varied responses they managed to organize despite these circumstances. If any analytic conclusions can be drawn from the chapters that follow, they are that elite preferences combined with groups' ability to circumvent them matter a great deal. Boldly stated, women's groups in the United States were undermined by the social conservatism of the 1980s and following, a phenomenon that cut across executive, judicial, and legislative branches of government and extended its influence to think tanks, the mass media, and other opinion-leading institutions. British and Canadian activists were advantaged by the relative disinterest of Thatcher and Mulroney in social issues and by access to European Community levers in the case of the United Kingdom and constitutional equality rights in the case of Canada. In short, cross-national variation hardly unfolded in such a way as to privilege the American women's movement.

Before turning to the clash of ideas, it is important to stress that this account of Britain, the United States, and Canada cannot cover every facet of the conflict between feminists and conservatives. The goal in each case is to present the general picture at the national level in the hope that others will tell more of the story. From this juncture, one pattern is clear. After 1979, women's organizations hardly possessed the awesome power attributed to them by opponents on the political right, who had their own reasons for exaggerating the other side. Nor had these groups retreated en masse, reeling from the effects of a conservative surge. Feminism neither took over nor fell apart; as usual, reality was a somewhat more complicated mixture of steps forward and backward. The irony remains that while leading groups were locked in a sustained, bitter conflict with Thatcher, Reagan, Mulroney, and their successors, some women in the general public were doing extremely well while others—and far more of them—were falling through what was left of the social safety net. In the same period as the death of feminism was announced, public opinion polls showed widespread support for many movement claims.

Women on the Defensive presents a story of contradictions, a blend of ups and downs in which women as a group were both influential and challenged, effective but embattled.

CHAPTER ONE Ideas Collide

Do ideas matter? Emphatically, yes. Witness the bitter conflict between conservative leaders and women's groups that unfolded after 1979 in Britain, after 1980 in the United States, and after 1984 in Canada.

Why the collision? Early women's organizations grew out of pro-reform, pro–social welfare ferment during the early part of the twentieth century. Leading women's groups in the Anglo-American world retain a similar outlook through the 1990s. They continue to see governments as contributing to the larger social good—as fulfilling a useful purpose, for example, when they regulate the workplace, provide health care programs, or finance public pensions. Conservatives of the Thatcher, Reagan, and Mulroney variety, however, begin with a very different approach. Not only did fiscal realities since the 1970s make social welfare programs unaffordable, in their view, but also these projects amounted to state meddling in the lives of individual citizens. New or neoconservatives believe government regulation and expansive social programs should be resisted and dismantled rather than celebrated. The less the state does, from their perspective, the better.

This clash of ideas threw into bold relief the fundamental denial of an inclusive social unit by new conservatives. In rejecting the collective values central to conventional Toryism in Britain and Canada, Margaret Thatcher and Brian Mulroney championed a profoundly individualist doctrine that had little to do with their parties' traditions. No longer was the notion of an organically integrated society at the core of the modern Tory ethos. In turning his back on the Republican embrace of unity and healing in the aftermath of the American Civil War, Ronald Reagan also turned away from the sense of social solidarity that preoccupied many of his predecessors. All three leaders elevated a new conservative individualism that downplayed social relations among citizens, and instead they highlighted personal achievement by seemingly anomic producers and consumers. Society, community, cohesion, and the bonds that bring people together were consequently devalued in a race to make not just economies but also individuals more competitive.

The elevation of the achieving, ambitious individual went hand in hand with direct attacks on collective action. Except for like-minded business groups, conservatives showed little patience for other organized interests. Efforts were made to diminish and ultimately demolish the other side, meaning those who defended some notion of a collectivity that transcended achieving individuals. The argument that no humane person can develop in a milieu that denies the common good was squelched in due course.

New conservatives made it unfashionable to defend all kinds of dissident collective interests, not just those of modern feminism. Margaret Thatcher's claim that unions did more to hurt than help workers heaped disdain on core collectivist values in Britain. In the United States, new conservatives undermined civil rights efforts to offer greater opportunities to blacks and other minorities. By the 1990s, it was possible to open a book written by an African American author that alleged liberalism was more menacing than racism.[1] Brian Mulroney's argument that continental free trade would enrich individuals denied nationalist claims that it would destroy Canada. In each case, new conservatives advanced a pro-achievement, pro-individualist position that ceded little room to competing traditions of collective action, social protest, and progressive political engagement. Women's groups, in short, were far from the only interests placed on the defensive after 1979.

The clash of divergent starting points led to sustained battles over laws, budgets, and court cases. In Great Britain, Margaret Thatcher's conviction leadership on the right clashed with a generally left-of-center feminist agenda. Conservatives and women's groups found little common ground in the United States, where social traditionalists and disgruntled ex-liberals found a powerful ally in Ronald Reagan. In Canada, Brian Mulroney was more of a pragmatist than an ideologue, but he borrowed enough from the Thatcher and Reagan scripts to antagonize leading women's groups. As the clash of ideas became clear in all three cases, feminists came to see each of these leaders as a serious opponent if not outright enemy of women's advancement.

What were the core assumptions of women's groups and conservative leaders? This chapter contrasts the main views of both sides to reveal how the collision of ideas unfolded in each country. In Britain, the government's role in the economy in addition to questions of social order and welfare policy were bitterly contested. In the United States, social norms, public spending, and the role of the federal government formed a crucial pivot. In Canada, ideas about the primacy of both the federal government and business interests sharply diverged.

Because leading conservatives and women's organizations differed on so many key principles, policy battles between the two sides were bitter, sustained, and virtually unavoidable. Both Thatcherism and British feminism were entrenched worldviews to which their adherents held firm. Much of the British women's movement had its origins in oppositional social protest, far from the well-connected Establishment that surrounded Thatcher in the Conservative party. After 1979, feminists faced this uncompromising prime minister at the helm of a highly centralized political system. Local government was essentially stripped of decision-making authority during the Thatcher years. Therefore, except for levers that were available through the more pro-intervention, pro-regulation European Community, British activists had few opportunities to make their point, because Conservatives controlled most key positions inside the country.

Women's groups in the United States tended to be more pragmatic; many engaged in fund-raising, lobbying, and other interest group activities during the 1970s. American women worked in a relatively decentralized environment in which federalism and the separate sources of power (judicial, legislative, and executive) at the national level served to limit the president's influence. Yet these circumstances hardly mattered as the Reagan and Bush administrations grew more and more intransigent in their conservatism. Senior judges and bureaucrats were nominated based on their opposition to civil rights enforcement, abortion access, and government intervention in the economy, while presidential vetoes of legislation passed by Congress piled up. In short, factors other than the clash of ideas seemed irrelevant.

In Canada, women's groups contended with a far less ideological conservative but one who deeply admired Reagan and Thatcher. Brian Mulroney governed a weak federation in which a great deal of power had already been dispersed to the provinces. He attempted to decentralize the country further despite strong opposition by groups in English Canada. These same interests protested Mulroney's efforts to make Canada "open for business" by building closer economic ties with the United States.[2] Canadian women's groups, however, depended heavily on government support. As their conflict with Mulroney reached its crescendo, federal funding for leading organizations fell under the axe.

Many of these contentious policy fights are recounted in subsequent chapters. They reveal why, during the late 1960s and following years, women's organizations contested a wide variety of laws that denied basic justice. British employment rules, for example, established different retirement ages for men and women. Some American states denied unemployment benefits to pregnant women. Canada's abortion provisions remained embedded in the criminal law. Before examining the struggle to challenge these laws, we need to lay out the basis for later battles, the clash of ideas.

Movement Beginnings

What ideas propelled women as a group to the forefront of social activism? Would that the answer was more simple. Instead of one single perspective, a variety of claims and beliefs multiplied over time to form large, intricate tapestries. Women's organizations in North America and Great Britain shared important common threads as well as striking divergences in their patterns.

A crucial link among feminisms was their common history. In most Anglo-American democracies, group efforts focused on winning the right to vote from the late nineteenth century through the period of World War I. These suffrage campaigns often began with political justice or equality claims that challenged discrimination in virtually all sectors of society—from the electoral system to the workplace to the family. A less direct argument, the social or maternal view, held that women should extend their purifying influence from the private hearth to the sordid world of politics. Whatever their basis for demanding the vote, suffragists held high expectations of the future. As one American advocate, Frances Dana Gage, predicted in a song composed in 1852:

> One hundred years hence, what a change will be made
> In politics, morals, religion, and trade,
> In statesmen who wrangle or ride on the fence
> These things will be altered a hundred years hence.[3]

Much of what activists believed in remained unknown, "hidden from history," in the words of British writer Sheila Rowbotham, for nearly a century.[4] Some who participated in suffrage campaigns saw women's rights as essential to social progress and maintained that inequality limited the ability of both sexes to build a better world. According to this maternal perspective, problems like alcoholism, urban decay, and poor sanitation had been neglected by generations of corrupt politicians. It was the responsibility of new women voters to cleanse and reform. Although these views were well-received, suffrage claims gained a major boost with women's efforts in World War I. Most American, British, and Canadian women, as a result, won the national franchise by 1920.

The right to vote, stand for public office, and enter professions like law and medicine remained core goals of early groups. Organized primarily by white, middle-class women in urban areas, these struggles were both draining for their proponents and upsetting for their adversaries, who saw no end to the social chaos that would result from change. Heated opposition to female suffrage had clear echoes in later decades of the twentieth century, when modern antifeminists railed against threats to the family, the selfishness of women who sought rights for themselves, and the imminent demise of public order. In addition, some conservatives in both periods tried to link women's rights with communism. One American historian, Stanley Lemons, notes that early efforts to protect the health of pregnant women were treated as "part of a Bolshevik conspiracy against America."[5]

After 1920, activism in all three countries became far less visible. Suffragists had one clearly defined goal, widely agreed on within the movement and relatively easy to explain to those outside. The next step was less obvious; as Nellie McClung reflected on the situation in Canada:

> There never has been a campaign like the suffrage campaign. . . . But when all was over, and the smoke of battle cleared away, something happened to us. Our forces, so well organized for the campaign, began to dwindle. We had no constructive program for making a new world. . . . So the enfranchised women drifted. Many are still drifting.[6]

Women's groups in all three countries tried to define a new focus once they won the vote. Most worked to educate their members about public affairs, encouraged them to monitor the political process, and pressed for social reform legislation. The American League of Women Voters, for example, was established out of a leading suffrage group following 1920. The league defined its main purpose as educational, seeking to inform women in a nonpartisan way about the political process. The league also pressed for welfare legislation to assist mothers and children through campaigns against child labor and for maternity care and prohibition.[7] Similarly, the National Union of Societies for Equal Citizenship (NUSEC) grew out of a British suffrage group. After 1919, NUSEC pressured for legislation on equal pay, women's access to the professions, widows' pensions, and limits on child labor.[8] Suffrage interests in western Canada formed the New Era League of British Columbia once they had the vote. This group emphasized prison and family law reform, mother's pensions, minimum wage legislation for women, infant protection, and industrial health and safety.[9]

Although the period between the end of the suffrage fight and the second wave of activism in the late 1960s seemed quiet, it was not a time of quiescence. The Great Depression meant little work was available for men or women, and prevailing views held that whatever jobs did exist should go to male breadwinners. Yet as more middle-class women had access to higher eduction, these assumptions came under close scrutiny. What political scientist Mary Katzenstein calls "unobtrusive mobilization" began among new groups of college graduates.[10] Not just in organizations like the League of Women Voters, NUSEC, and the New Era League but also in national and local councils of women, YWCAs, university women's clubs, peace organizations, and business and professional groups, a polite but consistent advocacy of both women's rights and social reform developed. As in the suffrage period, these groups continued to advance both equality (or justice) and difference (or social) claims. Some emphasized the importance of women's maternal roles and staked out a distinct, protected position vis-à-vis men, whereas others pursued an Enlightenment argument that sought legal equality. In 1921, American proponents of the justice view introduced the Equal Rights Amendment (ERA), a constitutional provision that became a focal point for activity during the 1970s.

In Britain and Canada, women's claims were gradually reshaped on the political left. Although party auxiliaries existed in all three countries, it was in organizations like the British Labour party and the Canadian Cooperative Commonwealth Federation (CCF) that women began to question both the suffragist model of incremental social reform and the party model of something less than equality. Because left parties held far more sway in parliamentary systems than in the United States, it was in Britain and Canada that influential groups of socialist women began to emerge; socialist feminism, as a result, developed deeper roots in these cases than in the United States. CCF women, for example, demanded leadership training programs, publicly accessible birth control clinics, and equal pay laws as early as the mid-1930s.[11] For feminists on the left, equality went hand in hand with social change; there was no tension or contradiction between the two.

Even though they presented disparate arguments based on justice and rights, or maternal purity and social reform, early activists agreed on at least two key points. First, women belonged in the public sphere and had useful contributions to make to democratic life. Although this claim hardly seems controversial, it challenged the dominant view at the time of females as private, diffident beings—if not totally silent and invisible ones. Second, early groups were convinced that government could and should play a positive role in improving society and regulating the economy. Whether they pressured for pure food and drug laws, child labor legislation, mothers' allowances, or industrial safety provisions, activists believed the state had a responsibility to advance the public good. And although their role in achieving much of the progressive legislation of the 1920s was not widely recognized, women's organizations were of crucial importance. Their political engagement demonstrated a clear overlap among women's rights claims, social reform, and state intervention. As part of a broader progressive impulse during the early decades of the twentieth century, these efforts held out great hope not just for women's advancement but also for social improvement via active good government.

Much of this social reform came to pass in the guise of new programs, rules, and, in Britain and Canada, the establishment of state enterprises. Franklin D. Roosevelt's New Deal was the best-known example of creating a modern welfare state, but the American version was less expansive than its British and Canadian counterparts. In all three countries, public works projects during the Great Depression expanded into a variety of permanent schemes involving income support, housing supplements, food allowances, and the like. Rules governing minimum wages and working conditions were established, along with regulations on pensions and the right of workers to organize in trade unions. In Britain, Canada, and, to a lesser extent, the United States, public health care provision became a major part of welfare state development. These varied programs were embedded in what eventually became the postwar consensus, the web of compromises between free market capitalism and government intervention that originated in the Great Depression and dominated most Western democracies through the 1970s.[12]

If this settlement was the middle ground around which most political debate evolved during the mid-twentieth century, then both modern women's movements and new variants of conservatism diverged from that consensus. Writing in 1963, American journalist Betty Friedan described the still very real constraints on middle-class women in terms of "the problem that has no name." Formal political rights had been granted, access to university education widened, and, throughout the Western industrial world, ever more consumer goods became available. Friedan saw an uneasy contradiction between postwar myth and reality, between the "feminine mystique" of contented and conventional domesticity, on the one hand, and a growing restiveness and questioning among university graduates, on the other.[13] By arguing that outdated social values continued to limit women's opportunities, Friedan challenged the view that women's roles were a fixed or settled part of the postwar order.

The Feminine Mystique proved to be enormously popular in North America and Western Europe. Friedan's ideas were discussed in older women's organizations in addition to newer, more informal women's liberation groups that emerged later in the 1960s. As the influence of Friedan, Simone de Beauvoir, and other writers widened, a sense of shared consciousness began to emerge among growing numbers of women.[14] Some were well-educated veterans of older organizations; others were younger, more militant participants in student protests of the Vietnam war years. Antiwar, black radical, and countercultural groups were part of a powerful new left mobilization in which many women found they were treated as far from equal participants.[15]

With astonishing speed and in enormous variety, new organizations sprang to life on campuses and in coffeehouses, church basements, and private homes. As groups and group consciousness continued to form, this second wave became the quintessential new social movement of North America and Western Europe, spreading a strong sense of collective identity among growing numbers of women. Gradually, over time, this challenge to the status quo drew older as well as newer women's organizations together under its own broad banner that read "women's movement." Ideas about change, demands for action, and claims on public attention came fast and furious from within this coalition, as the numbers of new recruits and new groups continued to multiply. By 1975, when the United Nations recognized the International Year of the Woman, it seemed that the banner was high in the air.

The banner seemed to land with a thud soon afterward, however, as a series of new political leaders was elected. After 1979, top conservatives held a very different view of the postwar settlement. While prominent feminists attacked it from the left as not going far enough, many right-of-center politicians insisted government meddling in the name of what they called social engineering was a huge mistake. The stage was set for a direct confrontation between women's groups, historically among the leading advocates of social reform in Anglo-American systems, and new conservatives, who were determined to return to a nineteenth-century model of private charity and minimal government.

Conflicts with Thatcherism

Such an enormous gap separated British Conservative and women's group positions after 1979 that almost no common ground existed between the two perspectives. In the first volume of her memoirs, Margaret Thatcher described with great conviction the evils of socialism, the perils of market intervention, and the glories of individual liberty. She attributed Britain's decline to a long series of leaders from across the political spectrum, each of whom was afraid to challenge the nation's leftward drift. Her own Thatcherite philosophy had its origins over the family grocery store in Grantham. It was a fiercely individualist creed that challenged the postwar consensus and "put its faith in freedom and free markets, limited government and a strong national defence."[16]

Thatcher's ideas represented a clear turn away from the traditions of both the postwar Labour party and her own Conservative party. Breaking with both the Labourite emphasis on collectivism and worker organization via trade unions and the Conservative view of a Britain united by solidarity and convention, Thatcher saw individuals and families as the sole units of social organization.[17] She rejected the tendency of her predecessor as Conservative leader, Edward Heath, to compromise with union leaders to secure a measure of industrial peace. Consensus and compromise were characterized by Thatcher as weak-kneed groveling by "wets" in the Conservative party, whose involvement in cabinet government became less and less after 1979.[18] Wendy Webster describes the prime minister as exhibiting "a marked preference for conflict, confrontation and combat over compromise, negotiation and conciliation," with the former conviction characteristics sharply distinguishable from the latter "wet" or spineless ones.[19] In short, there was no room for muted shades of gray in the new Conservative Britain.

Four main pillars supported the Tory outlook after 1979. First, Thatcher believed that both individuals and businesses should enjoy broad choice and liberty within a free enterprise economy. In *The Downing Street Years,* she maintained that high levels of state ownership, restrictive trade union practices, and economic planning attempts had undermined private initiative to the point that Britain was an inefficient, unproductive "sick man of Europe."[20] Bloated public bureaucracies made high rates of taxation necessary. They also created so many regulations that business could neither innovate nor compete in an increasingly global economy. Privatizing state corporations and deregulating economic activity became watchwords of the Thatcherite creed. Not surprisingly, each of these claims implicated the prime minister in heated conflicts with British unions.

Thatcher's second pillar rejected universalist approaches to social welfare. Providing open access to government programs, according to Thatcher, celebrated

> the virtues of dependence. . . . Welfare benefits, distributed with little or no consideration of their effects on behaviour, encouraged illegitimacy, facilitated the breakdown of families, and replaced incentives favouring work and self-reliance with perverse encouragement for idleness and cheating.[21]

In *The Downing Street Years,* Thatcher claimed that people who collected benefits were unlikely to lead productive work lives because they absorbed "a deeply rooted anti-enterprise culture."[22] Social benefits needed to be made less attractive and more narrowly targeted. Because Thatcher believed too many Britons lived in public housing, she proposed a strategy for residents to own their homes through the "Right to Buy" program.

Thatcher's third key claim emphasized social order and hierarchy. She saw herself as an outsider in the elite world of inherited (and largely masculine) privilege but acted in power with a firm hand and a tight cadre of male advisers. The statement in her memoirs of power, "give me six strong men and true, and I will get through," reflected a highly structured, top-down view of leadership success.[23] Social decay, she argued, required a return to principled morality and traditional institutions. The perspective on urban riots in *The Downing Street Years* claimed

> welfare arrangements encouraged dependency and discouraged a sense of responsibility, and television undermined common moral values that would once have united working-class communities. The results were a steadily increasing rise in crime (among

young men) and illegitimacy (among young women). All that was needed for these to flower into full-scale rioting was the decline of authority and the consequent feeling among potential rioters that they could probably get away with mayhem.[24]

Leadership by executive conviction rather than the prevailing social consensus became a hallmark of Thatcherite government. Stern resolve was also at the core of Thatcher's foreign policy forays, notably in the 1982 Falklands conflict with Argentina. The fact that Britain emerged victorious from the crisis meant Thatcher's reputation as the committed, resolute Iron Lady was assured.

State centralization, the fourth main pillar in Thatcher's worldview, was related to each of the earlier ones. In response to mostly Labour-controlled local governments, Thatcher lashed out at municipal councils as free-spending, inefficient, and out of step with her agenda. She established a limit on local tax rates, centralized control over school curricula, used the police to maintain order, and—most visibly—shut down the Greater London Council in 1986. Taken as a group, these actions had the effect of eliminating competing sources of political power in Britain. One of the most controversial proposals of Thatcher's government, and one which contributed to her decline as party leader, involved replacing local property tax rates with a flat-rate community charge known as the poll tax. This scheme was part of a larger effort to reduce the funds available to local municipalities. After massive public protests and divisions within government ranks, the poll tax was quickly dropped after Thatcher resigned in 1990.[25]

An additional challenge to central state power was the European Community, perceived by Thatcherites as interventionist, collectivist, and ultimately threatening to British sovereignty. Like the poll tax, relations with Europe were controversial and played no small part in weakening Thatcher's position as prime minister. At the core of both debates were questions of ideology and control, since for both Thatcher and her successor, John Major, the directions of Europe under the 1991 Maastricht Treaty were toward statism and ever higher social spending. The Major government eventually withheld support for the Social Chapter in Maastricht and continued Thatcher's practice of dismissing any ideas of continental integration. All told, Conservative actions on local government and the European Union served to weaken alternate sources of power in a highly centralized system.

Thatcher's efforts were also reinforced by the decision of John Major to introduce a Citizens' Charter. Designed as a hands-off, libertarian way of allowing individuals free choice in an open marketplace of services, Major's approach denied the existence of obstacles to that choice. As he announced in a 1992 address to the Adam Smith Institute:

> Of all the privatisations that this Conservative government conducts, the greatest and most far-reaching and the one to which I am most committed is the privatisation of choice. . . . Give people more choices and responsibility; trust the people, and you will have a more just and ordered society.[26]

Major claimed that by offering consumers greater choice, his Citizens' Charter would turn government agencies into efficient service providers. Critics, however, argued that it reduced citizens to consumers and removed issues of justice, equality, and representation from public debate.[27]

Overall, British Conservatives envisioned a minimal or residual welfare state modeled after the American one. This state would be led by a powerful political elite and supported by prosperous individuals in stable families. Each element in this outlook denied what Thatcher viewed as left dogma, including among moderates in the Conservative party. For example, her support for the American way was consistent with a rejection of continental welfare states and what she saw as the meddling, socialist tendencies of the European Community. Thatcher rejected prevailing views of urban decay that focused on poor housing, high rates of unemployment, and the resulting frustration of young people. She used police forces to impose order in the wake of street riots and emphasized the Victorian virtues of self-discipline and responsible behavior. Because motivated people living in traditional families made up society, there was no need to organize collectively to challenge this blissful arrangement. Thatcher ridiculed talk of "alternative lifestyles" among members of what was pejoratively called the loony left.[28] Clearly, her outlook diverged from women's group positions that saw poor single mothers as products of a deeply flawed and far from benevolent social order.

Thatcher fashioned herself in power as a committed crusader who intended to set things straight. She believed that as a female prime minister, her actions were scrutinized more carefully and challenged more often than those of her predecessors. Yet this sentiment hardly led Thatcher to promote other women as individuals, nor did it lead her toward an interest in issues brought forward by women's groups. The only other female member of her cabinet between 1979 and 1990,

Janet Young, was dropped as government leader in the House of Lords for what Thatcher described as her lack of "presence."[29] Similarly, she dismissed Labour initiatives on women's issues by telling the men on her 1983 campaign team, "If they have their way, you'll soon be having the babies."[30]

Most British feminists greeted Thatcher and her agenda with hostile suspicion. Unlike Conservatives, women who were active in movement groups tended to support collective action and government intervention, while they rejected pure individualism and pro–free market positions. The writings of Sheila Rowbotham and Juliet Mitchell reflected how many saw women's problems as far more than personal troubles. In *The Past Is before Us,* Rowbotham developed her vision of a humane socialist society, grounded in the values of cooperation, nurturing, and the empowerment of the marginalized.[31] Mitchell's ideas emerged from the left also and probed the cultural and psychoanalytic dimensions of identity.[32]

These views had direct parallels in the demands of the first national women's liberation conference at Ruskin College, Oxford, in 1970. British activists called for equal pay, twenty-four-hour child care, equal education and job opportunities, free contraception, and abortion on demand.[33] These claims involved government regulation of what workers were paid, how children would be cared for while their parents worked, and what access women had to schooling and jobs. The last two claims challenged traditional social norms, including what Juliet Mitchell saw as women's lack of control over their sexuality and fertility.[34]

As time passed, the movement agenda expanded. It grew to include issues of peace and nuclear disarmament (captured in the massive Greenham Common protest), violence against women, and the consequences of separation and divorce. The challenges facing women who had been beaten and were attempting to raise children on their own gained growing attention in Britain through the 1980s. Because the flight from violence often led to impoverishment, these issues reinforced older demands for equal pay and child care programs. Some groups engaged in a direct struggle with Thatcherism through Women against Pit Closures, a coalition that supported striking miners in their bitter dispute with the Conservative government.[35]

Many feminists were also suspicious of the British welfare state, however. Some argued that welfare benefits reinforced men's control, because the state used female social workers to cut off benefits for women who had "a man in the house."[36] Others criticized the public medical system known as the National Health Service, claiming that control by doctors left no space for a women's self-help approach.[37] Yet British groups clearly preferred a flawed system that offered decent, universal benefits to the bare-bones scheme proposed by Margaret Thatcher. As their model, feminists often looked to the expansive welfare states and publicly funded child care arrangements of continental Europe—not to the minimalist American system that Thatcher set as her standard.

On questions of order and hierarchy, the two sides again clashed. The lack of structure, order, and deference in new groups in Britain helps to explain this difference. As Anna Coote and Beatrix Campbell describe in their account called *Sweet Freedom,* women's liberation "was self-starting, self-regulating and self-directing, owing no allegiance to any other organization or set of beliefs. . . . There would be no hierarchies, no lines of authority, no leaders, no stars."[38] The emphasis was on small-group consciousness-raising as well as independent action mostly at the local level, which meant that women spoke with varied voices. Grassroots diversity became the defining feature of the British movement.

This rejection of national structures distinguished British from North American women's groups. The U.S. National Organization for Women (NOW) was established in 1966, the Canadian National Action Committee on the Status of Women (NAC) in 1972, but the British National Alliance of Women's Organisations (NAWO) only in 1989. The avoidance of hierarchy in Britain reflected a basic division between Thatcherism's emphasis on law and order, coherent ideas, and structure, on the one hand, and British feminism's focus on consensus, diversity, and local autonomy, on the other. The prime minister's response to urban riots in 1981 was to use the police to restore order and then call for a return to social tradition. The reaction of movement activists was to probe the racial side of police action and reject a return to the old order.[39] In this sense, British groups projected an antisystem or protest point of view.

Women's organizations also maintained that too much power was held by too few players. Captured in the term *municipal feminism,* they tried to build alternate sources of authority in local women's committees—most notably that of the Greater London Council between its founding in 1982 and its dismantling by the Thatcher government in 1986. The notion that the British state after 1979 was overly centralized, unresponsive, cut off from the everyday realities of women's lives, and, not incidentally, Conservative in orientation led them to pursue change at the local level. Municipal Labour governments had some funds and influence that could assist.[40] For a time, Sheila Rowbotham was employed in the Popular Planning Unit of the Greater London Council. Yet with the shutdown of the GLC by the central government, few avenues within Britain remained open to women's groups.[41]

One question that follows from this ideological collision concerns the electoral price paid by Conservatives. Did defying movement preferences make any difference at the polls? Survey data indicate the reverse, since women in the general public provided a loyal core of Conservative voters for most of the twentieth century. In 1993, for example, political scientists Joni Lovenduski and Vicky Randall contended that

> [n]o British political party has benefited more consistently from women's political and electoral support than the Conservatives. Women constitute 60 per cent of the members of the Conservative Party, and, during the years for which systematic records are available, women were regularly and significantly more likely than men to vote Conservative.[42]

This pattern continued through the 1992 elections, when British women remained more likely than men to vote Conservative, with 43 percent of females and 39 percent of males voting Tory.[43] Overall, rather than being punished by women voters, Conservatives often benefited from their support.

Explanations of this pattern vary. One line of argument suggests that, in general, Conservatives gained women's votes because unlike Labourites, they actively courted the traditional female electorate. According to Beatrix Campbell, "Conservatism appears to women to help them make sense of themselves and the world around them, and helps them find a way of being in a world they don't control. . . . The Conservative Party created a culture that embraced women, that celebrated their subordination."[44] This view suggests that underlining home, family, and social order more than other parties did attracted large numbers of women as loyal party members and voters. Conservatives thus cultivated a female support base that was unlikely to be swayed by modern feminism.

A second approach makes the reverse case for the Labour party. Building a solid trade union base in an environment where many unions were unwelcoming toward women workers meant that Labour had little prospect of building a female electoral base. In addition, the party's confrontational atmosphere during periods when a hard left faction was ascendant may have dissuaded women voters from supporting the party. These same factional splits, moreover, diverted the energies of feminist activists inside Labour.[45]

Lovenduski and Randall propose a third scenario, which is that centrist parties at times managed to avoid both traditional feminine (mostly Conservative) and masculine (mostly Labour) stereotypes. As moderate, consensual formations, the Liberals and Social Democrats during the 1980s actively sought out female candidates and stressed issues like education and equality at work. In both 1983 and 1987, data show these parties siphoned off a considerable bloc of women's votes from both the Conservatives and Labour. Some electoral payoff may therefore have existed for middle-of-the-road parties that adopted movement positions, particularly when the two older parties were locked in head-on confrontation.[46] The general case, though, was simply that Conservatives piled up parliamentary majority after majority with the support of both women and men.

Overall, the clash of ideas in Britain had three main bases. Movement activists and Conservatives differed first over the role of government in the economy; one side supported more intervention, whereas the other wanted vast reductions in state activity. Second, they failed to agree on social welfare policy. As women's groups pressed for program expansion, Conservatives believed in retrenchment to help only the neediest. Finally, there was no overlap on the question of social order. Tories embraced hierarchy and "the smack of firm government," whereas many feminists rejected structure in their own organizations and centralized power in the larger political system.[47] The two sides were headed for direct collision over fundamental principles *and* their implications.

Ideas Clash in the United States

Did Ronald Reagan or George Bush have many ideas? Lou Cannon, Reagan's biographer, wrote of a "delegative presidency," an administration in which the president "preferred to have 'the boys,' as he called the middle-aged and elderly men who were his advisers, settle differences on issues among themselves and bring a consensus recommendation to him for approval."[48] Other observers describe Reagan as an "anecdotal thinker"[49] and Bush as a "semi-sovereign" with little patience for domestic politics.[50] According to Steven Shull's account, "Bush gave little indication of what agenda direction he wanted, admitting he lacked the 'vision thing.'"[51]

Yet it is clear that Reagan arrived in power with a set of ideas that governed his actions as president. Some key features of this outlook were formed during his years of public speaking and politics on the West Coast, and perhaps even earlier during his youth in the small towns of the Midwest. Above all, Reagan resisted the notion that the United States was in decline, that high inflation, rising interest rates, and the taking of American hostages in Iran were somehow beyond the control of decision makers in Washington. Ronald Reagan advanced a populist patriotism, a sunny optimism that spoke of faith and human freedom. His orientation boldly challenged the malaise paradigm of Jimmy Carter's administration. As Reagan announced in his autobiography, *An American Life:*

> We had to recapture our dreams, our pride in ourselves and our country, and regain that unique sense of destiny and optimism that had always made America different from any other country in the world. If I could be elected president, I wanted to do what I could to bring about a spiritual revival in America.[52]

In Reagan's view, the United States remained a great land of promise. The crucial task of the president was to restore people's faith in themselves and their democratic traditions.

Reagan believed that individual initiative rather than government action represented the best way to solve problems. In *An American Life,* he celebrates what people did for themselves and each other during the Great Depression, while harshly criticizing the growth of a large and ineffectual federal bureaucracy under Roosevelt's New Deal. In Reagan's words,

> FDR in many ways set in motion the forces that later sought to create big government and bring a form of veiled socialism to America. . . . One of his sons, Franklin Roosevelt, Jr., often told me that his father had said many times his welfare and relief programs during the Depression were meant only as emergency, stopgap measures to cope with a crisis, not the seeds of what others later tried to turn into a permanent welfare state. Government giveaway programs, FDR said, "destroy the human spirit," and he was right.[53]

Reagan set about as governor of California and as president of the United States to dismantle what he saw as big government and the loss of freedom by the American people.

Reagan's worldview offered a road map toward building a stronger country with less government. It emphasized the need to lower taxes, cut public spending, reduce government regulation, and eliminate the control exerted by what he called special interests over the national agenda. Cutting taxes had long been a priority for Reagan, dating back to his early years in Hollywood when well-paid actors had no incentive to complete more than a few films a year. It continued through his famous 1964 speech supporting Barry Goldwater as the Republican presidential candidate. Reagan was particularly credible on this issue because he had grown up in a Democratic household and only changed his registration to Republican during the early 1960s.[54]

Much of the public spending that Reagan planned to cut was in the social policy field. Welfare expenditures by the federal government, in his view, had created a vast bureaucracy that did nothing but undermine families and remove the incentive to work.[55] As governor of California, Reagan pioneered the workfare approach to welfare policy. He declared war on "welfare cheats" and, later, "welfare queens" who were sending government spending through the roof.[56] Again, these efforts were credible because they came from an elected politician who had Democratic origins, who said in his memoirs that he "believed we should not take aid from the people who really needed and deserved it, the truly impoverished elderly, blind, and disabled. I just wanted to stop the abuses."[57]

Reagan maintained that private enterprise, the motor for economic growth, was throttled by government regulations. In his successful career as a public speaker before becoming governor, Reagan developed a lively repertoire of anecdotes about too much government, or what Lou Cannon called a "portfolio of antigovernment horror stories."[58] As president, Reagan continued to entertain audiences with these tales of ridicule—each of which pointed to how little constructive action governments (and especially the U.S. federal government) could actually take.

When the public sector did act, according to Reagan, it was usually because of concerted pressure from some "special interest" that was at odds with the broader "public interest."[59] During his two terms as president, Reagan accused the U.S. Congress of caving in to narrow-minded interest groups. He consistently blamed Democrats on Capitol Hill for the rise in public spending and the lack of a balanced budget between 1980 and 1988.[60] Yet Reagan's own commitment to restoring national confidence and international strength proved to be very costly, especially in terms of military budgets. When it came to a choice between fiscal prudence and what he saw as the defense of freedom, Reagan endorsed Pentagon spending. In the field of civil rights, his early commitment to "guaranteeing equality of treatment [as] the government's proper function" was trumped by a more deep-seated opposition to social welfare spending, federal regulation, and especially employment quotas for blacks and women.[61]

These tensions revealed a major shift of political ideas on the American right. Some currents had long been tied to the old right, whereas others evolved from a revolt against the new left by traditional liberals. Both old conservatives and disgruntled liberals came together under the umbrella of the Reagan administration. Fiscal conservatives like budget chief David Stockman, social or new right conservatives like communications director Pat Buchanan, and neoconservative intellectuals like United Nations Ambassador Jeane Kirkpatrick reflected the varied streams that brought Reagan to victory in 1980 and kept Republicans in the White House through 1992.[62]

What made the modern Republican coalition different from the party in earlier periods was its move away from the moderate center. Much in the same way Margaret Thatcher effected changes in the British Conservative party, the Reagan team edged aside centrist Republican elements and replaced them with true believers in a new conservative doctrine. Pragmatists who wanted to avoid unyielding positions on issues like abortion or military spending were shunned in the Republican haste after 1980 to court hard-line social conservatives and anticommunists. Compromise, moderation, and centrism were pushed toward the margins as part of this decisive shift to the right.[63]

The language of the Republican party beginning in the Reagan years dismissed American liberalism in no uncertain terms. Parallel with Margaret Thatcher and her disdain for Tory "wets," Ronald Reagan scorned the big government, heady interventionism of his predecessors—be they Democratic or Republican. Civil rights, women's rights, welfare rights, and so on, were treated as ineffective, unnecessary, and expensive vestiges of the liberal past that were rotting the core of the American dream. Instead of government handouts and social programs, the United States needed a regime that got off people's backs and out of their wallets. This approach would allow individual motivation to triumph, making "the land of the free" truly free once again.

Although it also had many streams, the American women's movement was mostly at odds with the Reagan worldview. The statement of purpose of the National Organization for Women (NOW), adopted at its founding conference in 1966, offered a conciliatory vision of men and women working together:

The purpose of NOW is to take action to bring women into full participation in the mainstream of American society now, exercising all the privileges and responsibilities thereof in truly equal partnership with men.[64]

NOW's founders included prominent writers (notably Betty Friedan), trade unionists, and members of nascent federal and state equal opportunity bureaucracies. NOW organizers included men and women who believed in the need for equal opportunities and a partnership of the sexes. Most had simply lost patience with the inaction of the Equal Employment Opportunities Commission (EEOC), established under the terms of Title VII of the 1964 Civil Rights Act. Early NOW activists argued for *more* government action to ensure equal opportunities at work. They maintained that women required a collective, credible voice parallel to that developed by blacks in the National Association for the Advancement of Colored People.[65]

Because NOW chose to work inside existing institutions, much of its early issue agenda was moderate and reformist. As the organization's historical statement published in 1972 reports:

The watchword was "action" as NOW waged war on all aspects of sex discrimination. Task forces were set up to deal with the problems of women in employment, education, religion, poverty, law, politics, and women's image in the media. Committees were also organized to handle finance, membership, public relations, legislation, and legal activities.[66]

At its second conference in Washington, D.C., in 1967, NOW expanded this agenda, calling for child care and maternity leave programs, the repeal of all abortion laws, and passage of the Equal Rights Amendment (ERA). The ERA was an amendment to the U.S. Constitution that some women's organizations had wanted since the 1920s. It said, "Equality of rights under the law shall not be denied or abridged by the United States or any state on account of sex," and it awarded powers to enforce equal rights to the U.S. Congress.[67] Supporters believed that passage of the amendment would in one swoop strike down all discriminatory laws and practices across the country, meaning it would no longer be necessary to challenge them one by one.

Growing numbers of consciousness-raising and self-help groups gave the movement a widened issue focus and grassroots presence through the 1970s. Many local organizations focused on problems in the legal system, after their members became frustrated with the handling of rape, divorce, and child custody cases. Others worked on improving access to education and jobs, in the belief that women in the workforce needed day care programs for their children and training opportunities to advance themselves. In terms of public policy, a consensus emerged that little would change without affirmative action and comparable worth laws that guaranteed fair hiring and fair pay for working women.[68]

Much of NOW's early issue agenda seemed to be moving forward through the 1970s, as a growing network of local and state affiliates brought in more members. Record numbers of women and men participated in demonstrations and marches. In 1971, NOW established a Legal Defense and Education Fund (based in New York City) to focus on changing laws, litigating in key issue areas, and educating the public. A wide array of similar litigation organizations and think tanks was also founded during the 1970s, including the National Women's Law Center, the Center for Women Policy Studies, and the Women's Legal Defense Fund, all based in Washington. Pressure to change abortion laws came from Planned Parenthood and the National Abortion Rights Action League (NARAL), often in coordination with NOW and other groups.[69]

These organizations, for the most part, used the rhetoric of equal rights and the strategies of interest groups. Through 1980, NOW and other Washington-based groups worked on passing laws, winning court cases, obtaining friendly executive orders, and ensuring pro–civil rights appointments and actions in the federal bureaucracy. Although other parts of the American movement had a more radical, transformative approach, this militant stream largely merged with the reformist one by the late 1970s. In ideological terms, Betty Friedan's account of "the problem that has no name" opened up a fairly fluid agenda.[70] It provided space for many provocative ideas, including Kate Millett's on sexuality (presented in *Sexual Politics,* 1970), Shulamith Firestone's on motherhood (in *The Dialectic of Sex,* 1970), and Susan Brownmiller's on rape (in *Against Our Will,* 1975).[71] If tensions existed in women's groups, they evolved from diverse voices within the movement. Organizations including NOW came under criticism in the late 1970s for having predominantly white, middle-class leadership and for neglecting the class and racial dimensions of women's experiences. The movement had many stars, but few attained the public profile of Bella Abzug, Betty Friedan, or Gloria Steinem. As more groups emerged among African American, Hispanic, and Native American women, these leaders faced a growing challenge not only to their stardom but also to the moderate approach they championed.[72]

American women's groups had one important advantage, however.

Unlike in the British case, voting patterns in the United States after 1980 showed Republicans paid a tangible price for defying movement preferences. NOW President Eleanor Smeal wrote in December 1980 about what she called the gender gap, the pattern by which roughly 8 percent fewer women than men voted for the Reagan-Bush ticket in the fall presidential elections.[73] The gap continued through the 1982 midterm elections, when about 6 percent fewer women than men voted for Republican candidates nationwide. Studies conducted during Reagan's first term in office confirmed this pattern, showing gaps in support for the president as high as seventeen percentage points in one 1983 Gallup poll.[74]

NOW and other groups worked to mobilize women to defeat Reagan in 1984, arguing that his policies on military spending, social welfare, and equal rights were antithetical to those of many female voters. These organizations helped to secure the vice-presidential nomination of Geraldine Ferraro, the first woman on a major party ticket in U.S. history. Ferraro's presence with presidential nominee Walter Mondale won Democratic endorsements from NOW, NARAL, and the National Women's Political Caucus.[75] Women's groups worked to increase voter registration among females, but the rise in turnout they effected and the continuation of a gender gap in the 4 to 9 percent range were not enough to defeat the Reagan-Bush reelection bid.[76] Republicans won a second presidential term by a landslide.

These developments helped to stimulate the growth of campaign organizations that supported pro-choice, pro-equality women candidates. As part of an explicit attempt to challenge new conservatives, the bipartisan Women's Campaign Fund (established in 1974) and the Democratic political action committee known as EMILY's List (standing for Early Money Is Like Yeast, founded in 1986) raised money to support women nominees. Their efforts were successful in the sense that more pro-feminist women contested and won office over time, including during the Reagan-Bush years. In addition, women voters contributed to Democratic efforts to win back control of the U.S. Senate in 1986 midterm elections.[77]

Early polls from the 1988 campaign hinted that the gender gap would help to move Republicans out of the White House. Surveys showed George Bush trailing Democratic nominee Michael Dukakis by as much as twenty-eight percentage points among women during the first half of the year, but this difference dropped off by election day.[78] As was the case with Reagan, support for Bush was about four to seven percentage points lower among women than men, but he still carried the bulk of female votes.[79] The American situation was in this respect similar to the British one. Although women's groups had identified the gender gap and spent a great deal of energy trying to mobilize it in electoral terms, they remained unable to defeat Republican presidential nominees in 1980, 1984, or 1988. As in Britain in 1979, 1983, 1987, and 1992, many women's votes remained parked with conservative candidates.

Despite internal strains, the American movement staked out a clear set of demands by 1980. Feminists became expert policy insiders who successfully lobbied, testified before congressional committees, wrote legislation, and influenced the wider public. It was just when they reached this point that the Reagan revolution came to town. Unlike leading Republicans, movement activists emphasized principles of privacy and personal choice on the question of abortion. In addition, feminists tended toward an interventionist view that saw economic problems as requiring government—and especially presidential—action. Federal involvement was viewed as necessary, for example, to address inequality in the workplace and the poverty of single mothers and their children. Governments needed to regulate employment conditions and spend more on education and job training. Movement activists wanted to enhance rather than reduce the federal state, by increasing instead of cutting public spending. Their take on social change saw too little occurring too slowly, in contrast to conservatives who saw too much happening far too quickly.

Conflicts in Canada

After leaving public office, Brian Mulroney devoted much of his time to working as a lawyer and corporate board member. Unlike Thatcher and Reagan, he did not immediately prepare an account of life in power. Yet Mulroney's key positions can be gleaned from biographies, speeches, and news stories. These sources show he was not a disciplined ideologue, not the carrier of a clear worldview comparable to Thatcher's Thatcherism or Reagan's Reaganism. If Mulroneyism meant anything to Canadians by the early 1990s, it seemed to be unbridled personal ambition tainted by allegations of corruption. *On the Take,* the title of a best-selling book by journalist Stevie Cameron, summarizes one popular view of Mulroney's principles.[80]

Brian Mulroney entered politics with a commitment to avoiding the rigid style of his Liberal predecessors. This emphasis on openness and consensus building followed from Mulroney's early career as a Quebec labor lawyer, in which solving problems was more helpful than scoring doctrinal points. In interviews with political scientist Donald Savoie, a number of senior government officials described his prime ministerial approach in parallel terms:

> Contrary to what is commonly believed, Mulroney is not an ideologue. He likes to cut a deal. This is what he did for a living before he came to politics. . . . He looks at problems one at a time and also looks to one solution at a time. . . . Once in a while, he would declare that one issue—say, the deficit—was the priority issue for the government. That would hold for a while, or until another issue that caught his attention came around.[81]

As a pragmatic deal maker, Mulroney attracted right-of-center Conservatives in English Canada along with left-of-center nationalists in Quebec. This broad coalition meant no clear political ideology emerged during his ten years in Parliament.

Mulroney's approach to public office merged five important elements. The first was creating an alternative to the Liberals who had governed Canada for decades. His commitment to this task grew out of experiences in Quebec, where the Conservatives were relatively weak. Mulroney devoted enormous energies beginning in early adulthood to fund-raising, networking, and building a victorious party coalition. As he explained in *Where I Stand,* a collection of early speeches:

> With few if any exceptions, the Conservative Party has been consigned to the Opposition benches for one reason alone—its failure to win seats in the French-speaking areas of the nation. From northern and eastern Ontario through Quebec and into northern New Brunswick, the electorate has rejected the Conservative Party with a consistency that is at once staggering and overwhelming.[82]

Mulroney's primary challenge on becoming party leader in 1983 was to bring the federal Conservatives from the political wilderness to power. He zeroed in on key Liberal failings, including the size of the federal bureaucracy and the mass of patronage appointees in elite positions. In his campaign speeches, Mulroney promised to make government leaner and more businesslike by offering "pink slips and running shoes to bureaucrats."[83]

Mulroney's second theme borrowed selectively from the Thatcher and Reagan scripts. Like his counterparts in the United Kingdom and the United States, he defended deregulation, privatization, and individual initiative. Mulroney vowed that government cooperation with the private sector would replace the confrontation of the Liberal years, declaring:

> The tragic process of swedenizing Canada must come to a halt. . . . I am a Canadian and I want to be free, to the extent reasonably possible, of government intrusion and direction and regimentation and bureaucratic overkill. . . . It is absolutely clear that the private sector is and must continue to be the driving force in the economy. . . . The role and purpose of government policy will relate primarily to how we can nurture and stimulate the Canadian private sector.[84]

As former president of the Iron Ore Company of Canada, an American mining subsidiary based in Montreal, Mulroney said he would bring a bottom-line perspective to government. This emphasis on scaling back the state and improving ties with business were key parts of the Thatcher and Reagan agendas that Mulroney adapted to a Canadian setting.

Third, Mulroney supported closer and more cordial relations with the United States. Continental cooperation would stimulate investment and job creation on both sides of the border. In a major address after becoming prime minister, he announced in New York, "Our message is clear. Canada is open for business again."[85] Opening up investment flows set the stage for Canada-U.S. free trade beginning in 1989. Related to his pro-American strategy, Mulroney's fourth theme blamed government intervention for the high cost of living in Canada. Whether he was referring to heavy regulation of business, limits on foreign investment, the lack of research and development, low worker productivity, or conflict between labor and management, Mulroney maintained Canadians paid a high price for overgovernance. He promised "hundreds of thousands of new jobs" and said Conservatives would eliminate the federal deficit by 1990.[86] However, reducing the deficit would not endanger social programs, which Mulroney described during the 1984 election campaign as a "sacred trust."[87]

Finally, Mulroney said he was committed to "national reconciliation," meaning he was willing to address the grievances of Quebec, western Canada, and the Atlantic region.[88] Each of these areas had long felt left out of the Canadian system, believing the political process was dominated by Ontario in particular. As Mulroney told reporters during the 1983 party leadership race, "We'll find a serious and eloquent formula to meet Quebec's legitimate and historical responsibility to safeguard its language and culture."[89] The ten points he outlined during that campaign shaped subsequent developments in the Meech Lake and Charlottetown constitutional rounds, when Conservatives proposed vast reductions in the power of the federal government.

Mulroney's core beliefs as Conservative leader were, like those of Thatcher and Reagan, at odds in many respects with his party's history. Canadian Tories had long advocated a strong federal state with its own public or crown corporations in broadcasting, transportation, and other sectors. Conservatives were traditionally the party of English Canadian nationalism, opposed to the continentalist or pro-integration impulses of the federal Liberals. Mulroney's attempts to shed federal responsibilities, sell off public corporations, and pursue Canada-U.S. free trade thus represented a sharp break from Conservative tradition. The most direct repudiation of convention in the Mulroney worldview, however, rested in its elevation of the individual above the interests of society in general. By adopting neoconservative emphases on personal achievement and market forces, Mulroney undermined the pro-community element of Canadian Conservatism. In particular, the "red tory" streak in the party that saw a role for government intervention in the economy gradually weakened after he became Conservative leader in 1983. This stream was wedged aside by a firmly pro-business and pro-U.S. orientation that displaced the collectivist element of older toryism.[90]

Perhaps because he was younger and more pragmatic than either Thatcher or Reagan, Mulroney had some tolerance for women's movement claims. When he participated in a televised debate on women's issues in 1984, sponsored by the National Action Committee on the Status of Women (NAC), Mulroney surprised viewers with his knowledge of problems facing women in the professions and on native reserves. Simply engaging in such a debate would have been unthinkable for both Margaret Thatcher in 1979 and Ronald Reagan in 1980. Yet what enraged Canadian movement activists was not Mulroney's performance as a campaigner in 1983–84. Instead, NAC and other organizations targeted the economic damage and social conflict which in their view resulted from his actions as prime minister.

The establishment of a national women's umbrella group in Canada dates from 1972, when NAC was founded at a convention in Toronto. Its purpose was to pressure governments to implement the recommendations of the 1970 *Report* of the Royal Commission on the Status of Women. NAC's organizational base included older middle-class groups like the Canadian Federation of University Women, the alliance of Quebec women established in 1966 as la Fédération des femmes du Québec (FFQ), and newer women's liberation groups that began in student and antiwar activism. From a steering committee that represented fifteen organizations, NAC grew to 120 member groups by 1977, 280 by 1984, and 586 by 1988.[91] This last figure meant that about five million women belonged to NAC affiliates by the late 1980s. Over time, NAC depended more and more on federal government funding. By the mid-1980s, at least two-thirds of its annual budget came from federal sources.[92]

The group focused on national policy issues that, from its perspective, required federal government action. NAC initially demanded better child care programs, legal changes to end discrimination on the basis of sex, and the removal of abortion from the Criminal Code. Equal pay was added as a fourth goal in 1975, and, during the late 1970s, divorce and other family law issues were highlighted to protest a proposed shift from federal to provincial control. In general, NAC envisioned the federal government as the primary vehicle for the changes it desired, believing that one national standard was preferable to a ten-province patchwork quilt.

NAC's early steering committees were dominated by members of older, established women's organizations. As the umbrella widened to include more groups, NAC hired paid staff and began to elect its executive committee. As in other Canadian interest groups, efforts were made to include representatives from each region. Through the mid-1980s, NAC attracted a series of prominent party, academic, and trade union women to serve as president. Much like NOW in the United States, NAC sponsored lobbies on Parliament Hill, met with cabinet ministers, presented submissions to legislative committees, and held press conferences designed to educate the public about its policy demands.[93]

What appeared to be a smooth pattern of growth, however, masked growing internal conflict. Some activists who joined NAC in the 1980s wanted to take on broader issues. Socialists challenged women's economic status, especially in the workplace. Radical feminists raised questions about sexuality and violence that followed from their work in rape crisis centers, shelters for battered women, and abortion clinics. By the mid-1980s, violence against women had become a core issue for NAC along with legal equality, family law reform, abortion, employment, and child care.

As radical and socialist views grew more influential, the position of moderate or liberal women began to weaken. This shift occurred as activists from disabled, aboriginal, and immigrant women's groups became involved in NAC. These diverse interests challenged what they saw as control of the movement by white, able-bodied, middle-class women—who in fact had differences of their own. When Quebec and English Canadian feminists could not agree on constitutional issues during the early 1980s, the FFQ resigned from NAC. Yet women's claims did receive growing attention, including in 1981–82 constitutional discussions, when strong equality language was entrenched in sections 15 and 28 of the new Charter of Rights and Freedoms.[94] If the demise of a moderate stream in NAC can be pinpointed, it was during the first Mulroney term. In the mid-1980s, an internal review process disrupted group activities and gave militants an edge.[95] NAC over time became less of an interest group and more of a protest movement.

Although some common ground existed between the moderate stream dominant in NAC through the early 1980s and the Mulroney outlook, this shared terrain gradually disappeared. Mulroney's commitment to a leaner, less powerful federal state contradicted movement demands in English Canada for an active federal government. Women's groups supported a generous welfare state with firm national standards rather than a decentralized scheme in which, in their view, provinces would compete to see how little they could provide. Mulroney's close friendship with Ronald Reagan set off alarm bells on this point, because it led Canadian Conservatives to import antigovernment, anti–welfare state rhetoric. Mulroney's decision to pursue Canada-U.S. free trade became the key pivot for much of this debate. As negotiated, free trade stood to strengthen business interests and limit the ability of future governments to tax, spend, regulate, and otherwise act in the national interest.[96]

Canadian women's groups were able to point to significant attitudinal differences on many of these issues. Polls showed a consistent gap whereby females were more supportive of social welfare spending, less inclined to endorse the use of military force, and less approving of free trade policies. In terms of political parties, public opinion surveys showed that traditionally lower levels of support among women for the left-of-center New Democratic party (NDP) disappeared in the late 1970s so that by 1984, there were no gender differences in NDP support.[97] This shift was quite different from trends during the same period in Britain, where Labour remained considerably stronger among men than women.

Canadian Liberals were historically the beneficiaries of solid female support. In federal elections since the mid-1970s, Liberal strength among women voters was consistently three to nine percentage points higher than among men.[98] As a centrist vehicle for social reform through much of the twentieth century, the Liberal party saw more male than female voters defect in 1979 and following. This erosion in the Liberal base, parallel with the Democrats' loss of male voters in the United States during the same period, meant Conservatives in 1984 won about 59 percent of men's and 56 percent of women's votes, whereas the Liberals gained 27 percent of women's and 23 percent of men's support. After four years of Conservative government, the federal election results of 1988 showed a massive decline in Tory support among both sexes but especially among women. Only 39 percent of females voted Conservative in 1988 compared with 46 percent of males, for a gender difference of 7 percent. Much of this gap was attributable to far less support for Mulroney's free trade policy among Canadian women. Approximately twenty percentage points separated male and female approval ratings for free trade in October 1988, when the federal election campaign largely revolved around this issue.[99]

Yet Mulroney, like his counterparts in the United Kingdom and the United States, was able to win reelection despite challenging many movement positions. The 1988 campaign saw both major opposition parties in Canada, the Liberals and NDP, chasing anti–free trade voters, while Conservatives held a political monopoly on their side of the divide. Opposition parties in Canada also vied with each other to show how pro–social welfare and pro-feminist they were, painting the Conservatives as Reaganesque supporters of a right-wing agenda. Once again, this strategy helped to split the anti-Tory vote and secured another majority government—albeit a somewhat reduced one—for Brian Mulroney in 1988.

Comparing Collisions

If a clash of visions occurred in Britain, the United States, and Canada, what can be said about the impact of this conflict? Was there a best- or, conversely, worst-case scenario for women's groups? Which variant of modern conservatism had the most to gain from directly opposing movement claims?

American feminism seemed to have both the most going for it and the most going against it. In terms of advantages, activists in the United States had long accepted the rules of the game to an exceptional degree. Leading groups were committed to lobbying Congress, meeting the mainstream media, and raising money from private individuals, corporations, and foundations—all activities of mature, moderate interest groups. Feminists in the United States had built dense webs of public support for their claims, as measured by solid approval in opinion polls and diverse organizational vehicles.[100] In Washington, groups tried to cultivate a staunch bipartisanship, a willingness to work with both Democrats and Republicans on Capitol Hill and in the White House.

Reagan's legislative record and that of his vice president, George Bush, calmed the fears of many. As governor of California, Reagan had signed one of the most liberal abortion laws in the country.[101] Bush had been a pro-choice, pro–family planning legislator on Capitol Hill.[102] Moreover, the Republican campaign in 1980 was not dominated by new right issues. As Jerome Himmelstein observes:

> Conservatism on social issues certainly was not central to electing Ronald Reagan to the presidency in 1980. Reagan's campaigns in the primary and general elections did not stress them, and voters did not often mention them in exit polls as a reason they voted for Reagan. . . . Ultimately the 1980 election was a plebiscite on an unpopular incumbent, not an ideological contest.[103]

In short, one could argue that women's groups in 1980 were not about to be moved to the political margins.

From a different angle, however, the clash of ideas in the United States seemed far more ominous. American feminism was very visible, very successful, and probably more effective at that point than feminisms elsewhere. Because it had developed a powerful constellation of stars whose lives and writings were themselves news stories, the U.S. women's movement loomed large as a target for conservative interests. If movements that have experienced the highest peaks of influence and growth also face the deepest valleys when they come under attack, then American feminism was poised to enter a long period of darkness after 1980.

Above all, the increasing clout of new right interests in the Republican party threatened to cut off women's group influence. Traditional free market, anticommunist conservatives had long questioned some movement claims; for example, they portrayed demands for publicly funded child care during the Nixon years as collectivist and soviet.[104] But relatively few old-line conservatives challenged the idea of legal equality. What marked the Republican transformation in 1980 was an official party platform that rejected the Equal Rights Amendment, endorsed a constitutional amendment banning abortion, and promoted an antiabortion litmus test for court nominees.[105] This platform was endorsed by an increasingly conservative Republican elite that saw male blue-collar Democrats, worried about social change and the decline of America, as ready to vote for Ronald Reagan. In the words of one party critic, the Reagan and Bush administrations actively courted a "Republican–Religious Right partnership [that] allows little possibility for women to be regarded as equal."[106] The ability of Republicans to mobilize social traditionalists, including antifeminist interests, thus made women's movement prospects far less promising after 1980 than before.

According to this perspective, social themes became closely meshed with Reagan's patriotism and fiscal ideas. Once moral conservatism met the Reagan worldview, women's movement isolation was just about assured. The joint emphasis of Reagan and the new right on restoring faith, comfort, and tradition directly contradicted feminist demands for social change—however limited that change was compared with movement claims in Britain or Canada. Reagan believed in unfettered individual initiative, whereas feminist activists saw their opportunities limited by bias and the absence of serious antidiscrimination measures. Women's groups looked to the power of collective action rather than toward individual solutions. They viewed inequality as a societal problem that could only be addressed by people working together. Finally, women's organizations assumed a positive rather than an inherently negative role for government. They viewed regulation, public spending, and interest group lobbying as useful rather than destructive activities.

The potential for serious conflict with the Reagan coalition was thrown into bold relief following the rise of antifeminism on the American right. Pressure to adopt anti-ERA and antiabortion positions in the 1980 Republican platform came from groups like Eagle Forum and Stop ERA. Both were founded by Phyllis Schlafly, who began her political career in the 1950s as an anticommunist crusader. Schlafly's opposition to abortion, school busing, and federally funded child care, together with her support for school prayer, merged in 1980 with the Reagan platform on private initiative and a rolling back of government.[107] According to that party manifesto, Republican appointees to the U.S. Supreme Court were to be vetted based on their positions on these issues; not surprisingly, Republican court nominees drew the ire of pro-equality interests. Attempts by the Reagan administration in

1987 to nominate Robert Bork, for example, led to sustained opposition by women's groups and civil rights organizations.[108]

Schlafly, however, was hardly alone on the right in her visceral rejection of the American women's movement. Neoconservative intellectuals provided a steady stream of denunciations, attacking affirmative action and the damage feminism had, in their view, caused family life. As Midge Decter declared in 1984 in *Commentary* magazine:

> All the demands for unneeded preference in admissions and hiring, all the absurd litigation, all the efforts at speech control and thought control, and most important, all the programs to manage and "improve" the behavior of the men in her life, whether husband, boss, roommate or date, have left [the American woman] more disaffected and more mentally self-indulgent than before.[109]

Concerns about what Jerome Himmelstein calls "the decay of the social bond" thus united varied conservatives in their attack on movement positions.[110]

From this angle, American women's groups faced a worst-case scenario after 1980. Opposition to them was becoming well defined and useful in electoral terms to conservative Republicans. Civil rights ideas so central to modern American feminism were weakening under pressure from the fierce individualism and antistate ethos of Reagan-era Republicans. Clear social divides along the lines of race were more deeply entrenched in the United States than in Canada or Britain, meaning that civil rights arguments were relatively easy to isolate.[111] Also, because the United States was arguably the most individualist liberal democracy of the three cases to begin with, any erosion of pro-group societal values was bound to have a devastating effect. In short, the polarizing rhetoric of new conservatives could find fertile ground in the United States.

It was nearly as difficult to predict good news for British groups after 1979. This women's movement had no national organization and operated in an environment where all forms of social protest faced a sustained challenge. In particular, Margaret Thatcher's attacks on trade unions cast doubt on every organized interest other than business. Even without Thatcher's rhetoric, the British parliamentary system favored a strong political executive, loyal partisanship, and virtually no dispersion of power beyond Westminster. At the polls, Conservative leaders were hardly disadvantaged by their opposition to movement positions, because the Tory party did consistently well among female voters. Overall, women's groups faced a neoconservative elite that virtually monopolized power in a highly centralized system. As the appeal of Thatcherism widened, moderate or what Thatcher called "wet" Tories became fewer in number and less influential. Parliamentary opposition to the Conservatives was often dispirited, as Labour activists blamed each other for defeat after defeat. Although they remained sympathetic to much of the movement agenda, trade unions were under direct threat from Conservative economic policy and hardly needed more confrontations with the government.

British activists held two key advantages, though. One was the absence of an organized antifeminist movement. Compared with groups in the United States, which faced fierce opposition, British organizations remained less visible and less useful targets for attack. Perhaps because the movement in the United Kingdom had not become a successful mainstream interest group, British activists had more room to maneuver and grow than did their American counterparts. No one inside or outside the British movement could reasonably claim in 1979 that women's groups posed a major political threat. In addition, social conservatives who imported antiabortion tactics from the United States saw them backfire in Britain.[112] Opponents on the political right, in other words, had little incentive to build an antifeminist movement.

Second, groups could look to a less politicized judiciary and to avenues outside the United Kingdom for progress. Unlike U.S. Supreme Court judges, British high court judges (known as the law lords) in the House of Lords were appointed based on their legal acumen rather than a Republican-style litmus test. The nine law lords could break with government policy by moving in new directions, because they were selected in a far less socially charged atmosphere. In terms of Europe, Conservatives were divided over Britain's involvement, but movement groups tended to endorse closer ties. The European Court of Justice was especially attractive because it could decide employment cases after they had gone through the court system in the United Kingdom. European judges generally began with a more interventionist, pro-worker framework than did judges in Britain—a prospect that pleased women's groups and annoyed Conservatives.

Circumstances seemed somewhat better in Canada. The Charter of Rights and Freedoms entrenched equality language that explicitly permitted affirmative action programs to help women and other disadvantaged groups. Women's organizations faced a relatively pragmatic Brian Mulroney, who offered a more flexible approach to their claims than either Margaret Thatcher or Ronald Reagan. Compared with the Reagan and Bush administrations, Mulroney's cabinet was less inclined to attack women's gains on issues like abortion and affirmative action. Unlike Thatcher and Major, Mulroney was not consistently interested in fiscal matters. Because his priorities rested in free trade and constitutional negotiations, women's groups did not see their core priorities on the chopping block. And because about nine-tenths of the Canadian workforce was governed by provincial rather than federal labor law, Mulroney had little leverage in the employment field.

Canadian interest groups worked in a parliamentary system that was less closed than the British one, in which American-style lobbying of politicians and bureaucrats had become more acceptable. The Canadian prime minister controlled the weakest national government of the three cases, because a great deal of power had gradually devolved to the provinces. Moreover, because he won election five years after Thatcher and four years after Reagan, Mulroney's every move was scrutinized by women's groups. If some British or American organizations had been naïve about conservative intentions early on, this was not the case in Canada after 1984.

A number of disadvantages, however, also faced the Canadian movement. Mulroney deeply admired Reagan and adopted much of his rhetoric despite rising public opposition. As a keen observer of the American political system, Mulroney recognized the value of establishing some distance between himself and organizations like the National Action Committee. NAC's status was challenged publicly during his first term in office by an antifeminist group known as REAL Women, meaning Realistic, Equal, Active, for Life. By applying in 1987 for federal government funding, REAL Women staked out a claim for both resources and credibility—during the same period as NAC was moving from moderate reform toward militant protest. Not surprisingly, the Mulroney government agreed to support a REAL Women conference, while it dramatically reduced funding for NAC and other groups.[113]

Clearly, Canadian women's groups faced the same potential for nasty consequences as did organizations in Britain and the United States. Modern conservatives seemed to be on a collision course with the core ideas of women's groups—not only from the second wave of activism but also dating back to the surge of social reform after World War I. In chapter 2, we examine the policy fights that resulted from this collision.

CHAPTER TWO

Policy Battles

Did the clash of ideas between women's groups and conservatives mean much politically? This chapter examines one set of consequences—bitter policy conflict in Britain, the United States, and Canada. Issue debates involved not only key items in the movement agenda but also larger questions about the role of government.

One way to evaluate policy battles is to compare what legislatures and courts decided before versus after conservative leaders won election. A straightforward coding scheme is used in this analysis (see app. A). Following the historical review in chapter 1, this chapter examines core feminist policy claims that were common to women's movements in all three countries and assigns positive (+), negative (−), or mixed (±) scores from the perspective of women's movement positions to national legislative and high court decisions.[1] As demonstrated by data in appendix A, this approach reveals different patterns in each of the three countries. During the Thatcher and Major years, British women's groups were less successful in formal terms than they had been before 1979. Yet access to the European Court of Justice, combined with the limited interest of British Conservatives in issues like abortion, meant feminist claims faced less erosion over time than they experienced in the United States. Under the Reagan administration, the momentum of American groups was clearly slowed. Later on during the Bush years, this situation deteriorated to the point that policy losses were nearly as frequent as policy wins had been before 1980. In Canada, equality provisions in the Charter of Rights and Freedoms came into force during the first Mulroney government, meaning women's group claims fared better in Parliament and especially the courts after 1984 than before.

This overall finding that policy reversals were most pronounced in the United States contradicts key assumptions in the comparative literature. Contrary to studies which view the American congressional system with its formal separation of powers across branches of government and limited party discipline as relatively advantageous, data presented in this chapter reveal very few benefits at the national level for U.S. women's groups after 1980.[2] In fact, evidence offered here points in the direction of measurable, sustained rollbacks in the American context as compared with relatively less policy damage for feminist interests in Britain and certainly Canada. The discussion suggests that a combination of formal institutional and informal elite preference factors explain the less eroded status of group claims during the conservative years in Canada and Britain than in the United States.

Decisions by high courts and national legislatures, however, tell only part of what happened to women's organizations in conservative times. Significant battles were fought in the streets and in media headlines, where groups took on the broader agenda of right-of-center politicians. In Britain, many feminists opposed changes to labor laws that abolished wage protection for the lowest paid and weakened the role of trade unions. In the United States, they struggled against conservatives who sought to limit access to abortion and who had no patience for federal regulations in the workplace. Women's groups in English Canada angrily rejected Conservative policies on constitutional change as well as free trade. Among these varied confrontations, the only one where movements won and elites lost was on the constitution in Canada, where organizations outside Quebec helped to defeat Conservative deals giving more power to the provinces. But in the longer term, Canada was decentralized by other means, and funding for women's groups was cut. As argued in the following chapters, nine years of Tory rule clearly cost Canadian feminism.

What lessons can be drawn from these defensive battles? On the positive side, women's groups were able to hold their own against conservative regimes under three conditions: first, when women already claimed full constitutional equality, as in Canada after 1985; second, when they could resort to levers outside the country, as with British groups using European Community channels; and third, when conservatives lacked the capacity to enforce their will, as the Mulroney government did on constitutional issues. Women in the United States faced especially hard times because none of these conditions applied. American conservatives blocked efforts to ratify the Equal Rights Amendment, so women in the United States did not obtain constitutional equality at a national level. No supranational body comparable to the European Union existed for American groups. And, finally, the Reagan and Bush administrations were more capable than the Mulroney government of getting their way, since the clout of federal decision makers in the United States was greater than in Canada. Even though the U.S. Congress was far less disciplined in partisan terms than were national legislatures in Canada and Britain, Republican presidents vetoed a number of its pro-movement decisions. Moreover, the politicized system of appointments to the U.S. Supreme Court meant women's groups faced a far from impartial high court bench.

On the negative side, a strong social (versus economic) conservatism in governing parties worked against feminist interests. If the story of policy battles is a relative one, then it was in the United States that women's groups faced the greatest threat from moral crusaders who shaped the preferences of elite decision makers. Access to abortion was a clear target for antifeminist interests, who succeeded over time in whittling away at the crucial precedent established in the 1973 *Roe v. Wade* decision.[3] Social conservatives managed to link the ratification of the Equal Rights Amendment with the disintegration of not just the family but also public order in general. Civil rights advances of the 1970s were undermined by a new language that called affirmative action "reverse discrimination."[4] In short, policies that affected American women and minorities were directly challenged by a sea change in the preferences of governing elites. By way of contrast, British Conservatives emphasized economic objectives as primary and had only a secondary interest in social issues. They paid substantially less attention than did their U.S. counterparts to rolling back abortion access, for example. Similarly, the Mulroney government invested far more political capital in its trade and constitutional agendas than in social issues.

In terms of relative damages, then, American women suffered the most decisive policy reversal of the three cases; this finding directly challenges assumptions in the comparative public policy and also women and politics literatures regarding the relative invincibility of diffuse interests in a U.S. congressional environment.[5] Losing the Equal Rights Amendment along with a series of employment and abortion decisions meant American groups were clearly set back in the years after 1980. Although the British and Canadian movements were hardly on good terms with their respective Conservative governments, they did not experience the same level of attack and defeat as that which occurred in the United States. Women in the United Kingdom could look to some progress in the employment field thanks to European Court of Justice rulings, and groups in Canada had a solid record of formal decisions to their credit. Even so, Canadian and British Conservatives prevailed in many important areas, including free trade in Canada and the weakening of worker rights in the United Kingdom. Damage to movement momentum in these core areas, in short, was most pronounced in the United States and less dramatic in Britain and Canada.

This chapter compares how women fared before Thatcher, Reagan, and Mulroney were elected with what happened while these three leaders held office. Because two conservative successors (John Major and George Bush) each governed for a lengthy period, their terms in office are considered as well. Overall, the record suggests sustained policy conflict in all three countries. In Britain, these battles entailed bitter debates over work and, more specifically, the Conservative government attack on trade unions and employee rights. Conflicts in the United States had as their pivot the conservative campaign against abortion and workplace regulation. In Canada, direct clashes between women's groups and Conservatives occurred over trade and constitutional issues.

In all three countries, the collision of ideas between feminists and conservatives led to a direct policy fallout. It was in the United States that this conflict entailed the most concerted attack on core movement ideas, meaning the stakes in the defensive struggle were extremely high. In the tale of policy battles, contrary to the assumptions of the scholarly literature, American women's groups hardly emerged unscathed. Then again, neither did their British or Canadian counterparts.

Policy Momentum in Britain

Because Thatcherism and British feminism began with starkly different worldviews, the clash between these two sides seemed destined to be harsh, direct, and damaging to the less powerful movement interest. The conservative outlook dominated a series of majority governments in a centralized political system. For the most part, British feminism was a disorganized protest movement, tied to a political opposition that seemed doomed to eternal opposition. But did women's claims suffer sustained policy reversal during the Thatcher and Major years? Were groups marginalized, unable to influence the national government, through the mid-1990s?

In answering these questions, we can imagine two large windows that open onto policy conflict. One reveals debate over specific move-ment goals, objectives held in common by groups in all three coun-tries. Through this window, women can be seen pressing their posi-tions on five main concerns that dominated second-wave feminism. They were (a) efforts to uphold legal equality in such areas as constitu-tional rights or access to education; (b) reform of family law to support women and children when marriages fell apart; (c) choice and repro-duction, to provide access to safe and affordable abortions; (d) violence against women, to address rape and assault; and (e) employment rights, to ensure equal pay for work of equal value, equal opportunities in the workplace, and decent child care programs.

A second window reveals conflict over the broader agenda of each conservative leader, in which movements related that agenda to wom-en's interests. Through this second window, groups can be seen strug-gling against conservative policy on more general terms than in the first window. During the Thatcher and Major years, these two sides engaged in policy battles over a variety of issues, many of them dating back to World War I. Debates over war and peace pitted antinuclear groups against the aggressive defense posture of the Conservative gov-ernment. This clash reached its peak when Thatcher agreed to station American nuclear missiles on British soil. A small march to Greenham Common in 1981 escalated during the next three years into a massive and well-publicized women's peace camp. Antinuclear demonstra-tions at Greenham involved as many as forty thousand women in one "Embrace the Base" mobilization.[6] Polls showed the Greenham protest was known to all but 6 percent of British survey respondents in 1983.[7]

Although Greenham Common involved direct conflict between women and Conservatives, this confrontation was less sustained than the fight over workplace issues. Struggles by British groups to intro-duce more government regulation of wages, hours, and conditions of work met a wall of official resistance for more than fifteen years. Poli-cies regarding women's work were highly contested through the Thatcher and Major years because group demands ran counter to Con-servative views on deregulation, privatization, and the need to tame trade union power. Because struggles over employment policy chal-lenged the broader Tory agenda, women were implicated in a pitched fight that extended far beyond the first window. The clearest evidence of this division was the formation of Women against Pit Closures, a coalition supporting striking miners in their showdown with Margaret Thatcher. One 1984 march organized by the coalition drew ten thou-sand women.[8]

Before we turn to these policy conflicts, it is important to sketch the

larger background. What progress were groups making in Britain before 1979? Did feminist organizations enjoy a strong wind at their
backs, a sense of policy momentum, in the years before Thatcher's
election? High court and parliamentary decisions on movement issues
in the pre-Thatcher period show group claims were moving forward
prior to 1979. More than twenty decisions came down in the decade
before Thatcher's first election, of which more than three-quarters were
favorable to movement interests and less than one-fifth were not. Although modern British women's groups had only begun to organize
about ten years before Thatcher's victory, they clearly built considerable momentum during this period.

In the area of equal rights, two laws passed by Parliament were opposed by women's groups. The 1971 Immigration Act established more
restrictive rules regarding citizenship for foreign husbands of British
women than for foreign wives of British men.[9] Five years later, the
Supplementary Benefits Act prevented married women or those living
with men from claiming welfare benefits.[10] In both cases, the assumptions underlying the legislation ran counter to the view that females
were autonomous individuals, the legal equals of males. Feminists argued that the partners of women and men should receive the same
legal treatment in immigration as well as welfare rules.

British family law before 1979 was generally moving forward. Legal
reforms granted women more open access to divorce, a broader claim
on property acquired during marriage, and additional child custody
rights. Because pressure to pass new laws came from a general shift in
public attitudes, these reforms were generally not contentious.[11] Although they enjoyed wide support in all political parties, they did not,
however, have unanimous support. Margaret Thatcher was one of a
handful of M.P.'s who opposed divorce reform in the late 1960s.[12]

It was on the abortion issue that women's groups organized their
most vigorous public campaign. A private member's bill introduced by
Liberal M. P. David Steel formed the basis for the 1967 Abortion Act.
This legislation, which passed through the House of Commons with
little difficulty, provided public funding for abortions up to twenty-
eight weeks. Some provisions of the 1967 act were restrictive; for example, two doctors had to certify risk to the mother or baby. In practice, though, the legislation was "interpreted more liberally" than its
formal terms stated.[13] Laws permitting local health units to offer birth
control materials also passed during the late 1960s, and, in 1973, Edward Heath's Conservative government established contraception as
an integral part of the health system.[14]

Arrayed against the Abortion Act were the Society for the Protection of the Unborn Child (SPUC), established in 1967, and a group known as LIFE, formed in 1970.[15] The National Abortion Campaign, begun in 1975 to counter SPUC's influence, was the leading women's group campaigning to retain the 1967 provisions. In 1976, an umbrella organization of sixteen groups formed as the Co-ordinating Committee in Defence of the 1967 Act. Known as Co-ord, it included the national Trades Union Congress, white-collar unions, female members of Parliament, leading medical associations, and women's organizations that had abortion rights as their core priority. Sustained conflict between the pro- and antichoice sides began in 1975 when Labour M. P. James White introduced a restrictive private member's bill. The National Abortion Campaign organized a demonstration in June 1975 against the White bill that drew about twenty thousand participants. This event, likely the largest women's rights demonstration since the suffrage campaign, helped to ensure the defeat of the bill.[16]

British judges and legislators began to recognize violence against women during the 1970s. A crucial case in this area was *DPP v. Morgan,* involving a pilot in the Royal Air Force and three male colleagues. Morgan allegedly told the men they could have sex with his wife, claiming that even if she protested, she really did not mind. Following a trial by jury, all four men were convicted of rape. They appealed the decision and were acquitted in 1975 by the House of Lords on the grounds they believed the woman had consented. This case raised serious questions about the treatment of rape victims and led Parliament to bring in new laws on violence against women.[17]

The 1976 Sexual Offences Act limited rapists' ability to claim consent and restricted the use of women's sexual history in courtroom evidence. Although groups including Women against Rape supported these changes, they were disappointed by other aspects of the act. It did not acknowledge rape within marriage and protected the identity of accused rapists as well as victims.[18] Some changes sought by feminists were incorporated in later pieces of legislation. The 1977 Housing Act made local authorities responsible for rehousing women with children in addition to battered women.[19] In 1976, organizations representing refuges, or shelters for women in violent situations, obtained terms allowing judges to arrest those who had inflicted physical harm and were likely to injure again. Two years later, they won the right to use magistrates' court injunctions to restrain a violent partner.[20]

Perhaps the strongest momentum for women's groups was in the employment field—the same area in which they faced solid Conservative resistance after 1979. Although one 1970 tax law defined a wife's income as that of her husband, 1972 legislation brought in separate taxation of married couples.[21] A very significant employment law affecting British women was passed in 1970. Known as the Equal Pay Act, this legislation came into effect in late 1975. It set out to ensure that women doing the same work as men were paid the same, and it permitted those who were paid less to appeal to industrial tribunals staffed by labor and management appointees. Women's groups and trade unions endorsed the legislation, although many believed it should go further to cover inequality in pensions, job recruitment, and training. This was *not* the position of the leading business lobby in the United Kingdom, the Confederation of British Industry, which opposed the Equal Pay Act.[22]

Three significant bills passed in 1975 were also supported by women's groups. The Social Security Act gave employees who had been in and out of the workforce—most of them women—the opportunity to earn a pension of their own.[23] The Employment Protection Act created statutory paid maternity leave, protected a mother's job for twenty-nine weeks after the baby was born, and, under a 1978 amendment, prohibited the dismissal of pregnant employees.[24] The Sex Discrimination Act, a companion piece to the Equal Pay Act, outlawed workplace discrimination on the basis of sex or marital status and introduced the concept of indirect or unintentional discrimination. It also established the Equal Opportunities Commission, a government agency charged with enforcing the terms of both the Sex Discrimination and Equal Pay Acts.[25]

In setting the stage for the Thatcher period, this background reveals how British women's groups were moving their issues along. Often in coalition with trade union organizations, they managed to secure important progress in the employment field and staved off a direct threat to abortion access. On their own in the area of violence, women's organizations moved the rape issue into the public realm and won some of what they sought in new legislation. Overall, the pre-1979 record shows steady progress for women's group claims.

The Thatcher Years

Although this momentum was not stopped after 1979, it was clearly slowed. Among more than twenty-five decisions during the Thatcher years, less than two-thirds were favorable, and nearly one-quarter went against movement positions. Seven pro-group actions after 1979 re-sulted from either pressure on the government by the European Com-munity or direct appeals by British women to the European Court of Justice. Because European provisions in the employment field were more progressive than British statutes were, women's groups were able to obtain better results using Community rather than domestic levers.[26] The British record in the Thatcher years *without* European Community influence would have been only 53 percent rather than more than 65 percent favorable outcomes, and one mixed result during this period would have been completely negative had it not been for European pressure.[27] Moreover, the record of Parliament versus the law lords was distinctive, because more than 90 percent of high court and less than half of House of Commons decisions were pro-feminist. With Euro-pean and British judicial influence brought to bear, the situation was considerably better than that without such leverage.

In terms of legal rights, the Thatcher government equalized nation-ality statutes for women and men in 1981, after 1980 Nationality Rules prevented foreign women (but not foreign men) living in Britain from bringing partners into the country.[28] A 1986 decision by the European Court of Justice said Jacqueline Drake, a married woman, was eligible to receive the Invalid Care Allowance while she looked after her ailing mother. When the allowance was introduced in 1975 as a way to com-pensate people for giving up paid work to be carers, it assumed that only married men were eligible.[29]

In the field of family law, three bills liberalized access to divorce and offered some assistance to children. Changes introduced in 1984 made it possible to divorce after one rather than three years of separa-tion, and 1987 reforms ended the disadvantage facing children born outside marriage.[30] The 1989 Children Act came in the wake of the Cleveland affair involving the sexual abuse of minors. Although this act attempted to balance the interests of children, parents, and the state, it gave responsibility for regulating child care to the same local authorities that had been stripped of power and funds by the Thatcher government. Given the increasingly weak position of municipalities, women's organizations questioned who, if anyone, was minding the child minders.[31]

More private members' bills on abortion were introduced during the Thatcher years. Efforts to restrict access, all unsuccessful, were made by Conservative M. P. John Corrie in 1979, Liberal M. P. David Alton in 1988, and Conservative M. P. Ann Widdecombe in 1989.[32] Although the Thatcher government refused to grant additional time to debate the bills, it did enact a system of regulating sex education that was opposed by women's groups and endorsed by the Catholic Church. The 1980 Education Act required local education authorities and school governors to publish details of sex education courses. The purpose of the act, defended by Conservatives and condemned by women's groups, was to ensure that courses conformed to local values and were regulated by local authorities. Opponents of sex education could thus ensure the demise of these programs by arguing that they violated local standards.[33] Provisions of the 1986 Education Act pushed this argument further by giving control to school governors, who could permit parents to withdraw their children from sex education classes. The Thatcher years also saw one positive court decision in this area. The *Gillick v. Minister of Health and Social Security* ruling by the House of Lords declared that contraceptive information and treatment could be given to patients under sixteen years of age without parental consent.[34]

The only significant action in the violence area during the Thatcher years was the 1985 Housing Act, which imposed on local authorities the responsibility to permanently house people in need. Studies showed women fleeing violence at home formed the third largest category of homeless persons.[35] This responsibility for local authorities to permanently house battered women was reversed by a subsequent bill during the Major years.

The bulk of activity took place in the employment field. Among fifteen decisions dealing with work between 1979 and 1990, seven resulted from European Community influence, and six of these were pro-movement. Among the most notable were amendments to the Social Security Act ensuring equal treatment of married women and men on welfare and, in the wake of the *Drake v. Department of Health and Social Security* decision, permitting the Invalid Care Allowance to be paid to married women.[36] Under European Court pressure, the Thatcher government was forced to pass amendments in 1983 to the Equal Pay Act. These changes recognized equal pay for work of equal value, meaning that different jobs requiring the same skill, effort, and responsibility had to pay the same. If they did not, employees from the underpaid group could file a grievance.[37]

The European Court's 1986 decision in the *Marshall v. Southampton Area Health Authority* case said the two retirement ages for British women (at age sixty) and men (at sixty-five) were a breach of Community law. This ruling that British employment law violated the European Community's Equal Treatment Directive prompted the Thatcher government to introduce the 1986 Sex Discrimination Act. The act extended antidiscrimination rules to cover small employers, professions, and collective agreements and said women could not be dismissed at age sixty if men were allowed to work until sixty-five. Women's groups objected to the deregulatory aspects of the act that sought to limit burdens on employers. For example, the 1986 legislation ended limits on hours of factory work by women and said workers had to file discrimination complaints within three months of any occurrence. Like most Conservative responses to European pressure, the 1986 Sex Discrimination Act was a convoluted piece of legislation designed to protect employers as much as possible.[38] European Court judgments in this period also limited the ability of employers to pay part-time workers less than full-time ones (*Jenkins v. Kingsgate Clothing Productions*) and to exclude women from particular job categories (*Johnston v. Chief Constable of the Royal Ulster Constabulary*).[39]

Decisions about women's work that did not involve European influence were far less favorable. British groups opposed changes in 1980 to the Employment Protection Act that weakened and vastly complicated the rules on maternity leave.[40] They objected to many aspects of the 1986 Social Security Act. This act reduced public pensions, replaced grants to welfare recipients with loans, and said state pensions would no longer be based on people's best earning years but instead on average lifetime earnings.[41] As the Institute for Fiscal Studies pointed out in its analysis of the 1986 act, women stood to lose the most from the Thatcher government's shift from public toward private pensions.[42] The 1988 Local Government Act was also considered a loss because it allowed municipalities to continue awarding contracts only to firms that hired and promoted members of racial minorities. The act discontinued the use of this practice, known as contract compliance, with respect to women and, in its infamous clause 28, said public money could not be used to promote homosexuality.[43] Overall, employment laws sponsored by the Thatcher government on its own emphasized less public spending and more private initiative.

The only official avenue inside Britain that was more sympathetic on these issues was the judicial one, since four House of Lords decisions during the Thatcher years supported movement claims. The *De-Souza v. the Automobile Association* ruling treated sexual harassment as discrimination in the workplace and held employers responsible for the actions of their employees.[44] The *Hayward v. Cammell Laird Shipbuilders* and *Pickstone v. Freemans* decisions upheld equal pay for work of equal value, and the *Brown v. Stockton-on-Tees Borough*

Council judgment said employers could not single out pregnant workers for layoff.[45] In other words, the actions of European and British
judges helped to stave off the erosion of women's gains that would
have otherwise occurred during the Thatcher years. In Britain, it was
particularly ironic that the law lords did more to advance women's
rights than did the country's first female prime minister.

The Major Years

The shift in pro-movement decisions from 78 percent before Thatcher
to 65 percent after 1979 dropped to about 57 percent during the Major
years. If European influences are excluded, the number of positive actions under Major falls to only seven of fifteen—most of them court
decisions rather than legislation. British groups viewed seven of nine
Major-era laws as a mixture of wins and losses. In short, women's
group claims fared demonstrably worse after the Conservatives came
to power, and they fared worse over time given the slippage from
Thatcher to Major.

One of the most contentious pieces of legislation in the Major years
imposed limits on public protest. The Criminal Justice Act was widely
criticized, including by feminists, because its provisions could be read
as prohibiting peaceful gatherings like those for abortion access or
against nuclear missiles or, even earlier, in favor of the right to vote.
This same law did contain a provision declaring rape within marriage
illegal, which women's groups had long sought. Efforts to press the
government to define consent more narrowly in sexual assault cases
and to shield the sexual history of rape victims from court questioning,
however, were not successful.[46]

After Thatcher's resignation in 1990, the Conservative government
passed a controversial Child Support Act. The act's stated purpose was
to compel absent fathers to pay child support. This goal was initially
shared by economic conservatives who wanted to reduce government
spending, by social conservatives in the Tory caucus who organized
in 1982 as the Family Policy Group, and by women's organizations
that believed single mothers and their children needed support.[47] The
terms under which the act was implemented beginning in 1993, however, provoked harsh criticism. Single parents on income support—
more than 90 percent of them mothers—were compelled to name their
child's father so that the agency enforcing the act could obtain payments from him. Any maintenance received from the father meant wel-

fare benefits paid to the mother were reduced by the same amount. Women's groups argued that the act was punitive because it reduced benefits to single mothers and dangerous because it encouraged contact with partners who had been violent. In response to this challenge, the government insisted the act was written in such a way that it did not endanger anyone.[48]

In this same area, a landmark decision by the House of Lords awarded one divorced woman, Anne Brooks, a share of her ex-husband's pension following their divorce.[49] The broader question of marital breakdown was addressed in a controversial piece of legislation known as the 1996 Family Law Act. The act moved English and Welsh divorce law closer to a no-fault approach under which "the irretrievable breakdown of the marriage" formed the sole grounds on which partners could split.[50] After long and acrimonious debate—including among Conservatives—the legislation passed in a form that encouraged divorcing couples to act slowly and to pursue mediation and marriage counseling as part of the process. Although women's groups generally disagreed with the conservative "family values" rationale behind that part of the divorce bill, they tended to support the provisions on domestic violence embedded in section 4 of the 1996 act (discussed later in this chapter).

On questions of reproduction, women's groups rated the 1990 Human Fertilisation and Embryology Act as mixed. Antichoice groups used a campaign strategy imported from the United States to communicate their point of view. They mailed each member of Parliament a plastic fetus, an action viewed in Britain as vulgar, distasteful, and ultimately helpful to the other side. Women's organizations were critical of the act because it limited access to artificial insemination by single women and said abortions could not occur after twenty-four weeks. On the positive side, the law removed any time limit on abortion when danger to the mother or serious fetal abnormality existed. Subsequent efforts during 1993 to organize antiabortion protests modeled on Operation Rescue efforts in the United States led to the arrest and deportation of leading campaigners. Although this last action did not involve a law or court case, feminists viewed it as a pro-choice move by the Conservative government.[51]

A number of important decisions during the Major years advanced women's claims in the violence area. The 1991 *R. v. Rawlinson* ruling reversed a long tradition among British judges by recognizing rape within marriage. It formed the foundation for revisions contained in the Criminal Justice Act three years later.[52] Amendments to the Sexual

Offences Act in 1992 banned the publication of information likely to identify rape victims,[53] and provisions in the 1996 Family Law Act extended the terms under which both adults and children could use the courts to remove an abuser from the family home.[54] These pro-movement directions were not apparent, however, in the 1996 Housing Act. That law removed a 1985 provision under which local authorities had to permanently house women in violent situations and replaced it with responsibility for temporary housing only.

As in the Thatcher period, the vast bulk of activity during the Major years had to do with work. Four decisions by the European Court of Justice accepted women's movement claims while one did not. In the *Barber v. Guardian Royal Exchange Assurance Group* case, the court found that sex discrimination in pension payments made to laid-off workers was contrary to European law, even though this issue was not addressed in the Equal Pay Act.[55] The *Enderby v. Frenchay Health Authority* judgment upheld a female speech therapist's claim that her pay should be comparable to that of male pharmacists and clinical psychologists. The court rejected employer arguments that male-female differences resulted from market forces that placed differing values on their work.[56] The 1993 *Marshall v. Southampton Area Health Authority* decision ruled against the British statutory limit on how much women could be compensated because of sex discrimination. After the 1986 *Marshall* case struck down separate retirement ages for men and women, the 1993 judgment of the same name led the government to remove the ceiling on monetary awards in cases of sex discrimination.[57] The *Webb v. EMO Air Cargo* ruling overturned a negative House of Lords judgment by declaring employers could not dismiss replacement workers who were pregnant.[58] In a 1995 decision that disappointed movement activists, however, the European Court rejected Rose Graham's claim that the cut in her disability benefit at age sixty was discriminatory, because men continued to receive their benefits until sixty-five.[59]

British court decisions on work issues were also positive for the most part. In the *Scally v. Southern Board* case, the House of Lords ruled that employers had to provide workers with information on benefits. The judgment dealt with pensions but was seen by women's groups and trade unions as affecting other provisions such as maternity leave.[60] In a 1994 landmark decision, the House of Lords ruled that part-time workers—most of them women—should have the same statutory rights to claim severance pay and compensation for unfair dismissal as did full-time employees. This crucial case was pursued by the Equal Opportunities Commission in coordination with women's organizations and trade unions.[61] The following year, the House of Lords ruled in favor of females working in school lunchrooms who were paid less than male garbage collectors. The *Ratcliffe v. North Yorkshire County Council* judgment maintained that women's lower pay resulted from sex discrimination rather than market forces, as argued by the employer.[62] Overall, this push in the courts for equal pay and rights for part-timers was part of a concerted movement and trade union effort to improve the status of working women.

All three employment laws passed by the Major government received mixed reviews. The 1990 National Health Act recognized carers as a group by name and ensured that people who took care of others (a majority of them women) would be consulted when community care plans were drawn up. Yet this same legislation granted carers no new rights and established cost control as a key criterion for public health services.[63] Probably the most controversial law about work was the 1993 Trade Union Act known as TURERA. Because of a European directive on maternity rights, TURERA set up complex new rules that improved British provisions on maternity leave. Other sections of TURERA brought in limits on the dismissal and suspension of pregnant workers. What the law also did, however, was require that all union members reregister every three years. Furthermore, it eliminated minimum wage protection (via Wages Councils) for workers at the bottom end of the pay scale.[64] British studies estimated that about three-fourths of these lowest paid employees were women.[65] The 1995 Pensions Act responded to the *Marshall* and *Barber* decisions by establishing that men and women had to be treated equally in pension programs so as to meet the requirements of European law. The act set out a timetable for equalizing retirement ages for males and females at age sixty-five, not sixty as sought by women's groups and unions. The 1995 law did not explicitly define pension provisions for dependent spouses, most of them women, nor did it reverse the erosion of state pensions begun during the 1980s.[66]

In short, British decisions in the Conservative years were less promovement than those that came down during the early 1970s. A steady decline in favorable outcomes occurred over time, from more than three-quarters before 1979, to about two-thirds in the Thatcher years, to only 57 percent in the Major years. Had it not been for House of Lords rulings, European Community influences, and especially European Court judgments on employment issues, the situation facing British groups would have been considerably worse.

American Developments before 1980

Efforts by national women's organizations in the United States to advance their agenda on equal rights, legal reform, abortion, violence, and employment were generally successful before 1980. Some observers of this first policy window, in fact, suggested that the spread of feminist consciousness in the general population, coupled with a proliferation of movement groups and substantial policy change, meant the momentum of American feminism was largely unassailable.[67] Writing in 1989, for example, Joyce Gelb claimed that these factors plus the political independence of U.S. women's groups and their tradition of equal rights litigation led to "less erosion in the U.S. public policy arena" than elsewhere.[68] Yet the rise of organized antifeminism on the political right, particularly within the Republican party, was arguably a very potent threat to policy momentum. On issues like the Equal Rights Amendment, child care, equal pay, violence against women, and certainly abortion, pro- and antifeminist interests held vastly differing positions. Gelb and others thus seemed to dismiss the possibility that a resurgent social conservatism could challenge let alone reverse the gains made by organized feminism.

According to the following account, U.S. women's groups after 1980 had a hard time in both the first and second window of policy action, primarily because they struggled to defend core movement priorities that few had expected to find so endangered. American groups were more pro-system at their point of origin than were British movement organizations; the latter primarily grew out of ferment on the political left, whereas many of the former developed within a moderate, pragmatic political center. This centrist tradition meant American feminism often employed interest group strategies that diverged from the kind of radical political critique and vigorous, direct confrontation that characterized the British movement. Conflict in the second window in the United States was therefore more muted than in Britain, as American activists after 1980 directed much of their energy toward fending off bad news in the first window using the moderate strategies they knew best.

Particularly when compared with judgments in subsequent years, decisions on movement claims during the decade *before* Ronald Reagan came to power were generally pro-feminist. A flood of more than thirty-five decisions flowed from the United States Congress and Supreme Court in this period; of them, about 70 percent supported women's group positions. Although laws were more pro-movement than court rulings, at least two-thirds of both high court and legislative decisions before 1980 were consistent with feminist claims. The bulk of formal action at the national level, in short, paralleled movement demands even though modern feminism had only emerged about ten years earlier.

One of the most significant events was the March 1972 passage of the Equal Rights Amendment. The ERA had been introduced in 1923 by members of the National Woman's Party, but 1972 marked the first time—after many, many attempts—that it won approval in both houses of Congress. A minimum of thirty-eight states was then required to ratify the amendment within seven years, although this deadline was later extended to 1982.[69] Laws ensuring women's access to education, housing, and credit also passed during this period. Modeled after civil rights measures, Title IX of the 1972 Education Amendments prohibited discrimination on the basis of sex in any educational institution that received federal funds. Except for a debate over undergraduate admissions to private colleges, to which Title IX did not apply, this law passed with relatively little controversy.[70]

The 1974 Equal Credit Act said financial institutions could no longer use sex or marital status in deciding about loans. Introduced by a Republican senator from Tennessee, this act passed the Senate unanimously and received only one negative vote in the House of Representatives. Republican President Gerald Ford signed the bill into law.[71]

One of the most intriguing stories of equal rights legislation involved the Women's Educational Equity Act (WEEA). First introduced in the House to support women's studies programs, revise textbooks, and improve the status of women in education, WEEA was absorbed into a larger Senate education bill. The act received little attention from either a House subcommittee or senators during a floor debate. It passed into law and later became a prime target for conservative critics during the 1980s.[72]

Supreme Court decisions on equal rights generally also favored movement positions. Using rulings against race discrimination as their foundation, lawyers argued against sex discrimination in parallel terms. Ruth Bader Ginsburg, who was later appointed to the Supreme Court by President Bill Clinton, argued successfully in the 1971 case of *Reed v. Reed*. This decision involved an Idaho law that gave automatic preference to males over equally qualified females as executors of the estate of a deceased person. In a unanimous judgment, the Supreme Court overturned the state law.[73] The Court's ruling in the *Frontiero v.*

Richardson case declared unconstitutional a military statute that awarded benefits to the spouses of married men but not those of married women.[74] A provision of the Social Security Act that offered benefits to widows but not widowers with young children was found invalid in the *Weinberger v. Wiesenfeld* case.[75] Finally, higher pension contributions by women were ruled a violation of the 1964 Civil Rights Act (and specifically Title VII, prohibiting discrimination at work on the basis of sex and other categories) in the *Los Angeles Department of Water and Power v. Manhart* decision.[76]

Two other rulings were less favorable. The *Geduldig v. Aiello* judgment held that denying disability benefits to a pregnant woman under a state health insurance plan was *not* sex discrimination and thus was constitutional.[77] The decision in *Craig v. Boren* was mixed. It ruled unconstitutional an Oklahoma law that established different rules on beer buying for young women and men, arguing that sex discrimination in this instance was not related to an important government interest. The judgment was positive in that it advanced beyond the standard set in *Reed* to reach "a middle-level scrutiny test" for determining sex discrimination.[78] Because of the way it was formulated, however, this case established that judges could uphold sex discrimination elsewhere because of government interests. The *Craig* decision showed that the controversy over when and how equal rights would be supported was far from over.

In the field of family law, only a few decisions came forward, but most were pro-movement. The primary focus of American women's groups after 1972 was threefold: ratifying the ERA in the states, protecting abortion access, and improving conditions at work. As a result, questions of family law reform received less attention. In the *Gomez v. Perez* case, the Supreme Court struck down a Texas law denying illegitimate children the right to claim support from their fathers.[79] In the *Stanton v. Stanton* case, the Court struck down a Utah law stating parents had to support sons until age twenty-one but daughters only until eighteen, and, in *Orr v. Orr,* it declared invalid an Alabama statute that said only men had to pay alimony.[80] Although these decisions upheld equal rights arguments, Social Security changes from the same period began with a different motive. Much like the British Child Support Act and U.S. laws passed during the Reagan years, the Child Support Amendments of 1975 were designed to lower welfare spending. The amendments set up a joint state and federal system to enforce support payments, locate absent parents, and require people on welfare to turn over support monies to the government.[81]

Many of the most contentious decisions of this period concerned reproductive choice. In the 1972 *Eisenstadt v. Baird* decision, the Supreme Court struck down a Massachusetts law against distributing contraceptive materials to single people. Married couples' access to contraceptives was established by the Supreme Court's 1965 decision in *Griswold v. Connecticut.* This judgment defined marital relations within a "zone of privacy" beyond the reach of government regulation.[82] The 1972 case had been brought to trial by Massachusetts Planned Parenthood, which put the issue in motion by showing contraceptives and giving sample products to students at Boston University. Planned Parenthood successfully argued that individuals—whether married or single—had the right to be free from government intrusion when they decided about childbearing.[83]

This same right-to-privacy argument was crucial to the 1973 watershed ruling in *Roe v. Wade.* The *Roe* case began in 1969 when an unmarried woman in Texas, Norma McCorvey, found she was pregnant and unable to obtain a legal abortion. In the litigation that followed, McCorvey became known as Jane Roe to both the federal court in Dallas and the U.S. Supreme Court. Ultimately, Roe's lawyers convinced the high court that restricting abortion was unconstitutional because it violated a woman's right to privacy. The *Roe* decision struck down state laws restricting abortion in the first three months of pregnancy and allowed states to regulate during the second three months only to protect the woman's health.[84]

The same concept of personal privacy formed the basis for the *Doe v. Bolton* judgment, delivered on the same day as *Roe v. Wade.* In the former case, the Supreme Court invalidated a Georgia law that limited abortion to hospitals, required a committee of doctors to approve the procedure, and restricted services to Georgia residents only. According to a majority of justices, these kinds of statutes created unnecessary obstacles for women seeking abortions [85]

The stream of pro-choice decisions following *Eisenstadt* brought opponents out of the woodwork. After 1973, antiabortion interests challenged *Roe* and other precedents on many different levels. Some went after state funding of abortion, as in the *Beal v. Doe* and *Maher v. Roe* cases in the Supreme Court, whereas others contested federal funding through the Hyde Amendments in Congress.[86] Still others tried to define rigid time limits for abortions and impose parental and spousal consent rules, as in the *Planned Parenthood of Central Missouri v. Danforth* and *Bellotti v. Baird* cases. Notably, pro-choice organizations won both of the latter as well as the *Colautti v. Franklin* case, which struck down a Pennsylvania law that said doctors could be charged if they did not save a viable fetus.[87] Overall, antichoice interests were able to restrict abortion funding in the years before 1980 but were less successful in imposing time limits and consent rules. After 1980, these groups won support in state legislatures, the White House, and the federal courts for all kinds of restrictions.

In the area of violence, much of the activity by women's groups occurred at the local level, far from Congress and the Supreme Court. Attempts to establish shelters for battered women began during the early 1970s in a number of cities. A national umbrella organization was formed in 1978 as the National Coalition against Domestic Violence.[88] One of the first legislative efforts in this field occurred during the Carter years, when a Domestic Violence Prevention Act was introduced in Congress. The bill set out to provide funding for shelters, research, and a federal agency on family violence. Yet this legislation was vigorously opposed by conservatives who viewed it as government interference in the family. The provisions, critics claimed, would lead to more divorces, prohibit parents from spanking their children, and generally jeopardize traditional family values. Ultimately, the act was blocked by a filibuster in the Senate.[89]

In the employment field, U.S. court and legislative action after 1970 was generally responsive to women's group claims. Of the eleven decisions rendered, nearly two-thirds were consistent with movement positions. Among the most significant court rulings was in the 1971 case brought by Ida Phillips, who was rejected from a company trainee position because she had preschool children, although men with children of that age were accepted. The Supreme Court declared in a mixed decision that companies could not have different hiring rules for men and women because this would constitute sex discrimination. If a firm could show that family obligations hindered women's work, however, then it could use sex plus the family status factor in refusing to hire mothers of young children.[90]

In the *Griggs v. Duke Power Company* ruling of the same year, the Court set out a landmark distinction between the seeming neutrality of employer practices and their far from neutral effect. In *Griggs,* black employees at a power plant argued against a rule requiring workers to pass tests or present diplomas to qualify for better-paying jobs. Because these credentials had no bearing on a person's ability to do the job, they amounted to discrimination in favor of whites—even though the intent of the practice was not to discriminate. The Court's decision held that Title VII of the Civil Rights Act proscribes not only overt discrimination but also practices that are fair in form, but discriminatory in operation. The touchstone is business necessity. If an employment practice which operates to exclude Negroes cannot be shown to be related to job performance, the practice is prohibited.[91]

Women's groups in the United States were able to use the *Griggs* ruling as a precedent that made employers demonstrate business necessity when they instituted various rules.[92] In the United Kingdom, the *Griggs* judgment shaped the concept of indirect bias in the Sex Discrimination Act of 1975.[93]

Two other court decisions in this period also favored movement claims. In the *Pittsburgh Press v. Pittsburgh Commission on Human Relations* case, initiated by the National Organization for Women, the Supreme Court ruled against separate male and female help wanted columns. The Court said eliminating separate ads from newspaper classifieds did not threaten freedom of the press.[94] In the *Cleveland Board of Education v. LaFleur* case, the Court struck down a policy that established when schoolteachers had to go on maternity leave. Whereas the Cleveland Board of Education said teachers had to go on leave at least five months before their due date, the Court claimed this rule was too sweeping. Because it gave no opportunity for pregnant teachers to show they were still fit to work, the policy was deemed a violation of due process.[95]

Labor laws passed before 1980 generally advanced women's rights in the workplace. The Equal Employment Opportunity Act of 1972 gave greater powers to the agency charged with enforcing the antidiscrimination terms of the Civil Rights Act. The Equal Employment Opportunities Commission (EEOC) was allowed to take companies to court if they did not voluntarily comply with Title VII.[96] A number of large firms, including American Telephone and Telegraph (AT&T), were indeed served with EEOC lawsuits in the years before 1980. AT&T had to pay about $40 million to female and minority employees as a result.[97] Under amendments to the Equal Pay Act and Fair Labor Standards Act, sex discrimination in wages was outlawed across a broad set of job categories in the public and private sectors.[98]

Three negative decisions from the Supreme Court came down during this period, one of which led Congress to pass legislation protecting pregnant workers. In the *General Electric Company v. Gilbert* case, the employer successfully argued that excluding pregnant workers from the company benefits plan was not sex discrimination.[99] NOW together with a coalition of labor and women's groups immediately formed the Campaign to End Discrimination against Pregnant Workers. This coalition convinced Congress to enact the Pregnancy Discrimination Act of 1978, which said pregnant employees must "be treated the same for all employment-related purposes."[100] The second negative decision on women's work came in the *Dothard v. Rawlinson* case, which permitted the use of sex as an occupational category. The Supreme Court accepted the State of Alabama's claim that banning female jail guards was not sex discrimination. Instead, a majority of justices said it was protecting women's safety in crowded prisons.[101] Finally, the *Personnel Administrator of Massachusetts v. Feeney* decision of 1979 declared constitutional a state law that gave army veterans preference over all others for civil service jobs. Less than 2 percent of veterans were women, meaning that men virtually monopolized state jobs. Despite what it had ruled earlier in the *Griggs* case, the Supreme Court upheld the law in *Feeney* on the grounds that Massachusetts did not intend to discriminate against women.[102]

Overall, these decisions preceding Reagan's election show American women's groups were making significant progress in a variety of fields. Important advances on equal rights, family law, access to abortion, and women's work all occurred in this period. Although there were limits to what group pressure could accomplish, particularly in terms of violence against women, public funding for abortion, and equality at work, momentum in Congress and the courts was clearly with the feminist movement. What began to unravel after 1980 was support for workplace rules and the *Roe* precedent, not only in the White House but also in Congress, the federal bureaucracy, and especially the Supreme Court. A succession of conservative appointments to the bench by Presidents Reagan and Bush had a direct impact on the lives of American women.

The Reagan Years

Decisions from the Reagan years show a definite shift away from the progress of the 1970s. Among nearly thirty laws and court decisions, less than half were consistent with what women's groups wanted, whereas about 35 percent went against movement positions. This pattern represented a much less favorable tilt than before 1980. From a success-to-failure ratio for women's groups of 25 to 8 before Reagan's election, the record dropped to 14 to 10 afterward and, even more dramatically, to 4 to 16 during the Bush years. Many women's movement defeats after 1980 were significant, including the loss of the Equal Rights Amendment despite an extended deadline for state ratification in addition to further restrictions on abortion access and funding.

Two of the six equal rights outcomes went directly against group claims. The first and most notable was the ERA, which fell three states short of success at the June 1982 deadline for ratification. Women's groups maintained that the ERA in one stroke would end discriminatory laws at all levels and eliminate the need to change them one by one. Although former presidents Carter and Ford had urged ratification and Betty Ford had cochaired a last-minute push to ensure ERA success, the Reagan administration was not on board.[103] Reagan said he favored the *E* and the *R* but not the *A*.[104] This view signaled a profound opposition to federal regulation among leading Republicans, who stressed that Congress would enforce the terms of the constitutional amendment if it passed. Business groups, antifeminist organizations, the insurance industry, and prominent conservatives successfully argued that the ERA would endanger the American way of life. During long and heated debate, the ERA was linked to same-sex toilets, women in combat positions, homosexual marriage, and the end of alimony payments.[105] As political scientist Jane Mansbridge observes in *Why We Lost the ERA,* supporters of the amendment presented a general view of what could be gained from its passage, whereas opponents created profound unease about the specifics of what might be lost.[106]

The other notable defeat on equal rights was the *Grove City College v. Bell* case. This decision involved a small private college in Pennsylvania whose students received federal aid monies. The college refused to comply with the terms of Title IX (forbidding sex discrimination in higher education), arguing that only students, not the Grove City administration, accepted federal aid. After it was denied student grants and loans during the Carter years, Grove City began legal action against the U.S. government.[107] The case reached the Supreme Court tailor-made for Reagan administration appointees, who were working in all branches of the federal government to limit antidiscrimination provisions.

Not only did the Supreme Court decide in 1984 to narrow the reach of Title IX of the Civil Rights Act, but also the federal government changed sides on the case. From arguing during the Carter years that colleges should comply with Title IX if they received any federal funds, the Justice Department after 1980 filed briefs claiming this rule applied only to the specific program receiving government aid. According to women's organizations and civil rights groups, the *Grove City* judgment effectively opened the door to discrimination in education because it narrowed the reach of federal law. Efforts to reverse this decision via legislation were held up for years because of fierce Republican opposition in the Senate and White House.[108] Finally, the Civil Rights Restoration Act of 1988 passed after both houses of Congress overrode President Reagan's veto. The act made it clear that colleges could not discriminate in any area if they were to receive federal support, thus overturning the *Grove City* decision. This same legislation, however, contained an antiabortion clause known as the Danforth Amendment.[109]

The only pro-movement actions of the Reagan years on equal rights were the *Arizona Governing Committee v. Norris* and *New York State Club Association v. City of New York* cases. The first ruling outlawed retirement plans that collected the same level of premiums from men and women but paid out more per month to retired men.[110] The second declared that private clubs could not select members on the basis of sex or race. It upheld an antidiscrimination provision of the City of New York, rejecting club arguments that the municipal law was unconstitutional.[111]

On the surface, the formal record on family law during the Reagan years looks passable. The 1984 Child Support Enforcement Act, 1988 Family Support Act, and 1988 *Hicks v. Feiock* decision were designed to improve enforcement of court-ordered child support payments. The two laws pressed absent fathers to pay up and, in the 1988 act, required states to guarantee education, job training, and child care support to parents on welfare (most of them mothers). Yet as in Britain during debate over the Child Support Act and as in the United States during the 1970s, women's groups had different motives than conservatives on these issues. Whereas feminists endorsed payments by fathers and better child care funding, conservatives believed in parents rather than governments supporting children.[112] Movement organizations saw the 1988 act as part of the Reagan administration's efforts to transfer power from the federal to state level and to reduce welfare spending, all under the guise of welfare reform. As a result, this legislation was criticized as a punitive, mean-spirited bill that offered little to poor mothers and their children.[113]

It was on the issue of abortion that women's groups suffered the most setbacks during the Reagan years. Fully five of seven decisions went against movement positions. They included a series of judgments by the U.S. Supreme Court beginning with *Harris v. McRae* in 1980.

Following the lines of the *Maher* ruling, this case upheld the Hyde Amendments, which cut off federal funds for abortions. A majority of justices said a woman's right to have an abortion was separate from the question of who paid for it. If a woman was poor, this economic condition was of her creation and not the result of government rules.[114] The *H.L. v. Matheson* decision one year later upheld a Utah law requiring doctors to notify the parents or husband of any woman seeking an abortion. Contested by a fifteen-year-old who lived with her parents, the statute was declared constitutional. According to the Supreme Court, Utah had a legitimate interest in strengthening the family and ensuring that parents were consulted about such a major decision.[115] The 1983 *Planned Parenthood of Kansas City, Missouri v. Ashcroft* ruling upheld a Missouri abortion law that required both parental consent and the presence of a second physician to care for any fetus that was viable.[116] These judgments on parental consent differed from the *Gillick* decision in Britain during the same period, which ruled against parental involvement in contraception offered to individuals under sixteen years old.

Two bills signed into law by President Reagan were also antichoice. The Adolescent Family Life Bill was part of an effort to promote chastity among teenagers. It prohibited abortion counseling for young girls, funded religious organizations that spread the chastity view, and encouraged pregnant teenagers to have their babies adopted.[117] The bill survived a legal challenge in the *Bowen v. Kendrick* case, when the Supreme Court ruled that funding religious groups for this purpose did not contravene the separation of church and state.[118] During the same period, the Danforth Amendment was tacked onto the 1988 Civil Rights Act. It made overturning the *Grove City* decision bittersweet for women's groups by adding an antiabortion clause to the act. According to the amendment, hospitals that received federal funds did not have to provide abortions, and colleges did not have to cover abortion services in benefit plans.[119]

Two pro-movement decisions on abortion were also reached by the Supreme Court during the Reagan years. Notably, these were the last pro-choice rulings by the high court until after Republicans lost the presidency in 1992. The *City of Akron v. Akron Center for Reproductive Health* judgment threw out very restrictive terms that had been drafted by the Ohio Right to Life Society. They required abortions to be performed only in hospitals and only if parental consent for minors, written consent of the woman following a doctor's lecture on fetal development, and consent of the father were all obtained. Although the

Akron regulations were defended by the Reagan administration before the Supreme Court, they were ruled unconstitutional.[120] A similar judgment followed in the *Thornburgh v. American College of Obstetricians and Gynecologists* case. Like *Akron,* this decision found that limits on access to abortion were not supported by a legitimate government interest.[121]

The same piece of legislation that antiviolence groups tried to move forward during the Carter years remained blocked. The Domestic Violence Prevention Act would have funded services for victims of violence. This act was vigorously opposed by conservatives who said the legislation would both increase the size of the federal bureaucracy and threaten the family.[122] Although the White House reduced funds for women's shelters, it was unable to stop a later bill known as the Family Violence Act. This law renewed the flow of monies to women's refuges by creating a separate source of endowment. Fines imposed on people convicted of breaking the law were channeled into a fund for both shelters and victims of violence. Conservatives managed to present this legislation as part of a war on crime and the federal deficit, because much of the funding for shelters would come from fines paid by criminals rather than from tax dollars. Moreover, allowing states to evict batterers from the family home meant women and children could stay there; this arrangement was less costly than moving them to shelters or other housing.[123]

In the employment field, women's groups did reasonably well during the Reagan years. Of the eleven actions taken, seven were consistent with movement claims. Changes introduced in 1981 increased child care credits for lower-income taxpayers.[124] The 1984 Retirement Equity Act improved pensions for workers who were in and out of the workforce and continued benefits for spouses whose partners had died. This act was designed to meet the needs of older women and was not opposed by either the White House or business groups, which saw few new costs as a result of the changes.[125] During his last year of office, Reagan signed a law extending antidiscrimination rules to borrowing by businesses and creating a government program to assist women in small business.[126] Also in 1988, the Housing and Community Development Act set up subsidized child care in public housing projects.[127]

Three Supreme Court decisions during the Reagan years were also pro-movement. The crucial *County of Washington v. Gunther* decision ruled that female jail guards in Oregon were unfairly paid less than men for substantially the same work. The *Gunther* judgment upheld women's claims that segregation by sex in the workplace produced wage discrimination.[128] This 1981 ruling marked the first stage in a long battle for what American groups called comparable worth and what Canadian and British women referred to as pay equity or equal pay for work of equal value. The point was that obtaining the same pay in the same jobs as men was irrelevant to the vast bulk of working women in clerical, nursing, catering, teaching, and other female-dominated job categories. To conservatives in the Reagan administration, however, comparable worth was rejected as yet another costly and bureaucratic burden on employers.

Three years later, the *Hishon v. King and Spalding* ruling extended antidiscrimination rules to law firms and other professional partnerships.[129] The 1987 *Johnson v. Transportation Agency of Santa Clara* decision rejected arguments that a less qualified woman had been hired instead of a man to work as a road dispatcher. This was again a precedent-setting ruling, because it upheld a voluntary plan by Santa Clara County in California to begin hiring women in skilled jobs. As in the *Gunther* case, the high court judgment on *Johnson* went against Reagan administration claims, in this case that preferring individuals from underrepresented groups amounted to reverse discrimination against white men.[130]

Setting the stage for a torrent of antimovement decisions during the Bush years, two negative and two mixed high court rulings came down on employment issues. In the *Firefighters Local Union v. Stotts* case, the Reagan administration argued against goals and timetables, or what it called quotas, in the workplace. The ruling involved laying off firefighters in Memphis, Tennessee. Whites were laid off before blacks who had less seniority and who had been hired under an affirmative action program. The Court's decision against laying off the whites first was cheered by conservatives who opposed affirmative action. Women's groups and civil rights organizations, however, saw a direct threat to their agenda in both the *Stotts* decision and subsequent challenges by the Justice Department to hiring plans like the one in Memphis.[131] Equally bad news from the perspective of these interests came down in the *Wimberly v. Labor and Industrial Relations Commission* decision. It upheld a Missouri law that denied unemployment benefits to pregnant women, arguing that pregnancy was only one of a number of bases on which benefits could be refused.[132]

The first mixed decision of the Reagan years was the 1986 *Meritor Savings Bank v. Vinson* judgment. This ruling found sexual harassment on the job to be a form of discrimination under Title VII, which was a major step forward. Unlike the British ruling in the *DeSouza* case, however, the employer was not held responsible for creating a hostile work environment.[133] The last work-related ruling of the Reagan years came in the *California Federal Savings and Loan v. Guerra* case. Against NOW's position that favored gender-neutral provisions for employee leave, the Supreme Court was sympathetic toward California Federal Savings and Loan employee Lillian Garland, who wanted her job back after taking a three-month leave to have a baby. The high court's decision in *Guerra* endorsed job protection and maternity leave for pregnant women at both the state and federal levels. It is notable that the arguments advanced by NOW along with the League of Women Voters, the National Women's Political Caucus, and other organizations in this case differed from what comparable Canadian and British groups would likely have argued during the same period. Parallel with the relatively greater willingness of feminists outside the United States to pressure for specified maternity leave, some American activists sided with Garland in demanding targeted protections for pregnant workers.[134]

Overall, the Reagan years saw women's groups falter on the issues of equal rights, particularly given the failure to ratify the ERA, and abortion, in which consent rules and restrictions on funding and hospital access were all upheld by an increasingly conservative Supreme Court. What appeared to be progress in the family law and violence areas was in fact contingent on compromises with conservative interests. The war on crime and the attack on the federal deficit represented in many respects the driving force behind Reagan-era legislation that funded women's shelters with fines paid by criminals and that reformed child support rules. Establishing momentum in the employment field was probably the most notable accomplishment by women's organizations between 1980 and 1988. During this period, Congress and the Supreme Court appeared far more open to arguments about limits on women's opportunities at work than they were in the years that followed.

The Bush Years

The Bush presidency was generally not a favorable period for women's group claims in the courts, the Congress, or the White House. The pattern of decisions that emerged after 1988, in fact, is damning in its indictment of movement influence. Among twenty-four actions, two-thirds went against feminist positions. More than 75 percent of Supreme Court decisions and more than 40 percent of legislative actions between 1988 and 1992 were inconsistent with group claims. This strong negative record—even as compared with that from the Reagan years—resulted from two factors. First, George Bush inherited the conservative Supreme Court bench that Ronald Reagan had built and strengthened it further with the controversial nomination of Clarence Thomas. Second, given suspicions on the right that he was a liberal, President Bush pressed a firm conservative line against abortion and federal regulation of the workplace.

The sharp decline in feminist influence occurred across all policy fields, beginning with legal equality. The only pro-movement decision in that area during the Bush years was the *Metro Broadcasting v. Federal Communications Commission* ruling. This judgment upheld the right of federal regulators to promote diverse programming on the airwaves by increasing the number of minority-owned radio and television stations.[135] The other action on equal rights, the *Shaw v. Reno* ruling, declared unconstitutional a North Carolina electoral district designed to represent blacks. According to the Supreme Court, the district boundaries were irregular and amounted to segregation by race even though they were consistent with earlier federal laws. Civil rights organizations opposed this ruling, as did women's groups, which saw a direct threat to local districts that had elected minority women to Congress.[136]

The only family law ruling during the Bush years was negative. In the 1989 *Mississippi Choctaw Indians v. Holyfield* case, the Supreme Court upheld provisions of the Indian Child Welfare Act that gave tribal courts control over adoptions of Indian children. The twins whose adoption was contested were born off the Choctaw reservation, and both parents wanted them to be adopted by non-Indians. In this decision, the parents' adoption preferences were denied by a ruling that gave primacy to tribal courts.[137]

Probably the best-known decision of the Bush years was the *Webster v. Reproductive Health Services* ruling of 1989, which women's groups saw as a direct threat to the *Roe* precedent. In *Webster*, the Court upheld a Missouri statute that said human life begins at conception and that prohibited public employees, public facilities, and public funds from being used in abortions except when the mother's life was in danger.[138] This ruling followed massive demonstrations by pro-choice groups in Washington, D.C. Accounts suggest that more than 500,000 marchers converged on the U.S. capital to support the *Roe* precedent both in 1989 and again in 1992 in the period of the *Planned Parenthood of Southeastern Pennsylvania v. Casey* ruling.[139]

Despite these efforts, however, no pro-movement decisions on abortion came down during the Bush years. The 1990 ruling in *Hodgson v. Minnesota* upheld a state law that both living parents of a minor had to consent in writing to an abortion.[140] The *Ohio v. Akron Center for Reproductive Health* decision rendered on the same day said one parent had to receive twenty-four-hour notice from a doctor in cases involving a minor.[141] The 1991 *Rust v. Sullivan* judgment upheld a ban on abortion information and counseling in federally funded clinics.[142] This Reagan administration policy, continued during the Bush years, was known among critics as the gag rule. Efforts by pro-choice groups to defeat it were unsuccessful because legislation passed by Congress did not command the two-thirds support necessary to overturn a presidential veto.[143] Not surprisingly, the gag rule remained in effect until after the Clinton inauguration in 1993.

Two cases brought forward by Planned Parenthood during the Bush years also faced stiff opposition. In 1991, the Supreme Court upheld the right of the U.S. government to deny funding to international agencies that endorsed any form of family planning. Known as the Mexico City policy, this practice of using contraception and abortion as a litmus test for foreign aid paralleled the Republican system of assessing Supreme Court nominees.[144] In 1992, the Court delivered a mixed ruling in *Casey*, the only action on abortion during the Bush years that was not completely negative. This decision upheld a Pennsylvania law demanding spousal consent or parental consent, requiring the woman be counseled on fetal development by a doctor, and outlawing most abortions in public hospitals. Both sides claimed an element of success in the ruling: women's groups took some consolation in *Casey*'s emphasis on the basic right to choose in the early stages of pregnancy, while antiabortion groups celebrated the Court's willingness to uphold substantial restrictions on access.[145]

From the perspective of movement influence, an avalanche of unfavorable decisions on work issues came down during the Bush years. Eight of the fourteen actions on employment after 1988 went against feminist positions. This pattern began with five negative Supreme Court rulings in 1989, all of which placed obstacles in the path of workplace equality. The first of these was the *City of Richmond v. J. A. Croson* decision, striking down a provision that directed 30 percent of city contracts in Richmond, Virginia, to businesses owned by minorities.[146] Next came the *Wards Cove Packing Co. v. Atonio* ruling that undermined the *Griggs* precedent on burden of proof. Instead of employers having to show that discriminatory practices were necessary to do business, *Atonio* shifted the onus to employees, who had to prove company practices affected women or minorities differently than others.[147] The *Lorrance v. AT&T Technologies* judgment imposed a time limit on employees who wanted to challenge discriminatory practices.[148] The *Martin v. Wilks* decision allowed workers who alleged reverse discrimination to challenge affirmative action plans in the courts.[149] And the *Patterson v. McLean Credit Union* ruling rejected arguments that racial harassment on the job was discriminatory treatment.[150]

Although each of these judgments dealt with a specific and in some ways technical aspect of inequality at work, their combined effect was devastating. Together with the *Webster* ruling delivered at the same time and the Clarence Thomas nomination two years later, these employment cases confirmed a clear erosion of support for women's rights in the high court. As Representative Patricia Schroeder told a crowded rally in 1989, "You know what happened in the eighties? Ronald Reagan got elected and said 'Put down your picket signs and put on your little dress-for-success suits.' Well, a lot of people put down their picket signs and lost their rights."[151]

The question remained, What could be done about these decisions? Women's groups and civil rights organizations turned to Congress for action but found their efforts were stymied. President Bush maintained that the remedial legislation groups proposed, the 1990 Civil Rights Act, would place an unfair burden on employers by creating unwieldy rules and quotas. Bush ultimately vetoed the act, which ensured that efforts to reach a compromise dragged on and on.[152] As a result, the 1991 Civil Rights Act offered less than many groups wanted. It strengthened antidiscrimination rules for women and minorities and, after a 1992 Senate amendment, removed the ceiling on monetary damages that could be claimed.[153] The legislation, however, did not provide clear limits on how companies could use tests and other measures to decide about hiring and promotion.[154] Perhaps the most disappointing aspect of the 1991 compromise was that it did not prevent further backsliding by the high court. The *St. Mary's Honor Center v. Hicks* ruling of 1993, for example, flew directly in the face of *Griggs* by shifting the burden of proof back to employees. The *Hicks* decision set a new standard by which workers had to demonstrate the discriminatory intent of their employers.[155]

A few mixed judgments also came down during the Bush years. They included the 1989 *Price Waterhouse v. Hopkins* case involving the promotion to partner of Ann B. Hopkins. While Hopkins's performance at the firm was judged to be outstanding, her personal style was viewed as unfeminine—to the point that one colleague said Hopkins needed a "course at charm school."[156] Women's groups endorsed the part of the ruling that said defining how females behaved at work constituted sex discrimination. They were disappointed, though, by the Court's view that companies could refuse to hire or promote for stereotypical reasons (including a woman's personal style) as long as the sex of the candidate did not play a decisive role.[157]

Child care legislation from this period was also mixed. The 1990 Act for Better Child Care Services (ABC) followed a long history of unsuccessful legislation dating back to 1971, when President Nixon vetoed a comprehensive child care bill.[158] Not surprisingly, the legislation ultimately passed during the Bush years was full of compromises. The 1990 Child Care Act, quite unlike the ABC proposal, established a voucher system for parents that allowed them to choose secular or church-based child care. Most benefits were delivered through the tax system to parents rather than through the education system to day care providers. Some organizations, including the Children's Defense Fund, saw these compromises as the only way to win support in Congress and the White House. Other groups argued that the compromises went too far in pleasing both the evangelical church lobby and conservatives who wanted to extend the use of vouchers. Women's organizations maintained that the 1990 bill offered little to poor families who needed child care most.[159]

Only a few small moves on behalf of women's work occurred during the Bush years. The Job Training Act was not a controversial law. It targeted federal training funds to women over age forty and to minority women in an effort to improve their chances of finding employment. Like a nontraditional jobs act passed in 1991, this legislation began with a conservative view that making individuals more self-sufficient would help to reduce government spending.[160] The only positive court decision was the *United Automobile Workers v. Johnson Controls* case involving the exclusion of women from work where they were exposed to lead in batteries. The Supreme Court rejected the company's rule on the grounds that it only considered the reproductive systems of women and neglected the effects of lead on men.[161]

Much like the gag rule and the Mexico City policy in the abortion field, the situation on family leave was virtually unchanged until 1993. In 1990, President Bush vetoed legislation to allow employees to take up to twelve weeks of unpaid leave per year, including as maternity leave.[162] Once the bill was proposed in 1985, a coalition of business groups maintained it would cause intolerable disruption to the workplace. In particular, the costs to insure workers on leave and replace them in their jobs temporarily would be prohibitive for small firms. No president signed the modest piece of legislation known as the Family and Medical Leave Act, therefore, until after Republicans left the White House.[163]

Overall, the Bush years were in many respects a disaster for American women's groups. The steady stream of losses in the areas of equal rights, family law, abortion, and employment meant little progress was achieved either in the courts or in legislation. George Bush vetoed a bill to overturn the gag rule on abortion counseling in federal clinics, just as he refused to sign both the 1990 Civil Rights Act and the Family and Medical Leave Act. Laws that did go into effect on civil rights and child care were so full of compromises that women's organizations were hardly anxious to take credit for them. Perhaps most ominous of all was the ability of Republican-appointed Supreme Court judges to undermine access to abortion and equality at work. The Bush administration pressed a hard line on these issues and showed little sign of letting up even when it seemed to be under siege. As the confrontation between Anita Hill and Clarence Thomas before the Senate Judiciary Committee made clear, conservatives were in no mood to listen to the claims of American feminism.

The Canadian Record before Mulroney

Canadian women's groups faced the two windows of policy debate in differing ways. During the years before 1984, feminists confronted a series of judicial setbacks that they tried to remedy via legislation and, during the early 1980s, via insistence on equality language in the Charter of Rights and Freedoms. Organizations that focused on federal policy change in the first window thus worked through 1984 to shape the actions of a generally sympathetic Liberal government. Although the fight over Charter language was lively and contentious, at no point did the Liberals or any other federal party of that period reject the basic concept of constitutional equality, as did the 1980 U.S. Republican platform. Struggles in the second window before 1984 were far less intense than after that year, largely because federal social policy, constitutional decisions, and trade directions under the Liberals were essentially consistent with the then-moderate leanings of organizations like the National Action Committee (NAC).

This situation tended to reverse after 1984. Although feminist pressure during the Liberal years focused on moving policy forward in the first window, the presence of Charter equality language and sympathetic judges after 1985 made this less necessary. As demonstrated later in this chapter, Canadian women's organizations during the Mulroney years were less pressed to overturn negative court decisions through House of Commons legislation. The courts often became the venue for Charter activity by feminist legal specialists, primarily using a vehicle known as the Women's Legal Education and Action Fund (LEAF), a litigation organization established in 1985 and based in Toronto. Other groups worked on fending off Conservative abortion and child care bills in Parliament and the media. Much of this defensive work on legislation was done by NAC affiliates, including the Canadian Abortion Rights League (CARAL) and the Canadian Day Care Advocacy Association.

It was in the second window of action that feminists took on the broader agenda of the Mulroney government. Simply put, Canadian women after 1985 enjoyed constitutionally entrenched equality rights that women in the United Kingdom and United States did not have. Feminist organizations thus trained their sights on massive damage to women's lives which they believed would result from general Conservative policy rather than from the kinds of attacks on movement claims that were unfolding during this same period in the United States. Therefore, as the National Action Committee became more radical through the late 1980s, it participated in protests that directly opposed core planks in the Mulroney government project. Coalitions against free trade and the Charlottetown Accord were two of the best-known umbrellas under which NAC pressed a head-on policy critique of the federal Tories.

Opposition by women's groups to the government's agenda, however, did not take the same form as that in Britain and the United States. No specific events comparable to the Women against Pit Closures or Greenham Common demonstrations in the United Kingdom or the massive pro-choice rallies in Washington, D.C., were organized. Instead, NAC generally worked with other groups that opposed Conservative free trade and budget policies, most notably in a coalition known as the Pro-Canada Network. This network, which changed its name to the Action Canada Network in 1991, drew together leading trade union, antipoverty, feminist, and aboriginal groups for joint activities.

These organizations raised about $750,000 to fight free trade in the 1988 federal elections.[164] After the Conservatives won another majority government, network activists staged ongoing protests against Tory budget cuts. For example, a cross-Canada "De-Rail the Budget" campaign in 1989 featured events at both ends of the country and culminated in a rally of four hundred in Ottawa.[165] A May 1993 protest against Conservative actions on free trade, unemployment insurance, and child care drew more than ten thousand demonstrators to Ottawa.[166] Each of these actions implicated the National Action Committee in a broadly left-of-center, extraparliamentary effort to oust the Mulroney government.

Was the Canadian women's movement influential before 1984? In terms of legislation, considerable progress occurred during this period because 80 percent of House of Commons actions were consistent with group claims. All six decisions by the Supreme Court of Canada during this time, however, went against movement preferences; this pattern led feminists to demand stronger equality provisions in a revised constitution. One of the most widely publicized losses by women's groups came in the 1974 *Attorney-General of Canada v. Lavell* and *Isaac v. Bédard* cases, decided in a single ruling by the high court. The Supreme Court rejected arguments that denying Indian status only to aboriginal women who married non-Indian men, not to native men who married non-Indian women, violated the 1960 Bill of Rights. Because the Bill of Rights was not constitutionally entrenched, it could not supersede the Indian Act. Moreover, the Supreme Court declared it was permissible to deny status to aboriginal women because this practice had continued "for at least one hundred years."[167]

Growing frustration over this ruling and a series of similar ones led Canadian women's groups to mobilize during the debate over constitutional change in the early 1980s. Although the federal government of Pierre Trudeau and most provincial governments at first resisted the equality language feminists proposed, these elites eventually agreed to include sections 15 and 20 in the new Canadian Charter of Rights and Freedoms (CCRF):

> 15(1). Every individual is equal before and under the law and has the right to the equal protection and equal benefit of the law without discrimination and, in particular, without discrimination based on race, national or ethnic origin, colour, religion, sex, age or mental or physical disability.
>
> 15(2). Subsection (1) does not preclude any law, program or activity that has as its object the amelioration of conditions of disadvantaged individuals or groups including those that are disad-

vantaged because of race, national or ethnic origin, colour, religion, sex, age or mental or physical disability. . . .

28. Notwithstanding anything in this Charter, the rights and freedoms referred to in it are guaranteed equally to male and female persons.[168]

These provisions constituted a very significant step forward for women's rights, but they did not come into effect until 1985.

In the meantime, a pattern of favorable legislation and negative court decisions continued. At least one widely publicized court loss by women's groups occurred in each policy field. In the family law area, Irene Murdoch attempted to claim part of an Alberta ranch at the time of her divorce. Although the property was registered in her husband's name, Murdoch argued that she had worked the land by "haying, raking, swathing, mowing, driving trucks and tractors and teams," and so on, up to five months a year on her own in some cases. The Supreme Court ruled in 1973 that she was not entitled to any of the property because what Murdoch contributed was, in her own words, the labor of "any ranch wife."[169] Instead, the Court awarded Irene Murdoch a lump sum payment.

The Trudeau government eased access to abortion somewhat with 1969 changes to the Criminal Code. These revisions permitted legal abortions under specified conditions: when the woman's health was in danger, when a therapeutic abortion committee of at least three doctors so certified, and when an approved hospital would perform the abortion. Even though these changes loosened the previous terms governing access to abortion, women's groups opposed them on the grounds that doctors and local hospital boards remained in control. In response to the 1969 amendments, movement activists organized an Abortion Caravan beginning in Vancouver, British Columbia, and traveling to the House of Commons in Ottawa. The caravan arrived in 1970 and featured a demonstration by four hundred protesters who chained themselves to the railing of the Commons visitors' gallery. A growing number of pro-choice organizations led by the Canadian Abortion Rights Action League demanded that abortion be removed from the Criminal Code.[170]

Efforts to challenge the law attracted public attention once again in 1970 when Dr. Henry Morgentaler was issued the first in a long series of criminal charges. In a number of cities including Montreal, Toronto, Winnipeg, and Halifax, Morgentaler was alleged to have performed abortions outside an accredited hospital, without the certification of a therapeutic committee.[171] These legal challenges worked their way through the system and, in 1975, Morgentaler asked the Supreme Court to overturn his Quebec Court of Appeal conviction. Notably, this conviction had reversed Morgentaler's earlier acquittal by a Quebec jury. His presentation to the Supreme Court of Canada closely paralleled the right to privacy argument that underpinned the *Roe* precedent in the United States. Morgentaler maintained that the Canadian Bill of Rights upheld individual freedom and privacy, but the Court unanimously rejected this claim and drew a clear line between protections for privacy in the United States and the lack of constitutionally entrenched rights in Canada. Morgentaler was sentenced to ten months in prison, and women's groups were once again reminded of how limited rights protections were in Canada. The only immediate change following this 1975 ruling was federal legislation to prevent a future provincial court of appeal from overturning a jury acquittal.[172]

The high court decision that mobilized Canadian women's groups on violence issues, as the *DPP v. Morgan* case had done in the United Kingdom, was the 1980 *Pappajohn v. The Queen* ruling. This judgment involved the rape of a real estate agent by a man who said she had consented to have sex. The Supreme Court upheld the man's claim, arguing his mistaken but honest belief that she had consented is a valid defense in cases of rape.[173] A national campaign by women's organizations led to 1983 changes to the Criminal Code. These amendments placed limits on the use of consent as a defense, redefined rape as violent sexual assault, and acknowledged that rape can occur in marriage. Some restrictions on the use in courtrooms of a victim's sexual history were also introduced.[174]

Nearly half of the decisions on Canadian women's claims before 1984 related to employment. These included three pro-movement laws passed by the House of Commons during the 1970s. Legislation from this period provided eleven weeks of paid maternity leave for a woman who had worked at least twelve months for her employer. Mothers returning to work were guaranteed the same pay and seniority as when they began the leave, which was paid from a general unemployment insurance fund.[175] Pension changes passed in 1977 allowed divorced couples to split pension credits and protected women who left the labor force for up to seven years to raise their children.[176] Later amendments to the Labour Code prohibited companies from laying off or dismissing pregnant employees and established a refundable child tax credit. This credit was a benefit paid to middle- and lower-income families under the income tax system, to assist parents with the costs of raising children.[177]

The 1977 Human Rights Act proved to be more contentious. This legislation outlawed discrimination at work on the basis of sex, marital status, and a series of other categories and established equal pay for work of equal value within the federal civil service. What women's groups questioned, much as those in Britain did during this period, was the enforcement of pay equity and the numerous exceptions to this policy. The Canadian law was complaints based, which meant individuals had to file briefs alleging discrimination in pay or promotion against their employers. Equal value complaints needed to demonstrate that skill, effort, responsibility, and working conditions were comparable across job categories. Finally, the law excluded pensions and other benefits from its purview and said pay differentials were allowed when there was a reason to justify the difference.[178]

Probably the most memorable decision on work during these years was the 1978 *Bliss v. Attorney-General of Canada* ruling. This case was widely viewed as the last straw, the judgment that exhausted the patience of women's groups in the pre-CCRF period. Stella Bliss worked in Vancouver, lost her job while she was pregnant, and could not find other work after the baby was born. She then applied for unemployment benefits. Bliss was refused on the grounds that she was pregnant when she lost her job and had not worked long enough to qualify for maternity benefits. The Supreme Court upheld the denial of benefits, arguing that Bliss had been refused because she was pregnant and not because she was a woman. The ability of women and not men to conceive, according to the justices, resulted from nature rather than law. The *Bliss* decision galvanized feminist interests, which in turn pressed for two legislative changes passed in 1983. One amendment altered human rights legislation so that companies could not discriminate against pregnant employees, and it defined sexual harassment as discrimination at work. The second change revised unemployment insurance rules so that paid maternity leave required the same qualifying period as other benefits.[179]

In general, women's organizations came out of the Trudeau years with a sense of solid momentum. Each setback in the courts—and there were five well-publicized losses—led to political action that helped to reverse the judicial precedent. The *Lavell* and *Morgentaler* rulings strengthened women's groups' resolve to win equality language in the new Charter. The *Murdoch* case was followed by a flood of family law reforms in the provinces, which controlled how property was divided after divorce. *Pappajohn* led to significant changes in the Criminal Code, and *Bliss* stimulated some of the most progressive rules on maternity leave in the Anglo-American world. Moreover, during his last term in office, Prime Minister Trudeau appointed Bertha Wilson as Canada's first female Supreme Court justice; Wilson's interpretations of the Charter proved crucial to the success of feminist litigation in later years.[180] In short, Canadian women's organizations entered the Charter period with tremendous optimism.

The Mulroney Years

Perhaps the most remarkable aspect of the Conservative years in Canada was the gap between formal outcomes and the informal political climate. A total of thirty decisions on women's group claims came down during the Mulroney years. More than 85 percent of them were pro-movement, including nearly 90 percent of high court judgments and more than 80 percent of legislative actions. Yet the informal side of the record reveals a very different story. Canadian feminist organizations refused to credit the Mulroney government for these positive outcomes. Instead, progress in the courts was linked to Charter language that women as a group had struggled to put in place during the early 1980s and to interpretations by judges that the Liberals had appointed. Legislative progress on violence and employment issues after 1984 responded to concerted pressure from feminist interests, the same pressure that stopped Tory proposals on abortion and child care. As revealed in chapter 4, feminists refused to attribute the positive formal record of the Mulroney years to Conservative actions.

In the area of equal rights, pro-movement decisions resulting from the Charter included changes to the Indian Act in response to the *Lavell* case. These revisions restored aboriginal status and the right to apply for band membership to women who had married non-Indians.[181] The argument that sex discrimination in sports violated the Charter was upheld by the Supreme Court in its refusal to overturn the *Blainey v. Ontario Hockey Association* ruling.[182] In the *Andrews v. Law Society of British Columbia* judgment, the Court agreed with LEAF's position that section 15 was meant to apply to disadvantaged or vulnerable groups in society. As the first major high court decision to interpret the equality section, the *Andrews* ruling was seen as a crucial step forward from constitutional language to legal impact.[183]

In the area of family law, most federal decisions were again pro-movement. Legislative changes in 1986 allowed divorce after one year of separation and set out criteria for judges to use in issuing support orders. Although women's groups generally endorsed these reforms, they questioned how support orders would work. Experience in Canada and elsewhere suggested judges had little understanding of how household and child care responsibilities limited the economic independence of married women.[184] In the *Moge v. Moge* case, this issue arrived on the high court docket. Zofia Moge argued that caring for three children during the day and working six hours a night as a cleaner left her economically disadvantaged in the long term. Her ex-husband argued that after nineteen years of separation and twelve years of divorce, he was no longer responsible for paying support. Parallel with LEAF's argument, the high court said payments should continue indefinitely.[185]

Probably the most famous court decision of the Mulroney years was the *Morgentaler v. the Queen* ruling of 1988. After years of pro-choice litigation, this judgment struck down the existing abortion law as a violation of the Charter section guaranteeing security of the person. The decision was celebrated by CARAL, NAC, and other organizations that maintained *Morgentaler* meant no new law was needed in this area. Antifeminist groups including REAL Women (standing for Realistic, Equal, Active, for Life) denounced the ruling as an attack on the traditional family and the rights of the unborn. Antichoice groups were also upset over the 1989 *Borowski v. Attorney-General of Canada* decision, brought forward by a former Manitoba politician. Joe Borowski claimed that Criminal Code provisions on abortion violated the fetus's right to life. In its judgment, the Supreme Court declared the case moot because the code was no longer relevant in the wake of *Morgentaler.*[186]

Controversies surrounding the abortion issue continued in the *Tremblay v. Daigle* case. Chantal Daigle, a twenty-year-old living in Quebec, wanted an abortion, but her ex-boyfriend convinced the provincial Court of Appeal that she should not have one. Daigle appealed to the Supreme Court when she was more than twenty weeks pregnant and unable to obtain an abortion in Quebec. The case drew sustained attention from groups on both sides of the issue but ultimately became moot halfway through when Daigle entered New York state and had an abortion there. In a unanimous ruling, the court found in favor of Daigle on the grounds that no other person could interfere in a woman's decision to seek an abortion.[187] This ferment led to two attempts by the Conservatives to bring in a new abortion law. The closest they came was in 1991, when a bill to recriminalize was defeated in a tie vote in the Senate. The government's loss was widely attributed to effective lobbying of women senators by pro-choice organizations.[188]

Action in the courts and Parliament on violence against women was much more intense in Canada than in the United Kingdom or the United States. This activity was linked in part to the murder of fourteen young women at the University of Montreal engineering school, the École polytechnique, in December 1989. Among nine decisions about violence during the Mulroney years, seven were pro-movement. High court rulings defined sexual assault and consent more clearly (the *Chase v. The Queen, Reddick v. The Queen,* and *Norberg v. Wynrib* cases), protected the anonymity of assault victims (*Canadian Newspapers v. Attorney-General of Canada*), and recognized the battered wife perspective in a case in which a woman killed her abuser (*R. v. Lavallee*).[189] The only loss in this area by women's groups was on the 1991 *R. v. Seaboyer* case, which threw out provisions in the Criminal Code that shielded the sexual history of rape victims. After this decision, an unusual consultation brought together women's groups that wanted a better rape shield law with the federal justice minister, Kim Campbell. Leading feminist organizations endorsed Criminal Code amendments that Campbell later introduced.[190]

In the area of employment, most legislative outcomes were again pro-movement. Changes to the federal Labour Code defined sexual harassment more clearly.[191] The Employment Equity Act required federally regulated companies with more than a hundred workers to report on the status of female, minority, aboriginal, and disabled employees. This act was seen as an extremely weak form of affirmative action by labor and women's organizations.[192] Attempts to bring in a child care act that worked through the tax system and did little for working parents were blocked by the Day Care Advocacy Association.[193] Finally, changes to unemployment insurance in 1990 lengthened the leave period for new mothers and also extended coverage to fathers.[194]

All four court decisions on employment were pro-feminist. The *Action travail des femmes v. Canadian National Railway* ruling upheld the right of human rights tribunals to order companies to hire more women.[195] The *Robichaud v. Canada* and *Janzen and Govereau v. Platy Enterprises* cases on sexual harassment found in favor of women who had lodged complaints.[196] The *Brooks v. Canada Safeway* decision said company benefit plans could not discriminate against pregnant women and culminated what had been a long struggle for women's groups beginning with *Bliss.* As Chief Justice Brian Dickson commented in the *Brooks* ruling, "Pregnancy discrimination is a form of sex discrimination simply because of the basic biological fact that only women have the capacity to become pregnant."[197]

These formal decisions from the Mulroney years showed the judicial progress that could follow from constitutional equality. Judges appointed by the Trudeau government helped to shape a new set of pro-movement precedents on equal rights, family law, abortion, violence, and employment issues. Some legislation proposed by the Conservatives on abortion and child care was effectively blocked, whereas other efforts by the Conservatives to create a new rape shield law were supported by women's groups.

What outraged many activists was clearly not the formal record of the Mulroney years. Instead, NAC and other organizations rejected the general economic and constitutional principles of the Conservatives. Free trade with the United States and later with Mexico too was seen as endangering women's jobs and jeopardizing public health care, pensions, unemployment insurance, and other provisions of the Canadian welfare state. Many Canadian women worked in manufacturing sectors that were most vulnerable under free trade, including textiles, clothing, small electrical products, and sporting goods. The likelihood that these women would find new work was doubtful because many were immigrants with little formal education. The women's movement critique of free trade was part of a much larger protest by trade unions, cultural associations, church organizations, and antipoverty groups in English Canada. Margaret Atwood, one of Canada's most prominent writers, described her own reasons for opposing the deal:

> Canada as a separate but dominated country has done about as well under the U.S. as women, worldwide, have done under men; about the only position they've ever adopted toward us, country to country, has been the missionary position, and we were not on top.[198]

In 1987, NAC became one of the founding members of a national coalition against free trade.[199]

Taking on the Conservatives' core economic priority hardly endeared the English Canadian women's movement to the federal government. NAC and other organizations saw their public funding reduced immediately following the free trade protest. Yet the conflict between NAC and the Tories over free trade during the 1980s was only a prelude to their confrontation over constitutional change during the early 1990s. Despite Brian Mulroney's speeches about national reconciliation, women's groups in English Canada saw his efforts as part of a destructive exercise that alienated the public and bargained away federal powers. NAC opposed the elitist process that allowed federal and provincial politicians to decide Canada's constitutional future far from public view. Moreover, changes that came out of the Meech Lake and Charlottetown rounds of constitutional discussion were seen as jeopardizing the equality rights women had won in the Charter and as weakening the same national standards in social policy that were already under threat from free trade.[200]

For critics in English Canada, free trade meant both a fundamental loss of sovereignty and downward pressure on the Canadian welfare state. The federal government that had built Canada was, in their view, gradually disappearing in order for Prime Minister Mulroney to please not just President Reagan but also business interests hungry for higher profits and provincial politicians anxious to claim more powers. Mulroney's critics believed the rise of an individualist, make-it-on-your-own ethos would surely leave Canadian women at the bottom of the heap.

Policy Battles in Review

Some of the clearest evidence that the rise of conservative leaders affected movement momentum comes out in the simple box score data in appendix A. From eighteen positive decisions among a total of twenty-three in the pre-Thatcher period, this figure dropped to seventeen of twenty-six during the Thatcher years and thirteen of twenty-three in the Major years. The percentage of pro-women's movement actions thus declined from more than 78 percent before Thatcher's election to about 57 percent during the Major period, which meant post-1979 developments were clearly less favorable than pre-1979 ones.

More than 40 percent of the pro-movement decisions recorded during the time Margaret Thatcher and John Major lived at 10 Downing Street resulted from European pressure, and another 37 percent came from high court decisions. In other words, about 80 percent of the actions favorable to women's movement positions during the Thatcher and Major years had nothing to do with direct government preferences, because they came either from Europe or else a relatively autonomous high court. Of the twenty-one actions taken by the House of Commons on its own under Conservative prime ministers, only five, or about one-quarter, can be considered pro-feminist. The record of British Conservative governments, in short, was hardly as favorable as the overall record appears. Only because of European influences and the willingness of the law lords to move substantially beyond cabinet and government caucus positions were British women's groups able to make much progress at all after 1979.[201] Much of this change was of considerable importance, particularly to pregnant employees who did not want to lose their jobs or to part-time workers who had been denied benefits available to full-timers.

Results from the United States provide even more dramatic evidence of the link between movement policy reversals and changes of political leadership. From a box score of twenty-five wins in thirty-six decisions before 1980, this figure declined to fourteen of twenty-nine during the Reagan years and four of twenty-four during the Bush years. In terms of percentages, pro–women's movement actions dropped from about 70 percent before 1980 to less than 20 percent during the Bush administration—clearly a massive decline. American women had neither constitutional equality nor an equivalent of the European Community to moderate the impact of presidential actions, nor did they face a politically independent high court comparable to the House of Lords. To the extent that Reagan and Bush nominees to the U.S. Supreme Court were expected to pursue antiabortion, antiaffirmative action, and antigovernment regulation positions, the assumption of judicial impartiality remained in doubt.

Above all, the impact of leader preferences that contradicted movement preferences was reflected in a series of presidential vetoes to legislation passed by Congress. Legislation that did make its way through the House and Senate was often watered down by compromise with conservative lawmakers. Only after this process of twisting and turning on Capitol Hill were Republican presidents willing to sign bills on child care or civil rights. Women's groups found it difficult to take credit for much of this legislation because what emerged from Congress was so different, and generally so much weaker, than what had initially gone in.

Overall, American movement progress at the national level nearly ground to a halt after 1980. In terms of actual consequences, policy rollback in the United States meant a great deal. For example, before 1980 a pregnant woman could obtain a legal abortion during her first trimester, but by 1992, the procedure could not be publicly funded in most states, nor could it be advised in any federally funded health clinic.[202] The fact that crucial setbacks of this type occurred in the United States underlines the degree to which American feminism was vulnerable to the attacks of a resurgent political right. Contrary to the core expectations of the comparative literature, backward motion characterized the legislative and judicial experiences of American feminism during the Reagan and especially Bush years far more than it characterized those of the British and Canadian movements during the Thatcher-Major and Mulroney governments, respectively.

If box scores provide an account of what happened in the policy fights of the conservative years, then Canadian women's groups seemed to triumph. From eight wins in sixteen decisions before Brian Mulroney was elected, this ratio changed to twenty-six in thirty after 1984. The percentage of pro-movement actions rose steeply from 50 percent during the Liberal years to 87 percent in the Conservative period, which represents the highest level recorded in appendix A. In terms of concrete changes, maternity benefits improved, the terms of support after divorce were spelled out, and Canada developed some exceptional legal precedents in the area of violence against women.

One question remains, though. What factors explain pro-movement policy developments in Canada? A combination of four factors stand out. First, Brian Mulroney was not ideologically opposed to basic feminist demands in such areas as equal rights and employment, nor were most of his leading cabinet ministers. Second, the Mulroney government and the Canadian judiciary operated within the terms set by equality language in the Charter of Rights and Freedoms. Third, the Liberals had placed a series of progressive judges including Bertha Wilson on the federal bench, so Brian Mulroney inherited a Supreme Court dominated by Pierre Trudeau's appointees. Finally, two laws that were introduced by the Mulroney government (on abortion and child care) were blocked by pressure from women's organizations. This background supports activists' contentions in chapter 4 that the pro-movement record of the Conservative years in Canada unfolded more despite than because of the Mulroney government.

As the conflict over broader policy decisions indicates, women's groups and conservatives were hardly on good terms in Canada or elsewhere. It was in the debate over work, government spending, and public protest that the gloves really came off. This larger set of entanglements forms the focus of chapter 3.

CHAPTER THREE **The Money Crunch**

Beginning in the 1970s, lots of people in Britain and North America talked about the feminization of poverty. An American writer, Flora Davis, called the phenomenon "pauperization."[1] Scholars in Britain compiled multiple editions of a book titled *Women and Poverty.*[2] One Canadian author claimed women were "shock absorbers" during times of economic change and spending cuts.[3] However it was described, the pattern was the same. Many women's lives seemed to be getting worse and worse. How was this happening? Were government actions part of the story? This chapter argues that policy decisions by conservative leaders had a direct and often negative influence. A three-pronged money crunch outlined here both impoverished the lives of many women in the general public, particularly those who were pensioners or single parents, and challenged feminists' ability to speak for those women.

Important changes occurred in all three countries during the postwar years. Over time in each case, more women entered the labor force, and more were single or divorced than in earlier generations. Better nutrition and advances in health care led to lengthier life expectancies. The fact that more women worked for pay, were not married, and lived longer meant any shift in jobs or public pensions had a massive impact. Alterations in the family unit and especially increases in the divorce rate fueled the growth of an identifiable and often very vulnerable group—single mothers and their children.[4]

The money crunch, we maintain, emerged along three dimensions. First, shifts in patterns of work, pay, and taxation resulted in large part from the actions of conservative leaders. Particularly in Britain and the United States, these trends created a more economically polarized society. Greater government reliance on indirect rather than direct forms of taxation, for example, eroded traditions of fairness and progressivity. New jobs that were created tended to be temporary, part-time ones that offered low pay and few fringe benefits. Differences between the lives of better-off haves and poorer have-nots widened because of changes introduced after 1979. Not only did many women labor long hours at low pay to try to support their families, but also these women sacrificed much of the leisure time available to working men. We refer to this bundle of pressures as the *work crunch.*

Second, women's lives were directly affected by changes in government spending. Decisions by conservative leaders about how unemployment, welfare, and pension systems would operate had a direct effect not only on those women who used social programs but also on others who worked for the state to provide them. Conservatives in all three countries moved to target very narrowly those programs that did survive their cuts. Eligibility rules were tightened in all three cases. The motto "lean and mean" said it all, because reductions to government spending were particularly severe in the social policy field. Women suffered as both clients and providers of public services. This pattern of government cuts formed the spending crunch.

Third, conservative decision makers reduced the flow of public money to feminist projects. In Britain during the Thatcher years, the central government shut down municipal governments that were friendly to movement organizations and placed a ceiling on local tax rates that served to prevent future public spending on groups. The Reagan and Bush administrations worked to cut programs passed by Congress before 1980, including initiatives under the Women's Educational Equity Act. In Canada, the National Action Committee on the Status of Women (NAC), the leading national umbrella organization, saw its federal funding sliced in half by the Mulroney cabinet. Canadian Conservatives also eliminated a government program that funded Charter of Rights litigation by women's groups. Efforts to defund feminist activism created an advocacy crunch.

How did the money crunch unfold in each case? In Britain, work pressures were arguably most significant because Conservative governments were loath to regulate employers. The Tory attack on trade union power and a general decline in manufacturing and mining meant little permanent, well-paid work was available to men or women. During his term as prime minister, John Major abolished minimum pay rules under a system of Wages Councils.[5] This combination of minimal regulation and few decent jobs meant the work lives of many British women after 1979 were difficult. The spending crunch was also important, though, because both Thatcher and Major opposed universal social benefits. British Conservatives preferred a more privatized, selective, and means-tested approach that was modeled on the American case. Changes to pension programs in Britain, for example, led to very negative consequences for millions of elderly women.[6] The advocacy crunch in the United Kingdom seemed less direct than elsewhere, but its effect was still to cut support for women's groups.

In the United States, growing economic polarization resulted in large part from tax changes introduced during the Reagan years. Businesses and wealthy households tended to benefit from Republican reforms, whereas moderate- and low-income families generally lost ground.[7] As in Britain, additional pressures were caused by a national leadership that refused to intervene on issues like child care and workplace regulation. Yet many American women probably suffered most directly from the spending crunch. As political executives, Ronald Reagan and George Bush mounted a punitive attack on social benefits that clearly demeaned welfare recipients. Over time, their rhetoric helped to shift the broader climate of opinion, including on Capitol Hill and among the mass media and general public. The angry language of Republican leaders ultimately gave welfare mothers and welfare programs a bad name—not just in the United States but often spilling over into Canada and Britain as well. In turn, women's units in the American federal bureaucracy faced cuts themselves.

The advocacy crunch was probably the most lasting legacy of the Mulroney years. Because about 90 percent of Canadian workers were subject to provincial rather than federal labor law, progressive reform did occur in many provinces during the 1980s and early 1990s. Ontario, for example, introduced equal pay for work of equal value (or pay equity) legislation that meant women no longer had to file individual complaints of wage discrimination against employers. Yet free trade and economic recession clearly threatened good jobs in Canada, and Conservative economic policy played no small role in creating these circumstances. Spending cuts also occurred after 1984, but not to the same degree as in Britain, the United States, or later on under the Liberals in Canada.

What Canadian women's organizations experienced most directly was an advocacy crunch. Both the Women's Legal Education and Action Fund (LEAF), which conducted much of its Charter litigation with the support of federal grants, and NAC, which relied on the Secretary of State Women's Program and other agencies for about two-thirds of its annual budget, saw their public funding sharply reduced. These cuts in government support hit particularly hard because Canada's roughly twenty-six million residents were spread out over a vast geographic area. The costs of operating a national organization were virtually prohibitive except for business lobby groups that had an affluent support base and thus did not need government subsidies.

Overall, this chapter reveals a triple whammy effect in all three countries. Work pressures, cuts to government spending, and the advocacy crunch—taken together—meant many women faced low pay, no job security, less of a government safety net on which to rely when they were old or sick or unemployed, and fewer opportunities to protest. Changes in the terms of employment, government programs, and advocacy thus produced a compound money crunch in all three cases.

A Quick Snapshot

By the 1980s and 1990s, government decisions about work and social services affected huge numbers of women. Greater access to formal education meant more were employed when they left school. This was particularly clear in the United States, where higher education had long been seen as the key to upward mobility. By the mid-1980s, approximately 20 percent of American women had obtained at least one postsecondary degree.[8] This figure compared with about 10 percent of females in Canada and 5 percent in Britain at that time.[9]

Women's entry to the paid labor force also followed from a decline in real wages. In all three countries, families were less and less able to live on the income of a single earner. High rates of inflation, especially during the 1970s and early 1980s, reduced what wages could buy and lowered the value of people's savings. Many well-paid jobs that men held, including in unionized industries like steel, automobiles, and mining, began to disappear. The overall level of union membership declined markedly in the United Kingdom and the United States between the late 1970s and early 1990s, from nearly 60 to about 40 percent of workers in Britain and from approximately 25 to 15 percent in the United States.[10] Rates of unionization in Canada remained steady at about 37 percent.[11] In each case, large numbers of women went to work to keep their families afloat. What few found available were full-time, permanent jobs with benefits, because all three economies seemed to be creating lots of part-time, temporary work, especially in the service sector.

Working women in the late twentieth century differed from those in earlier generations because so many were mothers of young children. In Canada, about two-thirds of females with children under school age worked by the end of the Mulroney years, and most held full-time jobs. In the United States at the end of the Bush administration, nearly 60 percent of mothers with children under age six worked for pay, again primarily full-time. In Britain, about 40 percent of women with preschool children were in the labor force by the point Margaret Thatcher left office, but most held part-time positions. Much of this variation was due to differing maternity leave and child care systems. Moreover, Canada, the United States, and the United Kingdom had not developed a comprehensive policy—like that in France and Sweden—to actively help mothers reenter the workforce. All three countries developed patchwork child care arrangements without national standards. Yet among these cases, Canada offered the most generous system of paid leave that ensured new parents the same or a comparable job on their return. In addition, incentives for single mothers to supplement their welfare benefits by working were stronger in North America than in Britain. And because child care expenses were more broadly tax deductible in the United States and Canada than in the United Kingdom, North American women had an additional incentive to work for pay.[12]

One of the most contentious questions in the 1980s and 1990s was how many mothers were unmarried teenagers. Conservatives in all three countries contended that rising numbers of young unmarried mothers and their children depended on welfare benefits. Ironically, this debate occurred at the same time as overall fertility rates declined in Britain, the United States, and Canada and as demographers questioned who would support their increasingly aged populations in the future. Data on teenage pregnancy showed the highest rates in the developed world in the United States, compared with far lower levels in continental Europe. Canada and Britain ranked in between. During the 1980s, the pregnancy rate was approximately 15 per 1,000 adolescents in the Netherlands, 30 in Sweden, 45 in Canada, 65 in the United Kingdom, and 110 in the United States.[13]

Research in this area links the availability of contraceptives and sex education with levels of adolescent pregnancy. In countries like Holland and Sweden, access to contraceptives is relatively open, and sex education is straightforward and far less politically contested than in Anglo-American cultures.[14] Teenage birth rates in Canada have tended to fall over time with greater access to contraceptives, more sex education in the schools, and a universal health care system not available in the United States.[15] In Britain, teenage sexuality had been controversial since Victoria Gillick began her campaign against under-sixteen contraception during the 1970s.[16] Yet access to sex education and contraceptives has been most limited in the United States, where the religious right has imposed restrictive parental consent rules on contraception and abortion and where most students receive no sex education at school.[17] Curiously, the same social conservatives who condemned teenage pregnancy pressed for policies that appeared to keep levels higher in the United States and United Kingdom than elsewhere.

Common to women's lives in all three countries were continued patterns of low pay and job segregation. Nearly 40 percent of females in Britain held full-time jobs in 1990, but they earned less than 80 percent of male full-time incomes.[18] Although this earnings gap was less than in North America, it represented the largest spread in the European Community. In Canada, 40 percent of women worked full-time, but they earned less than 70 percent of male wages.[19] In the United States, about three-quarters of women worked full-time and were paid 72 percent of what men earned.[20] These pay gaps tended to narrow somewhat over time in all three cases as men's income declined and greater education gave women a chance at better jobs.[21]

Yet the segregated labor force hardly disappeared. About half of North American working women in 1990 held pink-collar service or clerical jobs, notably as waitresses, secretaries, and health care aides.[22] A 1989 British study showed more than 80 percent of employed females in similar positions as clerks, cleaners, and hairdressers.[23] Inside schools and hospitals where many women held better jobs, relatively few obtained managerial positions. As British author Kate Figes observes in a study of what she terms the equality myth, "women still have jobs, not careers."[24]

Figes's conclusion is significant for two crucial reasons. First, the fact that they were marrying later and divorcing more often than in the past meant lots of women had to earn their own livelihoods.[25] Second, the growth in life expectancy implied that these earnings had to support women longer.[26] In the United States, for example, a typical first-time bride in 1970 was less than twenty-one years old, but in 1992 she was more than twenty-four.[27] The ratio of divorced to married women in the American population tripled during this period from 60 in every 1,000 to about 180.[28] Female life expectancy in all three countries in 1992 was roughly eighty years, a major increase from only sixty-five years in 1950.[29]

These trends help to explain why more women were concerned about issues like wage discrimination, child care, and pensions. Because so many worked in segregated occupations, equal pay for equal work laws had little relevance. If no males worked with females as cleaners, for example, basic equal pay claims had no effect. In Britain in particular, many women took part-time, temporary positions because decent child care was hard to find. Compared with 23 percent of preschoolers in organized child care in the United States and 18 percent in Canada, this figure was only 6 percent in Britain—in each case during the early 1990s.[30] Moreover, the pensions issue loomed as a dark cloud. Studies in all three countries showed the vast bulk of old people living in poverty were women, largely because fewer females than males had private pension plans to supplement their public benefits.[31] Women thus depended more than men on the same social security schemes that came under direct threat from conservative governments.

Finally, this snapshot needs to address the racial dimension of poverty. Poor people were increasingly likely to be elderly women and young single mothers and the children who depended on them. Their faces were less and less likely to be white as time passed. In the United States in 1990, 31 percent of black, 26 percent of Hispanic, and 11 percent of white adult women lived in poverty, many of them at the two ends of the age range.[32] British studies showed far higher unemployment rates among Caribbean and Asian women than among whites, with about half of West Indian families headed by a single mother.[33] In Canada, many of the lowest paid were immigrant seamstresses from Asia who worked at home, often for long hours at below the minimum wage.[34]

Taken as a group, these patterns reflect the broad and often harsh shape of life for many women in conservative times. Although male-female pay gaps were shrinking and women on average had fewer children over time, these shifts did *not* make up for the consequences of vastly changed family structures in all three countries. More and more women became heads of household as time passed, a crucial pattern that was closely correlated with low income. Even in the United States, where levels of education among women were higher than in Britain and Canada, nearly 45 percent of female-headed households with children lived below the poverty line in 1989.[35]

The Crunch under Thatcher and Major

In Britain, working women faced a set of pressures related to low pay, low job security, limited child care facilities, and the unwillingness of government to intervene. The Thatcher and Major years saw a decisive effort by Conservatives to make Britain more economically competitive. Trade union power was directly challenged by the government's strong commitment to flexible, pro-business policies on employment. Rather than using older strategies that tried to reconcile labor and management interests, the Thatcher government rejected consensual or conciliatory approaches as slow, economically destructive, and fundamentally unfair to business. The Tory defiance of union power was reflected clearly in Margaret Thatcher's showdown with the leader of the coal miners, Arthur Scargill. Thatcher refused to be brought to her knees by the miners, arguing that she would not cave in to violence and threats of an electricity shortage. Conservatives eventually broke the miners' strike and introduced a series of changes that restricted closed shops, strikes, and work stoppages. Thatcher's rhetoric in the conflict with Scargill took direct aim at what she called "the hard left operating inside our system, conspiring to use union power and the apparatus of local government to break, defy and subvert the laws."[36]

The polarized climate after 1979 in Britain thus pitted Conservatives and their allies against trade unions. As a result, women's claims for better pay, greater job security, more child care, and decent maternity leave were raised within a setting that was far from welcoming. Among Tories and business interests, movement demands were rejected as leading to more government interference. Among traditional trade union leaders, these same claims were initially viewed as a curious departure from the norm—meaning the typical agenda of men working in mines or railways. British labor unions had long been dominated by men uncomfortable with women in the workforce, let alone in the union leadership. Many trade unions held fast to a male breadwinner argument, for example, that demanded a higher "family wage" for working men. Their assumption was that raising men's pay via unionization meant women would no longer need to work.[37] Moreover, British unions were less committed to a standard minimum wage than were their counterparts elsewhere. Once again, the belief was that unionization rather than regulation would raise the income of low-paid workers.[38]

These views offered little space for women's groups' claims about equal pay and the need for government to regulate wages. Over time, though, unions began to endorse more and more of the movement agenda. By the Major years, the Trades Union Congress (TUC) and its various affiliates recognized that they had to organize women workers, notably in the service sector, to survive into the next century. Informal estimates suggested TUC membership had dropped precipitously over time, from approximately twelve to seven million. At the same time, the patience of the government-appointed Equal Opportunities Commission (EOC) with the Conservatives had begun to wear thin. The TUC and EOC thus began to work together on employment issues.[39]

Low pay and limited job security affected many women in Britain after 1979. These were issues that made sense to trade unionists from all backgrounds, and both fell clearly within the mandate of the public agency charged with enforcing antidiscrimination laws in the workplace. The EOC, established in December 1975 to oversee the Equal Pay Act and Sex Discrimination Act, was based in Manchester and chaired by a government appointee. Although the EOC was obviously not a campaigning organization based in the women's movement, it did play a crucial role in gathering data, publishing reports, and sponsoring litigation on work issues.

Much of what is known about the work crunch in Britain comes from the research arms of the EOC and TUC. Figures gathered by these organizations, based on British and European employment statistics, show that working women in the United Kingdom were overwhelmingly clustered in part-time, temporary positions.[40] More than two-thirds of British women worked for pay by 1990, but less than 40 percent held full-time jobs. This meant that the part-time workforce was overwhelmingly female. Part-time jobs in Britain were not often unionized. They tended to pay less, offer fewer benefits, and provide little or no job security relative to full-time work. The earnings gap between men and women was therefore much greater than the 20 percent figure reported in comparisons of full-time employees. Accounts show that women in part-time work, especially in manual labor categories, were at the very bottom of the income heap. In 1993, Conservative legislation abolished a system of tribunals known as Wages Councils that set minimum rates for the lowest paid. The income of these employees fell even further.[41]

The wages of part-time women workers, however, were only part of the problem. According to British statute, employees had to be on the job for sixteen hours a week to meet the minimum threshold for maternity benefits or compensation due to redundancy (layoffs) and unfair dismissal. These terms of the 1975 Employment Protection Act meant companies could reduce expenses by keeping employees below the sixteen-hour threshold. In fact, many organizations including department stores, banks, hospitals, and local school boards employed large numbers of women in what were called unprotected part-time jobs. Many working women, in turn, took on multiple part-time jobs to help make ends meet.[42]

According to Conservatives, these arrangements were both good for employers and good for women. Firms could hire workers on a flexible basis without rigid union and collective bargaining rules. Wages would compete with those in dynamic economies like the high-growth "tigers" of South Asia. British women benefited because the shift to temporary, part-time work created many jobs that could fit a family schedule. Mothers of young children, for example, could get a break from life at home by working the same hours as their children were in school.[43]

Analyses by the EOC, TUC, and a number of independent researchers disputed this view. They demonstrated that flexible work did not advantage women, only employers. The government's notion that mothers worked for frivolous "pin money" while their children were in school denied basic realities.[44] First, about 15 percent of households were headed by a single parent, more than 90 percent of them female.[45] Second, many men were either unemployed or else unable to support their families on their own, which meant that women were key contributors to family income. Third, the fact that many mothers worked part-time during school hours was often a commentary on the lack of child care, not on women's job preferences.[46]

The child care issue was a source of endless frustration for organizations like the EOC and TUC and certainly for many working parents. Studies showed that one of the main reasons British mothers did not return to work after their children were born was the lack of affordable child care.[47] Alone among members of the European Union through the mid-1990s, the United Kingdom had no national child care policy.[48] Unlike the situation in North America, day care expenses were tax deductible only for children who attended a workplace nursery; in 1993, a separate tax allowance was introduced, primarily targeted toward single mothers receiving social benefits.[49] The United Kingdom was at the bottom of the European scale on public child care funding, with about 2 percent of children under age three receiving publicly funded day care compared with nearly 50 percent in Denmark.[50] A pilot project that distributed vouchers to parents of four-year-olds began in 1995, yet, according to Conservatives, child care remained a private matter best left to parents or employers—but surely not the state.[51] Efforts to establish workplace nurseries led to some change, with approximately 425 centers in place in the United Kingdom by the early 1990s. Yet these facilities were primarily in London and southeastern England, accommodating only one in three hundred children.[52]

Virtually the only substantial progress British women made in addressing the work crunch was through domestic or European courts. A 1994 House of Lords decision upheld EOC and TUC arguments that the qualifying hours provisions for part-time workers constituted sex discrimination. This ruling paved the way for employees who worked less than sixteen hours a week in the public or private sector to claim severance payments when they were laid off. In Britain, these were known as statutory redundancy payments. Also according to the House of Lords ruling, part-time workers could claim the same right to compensation for unfair dismissal as full-timers.[53] In 1994, too, the Trade Union Reform Act came into effect in part as a response to the European Pregnancy Directive. Under this act, all pregnant women were entitled to fourteen weeks of paid maternity leave, with jobs held for them for a further eighteen to twenty weeks after the leave period.[54] Yet the legislation was complicated, difficult to interpret, and of little use for the estimated four thousand women who lost their jobs every year because they were pregnant.[55]

Each of these trends in women's work lives unfolded during the same period as the Conservatives were introducing significant changes to the tax system. During the 1979 election campaign, Margaret Thatcher denounced high taxes as bad for business, a drain on individual initiative, and an excuse for too much government spending.[56] She proceeded while in power to reduce the top rate of personal income tax from 83 to 40 percent and the standard rate from 33 to 25 percent.[57] Much of the money to finance these cuts came from massive sales of state companies—including British Petroleum, British Aerospace, Jaguar, and British Airways—to the private sector.[58]

At the same time, Thatcher raised both the consumption tax known as the Value Added Tax and also payroll levies on employers under the National Insurance system.[59] This shift from reliance on direct to indirect taxation was regressive in the sense that it moved much of the burden from haves to have-nots. Moreover, the hike in payroll taxes gave employers an additional push to hire more unprotected part-timers, for whom they would not need to make insurance payments. Thatcher also brought in tax concessions for mortgages and private pension contributions. These programs encouraged more Britons to buy homes, rather than live in state housing, and to rely on their own savings in retirement, rather than on public pensions.[60] The combined effect of tax changes was a clear net benefit for wealthy households and a direct loss for poorer people.[61]

In short, the work crunch in Britain amounted to a sustained brake on women's economic equality. Patterns of low pay and limited benefits in part-time employment were coupled with strong Conservative opposition to any workplace intervention. Unions were under siege following government attacks on striking miners and labor interests in general. Tax changes helped to create a more divided society of haves and have-nots. These trends existed alongside a persistent leisure gap whereby working women continued to do most of the family's cooking, laundry, ironing, and cleaning—while their husbands relaxed.[62]

Conservative changes to social policy were nearly as drastic as their actions on work issues. The governments of Margaret Thatcher and John Major set in motion a series of shifts that replaced relatively generous, universal social benefits with a system of narrowly targeted, means-tested grants and loans. Public programs were gradually defunded to make room for private arrangements. This broad pattern of change affected the welfare, housing, health care, and pension systems. The details were often complex and hard to follow, but the purpose remained clear. Tories wanted to create a more individualistic, enterprising culture in which fewer people were dependent on the state.

One change that affected large numbers of women in the United Kingdom was in the pensions field. Britain had established a universal system of old age support early in the twentieth century but paid relatively low benefits under what was known as the Basic Pension. The Labour government in 1975 agreed to allow employees to participate in private or public pension arrangements. Because earnings-related state schemes were made compulsory only for workers who had no private plan, Britain already had a fragmented pension system before Margaret Thatcher came to power.[63]

During the Conservative years, the 1980 and 1986 Social Security Acts radically altered old age support. The first act changed the terms on which the Basic Pension was indexed, from a combined wage and price measure to prices only. Over time, this shift drastically reduced the real value of the only universal pension in Britain. The second act lowered state pension benefits by basing payments on workers' average earnings over a lifetime. The previous calculation was based on best earning years, a formula far more generous to women who were in and out of the workforce. In the 1986 act, the government encouraged employees to participate in private pension plans by offering a 2 percent subsidy for those who opted out of the state scheme. Because women on the average earned less than men and many held precarious part-time jobs, few were able to take advantage of this offer. Finally, the 1986 act established that surviving spouses—most of them female—could inherit only one-half rather than all of the earnings-related state pension of their partners.[64]

Taken together, these revisions had the effect of impoverishing large numbers of elderly women. Traditional pension schemes were based on the model of full-time, life-long paid employment, a feature of many men's lives but characteristic of very few women's experiences in the United Kingdom. Changes introduced by the Thatcher government set out to channel retirement planning away from a state responsibility and toward a private, personal one. Here women as a group lost out because very few were in a position to divert current earnings toward future investment. By the early 1990s, studies showed that three-quarters of the elderly poor were women, with more than four in ten female pensioners living on less than £50 a week.[65]

The Thatcher government also worked to limit the role of the state in the housing field. About 30 percent of British families lived in public housing in 1979, and many were anxious to participate in the Conservatives' Right to Buy program. This popular initiative gave tenants the opportunity to purchase their homes at a discount, and about one in every five public units was sold off by 1990.[66] Changes in housing policy, however, also weakened rent controls and tenant succession rules in the private market. Rental fees imposed by local councils increased so that people who remained in public housing effectively subsidized the discounts given to new owners under the Right to Buy scheme.[67] Race discrimination was no longer prohibited in many categories of public, private, and nonprofit housing.[68] Because the stock of rent-controlled private housing and affordable public housing declined, the number of homeless grew over time.[69]

Conservatives proposed a different explanation of homelessness. According to Margaret Thatcher, the problem was "young single girls who deliberately become pregnant in order to jump a housing queue and get welfare payments."[70] The goal of government policy was therefore to eliminate the incentive to claim attractive social benefits. Lowering the level of payments and tightening eligibility rules offered a way to clamp down on queue jumpers. Conservatives worked to cut benefits and change rules across a wide swath of social programs. Housing allowances paid to low-income tenants became much less generous.[71] Unemployment benefits were reduced and rules tightened at least fifteen times during the Thatcher years, the same period as rates of unemployment rose sharply.[72] The universal family allowance known as Child Benefit declined in value because it was deindexed and later frozen.[73] Supplementary payments to welfare recipients were usually made as loans rather than grants.[74] Benefit levels for general welfare and low-income working families declined. All told, Conservatives cut an estimated £700 million from social spending by the late 1980s.[75] As political scientist Paul Pierson comments in his account of the Thatcher years, "This is a substantial sum, and it will come almost entirely from those living near or below the poverty line."[76]

The effects of spending changes on women who worked for the welfare state were considerable. About 45 percent of British public sector employees in 1981 were female; of these, more than 80 percent held positions in the health, education, or welfare fields.[77] A succession of Conservative governments worked to privatize what had been public sector work, including jobs in hospitals and schools for food services and cleaning. This practice of contracting out services that had previously offered public sector, unionized work meant lower wages and limited job security within a new employment "contract culture."[78] Over time, the size of the public sector labor force declined, and more women than ever found themselves in part-time, low-wage, temporary jobs.[79]

About two-thirds of adults on welfare in Britain during the 1980s were women, most of them single mothers.[80] The cuts to social spending by Conservatives directly affected this group and the children who depended on them. At the same time, the quality of public health care under the National Health Service deteriorated, and changes to pensions meant many women would be worse off in old age than during their earning years. Overall, the spending crunch amounted to a bad-news scenario for Britons who were poor, old, or sick. Core government programs that had existed in the past were in some cases replaced by private plans. In others, they remained as vastly eroded, minimalist arrangements. The practice of contracting out reduced women's access to well-paid unionized jobs. In short, the United States rather than continental Europe became the model for social policy in Britain after 1979.

The campaign against feminist advocacy in the United Kingdom was indirect, often unnoticed, but very effective. One way it occurred was through reductions to the budget of the Equal Opportunities Commission (EOC). As an agency dependent on central government funds, the EOC was charged with the task of enforcing equal rights at work. Conservatives had vigorously opposed both the specific legislation that created the EOC and also the general idea of government intervention in the workplace. After Margaret Thatcher took power, the Conservative budget of 1980 reduced funds going to the agency. The EOC drastically cut its staff from 400 to 148 as a result, and critics argued that the organization could not fulfill any useful mandate with so few employees.[81] Conservatives apparently preferred to avoid the public outcry that would have followed from eliminating the EOC. Instead, they chose in 1980 to cut transfers, gradually rendering the agency less and less effective in the eyes of its own supporters.

A second means of undermining advocacy work was through Tory attacks on local government. Feminism in the United Kingdom developed through a network of small groups that in some cases received support from municipal councils controlled by the Labour party. This stream of municipal feminism was very active, for example, inside the Greater London Council (GLC) after the Labour party won control during the early 1980s. The conflict between Margaret Thatcher and the GLC leader, Ken Livingstone, paralleled the Thatcher-Scargill confrontation. It arose in large part from the prime minister's unwillingness to tolerate any challenge to central government authority. Thatcher took to identifying both Scargill and Livingstone as extremists who were part of "the enemy within," meaning they posed a threat to the directions she intended to pursue.[82] Livingstone was especially dangerous as an articulate and charismatic advocate for Labour interests. Tories nicknamed him Red Ken.

The 1983 Conservative party manifesto called for abolishing the GLC and five other metropolitan councils on the grounds that they were fiscally irresponsible and politically out of step.[83] Thatcher condemned Red Ken and his allies as part of a "loony left" that wasted funds encouraging fringe interests and "alternative lifestyles."[84] Although women's groups hardly constituted the main target of the campaign against Labour-dominated local authorities, they were tarred with the same negative brush. Feminism was thus portrayed as part of a misguided, immoral effort to destroy the traditional family. As a result, the broader women's movement became a frequent object of media ridicule.[85]

It is difficult to measure the damage to women's activism caused by the shutdown of the GLC and the overall weakening of local government. Estimates of the funding available to the GLC Women's Committee indicate an annual budget of £7 to £8 million in the early 1980s. Approximately four hundred women's organizations received support from the GLC during the three years after the committee was established in 1982, and, of these, about three hundred were from minority and immigrant communities.[86] The GLC Women's Committee attracted trade union and women's movement activists in addition to others with no political experience. It focused on a number of initiatives including providing day care for the children of local government employees and improving training opportunities for women workers. Like women's committees established elsewhere by Labour councils, the GLC group campaigned to widen access to child care. Funds went toward a full-time worker in the National Child Care Campaign, for example, who was paid to pressure for more day care facilities. Issues like violence and health care were also highlighted by local committees along with child care, because many urban women believed the central government had no interest in raising let alone acting on these concerns.[87] According to Joni Lovenduski and Vicky Randall's account, however, no more than one-quarter of Labour-led local councils had committees focusing on equality issues during the 1980s.[88]

The obvious question about advocacy is what happened when Conservatives clamped down on local government. In 1986, the GLC and five other metropolitan councils were abolished. By the late 1980s, local governments that remained in place had lost control of education and housing policy and were forced to seek competitive bids for all services.[89] Under the terms of Conservative legislation on contracting out, municipal councils were compelled to accept the lowest bidder.[90] Local tax rates were limited by the central government under a scheme known as rate capping. Overall, these restrictions on what and how local governments could spend meant far less money flowed to women's groups.[91] Campaigning activities had to be organized by volunteers once again rather than by paid workers. The reduced monies that were available after 1986 came either from central government departments or else from quasi-independent nongovernmental organizations (known as QUANGOs) supported by local councils. These new sources of funding supported short-term, specific projects rather than long-term organizational work.

In short, the stable core funding provided to women's groups by the GLC during the early 1980s virtually disappeared by the 1990s. The assumption of both the Thatcher and Major governments was that taxpayers had no responsibility to fund "loony left" issue campaigns. In fact, under the terms of John Major's 1994 Criminal Justice Act, a great deal of protest activity by organized groups could be deemed unlawful—which went far beyond claiming groups were undeserving of public monies.[92]

The squeezing out of women's advocacy work in Britain was an integral and perversely effective part of the money crunch. Conservative budget cuts to the EOC led to a torrent of criticism by feminists, not so much of government spending reductions as of the agency's questionable influence.[93] By ensuring that activists were busy attacking an agency that the government itself disliked, Conservatives took the spotlight off themselves and managed to contain the story of work pressures and spending cuts. Issues like low pay and reduced social benefits remained women's private troubles as long as they were not the focus of well-organized, well-publicized protest campaigns. Controlling advocacy by diverting and defunding it meant the impact of the Thatcher and Major governments on many women's lives remained unknown to all but a small core of committed activists. To make matters worse, these militants were widely portrayed as crazed campaigners from the lunatic fringe. If it was any consolation, though, the challenge to women's advocacy in North America was remarkably similar.

The Crunch under Reagan and Bush

In the United States, conservative leaders had somewhat less of an effect on women's work than did their counterparts in the United Kingdom. American women were far more likely than British ones to hold postsecondary degrees by the mid-1980s, roughly twenty in one hundred versus about five in one hundred.[94] This formal training meant women in the United States had greater access to good, full-time jobs that allowed them to pay for child care and save for their retirement. Because the United States was a federal system in which other levels of government retained significant control over employment policy, it was not possible for Republican presidents to stop progress in its tracks. The Minnesota and Washington state legislatures, for example, passed laws assuring equal pay for work of equal value during the 1980s.[95]

That being said, the Reagan and Bush administrations worked hard to weaken unions and eliminate federal regulations on employers. Much as Margaret Thatcher had attacked British miners, Ronald Reagan took direct aim at American air traffic controllers during his time as president. He endorsed the idea of contracting out what had been public services to private business.[96] Presidents Reagan and Bush both accused unions of representing "special interests" rather than public ones. Reagan moved quickly to loosen a series of occupational health and safety, environmental, and labor relations rules. His administration vastly weakened the federal agencies charged with regulating in these areas.[97]

Much of the bureaucratic machinery put in place to enforce equal opportunities at work rested in the hands of the Equal Employment Opportunities Commission (EEOC). The EEOC was established under the terms of Title VII of the 1964 U.S. Civil Rights Act and served as the model for Britain's EOC. The American agency was staffed after 1980 by a series of appointees who opposed government intervention, active civil rights enforcement, and especially affirmative action programs. Reagan's nominee to head the EEOC was Clarence Thomas, later appointed to the Supreme Court by George Bush. Thomas and others reduced the amount of enforcement work carried out by the EEOC—a task they accomplished by devoting less money and fewer staff to equal employment policy.[98]

After 1980, federal civil rights work in the EEOC and Department of Justice changed directions to the point that these agencies reversed sides on key cases. In the *Grove City College* case, for example, the Carter administration defended arguments that colleges receiving any federal funds should comply with civil rights provisions. Yet once Reagan appointees were in charge, the federal government switched positions to side with the college, claiming civil rights rules amounted to heavy-handed federal regulation. Instead of defending civil rights precedents, the federal government in this case and others attacked its own rules.[99] The shift over time in how regulation was viewed had direct effects on the workplace. During the Reagan years, complex revisions to administrative codes took place to limit employees' ability to prove discrimination. Republicans criticized the goal of hiring more women or minorities as involving a quota that endangered the principle of merit.[100] Over time, conservatives succeeded in equating quotas, federal regulations, and what they called special interests in the public mind.

The unwillingness of Reagan and Bush to regulate was reflected clearly in their stand against unpaid family leave. The first attempt to introduce what became the Family and Medical Leave Act was made in 1985 by Democratic representative Patricia Schroeder. Women's groups including the National Organization for Women and trade unions supported Schroeder's bill. The U.S. Chamber of Commerce vigorously opposed it, claiming unpaid leave would raise the costs of doing business and open the door to more federal regulations on employers. Conservatives insisted family leave and child care were issues for workers and not government to look after. As a result, President Bush vetoed the family leave bill, and Congress failed to override his decision.[101]

Changes that Reagan and Bush made in this area tended not to involve direct federal intervention. In 1981, for example, the administration used the tax system to encourage private companies to set up day care facilities.[102] Tax credits for child care that originated during the 1950s and benefited primarily the middle class were continued. They allowed a maximum $2,400 tax credit per child per year, which was far below the actual price of care. The cost of these credits constituted about one-third of federal spending on day care in 1980.[103] Efforts to introduce more comprehensive legislation during the Reagan years were not successful. Social conservatives and antifeminists, notably anti-ERA crusader Phyllis Schlafly, effectively argued that mothers provided the best care for their children.[104]

During the Bush years, compromise legislation passed that met the demands of the conservative right. First, Schlafly won provisions that gave tax credits to families with mothers at home. Second, parents were given vouchers so that choice rested in their hands. The vouchers could be used for care by relatives, neighbors, churches, or private day care centers. Third, the program of federal block grants was to be administered by the states.[105] Republican senator Orrin Hatch, a leader of the social right who consistently opposed abortion, explained why he supported a 1989 child care bill:

> [It] does not make the federal government a child care provider; it does not give the government a monopoly on child care; it does not prohibit participation by religious institution[s]; and, it does not require the licensing of close relatives who provide care.[106]

Hatch's reasoning demonstrated how child care debates during the Reagan-Bush years had little to do with the needs of working women.

As in Britain, tax changes introduced in the United States helped to create a more polarized society. The record tax cuts of 1981 were driven by conservative arguments that once individuals and firms were taxed less, they would spend more, which in turn would stimulate economic growth and more jobs. Generous depreciation and expense allowances were introduced for business, and the principle of progressivity in rates of personal income tax was weakened. Payroll levies under the Social Security system were raised.[107] Unlike the United Kingdom, however, the United States had no national consumption tax and no mass of public corporations that could be sold off to generate revenue. Instead, American conservatives used ever-higher government deficits as leverage against any programs they opposed, while they conveniently forgot about deficits when it came to things they supported, like military spending. Accounts indicate that U.S. defense budgets doubled during the Reagan period to reach about $300 billion per year during the Bush administration.[108]

Overall, the work crunch facing many American women was hardly eased by the actions of Republican presidents. Federal regulations affecting employment were weakened and key agencies placed in the hands of foes like Clarence Thomas. Unpaid family leave legislation was blocked by presidential veto. Child care provisions that did pass were so watered down by compromise that they offered little to working women. And, as in Britain, research on family leisure showed the pressures on women at work did not let up at home. A 1985 study by the School of Social Work at Boston University reported married mothers had nineteen fewer hours a week of leisure time than did married fathers.[109]

Any discussion of what happened to American social programs must be placed in context. The United States had no universal public health care system. Public pensions were funded by payroll taxes, meaning the Social Security system was a selective, earnings-related scheme that did not provide universal payments. Unemployment benefits in the United States were very limited compared with those in the United Kingdom or Canada, and they involved both state and federal governments. Virtually all welfare programs were means tested and organized under a complex system of shared jurisdiction.[110]

The damage that could occur within this setting was potentially enormous. Accounts of developments during the Reagan and Bush years demonstrate that the human costs were indeed staggering. Low-income American women arguably suffered more as a result of the spending crunch than did their counterparts in Britain and Canada because the programs in place in 1980 were already so minimal and so decentralized. Cutting back the bare-bones, residual U.S. welfare state was simply more painful in human terms than reducing the relatively developed and expansive social systems of Britain and Canada.

Reductions to social spending by Republican presidents occurred in an environment of middle-class tax revolt. Proposition 13, a California ballot initiative that passed in 1978, offered one clear example of public resistance to tax increases. Fueling this antitax sentiment was the rhetoric of conservative politicians, who denounced not just welfare programs but also the people who depended on them. According to Republican senator Jesse Helms, food subsidies to the poor had become a "fiscal monster" supporting "parasites who have infested the . . . program."[111] Ronald Reagan consistently claimed that welfare programs caused poverty because they led people away from work and traditional forms of family organization.[112] Because Republicans held a majority in the U.S. Senate between 1981 and 1986, many of the most drastic changes to social spending took place during that period.

In particular, dramatic reductions to food subsidies and welfare occurred during the Reagan honeymoon period. The food stamps program had begun in the 1960s as a means-tested system of providing coupons to low-income households. The coupons could then be used in stores to buy essential items. The food stamps budget in the federal Department of Agriculture was cut 13 percent during the early 1980s, with a drop of $1.5 billion for fiscal year 1982. From covering about 65 percent of poor households in 1980, this level fell to less than 59 percent by 1988.[113] Much of the change effected by the Reagan administration occurred through the tightening of eligibility rules. As in Britain, this narrowing of access was far more likely to affect poor rather than middle-class or affluent citizens. Parallel with the situation in the United Kingdom, more than three-fourths of poor Americans in 1980 were women and children.[114]

The primary vehicle for providing income support to this group was Aid to Families with Dependent Children (AFDC). AFDC was a joint federal/state program since its inception in 1935, the same year as the national pensions system known as Social Security was introduced. Unlike the Social Security program, which benefited middle-class wage earners and survived relatively unscathed through the Republican years, AFDC was a touchstone for conservative critics of welfare spending. The program was designed to support children who had one absent parent and whose custodial parent had little or no income. The means test for AFDC, as for food stamps, was difficult and geared to minimal assets in the less-than-$2,000 range.[115] Approximately one-half of all families headed by women in the United States received AFDC payments in 1979.[116] After 1980, a series of Reagan budgets narrowed eligibility rules for AFDC recipients, cut cash grants to states to pay for the program, and, as a result of removing people from AFDC, limited eligibility for public health care under the Medicaid program.[117]

These changes occurred at the same time as federal budgets reduced subsidies for school lunch programs, job training projects, and public housing. The Comprehensive Employment and Training Act (CETA) of 1973 was superseded during the first Reagan term by the Job Training Partnership Act (JTPA). The latter focused on increasing local, state, and business involvement in training low-income people, including welfare recipients. According to sociologist Sara Rix, CETA's 1980 training budget was $3.9 billion, versus only $2.6 billion for JTPA's training budget four years later.[118] The flow of funds to build new housing developments was shut off, and tenants were forced to contribute a higher proportion of their income toward rent.[119] Simultaneously, the criteria for extended unemployment benefits were tightened, and all unemployment payments were made subject to tax as of 1986. Over time, the proportion of out-of-work Americans who were eligible to collect unemployment benefits declined from 50 percent in 1980 to only 32 percent in 1988.[120]

This combination of reductions in federal spending on food stamps, AFDC, Medicaid, school lunches, housing, and unemployment benefits largely occurred under the guise of New Federalism proposals. Although many of its most radical elements were never implemented, the New Federalism concept was geared toward downloading major social policy responsibilities from the federal level.[121] Ronald Reagan and leading members of his administration maintained that lower levels of government, meaning states, cities, and towns, knew better what their residents needed than did some distant federal bureaucrat in Washington. Because state and local governments could identify what people needed and direct money where it mattered, according to Reagan, spending programs needed to be devolved further. The essence of New Federalism was thus a push toward decentralization in an already fragmented and minimalist welfare state.

One of the most obvious effects of decentralization was a state-by-state race toward the bottom of social spending. What analysts called "interstate economic competition" amounted to an effort to keep taxes low and benefits limited.[122] These conditions would encourage businesses to invest in a given state, while they discouraged poor people from moving there to get higher welfare payments. As a result, proposals designed to move welfare recipients into the workforce, incorporated in the 1988 Family Support Act, were ineffective because many states lacked the necessary funds.[123] The 1988 legislation aimed to provide training and child care benefits for single parents, following the idea that assistance with education and day care would get many households off AFDC.[124] Yet most states that signed up to participate in the act could not claim full federal funding because matching state monies were not available. The amount the federal government could provide was in turn limited by tax changes in 1981 and 1986 that reduced revenues from middle- and upper-income households. In other words, further decentralization in an American environment of tax revolt and punitive attitudes toward the poor meant the spending crunch grew more severe as time passed.

The difficult situation facing many American women can be measured in terms of welfare spending and welfare jobs. Data show that roughly two-thirds of the reductions to social spending effected in President Reagan's budgets were made to programs serving low-income households.[125] Poor women and their children were the main recipient groups for these programs. At the provider end of the system, more than 30 percent of employed women in the United States held positions in the social welfare field. These women, many of them African Americans, worked as teachers, nurses, social workers, health care aides, and so on, whether for government, nonprofit agencies, or the private sector.[126] Research suggests that about half of social welfare spending in the United States at the point Reagan took office came either directly or indirectly (via grants to states and cities, or through transfers to individuals) from the federal government.[127]

Once Republican presidents began to cut social spending in a serious way, women stood to lose significantly as both welfare recipients and service providers. In Alabama, for example, a single mother with two children and a monthly income of more than $183 was not eligible for welfare benefits by the late 1980s.[128] Because AFDC payments were not indexed to prices by any of the fifty states, the real value of welfare benefits declined steadily over time. Among families with a black female head of household, more than half lived on an income of less than half the federal poverty line in 1987.[129] One-third of poor and 28 percent of low-income women in 1990 had no health insurance coverage.[130] It is not surprising that efforts to follow the British example by selling off subsidized housing to existing tenants went nowhere because most Americans who qualified for public housing were simply too poor to participate.[131]

On the provider side, an estimated 2.5 women for every 1 man were laid off as part of federal cuts to senior administrative staff in the 1980s. This imbalance occurred because the Reagan administration targeted its public service reductions on four key social welfare departments, where women were more numerous and more senior than in less affected areas like the Defense Department.[132] Staffing levels in the

Women's Bureau in the Department of Labor were reduced by more than one-quarter during Reagan's first term in office.[133] Around the country, organizations that relied on federal dollars to pay job trainees and legal workers (under the CETA and LEAA programs) lost those funds as a result of federal budget changes. Shelters for battered women in particular reduced their staffs and, in some cases, closed because of cutbacks by the Reagan and Bush administrations.[134]

Taken as a group, reductions in federal spending after 1980 imposed a heavy burden. Although Republican administrations had to compromise more over time to pass their budgets through Congress, they still established very fixed limits that would shape social policy far into the future. Lower taxes on business and the wealthy largely dictated lower benefits for the poor. The more fragmented funding and delivery system created after 1980 meant that crucial responsibility rested with state governments. Many of them were competing to see how little they could provide. The growth in defense spending created a higher federal deficit, which remained a clear barrier to social program expansion. American women who depended on federal social outlays were thus in the vice grip of a long-term spending crunch.

Feminist advocacy work in the United States was a also target for conservative politicians. Aided by a growing right-wing presence in the mass media, opponents of abortion, the Equal Rights Amendment, and equality in general hammered away at the feminist cause. As in Britain, the attack on advocacy occurred at the level of both language and money. But unlike their counterparts in the United Kingdom, American women's groups were able to find additional sources of funds in hard times, in many cases exceeding the amount that was available to them in earlier years.

Much of the effort to undermine women's group activism unfolded as a rhetorical campaign. Ronald Reagan consistently referred to labor, civil rights, and women's organizations as single-issue groups or special interests, meaning they were less legitimate and less credible than the Chamber of Commerce, for example. Terms like *equal opportunities* and *affirmative action* were turned on their heads so that opponents spoke only of reverse discrimination and quotas. The social right zeroed in on child care and abortion issues in arguing that feminists were antifamily and antilife, rather than pro-family and pro-life. Violence against women was degendered so that it became part of family violence, domestic violence, or some all-encompassing crime wave. This shift in language was at times subtle and at times fiercely direct, particularly when it came from committed social conservatives like

Paul Weyrich, founder of the right-wing Heritage Foundation. Weyrich viewed feminism as a source of radical ideas that threatened not only the American family but also Western civilization in general. The clear effect of the conservative counterdiscourse was to place women's groups on the defensive.[135]

At the level of dollars and cents, the Reagan administration worked to remove funds from the hands of advocates on the other side. One target within this campaign was the Women's Educational Equity Act (WEEA), a seemingly innocuous piece of federal legislation passed in 1974.[136] This act provided funds for educational projects including programs to teach women about their legal rights and to tutor them in mathematics. The purpose of the original bill was to end sex discrimination in education. The director of the WEEA when Reagan took office, Leslie Wolfe, became a focus of new right criticism. Wolfe was among the few senior female bureaucrats in the federal government at the time, and her program was the only national project that focused on educational equity.

The Reagan administration began by proposing to eliminate funds totally for WEEA. After vigorous lobbying by supporters of the program, a compromise was worked out with Congress that saw WEEA's budget cut by about 40 percent. In 1982, Wolfe was attacked in a number of conservative publications that described her as a radical, imperious "monarch."[137] Within the next two years she was reassigned in the Education Department, put back in charge of a WEEA staffed by hostile appointees from Phyllis Schlafly's Eagle Forum, and, finally, offered a demotion to the rank of clerk-typist. Wolfe resigned from the civil service and continued her career as head of the Washington-based Center for Women Policy Studies. The WEEA ultimately survived the Reagan years but in a vastly reduced form.

The advocacy crunch also affected violence against women programs. Pressure from the new right reduced monies going to women's shelters and led to the closing of the federal Office of Domestic Violence.[138] According to research by Joyce Gelb and Ethel Klein, one-quarter of rape crisis centers in the United States were forced to close because of Reagan administration budget cuts.[139] Supporters of these reductions argued that federal spending on antiviolence programs was both wasteful and likely to abet feminism and endanger the traditional family. It is no surprise that many of the same organizations that targeted the WEEA also worked to eliminate federal support for refuges, rape crisis centers, the Office of Domestic Violence, and the Women's Bureau in the Labor Department.

Conservatives assumed that once they diverted funds away from these programs, movement activities would gradually cease. The point about the Reagan and Bush years is that this did not occur. Instead, established women's organizations attracted a flood of private contributions from individuals and foundations to pick up where government left off. Many new groups including the Fund for the Feminist Majority, EMILY's List, and Republicans for Choice were created while Ronald Reagan lived in the White House.[140] During the Bush years, these organizations attracted record donations, memberships, and volunteers. The 1989 Supreme Court decision in the *Webster* case prompted increased contributions to many pro-choice organizations.[141] In 1991, Anita Hill's testimony before the all-male Senate Judiciary Committee did not prevent Clarence Thomas's appointment to the Supreme Court. What it did create, however, was a massive rise in public awareness of both sexual harassment and the absence of women in senior legislative positions. Donations to EMILY's List and other groups that sought to elect more women took off.[142]

In short, the campaign against feminist advocacy orchestrated by American conservatives did affect the language of public debate. Slowly but surely, the prevailing rhetoric shifted away from movement discourse. Where conservatives were less successful was in turning off the taps on movement advocacy. They tried to stop the flow of funds to the WEEA, for example, but were only partly effective. Ironically, by turning up the heat and targeting individuals like Leslie Wolfe, these opponents opened new doors for the very causes they were trying to block. As one movement activist commented, "The irony is that during the Reagan-Bush years, we had money falling out of the skies."

The advocacy crunch was therefore less damaging to women's groups in the United States than elsewhere. The fact that charitable individuals and foundations were prepared to support movement goals meant pressure for change did not stop just because Ronald Reagan and George Bush held the office of president. Yet record donations to feminist organizations during the Republican years did little to reverse the downward spiral in social spending. Pressed by administration cutbacks, for example, welfare recipients were worse off in 1992 than in 1980. Changes that might have been made in child care and family leave legislation remained unimaginable through the Reagan and Bush years. In general, the lives of many American women became increasingly difficult.

Some Americans looked toward a Canadian model of more generous social spending combined with tighter workplace regulation. Yet these very traditions were under threat, after 1984, north of the forty-ninth parallel.

The Crunch under Mulroney

Canadian Conservatives were generally less driven by ideological concerns than were their counterparts in Britain and the United States. Before running for office, Brian Mulroney practiced labor law in Quebec and developed a reputation as a skillful conciliator in various industries. This background made him relatively well disposed toward trade unions, meaning he took power in 1984 with no public vendetta against the labor movement. Mulroney's pragmatism was likely the basis for Margaret Thatcher's comment in *The Downing Street Years* that "[a]s leader of the Progressive Conservatives I thought he put too much stress on the adjective as opposed to the noun."[143]

Conservatives in Canada were also influenced by the terms of the federal system. Ottawa could only administer the roughly one-tenth of the labor force that worked for it or for federally regulated industries, leaving about 90 percent of workers under provincial jurisdiction. Women's groups and trade unions were therefore able to press for provincial laws to mandate equal pay for work of equal value and to limit the use of strike breakers. They did so quite effectively in Ontario, Quebec, and elsewhere during the same period as Conservatives governed at the federal level.[144] In addition, the equality language in the Charter of Rights and Freedoms was a reality for all governments after 1985. One case moving through the courts on paid leave for both new mothers and fathers, for example, led the federal Conservatives to broaden the terms of parental leave legislation.[145]

Yet the Mulroney years produced significant negatives that shaped the lives of many women. Probably the most crucial of these was the decision to pursue Canada-U.S. and later Canada-U.S.-Mexico free trade. Combined with the effects during the same period of a devastating recession and the government's high interest rate policy, free trade seemed to wipe out thousands of Canadian jobs.[146] As activists in the National Action Committee on the Status of Women (NAC) predicted, many of these positions were in sectors like clothing, textiles, small electrical products, and food processing in which large numbers of women were concentrated. Free trade, according to NAC, was a recipe for the deindustrialization of Canada and the impoverishment of Canadian women.

Government data on employment by industry offered some support for this position. They showed a trend over time toward more part-time, low-paid service jobs and less full-time, well-paid, unionized manufacturing work.[147] These same official sources indicated women were more likely than men to be looking for jobs through the early 1990s, because many females held part-time but wanted full-time employment.[148] The concerns women had about work were reflected in survey data from the early 1990s. When asked to name the most important issue facing Canada, females were significantly more likely than males to cite unemployment.[149]

As in the United Kingdom and United States, mothers in Canada had trouble with child care arrangements. Conservatives introduced a National Strategy on Child Care in 1987 that increased tax deductions for working parents and removed day care funding from the system of welfare transfers to the provinces. This complex switch in funding was opposed by feminist as well as antifeminist organizations. NAC and its leading affiliate in the field, the Canadian Day Care Advocacy Association, objected to the Conservative proposal because it threatened to reduce funds going to the provinces for day care. These groups also argued that the legislation as drafted would lead to government subsidies for profit-making centers and would not establish national standards either to train workers or to care for children. The antifeminist group known as REAL Women (standing for Realistic, Equal, Active, for Life) denounced the same legislation because it offered no subsidies to mothers who stayed at home with their children.[150] Not surprisingly, the Mulroney government went ahead with the tax deductions but dropped the other proposals. Canadian women were left with virtually the same patchwork of public, private, and workplace child care they had had earlier, in which expenses up to $5,000 per year per child could be deducted from taxable income.[151]

This tax arrangement and other changes introduced by the Conservatives were most helpful to upper-income Canadians. The child care benefit was a deduction rather than a credit, available only when working mothers had a full set of receipts to prove what they paid.[152] In 1991, the Mulroney government introduced a 7 percent national consumption tax known as the Goods and Services Tax. It replaced an existing manufacturers' tax. Like the British Value Added Tax, this was a regressive levy that placed its main burden on low-income consumers. Conservatives in Canada also reduced corporate tax rates, raised payroll levies, and introduced a $500,000 lifetime capital gains exemption to benefit the wealthy. Studies showed that the Canadian tax system became more unfair over time because the primary burden shifted from affluent households and private corporations to middle- and low-income families.[153]

In short, the Mulroney government's decision to pursue free trade and create what it saw as a welcoming environment for business was costly to many Canadians. High interest rates and continentalist trade policies coincided with growing levels of unemployment. More bad jobs than good ones were created in the restructured economy of the 1990s. Child care programs differed little from what was available earlier. Research showed a persistent leisure gap in the lives of women parallel to that in the United Kingdom and United States.[154] And the tax regime put in place by the Conservatives was arguably more imbalanced and more socially divisive than the one they inherited in 1984.

Compared with women in the United States during the same period, however, Canadian women were spared major changes at the national level in social spending. The Mulroney government, distracted by its free trade and constitutional agendas, devoted only limited attention to fiscal issues. The Conservative caucus contained a significant number of pro-intervention members, particularly from poor regions in Quebec, who were essential to Mulroney's political success. In other parts of the country, however, and especially in areas of western Canada and Ontario affected by the spillover from the U.S. system, Mulroney's caucus drew committed social and economic conservatives. When these interests decided to focus on social programs, they acted along the same lines as their American and British counterparts. Broadly based universal programs were turned into selective, means-tested ones. Spending that was already targeted became more so, in the sense that eligibility rules were tightened further. Fiscal transfers to the provinces were cut using rhetoric similar to the New Federalism language of the Reagan administration.

These shifts occurred in an environment where the Mulroney government was attempting to retain the support of its crucial electoral ally, the Liberal regime of Premier Robert Bourassa in Quebec. Mulroney's calculation that the Conservatives could not win federally without a base in Quebec was central to his political outlook. Once Bourassa defeated the separatist Parti québécois in 1985 provincial elections, Mulroney made it his business to keep the new government on his side. Conservative decisions to negotiate free trade and to embark on a series of ultimately unsuccessful constitutional discussions were taken with the support of Liberal elites in Quebec. In addition, the willingness of the Conservatives to chop transfers to other provinces like Ontario, British Columbia, and Alberta can be seen in the context of this political calculus. Overall, the Conservatives were unwilling to incur the wrath of the Bourassa government in the same way as they risked the anger of other provinces.

The fact that Canada at the end of the Mulroney years was even more decentralized than it had been in 1984 was understandable in this light.[155] Mulroney fundamentally endorsed the market forces argument that underlay his free trade policy. If Canadian social welfare standards were too high to survive economic integration with the United States, then they needed to come down a few notches to be competitive. If provinces like Quebec believed that they knew better how to deliver services to their residents, then the federal government should transfer more control to them. And so the story went until, as NAC and other critics claimed, Canada by 1993 seemed to be little more than ten feuding provinces economically annexed to the U.S. market.

The most significant changes made to federal social spending after 1984 affected family allowances, unemployment insurance, and transfers to the provinces to pay for welfare benefits. The first of these programs was established in 1945 as a universal system of baby bonuses paid to mothers. The amount paid out under the scheme was limited, about $35 per month for each child under the age of eighteen in 1992. Conservatives ended universal family allowances in a series of steps. In 1985, they ruled that payments would only be increased if inflation exceeded 3 percent. A system of taxing benefits was also introduced so that by 1992, one-third of the family allowances program was paid for through a "claw-back" of payments to middle- and upper-income families. In 1992, the Mulroney government eliminated universality altogether by creating a targeted Child Tax Benefit. This benefit replaced the Child Tax Credit created by the Liberals in 1978, for which Conservatives had already tightened eligibility in 1988. Full payment was made to low-income families who did not pay tax on the benefit but who only received an increase when inflation was more than 3 percent. An additional family supplement of $500 per year was paid to the working poor, but not to welfare recipients.[156]

Comparisons of universal with selective child benefit spending in Canada suggested the new means-tested scheme cost the government less money than did the older universal approach. It accomplished little for poor families and eliminated one of the only sure sources of monthly income for many mothers.[157] Moreover, by switching from a universal to a targeted scheme, the Conservative government moved from a system that was relevant to all families with children to one that addressed only the poor. This shift meant that the base of the family allowances program grew more narrow and, in political terms, more powerless as time passed.

Shifts in unemployment benefits after 1984 followed a similar pattern.[158] Although Mulroney promised a generous program for retraining Canadians who lost their jobs as a result of free trade, no such plan emerged. Instead, Conservative legislation tightened eligibility for unemployment insurance (UI) and reduced the level of benefits from 66 to 57 percent of insurable earnings. In 1991, federal government funds were withdrawn so that benefits were paid by employee and employer contributions only. This necessitated higher payroll taxes, shorter benefit periods, and lower benefit payments. Training programs for immigrant women and workers who were trying to reenter the labor force (most of them older women) were also reduced by the Mulroney government. Because women's wages on average were lower than those of men, women's UI benefits were hit hard by these changes. Moreover, parental leave programs were established under the UI system, and every time general benefits were cut, so were those for maternity leave.[159]

Probably the most complicated fiscal maneuvers of the Mulroney years involved transfers to the provinces.[160] Welfare programs in Canada had been organized since 1966 under the terms of the Canada Assistance Plan (CAP), which sent federal monies to the ten provinces and two territories to assist with welfare payments. Until 1990, Ottawa paid for one-half of all qualifying programs in all provinces and territories. After that point, the Conservatives enforced a "cap on CAP" that limited increases in transfers to the three wealthiest provinces to no more than 5 percent per year for five years. Alberta, British Columbia, and Ontario were thus made ineligible for matching federal monies that went to other governments, even though taxes collected in these three provinces were a primary source of all federal transfers.

Over time, the cap on CAP led key provinces including Alberta and Ontario to reduce social services to their residents and gave the federal government far less leverage over national welfare standards. As James Rice and Michael Prince conclude in their account of fiscal changes in Canada, "the most significant consequences of the Conservatives' social policy record have been a lowering of the safety net and a weakening of certain bonds of nationhood and citizenship."[161] Brian Mulroney's controls on transfers to the provinces were very similar to Ronald Reagan's attempts to bring in a New Federalism. Both strategies shielded the national government from responsibility for society's have-nots. Parallel with this change, they shifted the burden of criticism for what was going wrong from the federal to state or provincial level.

NAC along with leading trade union and antipoverty groups argued that Canada was becoming more and more like the United States.[162] By the time the Conservatives lost power in 1993, Canada no longer offered universal family allowances. The country had a much reduced unemployment insurance system and an increasingly decentralized regime of welfare spending. Taken together, these patterns confirmed suspicions that free trade would lead to downward policy harmonization in Canada, with lower U.S. standards gradually dominating the northern half of the continent. Mulroney's earlier claim that social programs constituted a "sacred trust" seemed to be just another hollow election promise.

Probably the most visible challenge to Canadian women as a group followed from the advocacy crunch. NAC vehemently opposed two of the most significant initiatives of the Conservative years, free trade and constitutional change. As a result, the women's movement in English Canada incurred the personal wrath of the prime minister from the time NAC first criticized free trade in the mid-1980s until Mulroney resigned in 1993. Canadian Conservatives, like their British and American counterparts, used a mixture of angry rhetoric and budget cuts essentially to punish feminists for stepping out of line. The key difference was that in Canada, women's groups were far more dependent on government support, so cuts to funding had a profound effect.

One reason federal Tories were so irate was because they had a strong record on female appointments. Upon assuming office in 1984, Brian Mulroney included six women in his first cabinet. He later named two female justices to the Supreme Court of Canada, bringing women's representation to a record one-third of the high court bench. Conservative appointments to federal agencies, the senior civil service, and the Senate were far more balanced in gender terms than those of any previous government. Tories in Canada believed that women's groups were captives of opposition interests if they failed to recognize these accomplishments.[163]

The tension between Conservatives and movement organizations reached its first peak during the period of the 1988 federal elections. Whereas criticism of free trade among francophone groups in Quebec was relatively muted, it was harsh and sustained among opponents in English Canada. As the leading umbrella for women's organizations outside Quebec, NAC began to raise arguments against free trade during the fall of 1985. Many of the position papers, newspaper articles, and parliamentary committee briefs presented by NAC were written by Marjorie Cohen, a social science professor who cochaired the NAC Employment Committee. Cohen's work argued that under free trade, women risked losing both their jobs and the generous provisions of the Canadian welfare state. She claimed health care, equal pay, and unemployment insurance standards were threatened by a more market-driven, privatized economy modeled on the U.S. system.[164]

Although Conservatives probably expected NAC to raise these kinds of questions, they were unprepared for the vigor of the organization's campaign. In 1987, NAC became one of the founding members of a national coalition against free trade known as the Pro-Canada Network. This group brought together many of the same trade union, anti-poverty, and cultural groups that opposed Conservative tax policies and spending cuts. During the 1988 election period, NAC produced a series of pamphlets that outlined why it opposed free trade. Marjorie Cohen wrote in a NAC newsletter that the organization was working "to mobilize women to oppose politicians who favour the deal."[165]

NAC's strategy was clearly to deny Mulroney a second term in office. This did not happen, as the Conservatives won another majority government in 1988 and free trade with the United States went into effect on a timetable beginning in January 1989. Once he had the second mandate, Mulroney appeared to punish those who had opposed his positions. Groups like NAC saw their federal funding dramatically reduced. At the point of the conflict over free trade, NAC relied on about $680,000 per year from Ottawa, or about two-thirds of its annual budget. These funds subsidized staff, publications, postage, and other expenses.[166]

The 1989 federal budget was the first to come down after the election campaign. It included a cut in federal funding to NAC of more than 50 percent over two years, which meant that annual federal support would drop to $300,000 by 1992. In 1989, too, the Conservatives became the first government in more than fifteen years to refuse to meet with representatives of the NAC lobby on Parliament Hill. The estrangement between women's groups in English Canada and the Conservative government grew over time. The 1990 budget eliminated an additional $1.6 million from the main federal agency that supported equality programs, the Secretary of State Women's Program. These funds would have gone primarily to women's centers and publications.[167]

NAC and other organizations protested these cuts, arguing that they would have to depend as a result on contributions from individual women—the same ones who faced unemployment and weaker social programs because of free trade. Higher rates of personal income tax plus higher consumption taxes in Canada than in the United States meant groups like NAC could not draw on the same pool of private funding that was available south of the border. Moreover, the costs of operating national organizations in Canada remained relatively high because a small population was spread over a very large land mass. Moreover, in opposing Conservative budget decisions, NAC maintained that the Women's Program after 1984 was hardly pro-feminist. About thirty members of the government caucus met representatives of REAL Women during the mid-1980s, when the group was attempting to obtain a grant from the Secretary of State. In 1989, antifeminists in REAL Women applied for and received approximately $21,000 in Secretary of State funds to hold a conference.[168]

The second high point in the conflict between government and movement occurred in the early 1990s. As prime minister, Brian Mulroney brought together all of the provincial premiers at a cottage on scenic Meech Lake, where they agreed in 1987 to a series of constitutional changes proposed by the province of Quebec. Over time, both the process and the content of the Meech Lake Accord came under intense scrutiny. In English Canada, the Ad Hoc Committee of Women on the Constitution—the same group that led the fight during the early 1980s for equality language in the Charter—was revived for the fight against Meech Lake. As an independently funded group, it argued that the 1987 deal was a misguided creation of eleven white men in a room, meaning Mulroney and the ten premiers. The Ad Hoc Committee insisted that the terms of the accord offered substantial new powers to all provincial governments, not just the government of Quebec. As in the early 1980s, groups in English Canada opposed decentralization on the grounds that it would render national standards in child care and other fields virtually unthinkable. Above all, the Ad Hoc Committee maintained that the terms of the Meech Lake Accord jeopardized Charter equality language entrenched in 1982. Meech Lake was ultimately unsuccessful as a constitutional deal because two provinces refused to ratify it by the 1990 deadline.[169]

Brian Mulroney then brought forward another set of constitutional proposals in the fall of 1992. This revised deal, known as the Charlottetown Accord, was more complicated than Meech Lake because it included provisions on aboriginal self-government. Notably, native women were not guaranteed Charter equality rights under the terms of self-government in the accord. NAC took a far more prominent part in the public campaign against the Charlottetown Accord than it had in the Meech Lake debate. The arguments the group raised were very similar to those developed in the Ad Hoc Committee's stand against Meech Lake.[170] What was different was that the Ad Hoc Committee was a group of feminist legal specialists who volunteered their time. NAC, however, was a more broad-based coalition of groups that had already seen its federal support cut in half. Conservatives were furious that women's organizations would once again dare to challenge the government on a core priority.

Mulroney lashed out in no uncertain terms against English Canadian feminists. He labeled them as "racist" and anti-Quebec "enemies of Canada."[171] Months before the Charlottetown Accord was defeated in a national referendum, the federal cabinet decided to eliminate the $2.75 million Court Challenges Program.[172] This project funded litigation by groups including the Women's Legal Education and Action Fund, established in 1985 to pursue test cases in the courts using Charter equality language. LEAF saw a crucial source of funding dry up as a result. It seemed more than a coincidence that many women active in LEAF were also associated with the Ad Hoc Committee. By punishing LEAF, the Mulroney government communicated its message loud and clear to constitutional critics. As time passed, activists noted, both Conservatives and Liberals who would succeed them in office began to label organizations that opposed their priorities as special interest groups. A number of women both inside and outside the governing party endorsed the Charlottetown Accord, and they modeled a large button that said, "NAC does not speak for me."[173]

The advocacy crunch in Canada, however, did have at least two unintended consequences. More money than ever poured into some organizations whose agendas were under direct threat. On the abortion issue, for example, Conservatives attempted to pass legislation that would recriminalize the procedure. This threat to limit abortion access led thousands of new supporters to join pro-choice groups during the early 1990s—the same period as Conservatives were attempting to marginalize women's groups through their language and their budget cuts.[174] In addition, NAC's willingness to challenge the government first over free trade and then on the constitution gave unprecedented public exposure to organized feminism. This level of attention only increased once the Conservatives tried to counter criticism from NAC and other groups.

Overall, Canadian women in the Mulroney years were to some extent insulated from the work pressures and social policy changes that faced their sisters in Britain and the United States. Conservatives in Ottawa had other priorities that held their attention longer, notably trade issues and constitutional deal making. Because provincial governments were extremely powerful within the Canadian federation, actions by Ottawa had only limited impact in areas like labor law. What the federal government did accomplish in the fields of work, taxation, and spending, however, was hardly helpful to many Canadian women. The federation seemed to be moving in an increasingly pro-market, antiregulation direction, as social standards weakened and tax policy shifted to favor the affluent.

Canadian women's organizations were well aware of what Brian Mulroney's friends in high places, notably Margaret Thatcher and Ronald Reagan, were doing elsewhere. They worked to set off alarm bells inside Canada about the real intentions of the Conservative government elected in 1984 and again in 1988. Yet this public advocacy campaign was limited by the realities of interest group funding—namely, that federal cabinets controlled how much money went to organizations like NAC and LEAF. Once English Canadian women's groups opposed the government on free trade, NAC's federal allocation was chopped. When arguments against the Meech Lake and Charlottetown Accords became too vocal for the government's liking, the entire Court Challenges Program was eliminated. In short, after 1988 the Mulroney government worked to limit feminist protest by stepping on the hose that carried federal funding.

The Effects of Change

How did conservative leaders affect women's lives beyond what might have happened in their absence? One view is that changes in the nature of work and government spending would have occurred in all three countries no matter what party was in power. Decisions by the Thatcher and Major governments to weaken trade unions and to eliminate wage floors for the most poorly paid, or by North American conservatives to tighten eligibility requirements for social programs and to download responsibility for many of them to states and provinces, were from this point of view a local consequence of economic globalization. Following this line of argument, the influence of market-driven economic forces was so strong that political leaders could no longer control the actions of private sector actors. Too much labor market regulation, too much personal or corporate taxation, or too much public spending, from this perspective, were intolerable to business investors who could simply pack up and move elsewhere. Because government indebtedness had reached critical levels, the prospect of investors and currency traders moving their bets elsewhere posed an ominous threat for all political leaders.

A different view of the same scenario, however, sees conservative elites as allowing businesses to roam around with impunity. The movement toward continental free trade in North America, for example, was according to this account linked to efforts by Ronald Reagan, Brian Mulroney, and, later, Carlos Salinas de Gortari (then president of Mexico) to reduce the powers of government and enhance those of the private sector. Their preference for open borders meant that the welfare of human beings inside national boundaries was far less significant than the profits of international investors. If minimum wage rules, unemployment insurance benefits, or health care standards interfered with this emphasis on market forces and business profits, then conservatives were anxious to act. They railed against the same supposed barriers to investment that in effect were supports for human dignity.

Because the Canada-U.S. and Canada-U.S.-Mexico free trade agreements included no language on social rights, they were quite distinct from the terms of the European Union—the same terms that British Conservatives so fiercely opposed. Each North American deal was portrayed by critics as a business bill of rights brought into effect by the neoconservative regimes of Reagan, Mulroney, and Salinas. From this perspective, European Community and later European Union provisions on equal pay, maternity leave, and so on, became the target of British Conservative wrath because they elevated such criteria as women's equality in the labor force above narrowly defined business interests. In other words, had British Tories constructed a European integration scenario of their own, it would probably have resembled the hands-off, pro–private sector model employed by Reagan and Mulroney.

The argument that conservatives in Britain, the United States, and Canada made a difference is most directly confirmed by evidence of the advocacy crunch. When it came to dealing with political protesters, pro-market, anti-intervention leaders seemed to lose patience with opponents who took on their agenda. Conservatives like Margaret Thatcher, Ronald Reagan, and Brian Mulroney preached at length about democratic freedoms and the need to defeat communism in Eastern Europe, but they showed little tolerance for their own domestic critics.[175] Language was twisted and rhetoric became heated as conservatives tried to undermine the influence of interests that held opposing viewpoints. As women's movement activists explain in their own words in chapter 4, the conservative years were tough times for those who opposed the new status quo. It was the language and the actions of conservative leaders that combined to make the crunch so severe for so many.

CHAPTER FOUR **Tough Times in Review**

What happened during the conservative years is captured only indirectly in the story of ideas, decisions, and money. Much of the flavor of this period comes out in the experiences of activists who worked to advance women's movement claims. Some pursued issues of basic legal equality or pressed for changes to family law that would help women and children after marriages broke up. Still others campaigned for access to abortion, action on violence against women, or better employment and child care policies. Many were involved in a variety of campaigns that crossed these areas.

More than one hundred activists in Britain, the United States, and Canada were interviewed for this study.[1] The British meetings were conducted in London and Manchester in August 1993 and August 1994, while John Major was prime minister. Because these women had pressured the Conservative government for more than ten years on the average, most could reflect on the Thatcher as well as Major years.[2] The American interviews were conducted in Washington, D.C., during March 1994 and March 1995, when Bill Clinton served as president.[3] Activists in the United States had been involved in movement work for about sixteen years on the average, which meant nearly all of them could reflect on some experience with the Clinton, Bush, and Reagan administrations. Interviews with Canadian respondents were conducted in Ottawa, Toronto, and Vancouver between August 1988 and March 1995.[4] On the average, these activists had been involved for more than sixteen years, so many could recall the Liberal period that preceded Mulroney's election. Most of the Canadian interviews were conducted after the 1993 defeat of the Conservatives, when it was possible for women's groups to assess the Liberal government of Prime Minister Jean Chrétien.

At least three common themes resonate through the approximately 110 interview transcripts. First, most activists described a clear sense of being on the defensive; in their view, conservative leaders had effectively isolated women's groups and many of their allies. Because new governments after 1979 tended to be suspicious of organized feminism, activists believed they were treated like political outsiders; as a result, their reflections reveal considerable bitterness and frustration. The expressions respondents used to describe their defensive posture during these years varied widely. In Britain, the talk was of "running hard to stand still," "sustaining rather than advancing," or being "listened to but not heard." American activists framed the situation in terms of feeling "alone, struggling uphill," reducing expectations, facing "a clear ogre, an enemy" in the White House, and struggling to preserve "what we had." Respondents in Canada felt frustrated, discouraged, and "very beleaguered" in these "grim times" because of the need "to expend energy to stop bad things from happening."

The defensive battles described by activists included messy fights over public funding in Britain and Canada, where the advocacy crunch described in chapter 3 meant like-minded groups competed among themselves for increasingly scarce government monies. The fact that so much effort was devoted to gaining so little funding while, in the process, groups were diverting their attention away from the conservative political target meant some activists felt immobilized. American respondents faced a not dissimilar challenge, namely, sustaining their membership levels and foundation grant bases in the same period as they could claim fewer and fewer victories in either legislation or court decisions. The scramble for resources thus created competition among groups and made life a bit easier for conservative governments. This was less the case on the abortion issue, however, in which feminist organizations in North America generally benefited from concern among the general public that access was under threat.

The sense that groups were on the defensive also reveals itself in activists' comments about the broader political climate after 1979. Many spoke of changes in language that gradually weakened the legitimacy of movement claims, notably in the growing use of terms like *special interest group.* In addition, activists described the challenge to such terms as *affirmative action* and *feminism* represented by more pejorative ones, including *quota* or *reverse discrimination* and *women's lib* or *loony left.* The sense that a great deal of momentum rested with conservatives rather than movements is also apparent in activists' comments about the unwillingness of other women to ally with organized feminism. One British respondent framed this phenomenon in terms of fear of rocking the boat, while an American talked about the problem of trying to change the world from under a box. The defensive climate was further revealed in allusions to the growing power of bottom-line perspectives in government. A number of respondents argued that as national leaders downloaded responsibilities to various agencies or subnational units in their haste to cut public spending, they were not transferring adequate resources to ensure these tasks were carried out. In the conservative atmosphere, respondents maintained, there was limited interest in the human consequences of fiscal offloading.

Second, activists emphasized what they saw as rays of hope in the darkness, notably more progressive public attitudes in key areas despite the influence of conservative leaders. Their claims on this point are backed up by poll data (presented in chap. 5) on consistent public support for access to abortion and equal opportunities at work and by growing public consciousness of violence against women. Third, a number of activists in the United States and Canada had limited faith in the governments that replaced conservative ones. In the British case, expectations of a possible Labour government were not very hopeful, either. The reasons for this unease with the Clinton administration, the Chrétien government, and a Labour regime in Britain are explored in more detail in chapter 6.

The reflections of movement activists also reveal significant differences across countries. British respondents' views of the Thatcher and Major years seemed to be based on gazing at government action from a distance, whereas their North American counterparts tended to project more of a policy insider perspective. American and Canadian activists spoke in terms of specific campaigns and contacts, often built around lobbying work and well-informed gossip networks in national capitals. Given the centralization of power in the British system, including the relatively weak position of newer organized interests, it is not surprising that British movement activists displayed a greater degree of political distance than their sisters in Canada and the United States. If applied to questions of unitary versus federal systems, this pattern reinforces the argument that divisions of power in the latter offer multiple points of access that are often not available in the former.

Distinctions between British and North American activists can also be discerned with reference to concepts of state and class. Whereas the British unitary state arrangement was seen by activists as creating an essentially coherent, cohesive unit, the two North American variants of federalism seemed to open up more possibilities for multiple political units and multiple political targets. Unlike the sense British activists revealed of a singularly focused Westminster process dominated by a single-minded prime minister during the Thatcher years, American and Canadian respondents could look to state or provincial as well as local governments—each with considerable degrees of political latitude. In keeping with their notion of the state as a single unit with a single leader, British activists also held fast to a relatively class-based worldview. This pattern is logical given the development of women's liberation on the political left in Britain, within a more hierarchical and class-based society than those of North America. To the extent that a class approach emerged among North American activists, it was more common among minorities, including African Americans in the United States.

In comparative terms, then, North American movement activists seemed less distant from power and the powerful and less likely to view political authority as a single unit dominated by a single political leader than were their British counterparts. Yet the talk about specific laws or legislators in these two newer systems also varied. In Canada, the Mulroney Conservatives were not as socially driven as Reagan- and Bush-era Republicans; as a result, the policy pipeline from movement interest to political executive remained somewhat more open north of the forty-ninth parallel. Canadian feminists' ability to cultivate contacts and sources of political leaks was also facilitated by their country's smaller population; although Canada stretches over more territory than the United States, it only contains about one-tenth the population of its southern neighbor. This difference, combined with the primary focus of Canadian Tories on issues outside the core concerns of the women's movement, meant the Mulroney government remained a comparatively indirect threat to organized feminism.

By way of contrast, the Reagan and Bush administrations presented a more direct challenge to movement groups; it was difficult for activists to get around the Republican threat as channels of communication narrowed. The clout of social conservatives in the Republican party through the early 1990s was in no way matched in the Canadian Conservative organization, nor did the ability of the American social right to influence judicial, bureaucratic, and legislative directions have parallels in Canada during the same period.

These patterns are in many respects inconsistent with what comparative public policy research would predict. The assumption, for example, that women's groups in the United States would benefit from a congressional system whereas those in Canada would be constrained by parliamentary arrangements is not sustained by the activists' reflections in this chapter. In fact, one could argue that the relatively closed or less porous character of parliamentary parties in both Canada and Britain offered an advantage during this period to feminist activists, because it limited the ability of far-right interests to capture these vehicles and, using them as a base, to then dominate a variety of other political institutions. Conversely, the obstacles described by activists in the United States demonstrate that the constitutional separation of powers combined with weak patterns of party discipline were hardly sufficient to ensure the continued influence of organized feminism after 1980.

Probably the best way to understand how activists saw history unfold is to listen to their words. The following pages present edited transcripts of interviews with five British, five American, and five Canadian activists. It must be emphasized that these reflections in no way represent all women's movement participants. Each respondent who was contacted as part of this study had a particular interest in shaping national-level policies, and many lived in national capitals. As a result, their perspectives on what occurred under conservative governments are filtered through a particular lens—usually a very political optic that gauged damage in terms of parties and national leaders. It is unlikely that grassroots activists working, for example, on issues that did not involve national governments would have seen things the same way.

The interviews presented here were chosen because they cover a wide range of ideas and policies. By providing fairly comprehensive accounts of life under conservative leaders, the activists who speak in the pages that follow offer a firsthand look at attempts to operate on a defensive posture while Thatcher, Reagan, Mulroney, and their successors held office. Names have been changed so that neither individuals nor organizations can be identified.

Views of British Activists

JULIA MURRAY had worked for about ten years on legal equality, violence, and child care issues when contacted in 1993. Although she was frustrated with the Thatcher and Major governments, Murray saw British citizens becoming more critical and more demanding over the years. Her views begin to explain why challenges to the Conservatives were so difficult to organize. Hard economic times, the spread of an individualist ethos that discouraged group activity, and divisions among women were key factors.

I hold the view that Margaret Thatcher in terms of policy was not at all interested in issues of concern to women. She downgraded the Equal Opportunities Commission and believed that women who had what it takes would make it on their own. She was not committed to women's equality at all. It was a side issue for her. She was committed to individualism based on experiences in her own life. She had no idea how merit was defined in a masculine way. She had conformed, and she had succeeded.

Yet in other areas during the Thatcher years, things were happening. Women continued to struggle in those other areas. For example, very good work was done on the nature and policing of domestic violence. But we lag way behind the United States and Canada on women's issues. The level of consciousness here is five to ten years behind. The issues do get on to the agenda eventually, though.

Our courts are rather resistant to these comparisons from elsewhere. The courts here have had to deal over time with a more vociferous public, and that's good. Women here are getting more demanding. For example, judges are not able to make the same comments that they used to make. Women in all parties and ages and races here believe the judicial system has failed women, especially in the areas of rape and domestic violence. For example, judges seem to feel that a woman's nagging of a man is equal to a man's beating of a woman. Women believe that their own lives are not understood in courtrooms. That criticism has begun to have an impact on how courts handle cases. This pressure has not come from government but has come from the changing status of women. People in Britain have become less deferential and are less convinced that our institutions are the best in the world.

The gains that have been made on domestic violence are mostly piecemeal. And these initiatives on violence cost the government less than universal child care, for example. Recessionary times prevent large changes. Governments want to cut taxes and expenditures, and things like child care cost money up front. Yet a real child care program would, over time, save money. If we had one, more women would be contributing to the economic system. The Labour party's manifesto for the 1992 elections was committed to better child care, but the women's vote kept the Tories in. This is shocking given the failure of the Conservatives to do much. Yet some women fear change, and the Conservatives present themselves as being a safe pair of hands, secure keepers of power.

In the U.K., we now have the highest level of part-time work in Europe. Women suffer from a lack of protection in part-time jobs, and this is a result of the Thatcher years. Women settle for these jobs in a world in which they have no child care and no readily available nursery education for toddlers. The work women do gives them a foot in on the career ladder. But no doubt exists that women are in low-paid jobs and are not given opportunities for training and often are not unionized. The Social Chapter of the Maastricht Treaty gives women additional improvements, and the Major government opposed it bitterly. The Conservatives won't change much for women or for working-class people generally. I must add, though, that I am realistic about the fair share of not very progressive men in the Labour party.

What we have changed is the numbers of women being educated. Half of our university students are now women, many in their midtwenties and older. What we are seeing is more vocal criticism of institutional failure, but this is by a minority of privileged, career-ladder women. The women's magazines in this country are now dealing with serious issues like child sexual abuse, rape, divorce, abortion, and spousal assault. Although large numbers of women may seem passive in groups like church organizations, they are actually less and less passive.

We've had Conservatives outraged this year, outraged about single mothers. But where are the good role-model fathers? A significant number of Conservative ministers are themselves divorced men, with multiple households. There is an enormous hypocrisy in the Conservative cabinet. Positive [affirmative] action ideas here are met by a paranoia among men and among women who have made it. They worry that merit will somehow be diluted. Yet quietly we are seeing increasing understanding that the presence of women must increase. The numbers game makes things easier for someone like John Major, who can easily find women who will fit the mold.

Ironically, the women's movement since Margaret Thatcher has become more interested in judicial decisions and parliamentary debates. The Conservatives' focus on consumer choice has actually made people more demanding as British citizens. The symbolic importance of having a woman prime minister cannot be neglected. Those changes are very positive. Yet Margaret Thatcher created the kind of backlash which said that demonstrations and so on are not effective. People now have taken off their blue jeans and put on suits. The women's movement has changed in that women can now get into institutions without being men. But these women have had a hard life in the professions. This means very few of them actively support women and women's issues. I think the softly, softly approach doesn't work because so many people benefit from the status quo. This keeps the number of people rocking the boat very limited.

* * * * *

JAN ROBINSON was a veteran activist in the family law and violence areas. Her comments criticize QUANGOs, or quasi-autonomous nongovernmental organizations, as agencies that have tied British advocacy groups in knots. Robinson focused much of her attention on the shutdown of the Greater London Council (GLC). Like Julia Murray, she saw problems in the legal system and differences among women as limiting what groups could accomplish.

I assess the damages in terms of things closing down, like women's bookstores. For example, one store in London closed, but another remains open. The closings of the bookstore and of a women's newspaper can probably be attributed to so many years of Conservative rule.

Once the GLC closed down, the government set up a QUANGO that has more or less kept us going. The financial hit we have taken as women's groups because of the closing of the GLC is hard to estimate. In the years since 1986, we are two-thirds of where we were. We would likely have kept on growing under the GLC. The QUANGO system has given us a tentative hold on funds. When the GLC started to fund women's organizations, some groups didn't take funding because they saw strings and conditions attached. These groups said the autonomy of the women's movement could be compromised.

The abolition of the GLC was a major problem because it meant we had to cut back on our work. In every round of funding competition during the Thatcher years, some groups were set up to get QUANGO money, and some were set up not to get anything. Doing application forms could take our entire staff's time for a full week, and then the money would only last twelve months. We are supposed to get our funding decision early in the year, yet often the QUANGOs don't call us until six months later because they don't have the financial commitments yet from the local councils. There has been a mega-uncertainty every year, and it causes us to lose workers quite often. We did get caught one year by having saved £10,000 which we were then docked for by our QUANGO. We all work more hours than we are paid for, so we have about twice as many people as full-time positions.

After the GLC was abolished, the government introduced the infamous clause 28. This was an attack on lesbian and gay men's funding from local councils. One group did a huge campaign against that clause that said, "We are not pretending [fake] families." Women's organizations had to sign forms saying they were not using local government money to promote lesbianism.

We usually work on family law issues with the refuge [women's shelter] movement, and with M.P.'s from Labour and from the Liberal Democrats. Occasionally, we get some support from a few Conservative women on the backbenches. But they are liberal individualist feminists who only talk about equality in institutions and not more broadly. Often the Tory party has homophobic and racist politics among its women. That creates lots of problems for us because our interests are not limited to white, middle-class, heterosexual women. We've also done a lot of work on employment questions. Sometimes we get trade union support and Labour party endorsement. The Labour party has taken a huge turn to the right lately, and that can mean trouble for us.

I think educational work has helped to change judges' behavior. People from the refuge movement and rape crisis centers are influencing the crown prosecution service plus the police. We did succeed in our campaign to get rape in marriage recognized as an offense. We have been working with other groups on a defense for women who kill their violent husbands. We are calling this the self-preservation defense. The problem here is that our judiciary is quite old and few judges have any experience in or of the women's movement. Race, class, and everything else intersect in a most peculiar way so that our legal profession is quite closed and the bench is even more so. Government cutbacks and the recession occurred just when more black women were coming out of law schools and beginning to get into the profession. This makes the system less open than we hoped it would be at this point.

What happened in the 1980s was a concern around identity politics. Different women claimed the right to organize autonomously. Lesbian and black working-class women, for example, claimed the same right to organize. This meant growing fragmentation and exclusion, but it also meant empowerment and an effort to build broader coalitions. We have had total disasters as far as coalitions are concerned, but some have worked. Our group has tried to get involved and still keep the focus on our issues.

* * * * *

C A R O L   D R E W was active in contraception and abortion campaigns. Like Jan Robinson, she was disappointed by the loss of the GLC and found it hard to recruit new activists in conservative times. Two factors made her hopeful, namely, progressive public attitudes and the limited impact of antiabortion protesters in Britain. Over time, she saw the United Kingdom becoming more like the United States and less and less like continental Europe.

We are running hard to stand still. It has been a very defensive period since 1979 in that we have been reacting rather than initiating. Abortion and contraception services have deteriorated. In terms of legislation, we have had some improvements. Since the late 1960s there have been many, many attempts to amend the Abortion Act. For us, the frustration has been their sheer number. What really rankled antichoice activists was that David Steel's bill in 1967 went through because of extra time, but the Tories did not give extra time on subsequent antiabortion bills. Space on the [Human Fertilisation and] Embryology Bill was given to an abortion debate, specifically to a time limit of twenty-four weeks. In effect, this clarified and liberalized the law on abortion.

Our side was tired. We'd had to fight so hard. This is not a fast- growing field, although we have some new recruits coming along. People do still rally, but it has been a tough fight. What's different about Britain is that the far right in our Parliament is pro-choice. Their radical libertarianism leads to women having the right to choose. In fact, it isn't always your liberal types who are most reliable. Your far right Tories here have no angst about voting for choice. Over 80 percent of our public wants abortion on request in the first trimester. We have got Conservative opinion behind twenty-five years of the legal provision of abortion.

We accomplished a great deal despite our fatigue. We are a pragmatic nation. We are much more muted here than the United States. Civil liberties and individual rights are less pressed here. As I see it, the other side made a major mistake by sending a plastic fetus to each member of Parliament. There were lots of complaints about that. It was totally tasteless. I think it was a crucial political error by the antichoice side.

The Conservative government is now arguing that women are having babies to get housing. This is a very sterile debate. Cuts to the National Health Service's support for contraception are part of an effort to cut spending. I believe younger women are having babies because they seek a purpose in life that is not available because of other Tory policies. It has nothing to do with wanting to jump the housing queue. The government is devolving responsibilities, and they have cut sex education provisions, for example. This contradicts health policy which says that to reduce teenage pregnancies, you need to offer sex education. There is no planning in our Tory government. It is just hitting out where it can. They see teenage mothers as being feckless. They blame radical feminism for teenage pregnancies. If we look at the way the Netherlands, for example, tackles it, we see we are moving backward in the U.K.

The government has lost its way. The debate on the Maastricht Treaty shows that the Major government has no plans whatsoever. The publicity stunts are evidence of no government. What lunacy now? The government plans to privatize facilities for troubled adolescents. Women's health services and women's issues generally get marginalized as this continues.

I think the Margaret Thatcher inheritance has bitten deep. We have lost a sense of social purpose that motivated most postwar public policy in all parties. It is proving to be a thread-bare perspective, this neoconservatism. But the Labour party hasn't captured the public imagination, either. It will take a long time to find an acceptable sense of social working-together that parallels what we had in the past in areas like education and health care. We now have ideas about privatizing policing, and that's hardly society coming together. On social security and health, the government is devolving responsibility away from itself, and that will take a long time to undo. The privatization of buses and trains is lunacy that parallels the loss of the GLC.

The lack of a federal system here has limited us. The Margaret Thatcher regime enormously limited the power of municipal government overall, not just in London. She imposed tax rate caps all over that prohibited local councillors who defied her from running for office. The Conservatives have divested responsibility in some areas and centralized control over other things like education. I think this government is attracted to a North American model of less and less government, but people are increasingly interested in more and more of the European Community's Social Chapter. John Major sells the U.K. as being cheap for labor, but this is very short-sighted. In the end, I hope things here will be less unfair and less destructive. Yet we have so many homeless people on the streets. We have a lot of disturbed people on the streets because we are trying to do things on the cheap via deinstitutionalization.

The backlash here is single parents that shouldn't be and so on. This is because the Conservatives have the wrong recipe and keep hitting soft targets. The old GLC did good things like provide cheap, plentiful public transportation. We need to remember that and emulate the continent more than North America.

* * * * *

When interviewed in 1994, **SELMA WATSON-BROWNE** was relatively new to movement activism. She had worked primarily on violence issues since becoming involved in organized feminism. Watson-Browne's comments range over divisions among women, government cutbacks, and her sense of having missed the good times in the movement before 1979.

I was very young when Margaret Thatcher came to power. I've never been politically aware under any other regime. Compared with others in the women's movement, I feel like I've missed the party. There was a sense of abundance and joy in the early women's movement experiences that's now been dampened. When I became active, I started to wonder how, during the 1980s, the movement got so involved in its own internal struggles. The sexuality and especially the race issues were very divisive since the late 1980s. Perhaps lately women have become less divided on these grounds, but it has been a long period of conflict. During the last few years, there is less and less to celebrate in the women's movement. There is less and less fun.

Part of this internal division resulted from Margaret Thatcher's decimation of the voluntary sector. Funding was cut, charities were cut off from political campaigning, and we lost influence. Margaret Thatcher tried to kill the voluntary sector via her brand of social engineering. Voluntary agencies started to fight with each other because they all wanted the same funding. Local authorities, Labour and Tory, used the divide-and-rule strategy too. People felt bitter and angry. That took a lot of the energy out of external campaigning. You have to be very committed to get involved in meetings, working with bureaucracy and all that, and we know the ever-elusive "ordinary woman" has lots of other things to do with her time.

Local governments want value for money. They want their own agencies to work at a standard, and they want the voluntary agencies they support to work at that standard too. It's all very difficult because the voluntary sector is just that, made up of volunteers. Women's units and local authorities have learned not to put their heads above the parapet. They don't use the L [lesbian] or F [feminism] words. Everyone has started to talk about equality and rights issues, not feminist or women's issues. Groups get pilloried every time they use the term *lesbian*. One organization tried to do a campaign that addressed shelter for women including lesbians and, of course, got hammered in the tabloid press. Another group offered something like £40 for a lesbian exercise class that became the notorious episode of the "lesbian gymnasts." One local government unit here is still recalled, ten years later, as the Leftie Loony Lesbian Unit.

I still believe local authorities are very important. Something like 60 percent of the people in my neighborhood depend on public housing. It's an aging population with clear social service needs. We need women's voices. We need central government funds to provide much of this, but it's only the local authorities and the voluntary sector that have pushed the central government to pay attention to things like violence against women. The staff of refuges [shelters for battered women] in this country rarely have time to work on the issue, in fact.

Was there any progress for women under Thatcher and Major? I have to laugh. I'm still thinking. There were tiny, tiny steps. Nothing very substantial. We took our successes in very small steps. We couldn't dream about anything big. Change doesn't feel possible to me because I grew up in the Thatcher years. I can't even hope for fundamental change. One small step was the slight increase in the number of women local councillors and the number of refuges. We have also swayed some judges on violence issues. A few rape crisis centers did stay open. Overall, the story is one of sustaining rather than advancing.

There's much more public awareness of domestic violence over time. When I began my activities during the Thatcher years, people had entrenched myths. One was that violence just happened in the working class. People are starting to let go of this myth, although they still think it's a little more common in the working class. There is a backlash that says women are abusive too, but few people say women do it as much as men. Most people say men do it more physically while women are emotionally difficult. They say women aren't blameless. But people are starting to see that violence is about power. Even government departments now say it's about power. We've won the war of ideas but not the war of resources.

One of the biggest effects of the Thatcher-Major years is that women are invisible. They're not on the agenda at all. Major's first cabinet had no women ministers. He has a white man responsible for women's issues, which Margaret Thatcher would never have even bothered with. It's interesting that John Major thinks he needs a minister. Perhaps he does this as a response to the Labour proposal for a women's ministry [government department].

Women I know think parliamentary politics isn't about them. Disabled women, black women, and lesbians especially feel this way. In business, women have made some progress, but the number of women managers actually decreased this year for the first time in forty years. We're listened to more over time, though we are not heard. There's often a sense among men in power that they can't ignore us but they often do nothing as a consequence of hearing. It buys people off because they think they've been heard. The police, for example, now know what to say about domestic violence, but their ideas are often the same as they were in the past. We aren't having much of a direct impact.

The most lasting Thatcher legacy is probably what she did to housing. She changed us from a nation of primarily renters of public and private housing, to a nation of private property owners. This has really had an impact on the mother with lots of children. If she has to leave her relationship, with three or four or six kids, she has to wait years for housing. These women can only get housing where no one wants it—where there are drugs and violence and prostitutes. What future is there for these women? That's why few of them leave. Homelessness is just appalling. It used to be just a few, mostly the elderly, and now it's mostly the young who have created cities of homelessness. The

Margaret Thatcher legacy around housing made people vote on taxes alone, because they have mortgages and think all the time about the risk that they too may become homeless. Doing away with council [public] housing also got rid of local government authority, which is exactly what Margaret Thatcher wanted. John Major has continued this, dumping more and more responsibility on local authorities but less and less money. This sets them up for failure.

The Margaret Thatcher effects are astounding, almost awe-inspiring. The decimation of the unions is another one of the lasting legacies. The decimation of the North is so clear. When I go to mining communities, I see what it's done. People there, in their thirties, have never worked. They've spent a life on benefits [welfare]. They've never had anything new or taken a holiday [vacation]. They're forced into a black economy to get by.

These issues are all connected. Local taxes can go to offer people a better life, and that would reduce what's paid for security services. At least the greedy me, me, me approach is less acceptable than it once was. People now want to be seen as more caring and considerate. Margaret Thatcher did her best *not* to seem that way.

*　*　*　*　*

PAT O'SULLIVAN was a trade union activist during nearly fifteen years of Conservative rule. Like Julia Murray and Carol Drew, she placed more faith in European Community pressures on Britain than in the government's willingness to make change on its own. O'Sullivan rejected above all the way Tories had altered British society along individualist lines.

In general terms, the only real progress we have made here since 1979 has been because of European pressure. The current prime minister is the same except for his style, which differs a bit from that of Margaret Thatcher. As chancellor under Margaret Thatcher, John Major made enormous funding cutbacks that have hurt people. He would like to be more pro-Europe, but he is squeezed by pressures inside his own party. The reality of the right wing within his own government means that Major's actions are more limited than if he were in a strong internal position, like Thatcher was.

The most damaging legacy of Margaret Thatcher is that she was seen as a great symbol of women making progress. There was lots of optimism. We thought there were real opportunities gender-wise. She was such a powerful figure that even if she had had an inkling of women's needs, she'd have made great progress. But she set us back a great deal. She has left such a legacy of being hated. No other prime minister has been so hated. She just personified the role of being an honorary man. In other professions as well, women have cut through the barriers, but then they have pulled the ladder away from other women following them up. Everyone needs to have a role model. Margaret

Thatcher could have been one. But she didn't select other women in her cabinet and just never helped other women.

The men who represent the parties in the House of Commons could easily be replaced by lots of women, but Margaret Thatcher didn't do anything about it. She has been very effective in terms of her own point of view and her policies. She didn't want people to disagree with her. Her push for market forces affected all aspects of public and private life. The National Health Service is now run as a business. The police service became the police force, and she gave them a huge wage increase. We also had the police force acting as an army to control demonstrations. Margaret Thatcher taxed trade unions, and that made it harder to organize lower-paid women workers. Her opposition to single mothers and to benefits was tied to an emphasis on the individual and not society. Problems of the homeless, drug abuse, alcohol abuse, and massive unemployment are in part related to Margaret Thatcher.

Large numbers of women single parents are in the uptake of benefits [welfare]. The more vulnerable they are, the more they are affected by what the Conservatives have done. It is difficult to get benefits now. You need to know the system. The suspicion now is that you're a leech, a crook, when you apply. As soon as you remove a universal benefit, you take away the citizenship aspect and make it instead a means-tested target. With targeting, the poor haven't been given more, and the lower middle class and upward get nothing. Universal school milk is now gone completely. When Margaret Thatcher was at the Education Department, she took that away.

This country has always been based on a high-quality, highly skilled workforce. Margaret Thatcher tried to turn us into a low-quality, low-pay, low-skill country. The emphasis under Margaret Thatcher was on the City, the financial elite who gamble with other people's jobs and pensions. The manufacturing sector was totally decimated.

The alternative to not getting involved is just standing back, knowing they'll do the same things anyway. We need women there when the decisions are being made. I don't think women want to stand back and let men make decisions anymore. More trade union women are getting involved. Issues that women prioritize are usually the same ones targeted by Labour. These are education and the health service. Tory ministers can go on television and talk about the millions of pounds spent on the NHS and hospital beds. Yet anyone walking down their high [main] street will see mentally ill people who should be in institutional care. Cases where former mental institution patients commit murder have now hit the news. The numbers of homeless in the cities and rural communities have increased. State attacks on education have meant turmoil for students at all levels.

Years ago, families looked after their elderly. The Margaret Thatcher I, I, I ethos helped to do away with that. Moving people from hospital geriatric wards to private nursing homes is another avenue for entrepreneurs. It has nothing to do with caring. Local authorities weren't given money to compensate for the loss of institutional care. What is left are often very terrible conditions in public homes for the elderly. Or else women are expected to give up their paid work to be carers. I can understand why people can be quite cynical about being involved in the system here. Lots of union women say they are industrial activists, not political activists.

I would imagine that the frontier for future union organizing will be immigrant women and ethnic minorities. One of the groups I've been involved in works with low-paid immigrant women. The GLC used to support us, but this was swept away by Margaret Thatcher. London has lost out because of transport changes and the loss of these grass-roots organizations. Margaret Thatcher concentrated more power in Whitehall [the central government bureaucracy] than had ever been in place before. This occurred despite all of her talk about individual rights. The European Community remains our only outlet given the centralization that has gone on in the Thatcher years.

American Activists Reflect

SARAH ANDERSON had worked on equal rights, abortion, and employment issues in the United States since the mid-1970s. She reflected on losing the Equal Rights Amendment (ERA) and sensing a climate of fear during the Reagan and Bush years. When we spoke in 1994, Anderson was convinced that the Clinton administration would do far more for women than its predecessors.

We had no idea that the country would lurch so far to the right. What happened with Ronald Reagan's election was that opposition to the ERA at the state level became ever so entrenched. We developed another agenda as a result, which was to get more women involved in politics. We saw how crucial women were in the state legislatures. We worked to recruit and support more women who would run for office, right away. We also tried to do more coalitions with like-minded organizations in this country. After the ERA campaign was over, for example, we saw that we shared lasting common interests with labor union women.

I was very disheartened when a family and medical leave bill was introduced during the Reagan years, gutted to no end, and then reintroduced in its totally gutted condition under Clinton as some big joke. Personally, I'm not driven by legislation. I think you need to mount judicial defenses as much as lobby Congress or the administration. Our organization is trying to increase the numbers of women candidates as well as educate the public.

I think on issues like abortion, it was easier to get people concerned during the Reagan-Bush years than it was before 1980. After George Bush was elected, women's groups started doing different kinds of things because there was great upset out there, given the state of the economy and the facade of helping people. The emperor started having no clothes. The Reagan idea of wanting people to feel good about their country was a brilliant idea. The Republicans built their base with the church, God, family, motherhood, and the flag symbolism. They played on people's fears.

I don't know if women made any progress in the Reagan-Bush years. The Supreme Court was not totally bad. We made some progress on sexual harassment, for example. The Republicans say they passed a child care bill that included some block money that was up to the states to spend. I don't know if that's a victory. EEOC [Equal Employment Opportunities Commission] guidelines on enforcing nondiscriminatory practices in employment went by the boards very quickly. People now see the impact of Reagan-Bush policies on the homeless, for example, but it's a very delayed awareness.

I don't know if much is changing under President Clinton. I think, in the middle of the fire, it's hard to see how it's spreading. What I see, in terms of who's writing policy and who is appointed, is people who *will* turn things back. Some of the policy coming down is good. We can harp about the details of the health care proposal, for example, but a few years ago the whole idea was unthinkable. It really is a small miracle that we are having the discussion at all.

There has been slight movement on allowing the abortion pill, RU-486. It's got to be better, worldwide, to have reversed the Mexico City policy [curtailing U.S. foreign aid for agencies that endorsed contraception or abortion]. Clinton's administration deals with things in a far more constructive way than previous administrations. We have to overturn twelve very horrendous years. Clinton is not perfect, but, in reality, we're glad change is being discussed. He's only into this for two years, and the Congress has not been all that helpful. There are Democrats on Capitol Hill who can't get together with the president. The judicial branch is terrible. Reagan and Bush appointed 40 to 50 percent of the federal bench. Eighty percent of their appointees were white men. That's going to be a telling problem. Clinton has done a good job of appointing women.

During the 1970s, Richard Nixon endorsed the Equal Rights Amendment. But he vetoed a significant child care bill that he said would sovietize American children. George Bush voted for the ERA and was pro-choice when he ran in 1980. I don't know if there are any moderate Republicans left. The party is so controlled at the national level by the new right types.

From my perspective, the most lasting Reagan-Bush legacy is the politics of intimidation. Our members are terrified to confront some of the lies and some of the threats. It is a foxhole mentality out there, but it's hard to change the world from under a box. The judiciary is also real scary. It will take forever to get some of those people off the bench. All it takes for tyranny to prevail is for a few good people to shut up. That's the problem with the foxhole mentality.

The Anita Hill story shows how it works when people turn a story around. The foxhole mentality is slow to change. People will now send letters or make phone calls, but doing petitions on the street and handing out literature in public is harder to do. People fear losing their jobs if they're found to be too close to a women's group.

* * * * *

CHARLENE MOORE worked on a variety of campaigns, including efforts to elect more minorities and women in the wake of the Republican years. She spoke about the sense of siege after 1980, arguing that the experience of tough times led many groups to change their strategies. Moore noted divisions among American women and questioned the extent to which any administration would address civil rights issues.

The basic problem in 1980 was that in an effort to highlight differences between the two political parties, Republicans felt they had to attack programs supported by black Americans. There was an all-out assault on affirmative action. The Reagan administration backed colleges and universities that were known to be racist. The U.S. Civil Rights Commission was undermined. Senior people in the Justice Department were on record as opposed to minority rights. In the areas of education, employment, and social programs, there was an all-out assault. I think black women have long voted more than black men, and this just continued under Ronald Reagan. Reagan made it clear he wasn't interested in the black community and didn't ever meet with us. Bush did meet with us, but whenever he was challenged by the political right, his attitudes hardened. This was unfortunate for the whole country.

The all-out assault of the Reagan years was mitigated somewhat during the Bush years. I don't think George Bush had the same ideological edge as Ronald Reagan. The two areas that managed to survive Reagan and Bush were voting rights and housing. Yet now the voting rights area is under attack by extreme conservatives. In housing, the main threat is time. Lots of subsidized housing was built about forty years ago, and the government is going to be confronted with expiring leases and no one to take them on. With women's issues, there have been real ups and downs. The ERA is dead, at least for ten years, in my view. The fight over abortion has dominated public policy discussion more than it ever should have.

During the Republican years, the federal courts were staffed by Reagan and Bush appointees. We found that judges were hostile even before we started. Up until Justice Brennan stepped down, there was a fragile 5–4 majority in favor of civil rights. There is now a fragile 5–4 majority against any race remedies. Having two women on the court may help on women's issues. After the courts, the last resort was Congress. I'd like to think our work helped to extend the Voting Rights Act in 1982 for another twenty-five years. This renewed act was signed into law by Ronald Reagan, but now it's under attack. One of the patterns here is that when there are programs benefiting blacks, you see lots of people coming out against them. That's complicating the debate now over welfare reform. The race, class, and gender issues really make it hard to advocate here.

There's a definite change in the White House now, certainly on women's issues. The Clinton administration has a more pro-women attitude than any other in the last twenty years. On black issues, there's been a lot of symbolism, but not much action. We have more blacks than ever at the top, but there are still lots of vacancies in crucial agencies. I think there's a problem for us. We like the symbolism but the substance is troubling.

In the Clinton administration, there is a combination of inexperience and a sense of not wanting to be too close to the blacks. Jimmy Carter was seen as too close to the blacks, and he was only a one-term president. The challenge for Clinton is to keep white support, including white middle-class support. I think that the fact the Reagan administration was so antifeminist hurt established women's groups but helped grassroots women's groups to mobilize at state and local levels. With all the budget cuts to cities where a lot of single mothers live, women found that they needed to mobilize for their own survival.

The most lasting legacy of Reagan-Bush has been the budget cuts. We constantly see homeless people, roads and bridges falling apart. The country is broke, but we're still spending billions around the world helping other countries.

* * * * *

SUSAN JONES worked on abortion, violence, and employment issues from a base in Washington. She was tired after twelve years of Republicans in the White House and wondered how different the Clinton administration would be. Jones's comments refer to differences among women that opened up during the 1980s and continued through the 1990s.

In my view, Reagan and Bush were the same. I feel like I have come out of a dark cave, like I'm recovering from the One Hundred Years' War. We had a bunker mentality during that period. We didn't know good times; we only knew bad times. A lot of our buddies are now in the Clinton administration, and we've had to ratchet down our expectations since they took office.

Our victories in the Reagan-Bush years were few and far between. They were very hard won. One win I recall was on basic pocketbook legislation that provided health insurance coverage for widows. We also changed the rules on pension vesting, and that was helpful. I worked on the Civil Rights Restoration Act in response to the *Grove City* decision, which was limited by Senator Danforth's amendment on abortion. We worked on voting rights and disability issues with other women's groups. Also, we did get the Women's Business Ownership Act passed. That was very middle-class too, to help women entrepreneurs.

The Reagan-Bush attack on civil rights had a direct impact on women. Yet the administration said women were doing just fine. I felt alone, struggling uphill, kind of like the old married couple who kept together in hard times but who wished they'd had more fun when they were younger. To live through the backlash was strange. We watched the Women's Educational Equity Act disappear via defunding. We were innocent and naive and thought we hadn't worked hard enough. I think Susan Faludi's book [*Backlash*] showed us what we were going through, that it wasn't just about working harder.

The backlash has loosened somewhat. People now refuse to let it get to them. I've seen it manifested in several ways. In response to people saying women aren't fit for public office, for example, we used to look for plus-perfect candidates. Now we expect women in public office to be good and bad, just like men. People outside the District of Columbia were busy working on battered women's shelters and rape crisis centers during the 1980s. These groups were alive and well.

I think the stroke-of-the-pen changes under Clinton, like the Family and Medical Leave Act and rescinding the gag rule [which prevented abortion counseling in federally funded clinics], were important. Yet Bill Clinton has to work with Congress. Congress doesn't want to do too much for women all at once. For example, Bill Clinton and Congress could make the abortion pill, RU-486, available right away. But members of Congress can only do one thing a year for women. I'd like to work more on health care and welfare reform, but there is no time. I think we're really going to have to make our point on pro-choice issues. Poor women are put in a particular situation here, a particularly punitive situation. The condition of mothers on AFDC [Aid to Families with Dependent Children] is crucial, and we see President Clinton's rhetoric as similar to the punitive state-level statutes. Lots of women on welfare are running from violence already, so why impose more punishments on them?

The most lasting Reagan-Bush legacy is probably greed or the antigovernment ethos. The free market capitalism of people who enjoy the benefits of the system is so two faced. I don't know if we'll ever recover from that greed and duplicity. The Reagan-Bush years felt like a ringworm, athlete's foot, or a stench of some sort. It's the savings and loans scandals, the money mania on Wall Street, and all the greedy people who never got caught. In spite of the Clarence Thomas–Anita Hill stuff, people still think they can get away with sexual harassment. In this country, we idolize guys like Rush Limbaugh. We listen to his show and buy his books. Yet look at how Rush Limbaugh talks about women! It's a problem because men can do as they please, but women are still so self-monitoring. That is what we said during the Reagan-Bush years, and we're still doing it. We reduced our expectations. We are still unsure how to go now that we have a friendly president in the White House and lots of new Democratic women in the Congress.

I enjoy the coalition work in the Clinton years, but it is still hard to get women together. Poor women don't trust organized feminism for its class biases, and, on the other hand, parts of the women's movement do see welfare women as lazy. The unions here are like the churches, the universities, and so on—dominated by men who are afraid AFDC women will take away jobs in the public sector.

The early 1970s were our most radically wonderful years. We had probably taken a lot for granted as a result. We assumed some massive things. We assumed public attitudes would carry us through. ERA isn't being pursued vigorously now. The right-wingers did their egregious homework, bringing up the divisive questions of women in the military, legalized abortion, and so on. We could not say that the ERA would not do those things. We need to change the climate so that we can get constitutional equality. Maybe Congress will get so sick of all the incremental stuff we push that they will *love* to see an Equal Rights Amendment.

It's true that lots of women got poorer in the Reagan-Bush years, but lots of others became successful entrepreneurs and got into advanced education, the professions, and higher and higher occupational positions. Lots of organizations are benefiting from the money of these women, and that's new since the 1980s.

* * * * *

KATHERINE RICHARDSON was a relatively young activist and had devoted most of her energy to violence, abortion, and work issues. She spoke about how much easier it was to get people to rally for abortion access than against violence. Richardson was quite critical of the Clinton administration in 1994. Her frustration over the treatment of teenage mothers echoed Carol Drew's comments about the British situation.

One of my first jobs was to develop a project on sexual harassment in the wake of the Clarence Thomas hearings. Sexual harassment is seen as an economic and employment concern, but it clearly became felt and known as a violence question. It is a violence issue that in my view has serious economic repercussions, and these effects are often violent in themselves.

We are working now on violence against women legislation as part of a larger crime bill. Legislators on Capitol Hill think the American people see crime as an epidemic, so they are willing to invest money that might not otherwise be available. We've had many discussions about linking our proposal to law-and-order questions. I wanted our part to be a separate piece of legislation, but the crime bill offers a secure basis of funding. It's the only way to ensure the appropriations.

George Bush was extremely weak on domestic policy. He didn't speak out at all on violence in the home. We didn't have any support in the White House, even though we knew we could get violence legislation through the Congress. On the other hand, Bill Clinton has consistently said he'd support our proposal. Violence wasn't a priority, or even a side issue, for Bush. There wasn't any support across the country for doing something. If the president talks about an issue, people write to their members of Congress. We were doing lots of work educating members of Congress and their staffs, but the president just didn't pick it up. We had to do all the communicating on our own. Some women did write in, and they told their members of Congress this was an issue to be addressed. But it's easier to do the work and get the appointments when you know the president is on your side.

The system now seems less adversarial. As a nation, we are going through a period of being revitalized, after twelve really long years. That's why we felt such a change. I remember clearly the inauguration of President Clinton. It was the first time I really cared who was in the White House. It was also the first time I thought the White House cared about people like me. My sense probably has much to do with a growing national awareness of violence against women. We've had a lot of high-profile cases covered in the media, and this means victims now have faces and experiences they're willing to talk about. Elected representatives are more responsive because more people are talking about it. It's all very cyclical.

Was there progress during the Reagan-Bush years? Sure, we moved up a bit in terms of the pay gap, and more women were elected to the House and the Senate. For the individual woman, I don't know. I was so young when Reagan came into office, it's hard to say. There are certainly avenues now that women have opened for themselves. Women have moved away from the stigmas about lifestyle choices. There are more personal freedoms. But there's still no Equal Rights Amendment.

What the courts were doing in the Reagan-Bush years had much more impact on choice questions than on violence issues. With increased attention to what was happening in local communities, lower courts became more involved. Now, most states have antistalking laws. The ability to introduce expert testimony on the battered woman syndrome is now greater. All of these developments have shaped what goes on in the courts. Media disclosure of victims' names became a big issue as well. Newspapers had to come up with policies about publishing victims' names.

It was easier under Bush for abortion rights organizations to mobilize. They were at risk, and they had a clear ogre, an enemy who was well identified. Abortion was framed as a straightforward middle-class issue of rights. Lots of people were mobilized to come to Washington. When I saw those demonstrations, I often wondered what it would take to get so many people out to oppose violence. The message still is that women are somehow responsible. This makes violence harder to take on. Women jurors in rape trials often have the most trouble believing the victim. Since we are children, we are taught what to do to keep safe, so when we meet a woman victim we just say, "You know you shouldn't have done that." There's a defense mechanism to keep the distance from women who are violated. It helps us deal with the fact that we're most at risk from the people we know, not from some stranger out there. How does a woman deal with that?

I think the whole Moral Majority, fundamentalist, conservative philosophy was so pervasive. It was the most lasting Reagan-Bush legacy. The legacy is also huge disparities between rich and poor, between poor and working poor. The welfare reform ideas of the Clinton administration are really quite conservative. Clinton thinks we need to keep young women with kids at home with their families, not let them get AFDC and a home of their own. But why do teenage girls decide to get pregnant? What happens if we leave them at home? The Clinton approach is very punitive. It just smacks of Bush. There really is a huge backlash against the poor. Clinton is so progressive on other things, but he just doesn't see progressive sides of the teenage mom issue. Clinton is saying what middle-class America wants to hear. People are outraged at the present state of the welfare system. People are full of backlash over the issue of homelessness. People are just saturated because the numbers of homeless are getting larger and larger. Clinton is aware of these messages. He's moving away from the real liberal look that he had. Even some of the women he appointed are full of the same ideas.

* * * * *

CARLA RUIZ worked on sexual harassment and employment campaigns and saw the U.S. movement set back quite severely during the Reagan-Bush years. She explained her view of how language was changed, how intolerance became permissible and even popular after 1980. Ruiz concluded her reflections with a plea for the movement to move beyond its white, middle-class origins.

Reagan conservatives arrived in Washington with a social agenda. Reagan had an active social agenda, not a negligent one. Twelve years of pounding by conservatives can change people's minds. We had an administration that didn't return our telephone calls. We were also dealing with larger and larger numbers of women who saw themselves as entering the workforce based on their own merit, their accomplishments. They thought they owed no allegiance to a women's movement. We had a constituency that thought things had already been done. It was horrible.

Most movements are propelled by moments of crisis. The 1984 elections, the Clarence Thomas hearings, and the failure of the ERA were our moments of crisis. We saw overall just a steady erosion. That we managed at all to sustain, to maintain our organizations, to keep our issues in the forefront, was due to the hard work of those women who stuck it out. The movement here raised the most money and had the most visibility around Anita Hill, the accidental heroine. It caused more women to vote and give money.

During the Reagan-Bush years we had a money crisis, except when there was a moment of crisis. There was a cumulative emergency, but that's hard to convey. Reagan was this nice man from Hollywood who had "Morning in America" public relations behind him. He was leading what we now know was a very greedy society in the 1980s but one that we said then was experiencing a huge economic boom. Our core agenda in the women's and civil rights communities was preserving what we had.

The court of public opinion was as hard as the legislative one. The attack on choice was well documented in this period. Forget ERA. We didn't dare make a major move because there was no political will. The Family and Medical Leave bill was vetoed by every Republican president. It was dead meat, as one Republican told me. A Republican woman in the cabinet said leaves would be abused and lead employers not to hire women. Employers lobbied strongly against any mandated benefit with their millions of dollars. For us, the leave bill was a crucial piece of legislation that recognized the double demands on working women.

The other side, the conservatives and fundamentalist Christians, handled the media well. They kept pounding their ideas in the press. If you say "family values" enough, then people start believing you. Women's magazines started talking about the new traditionalists, women leaving their briefcases and staying home. Yet over 60 percent of the poor in this country are women and children. The feminization of poverty happened in the Reagan-Bush years, and it's only become worse. We wanted pay equity, but that was a nonstarter. We wanted a study of the pay gap and couldn't even get that. The fight against Reagan's nomination of Robert Bork to the Supreme Court was the one successful fight we had. We all united and mobilized to get rid of this man. And we were so tired from that and so depleted that we didn't fight the Anthony Kennedy nomination to the Court. He was at least as bad as Bork.

One thing that did happen is we said, "Let's look to the states if we can't do anything at the federal level." We just kept the focus on where we could get things done. Politics, to people, often is local, and that shifting downward was crucial. The states of Minnesota and Washington began to address pay equity, and other states worked on family leave issues. They didn't have to wait for a federal mandate. This was our answer to Reagan's New Federalism.

I think maintaining visibility for our issues during the Reagan-Bush years was progress. Eighteen percent of Bush's senior appointees were female. We pressured him, and that had an effect. When the Republicans saw the gender gap in 1980, they knew they had to respond. That's why Reagan appointed Sandra Day O'Connor to the Supreme Court. After he did, his numbers shot up in the polls. The women's vote really registered after Anita Hill and after the threats to choice became so clear. Before that, women in the general public actually bought the same messages as men did from the Republicans.

The Clinton administration is nearing 40 percent women in senior positions. That creates depth. In terms of policy, all the bills that Reagan and Bush vetoed got passed after 1992. This includes the Family and Medical Leave Act, a provision to overturn the gag rule [preventing abortion counseling in federally funded clinics], and other laws. The national health care issue is critical to women. Training is something the president talks about, and that's very significant to women. Yet it was so much easier to be in the opposition. We could afford to be glib. We had no personal connection to most of the players. It was all good/bad in clear terms. Now there's a lot of gray areas. We have gradations of commitment. Issues aren't so clear anymore.

Clinton talked the same way on welfare reform when he was governor of Arkansas as he does now. He's a conservative, centrist Democrat. His welfare reform ideas continue this line of argument. Anyone who thinks you can change the discourse overnight is crazy. As well, he has to work with Congress, and with a society that largely agrees with him. No bill from this administration will be all that we want. For example, if I had my way, I'd like family and medical leave to be paid leave.

The most lasting legacy of Reagan-Bush is the climate that gives shelter to people's worst prejudices. People were more willing to come out with racist and sexist opinions in the last twelve years than ever before. That climate has stayed. What you see now is a very divided country, with fewer resources and people in the habit of saying things they would not have said a decade earlier. More than any executive order or legislative mandate, the Reagan-Bush legacy was social. They'd probably agree with that, but they'd view it in positive terms. They do it by talking about the family as father, mother, and children even though that's only 11 percent of American families. They talk about the return of the community, but I know it doesn't include me. It's a return to the church. It's a return to educational choice, meaning private schools because public schools are full of minorities. We on the other side try to capture family, community—and Clinton tried to do that. I think he needs to do that. He's probably one of our best politicians ever, but nobody's going to make it easy for him.

The biggest challenge for women's organizations here is to develop an agenda that embraces all women. It continues to be a white, middle-class movement. We need leaders in the future who come from lots of different constituencies.

Canadian Activists' Views

EVELYN CRONIN was an equal rights activist in Canada since the 1970s. Her reflections cover the fate of the Court Challenges Program, the rise of antifeminism, and the economic impact of the Conservative years. She was particularly concerned about the long-term effects of Brian Mulroney's appointments to the Supreme Court of Canada.

As I understand it, the strength of the Court Challenges Program was that it offered funds based on cases and it was steady, dependable money. When Mulroney came in, women's groups had lots of supporters in the civil service and the Secretary of State bureaucracy in particular. We had strong support from all three political parties. But over time there were lots of straws in the wind that suggested things were not going well. There were changes we made to deal with the Mulroney government. We started looking for different women to be our contacts. As well, the Court Challenges Program was surrounded by a huge row over endowments, and, in the end, the money went to a social policy think tank instead of to actual equality-seeking groups. The Conservatives would not let the groups themselves run Court Challenges. They wanted women to stay on a short leash.

One of the other things I noticed was the government started giving credibility to REAL Women [an antifeminist group], who had not got anywhere under the previous government. They were a small group that started using various channels to get information on women's organizations that received funding from the Secretary of State Women's Program. REAL Women tried hard to establish themselves as the other side of the story. The Mulroney government decided to practice what I call the doctrine of false equivalency. It suited them to have REAL Women around. They could do bad and slighting things toward the women's movement. It suited them to have the pro and con sides, even if NAC had millions of members and REAL Women was only a handful. This whole politics of false equivalency, of using women to turn against women, is ongoing. It's part of a much larger backlash.

I can't put my finger on when the funding for what we were doing started to go funny. In the late 1980s, the Secretary of State budget was cut, and it started taking a very long time, much longer than earlier, to get budgetary approval from the federal government. This really upset our organizational planning and our relations with our staff. This may not have been deliberate, but it happened. The other thing that started happening was the Mulroney government played invidious games with equality groups. They would encourage new organizations that undermined legitimate grassroots groups, especially if the new ones were pro–Meech Lake rather than critical of the government. Using funding as a lever, they set off one group against another. They said, "If you cooperate with us, you will advance and get the funds."

This process that I call the auction for compliance developed alongside the neoconservative economic doctrine of picking off the most vulnerable. Everybody all of a sudden started competing to be the most miserable. Part of the price for government attention and money was how compliant you were and how poor you were. Groups started competing to see how badly off they were. This fed into the Tory cry about "don't be so poorly off, you victims." They said we were always whining, but here they made us play a means-tested game, one where benefits were no longer universal. Groups were encouraged to behave in ways that would then be read back against them.

The other thing that happened was that private fund-raising money was going to services, to women's shelters, for example. The advocacy funding from the private sector was being directed toward things that used to be publicly funded. Women's studies in the universities, women's shelters, and others were all going to the private sector to raise money. This raised huge moral dilemmas. Can you pay for a court case by denying poor children a breakfast? Since then, we see an appalling funding problem. I saw the cuts as deliberate in the sense that the most obvious advocates were being whacked and then services were cut.

As far as cases were concerned, the Supreme Court was still very much on the rights-oriented trajectory of the 1970s and early 1980s. The case law was developing in a positive way, largely because of the courageous work of the court. They, the judges, were really out of step with the Mulroney ethos. In terms of abortion legislation, Kim Campbell as justice minister was very much a team player. She was going to lead the charge on that silly piece of legislation. Most of us saw it as a crock. We wondered why she would lend her name to the propagation of such foolishness. I think Kim Campbell's finest hour was in the aftermath of the *Seaboyer* decision when she held a consultation with women's groups to develop a new rape shield law.

Kim Campbell was justice minister as well when the Court Challenges Program was eliminated. She said something like, "We really don't need it any more because the developmental phase is behind us." That became a self-fulfilling prophecy because the equality-seeking groups lost their input into Charter jurisprudence. It will take a long time to breathe life back into the Charter. The late 1980s were exciting and unique because of who was on the bench. The current Supreme Court has occasional flashes of the earlier period, yet with Mulroney's appointments it is probably more obsessed than U.S. courts with the rights of the criminally accused. The coherent vision of the earlier era is gone. Mulroney has not appointed anyone who is more than a moderate on social issues. That Court will be with us for a long time. Overall, the development of Charter jurisprudence is at stasis with the shutdown of Court Challenges and with the Mulroney appointments.

The other thing that happened in the Mulroney years was we were getting good rights decisions from the Supreme Court, yet the economic bottom was being ripped out. The economic policies of the Mulroney government bought into a worldwide neoconservative agenda of making domestic economies safe for the roving capital of world corporations. They saw government's job as putting capital here. You need nothing of interest to workers. Labor must be cheap and taxes low. The bright signals on individual rights meant that neoconservative economic policies left nothing in terms of real victories. Years of work on employment legislation and pregnancy leave still left lots of senior women dumped from work after their leaves. Women were worried they would become known as troublemakers and never get another job if they took action.

The economic climate made the legal achievements of the seventies and eighties irrelevant. That's the real tragedy. A lot of organizations felt very beleaguered. It's been grim times, and what has surprised me is that people seem to have been struggling to maintain a positive vision, even though all around them are the horrible consequences. The most lasting Mulroney legacy is ruin. I think probably economic devastation is the biggest thing. I think that government consciously adopted policies designed to appeal to corporate capitalism. It wasn't an accident. They went into it with their eyes open, although they thought they would reap more economic benefits than they did. They made no effort to shore up the social safety net. That never occurred to them.

The other legacy, I guess, is the program cuts, the court appointments, and the other changes that limit legal progress. I do think things are better here now than they are in a lot of other places like the United States, but that's because people struggled here to move forward. Groups really pushed hard and asked, "Just because things are worse elsewhere, does that mean that we have to go along with this?"

* * * * *

ALEXIS SMITH refused to credit the Conservatives for any progress made by Canadian women's groups between 1984 and 1993. Her comments focus primarily on the limits of family law reform during the Mulroney years, but they also address her views of how language changed and how free trade cost women's jobs. Smith linked the record of the Mulroney Conservatives with growing cynicism about government.

A lot happened, despite Mulroney. Much of what women's groups obtained was despite Mulroney and despite the Conservative agenda. The Charter was passed in 1982 with a three-year moratorium on equality rights. The fact that it came into force in 1985 had nothing to do with the Conservatives. They were not, historically, the biggest Charter advocates. The Charter comes from the Trudeau years—it was a pre-1984 initiative that women's groups benefited from. The Court Challenges Program was part of the means by which the Charter was to be used, and it was eventually canceled by the Tories. So lots of the energy and money that went into litigation came from volunteers in the women's movement.

On the child care and abortion bills, it's true they were blocked, but the blocks were no credit to Mulroney. The abortion bill was largely stopped by Senate women, responding to what pro-choice groups said. On the child care question, Mulroney wasn't ready to listen to our groups at all. He said he had lots of women in cabinet, and they would tell him what he needed to know. He promised a great deal on child care, and what he came through with was something the child care movement could not accept. That need to expend energy to stop bad things from happening was awesome—it was hugely frustrating and required huge amounts of time and energy, especially on abortion.

The rape shield legislation was introduced after [Justice Minister] Kim Campbell worked something out with feminist criminal lawyers. That was a really positive outcome. Maybe that was because Kim Campbell was more willing to listen to women as justice minister. Although she was a woman and a lawyer with feminist leanings, it wasn't something she initially understood as an issue. But rape shield was a positive contribution on Kim Campbell's part.

After 1984, there was the overall feeling of frustration. We had a government in power that wasn't going to listen. That was frustrating. I had grown up with the sense that you could affect government, and here it was much more difficult. After 1984, it became a mixed picture on the progress question. Even when there appeared to be progress, there was bad stuff going on. We would move steps forward and backward at the same time. We'd have good legislation that wasn't implemented fairly for women, and vice versa.

Family law has mixed federal and provincial jurisdictions. In 1986, the federal government brought in amendments to the Divorce Act that said women would have to support themselves at an earlier stage than might be thought reasonable by sensible people. Sections of the act were interpreted to mean women must be immediately self-sufficient. This directly affected those women who had made the traditional bargain when they entered into marriage, that he would earn an income while she would support in emotional terms. We gradually gained for women a general principle of sharing of property, eventually a 50–50 division. But once women got property, there was the assumption they didn't need support. It has taken a few years to try to deal with that. During the 1980s, there were all kinds of court orders to end support after two to three years, even for a woman in her fifties who had never earned her own living. The *Moge* decision was crucial. It said women need lifetime support. The legislation didn't say we need to come to some of these common conclusions, and it has taken years to get us to where we are now.

In terms of public consciousness, people thought their own views were not being considered by the government. What also happened is that some people made feminism vaguely disreputable. It is an unfortunate view. I remember how the phrase *women's lib* got increasingly ridiculed over the years. But people now expect women to be paid equally with men. Most people want a good child care system. Lots of what feminists want is what people want, including free choice on abortion. Polls show that.

The most lasting Mulroney legacy is anger and frustration. To have to join some organization just to get issues heard, just to make those in charge listen, is too much. I think free trade was a bad move and a disaster for women. Free trade means a loss of jobs. Anger and frustration are accompanied by a cynicism about politicians. Mulroney promised that with the free trade agreement, there would be retraining programs, but he didn't create any. There's a lot of cynicism that came from the way Mulroney ran the government. Since 1993, Jean Chrétien has helped to reduce this cynicism. I don't know how democracy works when government doesn't listen. The Conservatives were self-aggrandizing and antidemocratic. That isn't what makes democracy work.

Overall, there can't be any improvement for women without a good child care system. Without that, everything else is just nibbling at the edges.

* * * * *

NATALIE SIMARD was an abortion rights activist who saw ongoing threats to women's access. She viewed the pressures of party discipline on elected women in Canada as limiting what could be accomplished in Parliament. Although she was pleased with the increasing private donations and favorable court decisions of the Mulroney years, Simard feared a spillover of more antichoice violence from the United States.

Our money increased incredibly during the Mulroney years. To be honest, it goes up and down depending on what is in the newspapers. All the things that happened in the Mulroney years increased our contributions—the proposals for new abortion laws, the boyfriends going to court, and so on. I would say our donations increased by one-quarter to one-third. The recession has cut us back so much, and we started to feel the pinch from the recession in the Mulroney years. Stopping the abortion bill in the Senate led people to think things were OK across the country, but they aren't.

The Mulroney years brought home a sense for me of how much this country works on the basis of party politics. I saw how much a leader's personal views shape what parties do. There were strong pro-choice women among the Conservatives, but they were drowned out. Party discipline really stymies women and affects who will go into politics.

The Conservative victory increased the amount of lobbying and education work we had to do. We also saw the Senate change in the Mulroney years, from a place that wasn't very partisan to one that was dominated by the party line. In the House of Commons, female members of Parliament agreed with us, but they had the party constraints put on them. Cabinet solidarity went far into the government caucus, even on so-called conscience questions like abortion.

With the Conservatives, we started to see that we needed to educate and lobby the bureaucrats behind the government. That's a really difficult task for a group of volunteers. What we also saw after 1984 were the enormous costs incurred, as well as some of the gains that could be made, by going to the courts. We knew that going to Parliament alone was not going to get us very far. So we started using the Charter and going to provincial courts.

There was progress, but not because Mulroney pushed for progress. The abortion bill backfired on them, even though they tried to use the backlash to fuel it. The progress women's groups had was in spite of them, not because of them. Some of the progress was following through from good things in the Liberal years, and some was from women in Parliament. But these women in the House and Senate did more to stop bad things than to initiate good things. We needed more women, and more feminist women, in Parliament. Their voice has to be strong enough to counter that of antifeminists and real conservatives in the Reform party, who think it is acceptable to ask women their marital status before employing them.

I think there were changes in public consciousness. The Mulroney era made people realize they can't be complacent. Abortion may be legal, but it's not available in many regions. The Charter may exist, but our rights may not be enforced unless we push governments to enforce. There are people across the country who would consider it quite alright to take some of those rights away. The Mulroney years pulled the women's community together on all sorts of issues. We had to pull together. It wasn't me or her—it was us. We stood together on issues like we hadn't before. It was a time of intense lobbying.

For the public, the most lasting Mulroney legacy is that the abortion bill was put to rest for a while. For me, the legacy is the opposite. It's the realization that access is either fragile or nonexistent. We need to find ways to ensure it is entrenched. We need lobbying, full-time, of bureaucrats everywhere and at all levels. We see the rationalization of health care in each of the provinces. How will that affect access for Canadian women? As I see it, the Conservative thought train leads to extreme right-wing violence. People on the other side have been frustrated in the courts, and this violence is the backlash coming from them.

* * * * *

PAMALA KHAN worked on violence and employment issues during the Mulroney years. She saw the Conservatives as shutting down pro-equality litigation and as shifting Canadian values away from caring, community-oriented views toward a rugged individualist ethos. Khan described the general growth of political cynicism and hostile language in addition to despair and infighting among movement activists.

The funding for Court Challenges came exclusively from the Secretary of State [department], so justice ministers weren't officially responsible for the program. After she was appointed to the [Ministry of] Justice portfolio, Kim Campbell went around the country saying test case litigation should not be driven by special interest groups. Just from her language, we could see there would be problems. Then she was upset that women's groups intervened in the *Schachter* case on paternity leave. Campbell did not like the fact that courts could pressure legislatures to change maternity benefits in a way that would permit both parents to use them. The government just wanted the existing law struck down by the courts. Campbell did not want benefits to be extended by court fiat, since in her view this was usurping the role of Parliament.

I would describe the Mulroney years as a major shift. The formal discourse on equality was there, but other criteria regarding economic rationality were brought into the picture. We saw the erosion of an egalitarian or humanitarian discourse. The economic profitability or cost criteria were brought to the fore under the Conservatives, to justify their policies. I think people felt very powerless under Mulroney. People did not think the government would listen.

I wouldn't say there was any progress during the Mulroney years due to the government. The court cases were won against the government, since their lawyers actively defended themselves against Charter arguments. We didn't get day care or pay equity as we wanted these policies to be. This offered the groundwork for the Liberals after 1993 to do what they're doing on social policy. We now see the criticism of political correctness, which to me is clearly directed against equality-seeking groups. It is easy to challenge people who are trying to create equality by calling them "politically correct."

We are also moving to the right because of a shift the Reform party has been able to impose on the Liberals. The only discourse that seems legitimate now is the bottom-line fiscal discourse, which was brought in by the Mulroney Conservatives. People are now convinced that having a deficit is like having an overloaded credit card. People say somebody has to suffer, and it is clearly the same people who suffer every time government cuts back. There has been an increased focus on blaming the victims, like people on welfare or unemployment insurance, as if they were the cause of the problem. We see that approach in terms of rape and spousal violence. The view is not challenged even though it is a fraudulent representation of reality. This shifts attention away from those who did cause the deficit. The Conservatives were lying to us. I feel a huge sense of outrage about this man, Mulroney, who lied through his teeth. The media refused to challenge him. The intellectuals were afraid to play their role.

Yet there was a huge change in public views on violence and choice issues. This was caused by the hard work of the women's movement. There has been a big change in perspectives on sexual assault and wife battering, although some people still blame young women who go out to parties for what happens. The idea that women work, that they require equal pay, became more entrenched. Perhaps that's why the Mulroney government felt it had to say certain things. We also obtained amendments to the Criminal Code on sexual assault that made Canada the most progressive common law country in the world. But these are changes that don't cost the government any money. Adopting policies that do cost money, like child care, is something the government won't do.

I would say the most lasting legacy of Mulroney-Campbell is that a lot of people got really discouraged. A lot of people dropped out, got burned out. We used to talk about despair, and I think there's quite a lot of that and a lot of anger. There's mistrust, cynicism, and a sense that the women's movement can't do anything. People just don't do political work any more. Instead, they fight among themselves because it's easier. Infighting hasn't destroyed the movement, but it has slowed it down a lot. There are limited resources, and this causes the infighting.

* * * * *

FRANCA ELIA emphasized employment and child care issues in her work as an activist. She argued that although public attitudes became more progressive in some areas, Conservatives were driven by a business agenda that left little room for any competing perspective. Elia also saw the language of equality replaced by a far less friendly discourse.

There is the question of how social policy gets played out. The cap on CAP [Canada Assistance Plan] and the changes to funding for higher education got worse in the Mulroney years. The devolution of spending to provinces and municipalities was quite damaging. One of the things that happened during the Mulroney era was that women's groups started to be called special interest groups. This has a marginalizing impact, and it continues in the discourse of the Liberal government. One minister in the Chrétien

cabinet, for example, says he wants to hear from "real people," as if people who participate in women's groups and unions are not real.

There's also a shift in the terrain. The economic turf really changed because the
business agenda became the public agenda. That affects what women's groups can do.
The Mulroney government was very good at entrenching this business agenda and con-
vincing people we need to be lean and mean. The Mulroney years were horrible. The
really bad parts began after the 1988 elections, when the free trade debate showed
clearly that our ideas differed from theirs. We thought up until 1987 that we might get
a child care bill we liked, but then we realized we couldn't with that government. We
had no bill because we had killed it. The government sure was mad at us. So, after 1988,
we engaged in underground guerrilla tactics, once we saw the Tories would not do any
good in terms of new legislation. We worked to keep them from doing worse. We were
also against the Charlottetown deal, since the potential for damage was even more serious than with the Meech Lake Accord. Everyone I knew was so browned off [disgusted]
by 1992, not just with the Tories but with the other parties as well.

Progress for Canadian women did occur, but it was inadvertent and only on specific
issues. Examples were the narrowing of the wage gap and the abortion decisions from
the Supreme Court. At the federal level, child care showed no improvements. But public
opinion on child care changed for the better. Attitudes around child care have become
more aware. The public, in general, understands the need for child care now more
broadly. We developed our own poll question on this. You don't have to explain child
care from scratch anymore. The public and media view it more knowledgeably now.
Women took the heat for economic dislocation coming out of free trade. In my view,
things improved and deteriorated at the same time.

The most lasting legacy is that business groups changed Mulroney. They shifted the
political terrain in Canada to the right. The center became the right on economic and
social issues. Privatization, deregulation, and taxation were all moved to the right. You
can hear it in the language people use. They talk of special interest groups, efficiency,
replacement workers, and not scabs. That's their most lasting legacy.

These accounts of life in conservative times suggest considerable variety across countries. Although movements in each case were arguably all on the defensive to some degree, the dynamics of that posture
differed. In Britain, activists generally framed their reflections in light
of Margaret Thatcher's dominant role as Conservative party leader,
prime minister, and ex–prime minister. After 1979, Thatcher served as
a lightning rod for critics of the new conservative individualism. The
frustration of British activists with the length of Tory rule was apparent, as was the sense that Thatcher had let women down by her actions.

Much of the progress cited by British respondents resulted from the courts, the institutions of the European Community, and increasing public responsiveness to movement claims. According to activists, British citizens seemed less passive as time passed, less likely to defer to what existed as a substitute for what could be. On issues of violence, child care, and women's work, activists believed change had occurred despite long years of Conservative rule. More groups learned how the system worked and found ways to manage despite government cutbacks and the emphasis placed by public agencies on project as opposed to core organizational funding.

Part of the defensive struggle they describe occurred at a discursive level. British activists commented in particular on the use of social or moral right rhetoric by the governing party. Julia Murray noted attempts to condemn single mothers, whereas Carol Drew, like other respondents, rejected Tory arguments that "women are having babies to get housing." This language, however, sat alongside what activists saw as a relative openness to abortion access in Conservative circles, in which Drew described a "radical libertarianism [that] leads to women having the right to choose." Compared with developments in the United States during the Reagan-Bush years, these patterns in Britain suggest a less aggressive social conservatism in which moral rhetoric became heated but in no sense overtook the economic core of government doctrine.

Over the longer term, British respondents lamented the decline in valuations of the broader society; this trend was seen as a consequence of rampant individualism, sanctioned since 1979 by the governing party. Carol Drew expressed the argument in terms of losing "a sense of social purpose." Many activists believed the damage caused by Conservative decisions would be difficult to reverse, even after the party lost power. Moreover, their faith in the ability of opposition parties to articulate an alternative vision was far from solid. The Labour party of the 1990s was turning to the right, according to Jan Robinson and many others, whereas the Liberal Democratic alternative seemed to fizzle during the 1980s. The view that politics was no longer about Parliament had become increasingly popular and fit with an entrenched sense among activists that no party could be trusted to do much for women.

The American system had a long tradition of weak parties and separate legislative, judicial, and executive powers, so activists in that system dealt with less centralized political institutions. The strength of interest groups in the United States also provided a different set of strategies with which to begin in the late 1960s. Reflecting on the situation nearly thirty years later, American respondents remained remarkably pragmatic. Getting more women involved at elite levels as candidates for public office, building coalitions with like-minded groups, and pressing forward in the courts, Congress, and the states were integral parts of respondents' agendas through the 1990s.

Twelve years of Republicans in the White House had certainly taken their toll on these activists, however. Sarah Anderson described what she termed "the politics of intimidation," meaning women's fear of speaking or acting publicly against powerful new right interests. She wondered whether any moderates remained in the Republican party. Charlene Moore spoke about the decline of public housing and the threat of homelessness, which in her view gave many low-income women an impetus to organize for the first time. The greed and deceit of the Reagan-Bush years are what Susan Jones remembered most, along with the ability of ERA opponents to pit women against each other. Carla Ruiz's comments spoke directly to this issue of social division, notably in her statement that conservatives "talk about the return of the community, but I know it doesn't include me."

American respondents were generally hopeful about the Clinton administration. White House decisions in early 1993 to allow unpaid family leave and to overturn the gag rule on abortion counseling in federally funded clinics were greeted with considerable relief, because these changes had been impossible during the Reagan and Bush years. What activists worried about was ongoing pressure to cut federal spending in areas of crucial significance to women—given that Republicans had bequeathed such a massive federal deficit. They also suggested public sentiment against government in general was a powerful brake on the actions of all American politicians.

The spillover of social and economic conservatism from the United States to Canada was a central theme in activists' thoughts on the Mulroney years. Both the rise of REAL Women and the willingness of Conservative M.P.'s to do business with that group represented an important change from the Liberal years. Interviewees criticized shifts in social policy away from universal benefits, toward targeted ones, as part of a weakening of the Canadian welfare state. Efforts to restrict abortion access and eliminate government funding for advocacy activities by NAC, LEAF, and other groups were linked to the same Conservative ethos.

At the level of language, Canadian activists including Alexis Smith spoke of the "vaguely disreputable" aura surrounding feminism during the Mulroney years and noted the increasing use of terms like *special interest group.* Canada's first female justice minister and, briefly, first woman prime minister drew a mixed response. Kim Campbell was commended for consulting with women's groups on a new rape shield law but condemned for her abortion law proposal and decision to eliminate the Court Challenges Program. For Natalie Simard, Campbell's situation reflected the dominant role of party discipline in the Canadian system. Squeezed within a more and more hostile rhetorical environment and a governing caucus that contained avowed antifeminists, Campbell had only limited room to maneuver. Like many others, Simard took heart from the defeat of the abortion proposal, commenting that "the abortion bill backfired on them, even though they tried to use the backlash to fuel it."

Canadian activists believed progress during the Mulroney years was more in spite than because of the government. The Charter of Rights together with sympathetic judges appointed during the Trudeau years accounted in their view for most positive judicial changes. Legislation on child care and abortion that activists opposed was blocked by pressure from groups including their own. What remained of the Conservative legacy, according to respondents, was severe economic damage resulting from free trade, plus profound public cynicism about government. The language of business profits and bottom lines became the dominant discourse, including for the Liberal government of Jean Chrétien elected in 1993. Activists grew tired, and, according to Pamela Khan and other movement veterans, many found it easier when placed on the defensive to fight among themselves rather than against the government.

This opening up of divisions among women, a crucial part of the story, forms the pivot of chapter 5.

CHAPTER FIVE **Driving a Wedge**

How did conservative leaders work to weaken their political adversaries? What strategies were available to unsettle and fragment protest groups?

These questions turn on two crucial concepts: social cohesion and political division. If cohesion is the glue that keeps a group of people united under a single banner, then division is what drives members of the collectivity apart to make their own claims and their own banners. Many sources of cohesion brought women together as an interest in Britain, the United States, and Canada through the 1970s. Discriminatory laws and court decisions plus a general sense of blocked opportunities led activism to surge. Women's groups multiplied rapidly in an environment of relative affluence, optimism, and openness to new ideas. Belonging to a larger group made sense in a setting where collective consciousness was growing, particularly among younger, well-educated, and employed women.[1]

This group cohesion, however, came under direct threat with the rise of conservative individualism. The ideas put forward by Margaret Thatcher, Ronald Reagan, and Brian Mulroney encouraged people to take charge of their own lives and throw off the shackles of groups, governments, and communities. Social divisions began to widen during the 1980s because an ascendant individualism challenged the value of collective action. Right-of-center elites worked to exploit emergent differences in a way that undercut group cohesion and added legitimacy to new conservative agendas. Although women as a political unit would likely have faced cohesion problems with or without Thatcher, Reagan, and Mulroney, internal divisions were far more severe because of these leaders. The tenor of the times after 1979 was decidedly individualist and offered many opportunities for women themselves to reject women's movements. It became more acceptable, legitimate, and indeed popular to stand outside the movement banner rather than underneath it. Over time, the incentive to be a group critic rather than a group participant grew as conservatives in all three countries worked to drive a wedge among their opponents.

Right-of-center leaders were able to exploit three main lines of division. The first was obvious: the very size of the constituency in question. Women were a large, diverse demographic category covering more than half the population and crossing multiple lines of social class, race, language, and so on. These powerful sources of internal difference were compounded by the rise of antifeminism, which showed how dramatically views among women about the women's movement could vary. In addition, in all three countries, considerable numbers of women voted for right-of-center parties. This fact permitted Thatcher, Reagan, Mulroney, and their party successors to claim that conservative policies enjoyed support among females in the general population. A crucial source of division, therefore, followed from feminist efforts to build a mass base in a diverse collectivity at the same time as conservative leaders worked to prove that women supported them and that groups were less legitimate than individuals.

The second source of cleavage was even more useful to governments. It involved divisions between women inside versus outside political systems. Feminists had long assumed that electing more women to public office would spread movement ideas and make governments more responsive to these claims. Yet political partisanship often overtook independent feminism as the guiding principle of elected women, meaning that insiders were toeing the lines for parties more than for women's movements. This issue was especially problematic in parliamentary systems like Britain and Canada, where party discipline constrained legislators far more than in the United States.[2] Although many female politicians in all three countries endorsed feminist claims, their support was not unanimous. The rise of women in conservative parties who were unwilling to serve as conduits for the movement—and the obvious example was Margaret Thatcher—showed the potentially deep chasm between political insiders and outsiders. This division helped right-of-center leaders to mount a state case by women against organized feminism.

Strategies within movement organizations also differed, opening up a third line of division. Over time, women who were moderate reformers had less and less in common with others who were militant protesters. Whereas the former tried to avoid polarization vis-à-vis conservative politicians, the latter pursued confrontation and protest as one of the only visible ways to keep up the fight in hard times. Moderates often sought to build bridges to female legislators, for instance, whereas militants were skeptical about working with or in the system. At some points, conservatives cooperated with moderate feminists to show how reasonable they were; at other times, they directed the spotlight toward militants to undermine the respectability of social movements more generally. The cooperative strategy was particularly helpful to right-of-center leaders before elections, when they tried to compensate for weak legislative records by emphasizing minor changes. The second strategy was useful at other times, when elites sought to weaken social critics by belittling and undermining them as a group.

Conservatives exploited each line of cleavage so that divisions among women in the general population *and* within women's movements opened up in all three countries. In Britain, organized feminism was considerably weaker than in North America and the backlash against it far less direct.[3] Divisions were most pronounced and easiest for Conservatives to exploit along insider versus outsider lines. Margaret Thatcher represented in towering terms the fiercely individualist insider who believed free market capitalism was the key to human freedom. As prime minister, Thatcher glorified women's traditional roles and worked to portray feminism as part of a threatening mobilization on the left fringe. Other Conservatives shared her economic values and her nostalgia for what they saw as a more orderly and moral past. Yet Tory efforts to drive a wedge were limited by changes in the women's movement, in the Conservative party, and in society generally. Overall, British feminism after 1979 refused to be conquered by the Conservatives.

In the United States, public support for movement positions was relatively solid through the 1970s.[4] National women's organizations were generally reformist in orientation, able to command a fair and often sympathetic hearing in the corridors of power before Ronald Reagan became president.[5] The success of organized feminism, however, provided a foil for critics whose views were more traditional and often grounded in fundamentalist and evangelical Christian belief. The rise of antifeminism on the American right was extremely useful to politicians like Ronald Reagan and George Bush. Republican leaders argued that they consulted with women and appointed them to cabinet positions, yet leading female insiders were in some cases antiabortion, anti-ERA, and anti–affirmative action.[6] Although these conservative women were critical of movement positions, their ability to divide and conquer could only go so far. In fact, the organized backlash against American feminism may have been so fierce as to be counterproductive by the 1990s. Moderate Republican women began to chafe as their party leadership grew increasingly intemperate vis-à-vis feminism.[7] Moreover, what members of the public perceived as a direct threat to equality attracted record dollars and members to movement groups during the Bush years.[8]

The situation in Canada blended elements of Britain and the United States, with a few twists of its own. As in the American case, public attitudes were relatively pro-movement, and this success encouraged antifeminists to mobilize. Organized opposition, however, was less vigorous and less successful in Canada than that in the United States.[9] Canadian Conservatives found it was more effective to use language as a wedge, since women's groups in English Canada and francophone Quebec held vastly differing constitutional visions. The Canadian case paralleled the British one in the use of one prominent woman to carry the government message. Brian Mulroney appointed Kim Campbell as Canada's first female justice minister at the federal level, and Campbell briefly held the position of prime minister in 1993. Yet Campbell differed from Thatcher and from lower-ranking women in the Reagan and Bush cabinets because she proclaimed she was a pro-choice feminist who had been unfairly treated by Tory men.[10] Although her statements were widely disputed, the fact that Campbell made them showed the limits of a divide-and-conquer approach in Canada. A female Conservative, in effect, insisted on registering her own group consciousness in public terms.

Political leaders in all three countries managed to foster a sense of rugged individualism that jeopardized social cohesion. Within this divisive environment during the 1980s, right-of-center elites worked to drive a wedge among all their critics, not just women's groups. The motive was obvious: to make governing easier and protesting more difficult by making critics weaker and ruling interests stronger. Conservative actions provided a seal of approval, an imprimatur of state legitimacy, for all sorts of efforts to undermine collective action. Journalists and academics who railed against organized feminism became more vocal, more credible, and certainly more numerous as time passed.[11] By changing the climate of ideas, Margaret Thatcher, Ronald Reagan, Brian Mulroney, and their party successors set out a welcome mat for varied critics of collective action. However effective these leaders were at the game of divide and conquer, though, their success had clear limits. For one thing, both feminist organizations and pro-equality attitudes more than survived the hard times.

The Thatcher-Major Wedge

The ability of Conservative leaders to divide British women was facilitated by many different factors. The historic ties between Toryism and women, polarized relations between left and right, relatively weak public support for feminism, and the rising numbers of females in prestigious occupations all opened up possibilities for the government to drive a wedge. Above all else, however, loomed the towering presence of Margaret Thatcher. The personal profile she cultivated remained the single most effective Conservative tool not just against relatively weak women's groups, which hardly threatened to topple the government, but against all opposition interests. Thatcher became the pivot for significant divisions between insiders and outsiders, between experts who knew power and critics who were consigned to the political margins. Other factors seemed secondary to this basic insider-outsider dynamic.

The United Kingdom was already a centralized unitary state when Thatcher took power. As prime minister, she concentrated control over political decision making even further by eliminating metropolitan governments like the Greater London Council and systematically weakening other local authorities. At the same time, opposition parties lost election after election. Taken together, Thatcher's command of the levers of power and the waning strength of any political alternative served only to heighten her stature.

Margaret Thatcher also stood out because her background was far from the norm. As the daughter of a small-town grocer in Grantham, she came from a place that biographer Hugo Young calls "the epitome of middle England."[12] Yet Thatcher's life was hardly confined to the ordinary, complacent world of her early years. In a milieu where upward social mobility was far from common, young Margaret Roberts went off with her father's encouragement to earn a degree in chemistry at Oxford. She quickly became an active partisan on campus and rose to the position of Conservative president. After completing her studies, she worked for about three years as an industrial chemist.

The formal beginnings of life as a Conservative campaigner date from 1949, when Margaret Roberts ran in the lost-cause riding of Dartford. As Young notes, "this impressive and dedicated young woman became, at twenty-four, the youngest woman to contest the 1950 General Election."[13] Although she lost in Dartford, Margaret Roberts met Denis Thatcher on the night of her nomination, and they married in 1951. The fact that Denis came from an affluent, Tory insider background and was the heir to a successful family business opened up broad new possibilities for Margaret. She was able to study tax law, give birth to twins Mark and Carol, hire a full-time nanny, pass the bar exams, build a law practice, and establish a political name for herself—all in about eight years. Her recollections of this period remain blissful. As she notes in *The Path to Power*, "to be a young married woman in those circumstances in the 1950s was very heaven."[14]

It was probably also very rare. Few women in postwar Britain had the political connections, education, and confidence of Margaret Thatcher. Female advancement through the universities and into prestigious occupations like law was much slower than in either North America or many parts of continental Europe.[15] Thatcher managed to thrive despite these factors and despite a broader environment that emphasized stasis and conformity, order and hierarchy. The profile she cultivated as the achieving political woman was virtually hers alone.

The orientation of the British movement also contributed in an ironic way to Thatcher's prominence. From its origins during the late 1960s, British feminism was a fragmented, radical phenomenon that focused more on theory and small-group consciousness than on lobbies, fund-raising, or electing more women. This meant Thatcher could virtually monopolize the stage as a visible, powerful female voice. When questioned about her feminist ties, Thatcher asked what the women's movement had "ever done for me."[16] This reply was less preposterous than it might have sounded in a different setting. British feminism lacked the mass attitudinal base that developed elsewhere, which made it easier for Conservatives to divide women. Poll data, for example, consistently showed weaker support for women's movements in the United Kingdom than in most other industrialized countries.[17] Moreover, British women had a minimal presence in the mass media, arguably less than in North America or elsewhere in Western Europe.[18]

If a comparative measure of movement density is constructed, it suggests that the percentage of active feminists in the U.S. female population was about three times greater than in the British female population at the point Reagan and Thatcher took office.[19] Moreover, no umbrella voice parallel to the National Organization for Women (NOW) in the United States or the National Action Committee on the Status of Women (NAC) in Canada was established in the United Kingdom until 1989, with the founding of the National Alliance of Women's Organisations (NAWO). Even after it was formed, NAWO was far less prominent in the media and less central to the lives of movement activists than its NOW and NAC counterparts.[20]

This problem of limited visibility and weak public support for feminism was compounded by historically warm relations between women and British Conservatism. As Beatrix Campbell demonstrates in her account of *The Iron Ladies,* women have constituted the core of the party volunteer base since the late nineteenth century. Although Conservatives remained more welcoming over the years to traditionalists than to modern feminists, they drew masses of both female voters and female party workers.[21] If British feminism had taken hold, it was among opposition interests that the Tories after 1979 tended to ridicule and isolate. Women's groups were linked at the level of ideas to the same collectivist ideology that Thatcher detested and at the level of practice to unions, local governments, and other troublesome interests. These opponents were wrapped together in a single rhetorical package by the government and its supporters in the tabloid press. Protest groups were castigated as "loony left," fringe advocates of both high government spending and morally decadent "alternative lifestyles."[22]

When Thatcher did single out feminists for derisive comment, it was to explain from the pinnacle of state power that merit was most important and that sex discrimination had ended long ago.[23] As she told a public audience in 1982, "the battle for women's rights has been largely won."[24] A number of trends other than her own success gave credence to this argument. Tory governments after 1979 were reluctant to improve women's status in the labor force and acted for the most part only in response to pressure from the European Community or from British courts. Access to child care altered little because systems of taxation, social welfare, and education were controlled by a central government that opposed public day care provision.[25] Despite these circumstances, however, growing numbers of British women obtained higher education, entered the paid workforce, and, in some cases, achieved elite positions. By 1994, Kate Figes was able to devote an entire chapter of her book on British women to "Life at the Top." It described their experiences as doctors, lawyers, scientists, and senior public administrators.[26] In the same year, a study by Lesley Abdela noted that the number of women who held seats in the House of Commons had more than tripled to sixty from only nineteen in 1980.[27] Abdela also reported that about one-half of newly admitted solicitors were female.[28]

Particularly during the Major years, Conservatives claimed they took unprecedented measures to help women succeed. Unlike a long succession of Thatcher cabinets that usually contained only one female (the prime minister), John Major's cabinet following the 1992 elections included two women.[29] Major also became a vocal supporter of the program known as Opportunity 2000, an initiative by private sector employers to train and recruit women managers. The program drew growing interest from business and generated considerable publicity around issues of child care, pensions, maternity leave, education, and part-time work.[30] Some employers established equal opportunity units within their management structures. All told, these developments suggested more and more women were moving up the economic ladder in Britain.

Thatcher presented herself as the achieving individualist titan who had already blazed the trail, overcoming prejudice among Conservatives and journalists, men as well as women. One passage in *The Path to Power* describes how local partisans during the 1950s often confronted her with the same set of questions:

> With my family commitments, would I have time enough for the constituency? Did I realize how much being a Member of Parliament would keep me away from home? Might it not be better to wait for a year or two before trying to get into the House? And sometimes more bluntly still: did I really think I could fulfil my duties as a mother with young children to look after and as an MP?[31]

Thatcher eventually obtained a winnable nomination in the north London riding of Finchley, where constituency activists seemed willing to accept a confident and knowledgeable woman. Her key political mentor upon arriving in the House of Commons was Keith Joseph, a cabinet minister in the Heath government who contributed much of the philosophical grounding for what became Thatcherism. With his analytic base plus the emotional and financial support of her father Alfred and later her husband Denis, Margaret Thatcher ventured forth on the political stage.

When speaking from that platform during the early 1950s, the aspiring candidate said she believed married women and mothers should be able to have active career lives.[32] Britain needed more women in

Parliament and senior cabinet posts. Yet Thatcher's later actions belied her words, as only one other female ever joined the many cabinets she named. That lone woman, Janet Young, lasted two years following her 1981 appointment as government leader in the House of Lords. Thatcher's substantive decisions on employment policy and government spending, reviewed in chapters 2 and 3, generally went against women's movement positions. It is not surprising that she recalls having "to push my way through protesting feminists chanting, 'We want women's rights not a right-wing woman.'"[33]

The prime minister became more outspoken in her criticisms of organized feminism as time passed. By the early 1980s, Thatcher was lambasting the "strident tones we hear from some Women's Libbers" and embracing the traditional roles of wife and mother.[34] Private life took on a hallowed place in Thatcherite thinking, as she argued "[t]here is no such thing as society. There are individual men and women and there are families."[35] Traditional roles were celebrated in regular interviews with women's magazines and television programs. With cameras rolling, Thatcher reminisced over family photographs and discussed improvements to the decor at 10 Downing Street.[36] She contended that growing numbers of single parents proved moral standards were in decay, threatening "our whole way of life."[37]

This emphasis on the Victorian values of order and morality, home and family, was reinforced by the nostalgic musings of other Conservatives. Keith Joseph gave a controversial speech in 1974 that set the tone for much of what followed. His attack on "the permissiveness of our time" targeted single mothers who "are producing problem children, the future unmarried mothers, delinquents, denizens of our borstals, subnormal educational establishments, prisons, hostels for drifters."[38] There was more than a hint of derision in Joseph's claim that "our human stock" was degenerating as uneducated teenage mothers "in social classes four and five" bore more and more children.[39] Three years later, M. P. Patrick Jenkin presented the following commentary:

> Quite frankly, I don't think mothers have the same right to work as fathers do. If the good lord had intended us to have equal rights to go out to work he wouldn't have created men and women. These are biological facts.[40]

Similar themes were adopted in the mid-1980s by cabinet minister Norman Tebbit, who linked Britain's troubles to "the debasement of standards" and called for a return to "decency and order."[41]

Much of this moral crusade, however, remained at the level of rhetoric rather than active policy change. The social right in Britain was a relatively weak political formation, built around individuals like Victoria Gillick who led the campaign against teenage access to contraceptives. Gillick and others failed to develop the organizational base necessary to displace economic conservatism in the governing party.[42] As a result, Thatcher and Major did relatively little on issues like abortion and contraception that would have pleased the religious right, nor did they act to restrict the employment of mothers. One of the only pieces of legislation in this area was the 1991 Child Support Act, which required fathers to pay support. The act was buttressed more by economic claims about the need to lower welfare spending, however, than by the moral claims of the social right. In fact, judging by the initiatives they pursued, both Thatcher and Major seemed far more wedded to economic laissez-faire than to the moral renewal arguments of the social right.[43]

Commitments to reducing government intervention also took precedence among women in the Conservative caucus. Edwina Currie, for example, directed her fury at the Equal Opportunities Commission (EOC). Known as the M. P. who told one journalist "I'm not a woman. I'm a Conservative," Currie described the EOC as "that ragbag of a body which finds it so easy to waste time and public money."[44] Her colleagues Ann Winterton and Teresa Gorman also railed against the EOC and the European Community as interfering, collectivist, and out of touch with the real world.[45] M. P. Angela Rumbold explicitly argued against placing moral issues at the forefront of the party platform. In 1991, she wrote "I don't think governments should have departments saying 'we are the ministry of the family,' then legislating or issuing circulars or guidance to people and saying this is how families behave."[46]

Laissez-faire views thus remained central to the new Conservative outlook. In adopting them, Margaret Thatcher rejected any element of conventional female caring when it came to the plight of the poor, the homeless, or the unemployed. During the Falklands crisis, her reputation as the Iron Lady was fixed in the public mind.[47] Thatcher in power became, in short, no more the traditional nurturer than the feminist soul mate of other working women. She emerged as a proudly assertive individualist with a "Queen Bee" image, far above the masses of both men and women. As Wendy Webster argues, Thatcher was one of the only women in Britain to meet her stated conditions for career success. These were having both a sympathetic husband and the means necessary "to employ a first class nanny-housekeeper."[48]

As the gulf widened between Thatcher's early statements and what she actually did for British women, movement activists grew more embittered and more hostile. Thatcher refused to strengthen employment legislation, approved cuts in funding for the EOC, and hammered away against women's movement allies in local government and the trade unions. She became a more determined, utterly incorrigible opponent than any man in power was likely to be. By denying women's movement claims in vigorous terms and still remaining a proper, feminine, well-groomed matron, Thatcher seemed to obviate the need for organized antifeminism in Britain. She was her own crusade against collective action, living proof that no qualified woman ever required a movement to get to the top.

The problem with this impression about women reaching the top was it remained just that. Better-educated women did enjoy wider employment opportunities than ever before, but their status relative to men in elite occupations remained weak. In fields like education or health care, women were still far from numerous as managers and directors.[49] As Kate Figes argues:

It is true that a handful of women have become stars, eagerly sought after for interviews and appearances. . . . But the price is often high. They still find themselves defined by their gender before their talents, and since they are doing jobs defined by men, they still face problems because of their sex. Meanwhile their speckled presence among the higher echelons of society supports the myth that we have equal opportunity.[50]

Figes and Abdela both present data showing a preponderance of unmarried, childless women among those at the top.[51] Clearly, their lives differed quite dramatically from those of women in the general population. According to interviews conducted by Figes, successful careerists ended up this way because unlike Thatcher, they found it was impossible to accommodate both work and family responsibilities.[52]

The impact of an initiative like Opportunity 2000 remained limited. As Figes observes, the program

still covers no more than roughly a quarter of the British workforce and can only do so much under current legislation. Opportunity 2000 focuses on individual success, on increasing the numbers of women within management and at the top, rather than on the poverty of working women within an increasingly segregated workforce.[53]

Yet the program was enormously useful in public relations terms to John Major, who appeared to be encouraging women at the same time as his government actively blocked pro-movement legislation and litigation. This gap between appearance and reality, between public relations and realpolitik, was hardly unique to British Tories. Similar patterns could be discerned in the United States and Canada under Republican and Conservative leaders.

Thatcher's example, though, and some Conservative ideas curiously inspired other women. For instance, the emphasis on citizens as consumers who can demand the means to take care of themselves remained central to government discourse through the Major years. This gave individuals a sense that they could break through barriers by dint of confidence and hard work. Even though Thatcher did not directly encourage others, her presence raised women's self-esteem and nurtured ambitions in the general public. Studies showed more British women took on higher education and professional employment as time passed.[54]

In addition, declining levels of fertility and increasing rates of divorce meant women on average spent less of their lives as married mothers of young children.[55] Public opinion studies showed British voters were increasingly egalitarian in their social attitudes and more receptive toward women in political life. Voters also remained tolerant on the abortion issue despite numerous efforts to restrict access.[56] As one equal rights activist explained, "I don't think Margaret Thatcher has stopped the vast changes in the status of women. A different government could have accelerated these changes and Thatcher certainly had no interest in accelerating this process."[57]

At the same time, a laissez-faire feminism was developing among some Tory women. Party appointees to head the Equal Opportunities Commission became more and more critical of government employment policy.[58] Pro-choice backbencher Teresa Gorman urged the government to develop better child care provisions through the tax system and to appoint more women judges. In Gorman's words, a "massive imbalance" on the bench needed to be corrected.[59] M. P. Emma Nicholson pressed the party to field more female candidates and update its treatment of working women.[60] Given what she viewed as a swing to the right by the Major government, Nicholson decided in late 1995 to leave the Conservative caucus and join the Liberal Democrats in the House of Commons.[61]

Women's movement organizations also became more willing to employ interest group strategies. Lobbies, coalitions, and press conferences began to be used in Britain during the Thatcher years in the same way they had been tried in North America since the late 1960s. In 1980, the 300 Group was formed to encourage more women to run for public office and win half the seats in the House of Commons. The National Alliance of Women's Organisations was formed in 1989, and a Labour women's campaign fund modeled on EMILY's List in the United States was established in 1993. Even activists who came out of one of the most radical streams of British feminism, the antiviolence movement, began to work inside the system. These campaigners gained growing public legitimacy, media interest, and, to a degree, governmental responsiveness for their work. By the end of the Thatcher years, rape crisis centers, refuges for battered women, and campaigns to secure the release from prison of women who killed their abusive husbands were all in the public eye. One harsh critic of Thatcherism summarized this shift as follows:

> Enormous changes in the treatment of violence against women have occurred, despite the Thatcher era. The problem has now been recognized in the public consciousness as male violence against women. Just the way we have been able to manipulate the media shows the change. Ten years ago we would have been much more purist in not letting the media sensationalize our issue. Now we are much more pragmatic.

Activists in the violence field spoke of working closely with police units and even with younger members of the royal family, to gain attention and funds for their efforts.[62] Child care groups found that while Conservatives opposed their demands, some large employers were introducing workplace facilities and lobbying the state for policy change. Organizations like the Equal Opportunities Commission and Trades Union Congress made considerable progress on employment issues through appeals to the European Community and British courts.

This shift toward moderate, interest group strategies and away from militant protest was helped by a change in British consciousness, the growth of what one movement participant described as "a more vociferous public." Another said, "Thatcher's focus on consumer choice has actually made people more demanding as British citizens." Because of these changes, activists believed their groups had managed to sustain some momentum through the days of darkness. Above all, the turn toward reformism blunted Tory claims that feminists were strident campaigners on the political fringe. More and more, they were respectable lobbyists whose goals seemed not inconsistent with Conservative arguments about hard work, individual achievement, and people taking care of themselves.

The turn away from militant protest, however, was not unanimous. Some activists in the mid-1990s remained committed to radical grassroots work and condemned what they saw as the cooptation of the moderate wing of the movement. Activists who worked in shelters for battered women, the lesbian rights struggle, and the black community were most likely to reject interest group strategies. One participant in an antiviolence group summed up the militant view: "Feminism changed under Margaret Thatcher from radical feminism to career feminism. Women started to think they needed to get a high-powered job in local government to survive. In short, women sold out."

Divisions between these two orientations often turned on the question of ties between feminism and the "loony left," which suggests that Conservative rhetoric indeed drove a wedge within the movement. One moderate explained the need to distinguish women's rights efforts from what she termed

> the "loony left" ideas of promoting lesbianism and nationalizing banks without compensation. . . . The Labour party wants to represent a wide range of conventional working people who don't want to pay to keep up a single mother with three or four children. The Labour party needs to recapture its working-class base, and through this we need to appear not too concerned with supporting the weakest at the expense of the next group up. President Clinton managed this in the United States. The left which took over the Greater London Council lost its marbles. They were so provocative in getting into nuclear free zones and policies on Northern Ireland. I don't regret the loss of the GLC as it evolved. It needed to be reformed and not abolished. It had become a vast and bloated bureaucracy with huge numbers of equal opportunities officers tripping all over each other.

In this way, pragmatists tried to distance themselves from militants, often in angry terms. One antiviolence activist stated, "The separatist feminists in Britain have a lot to answer for. They've helped to create a media culture in which all feminists are labeled as Man Haters." Another framed moderation in more measured terms: "We are very careful not to offend the government we've had for fourteen years. . . . We are in no way open to the charge that we are loony lefties running the organization on behalf of some fringe interests."

A number of writers predicted the death of the British women's movement after 1979. Their obituaries spoke of postfeminism, back-lash, and the end of organized activism.[63] Yet if the Thatcher legacy proved anything, it was that a powerful woman leader who rejected feminism could coexist with a women's movement that rejected her. Many British groups not only survived Conservative efforts to polarize women but also worked to transform themselves into moderate, pragmatic organizations that could mark some progress in the dark days. By keeping up the pressure from both moderate and militant directions, British women's organizations were neither totally coopted nor completely isolated by Conservative leaders. A varied set of strategies helped to ensure that the obituaries were premature, with elements of the British movement soldiering on despite the odds and the divisions. As the legislative and judicial record after 1979 indicates, women's organizations could celebrate a considerable number of pro-feminist decisions mixed with the less favorable ones. Tory rhetoric and actions may have splintered the broad constituency known as British women, but movement veterans simply refused to be conquered by tough times.

Splits in the United States

If any single factor cleared the way for Republicans to divide American women, it was the presence of a vigorous antifeminist movement. As efforts to turn back the clocks on women's rights spread among the ranks of evangelical and fundamentalist Protestants as well as traditional Catholics, the momentum that feminism built through the 1970s was placed in jeopardy. Unlike its counterpart in Britain and Canada, this push by the American social right began early and created a firm organizational base with plentiful resources. Moral crusaders led by Phyllis Schlafly condemned feminism as both selfish and dangerous. In Schlafly's words, "The claim that American women are downtrodden and unfairly treated is the fraud of the century."[64] As sociologist Rebecca Klatch explains, "Schlafly insists that females are in a favored position in America, the privileged beneficiaries of the Christian tradition of respect for women, based on the chivalry and honor bestowed on Mary, the mother of Christ."[65] The ability of new right interests to sustain a long and at times violent campaign against abortion access demonstrated their power in the United States, compared with the more limited impact of similar interests in Canada and Britain.

During the 1970s, antifeminism also emerged on the American economic right. Opponents of government spending, public regulation, and the state in virtually all its guises took on feminism as the source of yet more bureaucracy and interference in people's lives. The Equal Rights Amendment was criticized from this perspective as an effort to legislate and control personal liberties. In addition, adherents of a pro-market, individual freedom view shared important elements of the social conservative outlook. Both streams rejected women's claims as part of what they saw as a pernicious 1960s counterculture. Social rebellion endangered the traditional family according to moral crusaders and, in the view of economic conservatives, strengthened an invasive, overblown welfare state.

Ironically, it was fear of the progress feminists were making that led both sets of opponents into the fray. During the early 1970s, problems with the Nixon administration foreshadowed the trouble women's groups would later have with a series of Republican presidents. Richard Nixon vetoed a comprehensive child care bill in 1971 not on the grounds of cost, which would have been the usual turf of laissez-faire conservatives, but on the basis of its inherent threat to the American family.[66] This decision along with limits imposed by President Nixon on abortion in military hospitals showed the growing strength of social conservatism in the Republican party.

In 1972, Phyllis Schlafly presented her first public condemnation of the Equal Rights Amendment. Like the attacks that were to follow, this statement rejected "[w]omen's lib [as] a total assault on the role of the American woman as wife and mother and on the family as the basic unit of society."[67] Schlafly built a powerful movement under two umbrella groups she led, Stop ERA and Eagle Forum. Their overall purpose was to halt the momentum of feminist organizations, including at the 1977 International Women's Year Conference in Houston, Texas. Antifeminists held their own events in Houston at the same time as the conference was taking place, drawing about eleven thousand to a "rally 'for the family.'"[68]

Numbers and fervor were not the only sparks that made headlines for Phyllis Schlafly. Her solid credentials as a conservative anticommunist dated back to the 1950s and meant she was a force to be reckoned with on the American right. Moreover, the religious crusade of which Schlafly was a part proved to be electorally useful and financially indispensable to Republican candidates. Survey research during the 1970s showed both the erosion of a solid Democratic South as well as the possibility for Republicans to win support among northern Democrats who were fearful of social change. Direct mail appeals by the coalition known as the Moral Majority (established in 1979) mobilized masses of voters and attracted millions of dollars in political contributions.[69]

These developments assumed enormous significance once Ronald Reagan was nominated as the 1980 Republican presidential candidate. Reagan had a long history of close relations with social conservatives in the party. Schlafly along with a variety of right-wing senators and professional organizers had supported Reagan in his unsuccessful bid for the nomination in 1976. They were determined to win in 1980. The fact that Reagan obtained both the nomination and the presidency in that year meant he was beholden to loyalists from the moral crusade. In effect, Reagan brought the antifeminist baggage of the American right with him to the White House.

Once it was ensconced in this privileged position, the conservative campaign obtained more clout than ever before. Efforts to divide women by driving a wedge on controversial issues was made easier because political insiders orchestrated the attack. No longer did disgruntled individuals carp from the sidelines. Instead, Republican administrations between 1980 and 1992 worked consistently to undermine both the ideals and achievements of the U.S. women's movement. Although these efforts were not entirely successful, they did make considerable inroads.

In a book entitled *The Republican War against Women,* Tanya Melich lays out the complex and ultimately duplicitous strategy developed by her own party. While claiming they were committed to women and to elements of the feminist agenda, leading Republicans actively courted antifeminist interests. As described by Melich, the approach involved four main steps:

> First, say you're for women. Second, oppose any move that will give them real power but propose a measure or slogan that gives the appearance of doing so. Third, get some visible moderate women to agree publicly with your approach, but also ensure that they say the issue affecting women, whatever it is, is of lesser priority to the nation than other issues championed by the candidate, such as lower taxes and a strong defense. Fourth, firmly implement the antifeminist policy.[70]

As in Britain, the gap between administration rhetoric and action on movement issues was often large. This mattered little to Reagan, Bush, and their handlers, though, because the strategy worked for its intended purpose—to elect and reelect Republican candidates.

American feminists including Melich had many reasons to feel frustrated with Reagan and Bush. The 1980 Republican party platform turned its back on the ERA and endorsed a constitutional amendment outlawing abortion. It proposed using the abortion issue as a litmus test for judicial nominees. Once elected, Reagan and Bush weakened antidiscrimination initiatives in many agencies, including the Equal Employment Opportunities Commission, by reducing budgets and appointing people who were hostile to government enforcement activities. Programs established under the Women's Educational Equity Act were placed under a microscope by the administration and its friends on the social right, notably Paul Weyrich's Heritage Foundation. Welfare payments and housing programs were cut for poor women and children at the same time as tax changes helped many affluent Americans.

These policy decisions were only part of the story, however. Movement activists were at least as distressed by personnel decisions made after 1980. In terms of sustained influence within their closest circle, Presidents Reagan and Bush had few women around them except their wives. Some appointments of senior women were made, but in no case did they pierce the inner circle on domestic policy. Political scientist Jeane Kirkpatrick, for example, became ambassador to the United Nations. Kirkpatrick had studied women in state legislatures and national party organizations and supported the ERA. She gravitated toward the neoconservative stream, however, and became well known for her cold warrior stance in the pages of *Commentary* magazine.[71] As Melich observes, Jeane Kirkpatrick "would stay clear of women's issues during the Reagan years."[72]

Other loyal women were appointed to the Reagan and Bush cabinets, including Elizabeth Dole, Margaret Heckler, and Lynn Martin. Dole was initially a Democrat in the Johnson administration but switched to the Republicans during the Nixon years.[73] She also changed positions on the ERA.[74] Her husband, Senator Bob Dole, described his wife as "a 'sensible feminist' who 'doesn't threaten anybody.'"[75] Heckler had a long record in Congress and the Republican party of supporting national child care provisions and the ERA. During the early 1970s, she was a cosponsor in the House of Representatives of the Equal Credit Opportunity Act.[76] But Heckler remained firmly antiabortion and, during her time on Capitol Hill, tried not to become too closely identified with progressive Democrats in the Congresswomen's Caucus. By the Reagan years, according to Geraldine Ferraro, Heckler "vetoed whatever criticism the Caucus leveled at her President's policies."[77] This loyal record was not enough for the administration, however. After naming Heckler secretary of health and human services, Reagan sent a handpicked senior staff to accompany her.[78]

Lynn Martin was firmly pro-choice but had even less patience for working with Democratic women than did Margaret Heckler. One account of Martin's time in the House of Representatives indicates that she refused to pay full dues to the Congresswomen's Caucus. Martin explained that she "'believes in working from the inside' and 'has always been one of the boys.' She 'hates the term women's issues and wants to focus on people's issues.'"[79] Consistent with this perspective, Lynn Martin spent her time at the 1988 Republican convention assuring delegates that George Bush was a caring candidate who "would treat women fairly once he was in the White House."[80] As secretary of labor in the Bush administration, Martin encouraged private sector firms to promote more women to management positions. This focus on voluntary action to assist professional women was very similar to the Opportunity 2000 approach pursued by British Conservatives.[81]

In each case, these appointees behaved in a way that reflected their status as dutiful insiders. The tight constraints of the parliamentary party systems in Britain and Canada were expected to make new recruits prove their loyalty by toeing the government line. The fact that Kirkpatrick, Dole, Heckler, Martin, and others consistently placed their loyalty to Republican presidents ahead of whatever commitment they may have had to feminist positions demonstrated similar limits in the United States. These women assisted Reagan and Bush by blunting the sharp antiequality messages coming from Phyllis Schlafly, the Moral Majority, and the rest of the social right. Appointing cabinet members like Dole and Martin allowed Republican administrations to claim they included responsible moderates, women who had proven their commitment to other women even though they did little of the sort while in office.

This is not to say that Presidents Reagan and Bush failed to make sympathetic noises from time to time. In fact, whenever their poll numbers were particularly bad or an election was looming, the symbolic floodgates opened wide. For example, Reagan named Sandra Day O'Connor to the U.S. Supreme Court in 1981. Although O'Connor was not as antiabortion as social conservatives would have desired, she was likely as anti–civil rights as the administration that appointed her.[82] Concern about Republican electoral prospects apparently prompted Reagan to sign a number of laws including those on child support, family violence, and pensions in 1984 and on credit for women in business in 1988. The same motives seemed to underlay Bush's actions on child care in 1990 and on civil rights and nontraditional employment in 1991. In many cases, both fiscal and social conservatives opposed the ideas behind these laws. Operating on Capitol Hill, however, they ensured each piece of legislation contained very little progressive content by the time it reached the president's desk. Overall, implementing weak, watered-down provisions allowed Republicans to look compassionate and responsive in the face of public perceptions—especially among female voters—that they were uncaring and antiwomen.

As feminists watched some priorities including ERA go down the drain and others like child care become twisted beyond recognition, antifeminists saw similar problems facing their agenda. The Reagan and Bush administrations did not effect a constitutional amendment banning abortion, nor did they impose a watertight litmus test on judicial nominees. Priorities like preventing busing to achieve school integration and making school prayer compulsory seemed to assume secondary importance. Rebecca Klatch summarizes the frustration of moral crusaders:

> Since the early days of the Reagan administration, social conservatives have expressed dismay over Reagan's neglect to use state power to endorse traditional values. Social conservative critics charge Reagan with being preoccupied with economic and defense issues, ignoring the social issues that helped get him elected.[83]

In 1990, George Bush bitterly disappointed fiscal conservatives with his decision to raise taxes, despite promising not to do so.[84]

Obviously, these perceptions were at odds with women's movement views that Republican leaders were very true to their conservative roots. Gutting many pro-choice, antidiscrimination vestiges of the federal state showed feminists where administration priorities rested. Much like Emma Nicholson's frustration with the British Conservatives, some pro-choice women in the Republican party gave up trying to work from the inside. A number left the party in the period of the 1992 elections, when Republican attempts to curry favor with social conservatives became especially vigorous. Pat Buchanan's speech to the party convention in that year spoke of a "religious war going on in this country for the soul of America."[85] The wife of Vice President Dan Quayle, lawyer Marilyn Quayle, attacked "liberals who believe the grandiose promises of the liberation movement. They're disappointed because most women do not wish to be liberated from their essential natures as women."[86] Moderates who put feminism and equality ahead of the moral absolutism of the social right found staying inside the Republican party was increasingly untenable because of changes between the Nixon and Bush years. Tanya Melich reports that in 1992, she threw her energies into Bill Clinton's campaign against George Bush.[87]

This revolt against what the Republican party had become helped to make 1992 the "Year of the Woman" in American politics. Record numbers of female candidates were elected, in many cases with the support of other women. Groups like EMILY's List, which bundled together contributions for pro-choice Democratic women, raised record amounts. Donations to other pro-choice organizations grew rapidly as the sense of siege widened.[88] This mobilization happened in part because more American women had access to money in the 1980s and following. Just as the social right was organizing a more traditional constituency of older married housewives from Catholic and Protestant backgrounds, feminist groups tended to attract younger, better-educated women who held paid employment.[89] The latter group grew more and more as time passed. The numbers of women enrolled in postsecondary institutions in the United States more than doubled from about 3.5 million in 1970 to nearly 7.5 million in 1990.[90] During the same period, the numbers who worked for pay increased by about 60 percent to the point that more than one-half of American working women held full-time, year-round jobs by 1991.[91]

Poll data showed sturdy support for women's movement positions among the general public. Despite consistent efforts to marginalize it through the Reagan-Bush years, more American women identified with feminism in 1992 surveys than ever before.[92] About half of those polled in 1992 reported warm feelings toward the women's movement, and more than 60 percent of both men and women said they were angry at women's treatment on equality issues.[93] Opposition to the proposed constitutional amendment banning abortion increased over time, and support for measures to achieve equal pay for work of equal value reached nearly 85 percent.[94]

In short, feminism was gaining ground in the general public at the same time as it was under siege in the Republican elite. Susan Faludi gave a name to this phenomenon in her 1991 best-seller entitled *Backlash*. The pattern was a tale of contradictions, of steps backward and forward all at the same time. Membership levels in the National Organization for Women reflected much of this flux, as numbers went up sharply, down sharply, and then back up beyond the previous peak. From a base of only three hundred in 1966, NOW attracted more and more members to reach a hundred thousand in 1979. After two years of the first Reagan administration, NOW claimed 225,000 dues-paying members.[95] This figure dropped precipitously through the mid-1980s as the organization went approximately $1 million into debt.[96] Yet the *Webster* decision of 1989 coupled with Clarence Thomas's confirmation hearings brought NOW membership numbers back up—surpassing 1982 levels to reach 275,000 in 1992.[97]

At the same time as NOW membership was soaring during the early 1990s, so too were the numbers of conditional feminists. These were writers who said they were feminists but declared their opposition to a variety of movement positions. Most were affluent, well-educated individualists who sought to prove, like Margaret Thatcher, that they did not need feminism. Probably the best-known conditional feminist of the early 1990s was Camille Paglia, a provocative essayist who rejected the antipornography element of the women's movement in favor of sexual libertarianism. Paglia's essays in *Sexual Personae, Sex, Art, and American Culture,* and *Vamps and Tramps* were lively, direct, and often outrageous.[98] In one piece first published in *Playboy* in 1992, for example, Paglia began, "I am a pornographer." She went on to describe feminists who wanted to limit access to pornography, notably Catharine MacKinnon and Andrea Dworkin, as "obsessed, moralistic women" who were too prudish to appreciate fun and sexuality.[99]

Paglia rejected antipornography claims as part of a limiting, unenlightened feminism. Instead, she proposed

> [a]n enlightened feminism of the twenty-first century [that] will embrace all sexuality and will turn away from the delusionalism, sanctimony, prudery, and male-bashing of the MacKinnon-Dworkin brigade. Women will never know who they are until they let men be men. Let's get rid of Infirmary Feminism, with its bedlam of bellyachers, anorexics, bulimics, depressives, rape victims, and incest survivors. Feminism has become a catch-all vegetable drawer where bunches of clingy sob sisters can store their moldy neuroses.[100]

Much of Paglia's notoriety was attributable to her wildly unpredictable claims, such as denying sexual harassment was an issue for women at work or questioning "the feminist obsession with rape."[101] As an experienced performer on book tours, Paglia became a pop icon in her own right.

Rather than using sexual freedom as the pivot for her conditional feminism, Christina Hoff Sommers employed a critical take on women's studies programs.[102] Published in 1994, *Who Stole Feminism?* was an angry attack by a philosophy professor against academics close to the women's movement. Sommers maintained that the older tradition of liberal equity feminism had been replaced by a New Feminism that saw women as a besieged, victimized gender. In her words:

> When [New Feminists] speak of their personal plight they use words appropriate to the tragic plight of many American women of a bygone day and of millions of contemporary, truly oppressed women in other countries. But their resentful rhetoric discredits the American women's movement today and seriously distorts its priorities.[103]

Like Margaret Thatcher's views about the British situation, Sommers admitted that inequality was once a problem in the United States but believed it was no longer relevant. If "gender feminists" only opened their eyes, she claimed, they would see all the progress women have made and embrace "the equity feminist mainstream."[104]

A third conditional feminist, American historian Elizabeth Fox-Genovese, challenged the treatment of motherhood and children by women's groups. Her book entitled *"Feminism Is Not the Story of My Life,"* however, relied on neither personal experience as a mother nor any analysis of the policy claims of movement organizations. Genovese instead used a series of conversations with other women in the United States to argue that feminism fails to appreciate the glories and costs of raising children. This neglect, she maintained, follows from a misguided tendency by many feminists "to consider women as independent agents rather than as members of families."[105] In a bold distortion of the empirical evidence, Genovese condemned women's groups for not pressing vigorously enough on the child care issue.

The point about conditional feminism à la Paglia, Sommers, and Genovese is that it captured the dissenting voices of affluent, educated women during conservative times. On a less grandiose scale than that of Margaret Thatcher in Britain but certainly in very popular terms, all three American writers put themselves forward as achieving individuals who for one reason or another rejected organized feminism. The criticisms they presented were often personally nasty, particularly in the case of Paglia, and weak in interpretive and analytic terms, but they remained rhetorically forceful. At a political level, the willingness of these authors to drive a wedge among women showed the depth of their *conditional* feminism. In effect, Paglia, Sommers, and Genovese offered a shiny new patina to the antifeminist gloss first burnished by Phyllis Schlafly. These writers thrived on the Reagan-Bush legacy of rejecting groups and collective action, by building a veritable cottage industry of disgruntled critics who said no movement could speak for them. By pointing sharp arrows from so many directions, their writings tried to convey a particular individualist message: American feminism was not growing, not credible. Instead, the women's movement was portrayed as an embattled mess—unable to address even its core constituency of affluent white careerists.

In short, the new Republican ethos worked on many different levels to turn back the clocks on progress for women. Presidential administrations perfected the art of manipulation—appearing to be friendly to feminists or antifeminists depending on the circumstance. Republican leaders proved they could simultaneously court and offend not only the women's movement but also those who built a sustained campaign against it. The cult of the ambitious individual was raised to new heights to discredit progressive movements for social change. Traditional roles for men and women were reasserted with a vengeance. What Reagan and Bush did not accomplish was putting organized feminism out of business. As public opinion polls, NOW membership levels, defections by Republican women, and the results of the 1992 election showed, pro-equality interests remained a force to be reckoned with in American politics. Although all kinds of antifeminists and conditional feminists continued to divide the constituency known as women, the momentum for basic rights withstood the backlash of the Republican years.

Divisions in Canada

Upon taking power, Brian Mulroney seemed more conciliatory than either Margaret Thatcher or Ronald Reagan. He appointed record numbers of Canadian women to positions of responsibility and, unlike his counterparts, showed little evidence of wanting to undermine feminist groups or trade union interests. His regime, however, was arguably the most socially divisive of the three under consideration. Months after Mulroney resigned as party leader in 1993, Conservatives were reduced to only two seats in the House of Commons from a peak of 211 in 1984. The bulk of the electoral damage done to the Tories was by new parties that wanted to turn Canada upside down, in the case of the Bloc québécois through the separation of Quebec and in the case of the Reform party (based in Western Canada) by emulating American new right policies. Two years later, Canada came within a breath of falling apart as a result of the 1995 Quebec referendum. The vote breakdown gave a very slight margin of victory to opponents of Quebec sovereignty.

How did one leader manage to sow this degree of political discord? Obviously, the main forces of division were not attributable to Mulroney per se, because Quebec nationalism and Western alienation had long bedeviled the country. Yet Mulroney was responsible for creating a political coalition in the Conservative party that raised the expectations of both Quebec nationalists and western Canadian regionalists to dangerous new heights. When his promise of massive decentralization via constitutional change failed to materialize, Mulroney dashed the hopes of Quebeckers, Westerners, and Canadians generally that political consensus was achievable. In turn, he lambasted critics of his proposals, lashing out at adversaries in bitter, relentless terms. It was in the vindictive Tory rage against protesters that women's groups found themselves at the receiving end of government vitriol.

The gulf between Mulroney and his critics also widened because of the increasingly radical tone of social protest in English Canada. In the fight over free trade, federal spending cuts, and the constitution, established political parties were overshadowed by new issue coalitions. Trade unions, women's organizations, and antipoverty groups were outspoken critics of the Mulroney government and, as a coalition, kept up the heat through the late 1980s and early 1990s. Because protest groups were so consistently negative in their assessments both of Mulroney personally and of Conservative policy generally, distance between the two sides only grew over time.

One way the government tried to manage this situation was by discrediting its critics. Conservatives described protesters as knee-jerk, extremist opponents who lacked a coherent alternative of their own.[106] Party women worked to undermine feminist groups that opposed the government, notably the National Action Committee on the Status of Women (NAC), by portraying these organizations as marginal cranks on the political scene. In the words of the president of the national Conservative women's association, "NAC's leadership takes partisan views on just about every topic and is anti-everything."[107] Conservative women's groups threatened to leave the NAC umbrella in 1988. According to Tory women, this threat followed not just from NAC's handling of trade and constitutional issues but also from its generally oppositional stance vis-à-vis the federal government.[108]

During the 1980s, Conservatives attempted to paint themselves as reasonable moderates caught between two polarities, an increasingly radical left NAC on one side and a growing radical right antifeminism on the other. Surveys conducted during this period help to explain the strategy. Poll data showed more women over time identified themselves as feminists and more males and females believed obstacles faced women in the workplace.[109] Views that Canada would be better off if more women held political office were widely shared, with about 50 percent of survey respondents supporting this position in national polls.[110] For his part, Brian Mulroney held a fairly sympathetic position on basic rights issues. In 1984, he named six females to his first cabinet of twenty-nine members. Mulroney later told journalist Sydney Sharpe that he "became a one-man affirmative action course" as a result of tutoring by Conservative women.[111]

The same year as Mulroney became prime minister, organized antifeminism arrived on the English Canadian scene. REAL Women, standing for Realistic, Equal, Active, for Life, spent much of the next ten years lobbying *against* laws mandating equal pay for work of equal value, divorce reform, sex education for adolescents, affirmative action programs, and public child care provision.[112] The group was an active member of antiabortion coalitions, and, like Phyllis Schlafly's organizations in the United States, it argued for traditional sex roles in marriage and family life.

From its earliest beginnings in 1984, REAL Women contested the National Action Committee's voice as the representative of Canadian women. Although refusing to list either its members or benefactors, REAL claimed a base of ten thousand to twenty thousand adherents who viewed NAC as "a handful of radical feminists promoting their own personal extremist views purportedly on behalf of the women of Canada."[113] REAL Women took on NAC directly by applying for federal government support through the same agency that funded feminist groups. The willingness of the Secretary of State Women's Program to allocate monies in 1989 was likely due to REAL's ties with the Family Caucus, a group of thirty-five social conservatives who held seats as federal Tory M.P.'s.[114] Feminists viewed this decision to grant funds to REAL Women as part of a thinly veiled threat: NAC had to behave or else the Conservative government would shift support dollars to the other side.

The challenge posed by REAL Women was compounded by a spillover of conditional feminism from the United States. A number of journalists in English Canada worked away at the individualist theme, arguing that the women's movement was unnecessary, out of touch, and otherwise unworthy of their support. Danielle Crittenden gave an old twist to conservative arguments in the pages of *Saturday Night* magazine. Like Elizabeth Fox-Genovese in the United States, Crittenden condemned women's groups for not understanding the pressures on working mothers and claimed that publicly provided child care would do nothing to assuage their basic feelings of guilt. Crittenden reverted to traditional "pin money" assumptions in asserting that women she knew worked for frivolous extras—if not jewelry, then designer kitchens and exotic ski holidays.[115] Donna Laframboise, a columnist for Canada's largest circulation daily, echoed the ideas of Camille Paglia and Christina Hoff Sommers in condemning women's studies, Catharine MacKinnon, and the rest of what she termed "contemporary feminism's anger, self-obsession, extremism and arrogance."[116]

Efforts to marginalize NAC and other movement organizations went into full swing in 1988 and following, when protest coalitions in English Canada put the spotlight on Mulroney's free trade and constitutional agendas. As in Britain and the United States, much of the government campaign was conducted by female insiders—the difference being that in Canada, there were far more of them. Women comprised more than 13 percent of Canadian M.P.'s by 1988, roughly twice the corresponding level in the United States House of Representatives and British House of Commons. For the most part, female cabinet ministers in Canada were fiscal conservatives who said they were feminists. Like their counterparts in the United Kingdom and the United States, most placed their loyalty to the government far ahead of any commitment to the women's movement. Yet they did break ranks more often and more openly than women insiders elsewhere.

Two of the most influential ministers during the first Conservative term were Pat Carney and Barbara McDougall, both pro-choice M.P.'s from urban areas. Carney later defied the government that appointed her to the Senate when she voted against abortion legislation in 1991; her decision helped to produce a tie vote that defeated the new law. One of the most outspoken women in the Conservative caucus was Toronto M. P. Barbara Greene, a former municipal councillor who was assaulted in the House of Commons parking lot. Greene along with McDougall and women from opposition parties helped to form the Women's Parliamentary Association in 1988. The group worked to improve life on Parliament Hill, not just for women M.P.'s but also for support staff. In addition, Greene took a courageous stand within her caucus on issues of homosexual rights and violence against women.[117] She remained a committed fiscal conservative, however, who showed the hard economic face of Tory women. As chair of the House of Commons subcommittee on poverty, Greene put her energies into redefining the poverty line so that fewer people would fall below it.[118]

During his second term in power, Mulroney elevated Kim Campbell, a new M. P. who had built her political base in the Vancouver School Board. Campbell finished law school in 1983 and worked briefly in a commercial law firm.[119] During the mid-1980s, she left municipal politics to become first an adviser, then a leadership contender and provincial legislator in the Social Credit party. Social Credit at the time was a fiercely right-wing formation in the polarized world of British Columbia politics, and Campbell was among a handful of activists who held an urban seat. One of the best-known conflicts in her brief provincial career involved abortion, the same issue that was to color much of her reputation in federal office. After the 1988 Supreme Court ruling in the *Morgentaler* case, Campbell broke ranks with the Social Credit leader and premier, William Vander Zalm, who wanted to cut off public funding for abortions. As Campbell told a reporter, "It would be hypocritical to suggest I support the policy. My pro-choice views are well known."[120] The premier's position was rendered void by a British Columbia Supreme Court decision that sided with Campbell's arguments.[121]

Not surprisingly, Campbell was never appointed to the provincial cabinet, and, when approached about running in the 1988 federal elections, she agreed. Her combative, aggressive style worked well in the ensuing campaign. Campbell delivered a series of feisty speeches applauding Canada-U.S. free trade, never yielding an inch to critics who denounced the deal. As a rookie federal candidate in a swing riding, Campbell trained her sights on the two opposition leaders who were attempting to sway voters with emotional nationalist appeals. In her words, "Canadians must reject the appeals of those political leaders Jingo John [Turner] and Oshawa Ed [Broadbent], who wrap themselves in the flag while they not only sell Canadians short but sell them out."[122] After a very close race, Campbell won her riding for the Conservatives.

In quick succession, she was appointed to a minor portfolio and, at the age of forty-two, to major posts as minister of justice and member of the inner cabinet. Once inside the Mulroney government, Campbell did not endear herself to REAL Women and other social conservative interests. First, her attempt to steer a new abortion bill through Parliament was greeted with derision by antichoice groups that saw Campbell as more objectionable than the previous justice minister. In the words of a Campaign Life activist, "What we had in Doug Lewis was an apologist for the feminists. What we have in Kim Campbell is one of the radical feminists themselves."[123] Second, Campbell worked in the wake of the *Seaboyer* decision to develop a new federal rape shield law. This legislation, one of the only initiatives by Campbell that feminist groups endorsed, was decried as "anti-male" by REAL Women.[124]

These criticisms from the social right reflected the frustration of activists whose policy demands were making little headway. Because affirmative action programs were permitted under the terms of the Canadian Charter of Rights and Freedoms, at least one claim advanced by REAL Women was impossible without arduous constitutional amendment. Equal pay laws and child care policies were pressed by a variety of groups at both federal and provincial levels, and in each case REAL Women seemed to be outflanked by advocates on the other side. Divorce law reform enjoyed wide support including among Conservatives, so again opponents were frustrated. Similarly, the Christian right campaign against abortion, of which REAL Women was a part, remained ineffective in Parliament and the Supreme Court during the Mulroney years.

Kim Campbell, however, also had problems with feminist interests. Like Lynn Martin in the U.S. House of Representatives, she did not participate in cross-party women's activities in the House of Commons.[125] Later on, however, Campbell told a national journalism conference that life in Ottawa was "unspeakably lonely and very difficult."[126] Her closest ties remained to other Conservatives, who joined Campbell in denouncing NAC's critique of free trade and ensuring that a pro-trade argument highlighting women made the headlines. Once NAC reached beyond its standard issue focus to criticize free trade, Conservative women defended a round of harsh budget cuts that reduced funding for feminist groups and later eliminated the Court Challenges Program. In 1989, Barbara McDougall became the first federal minister responsible for the status of women to boycott NAC's annual lobby on Parliament Hill.

As feminist groups continued to challenge a series of other government policies, the common ground between them and Conservative women eroded even further. NAC targeted cuts to unemployment insurance and family allowances, along with efforts by Kim Campbell to return abortion to the Criminal Code. While the justice minister announced "I believe that this [abortion] bill is actually better than no law," pro-choice organizations along with leading medical doctors and legal experts denounced her proposal and ensured its defeat.[127] Government attempts to respond to the killings of fourteen young women at the University of Montreal engineering faculty were rejected as useless and ineffectual. NAC claimed Campbell's 1991 firearms control law was a victory for the gun lobby.[128] Subsequent Tory efforts to establish a task force on violence against women and a royal commission on new reproductive technologies were described as strictly symbolic moves. NAC refused to participate in either inquiry, claiming aboriginal and minority women were not adequately represented.[129] Overall, Canadian groups maintained that a gaping distance separated what Conservatives said and did for women.

Above all, constitutional matters became the most visible point of friction between Conservatives and NAC—and offered the greatest opportunity for Tories to drive a wedge among women. Like most left-of-center activists outside Quebec, English Canadian feminists during the 1970s and 1980s generally endorsed a strong federal government. This regime would not only counteract the continental pull of the United States but also ensure firm national standards in social policy. By way of contrast, Quebec women's organizations tended to be decentralist and nationalist, believing a committed leadership in Quebec City was more likely to act in women's interests.

The most vocal stand against Conservative constitutional proposals was taken by NAC president Judy Rebick in 1992, when she led the organization's campaign against the Charlottetown Accord. Rebick criticized the closed-door methods used to reach agreement and the threat to national standards implicit in the terms of the Accord. NAC's attempts to include equal numbers of men and women in a reformed Senate were rejected, as were proposals that Canada be reorganized along asymmetrical lines that recognized Quebec, aboriginal peoples, and the rest of Canada as three founding nations. In Rebick's view, the Charlottetown Accord was an unpopular proposal that would only divide Canada and make the country more like the United States:

> Instead of meeting the demands of the different regions of the country, we have an accord that does not meet anyone's demands. There is a lot of unhappiness with this accord. . . . In my view, far from unifying the country, the agreements that the first ministers have made will further divide us, further set region against region. . . . We have only to look south of the border to see how decentralized governments compete with each other for investment. The accord's social and economic union, because it is toothless, does not provide the necessary guarantees. This is

why the National Action Committee on the Status of Women believes that, in fact, a 'no' vote is a vote for Canada. We believe the
Charlottetown Accord will lead to a dismantling of national social programs and more division and disunity over the years.[130]

To the chagrin of Brian Mulroney and most leading federal and provincial politicians, the accord was defeated in a national referendum in
October 1992.

Opposition by NAC to the Charlottetown deal angered not only Conservatives but also every official party in the House of Commons. Brian
Mulroney labeled anglophone feminists as "racist," anti-Quebec "enemies of Canada."[131] Kim Campbell stated that the yes side in the referendum fight had been endorsed by educated voters, whereas only the
"civically incompetent" had voted no.[132] Echoing Mulroney's choice
of terms, she described critics of Conservative policy as "the enemies
of Canadians."[133] Printed buttons saying "NAC does not speak for me"
were worn by many yes supporters. Tory minister Barbara McDougall
explained her perspective as follows: "I joined the YWCA to use the
[swimming] pool, not to have NAC speak for me."[134] On the other side
of the House of Commons, deputy Liberal leader Sheila Copps and
New Democratic party leader Audrey McLaughlin also adopted insider
as opposed to outsider positions on the Charlottetown Accord. Both
publicly identified themselves as feminists, while disavowing NAC's
stand on constitutional change. Along with other elected politicians
on the center and left of the spectrum, Copps and McLaughlin criticized NAC as unrepresentative and out of touch.[135]

Clearly, Canadian women were a fractured lot by the early 1990s.
Organized antifeminism limited NAC's ability to speak in an uncontested way about core issues like equal pay and abortion. Differences
between English Canadian and Québécois feminists replicated broader
divides over the country's thorniest question, constitutional change.
Feminists in English Canada were themselves split between political
insiders and outsiders, between those like Kim Campbell who were
part of the party system and others like NAC president Judy Rebick
who had little patience for politics as usual.

Campbell's own experiences as Conservative leader capture much
of this conflicted tale. Brian Mulroney stayed on and on as party chief
until 1993, while support for his party dropped lower and lower. By
appointing Campbell as defense minister in his last cabinet, Mulroney
seemed to signal that she was his anointed successor. Yet Campbell's
inexperience led to major stumbles during both the party leadership

race and subsequent federal election. Conservative insiders including Mulroney were quick to fault Canada's first woman prime minister for what occurred, ignoring the imperiled state of the party which Campbell inherited. As Mulroney told a reporter in 1994, "Leadership is a series of unusual talents one finds in an individual. She didn't have them."[136]

Kim Campbell was not about to let this interpretation stand. In 1996, she published her own account of the 1993 debacle under the title *Time and Chance.* It alleged that the same male strategists who controlled the Conservative campaign remained in close contact with Mulroney throughout, yet all of them blamed Campbell once things began to unravel. According to *Time and Chance,* the "seasoned pros" called the shots but refused to take responsibility for the consequences—in this case, the worst ever Conservative showing in a federal election. To the horror of her former handlers, Campbell was open and unrepentant in assessing what went wrong. She described prominent Conservatives as wanting her to take the fall for a disaster that was caused by others and as expecting her to serve as the proverbial widow who "threw myself on the funeral pyre" to protect what was left of Brian Mulroney's reputation.[137]

If Tories blamed each other for these developments, moderate feminists outside the party worried about the larger implications. Pragmatists believed it would be difficult in the future to elect women as party leaders and difficult for women leaders to trust their own parties. These women also saw NAC as increasingly out of step in an environment where confrontational tactics had perhaps run their course. In the words of one pragmatist, NAC's behavior led "the federal government to lose patience with being insulted." Moderates claimed that sustained criticism of virtually every Conservative initiative risked movement credibility and cut off access to politicians and bureaucrats. Another commented on the lack of fiscal realism among militants: "The women's movement has refused to acknowledge the deficit. . . . They have never dealt with the fact that we are in a country that's broke." Others lamented the unwillingness of NAC presidents after 1986 to give government credit for anything, since the strategy alienated those who did not share the same outlook. Pragmatists emphasized the need to be realistic about the priorities of women in the general public. From their perspective, the fact that more and more Canadian women completed university and held paid employment would translate into support for NAC's basic goals, but not its approach.[138]

Feminism survived the Conservative years, but in a strained condition. Radicals in NAC and other groups celebrated in the belief that their efforts had helped to undermine the government's constitutional proposals and, not coincidentally, Brian Mulroney's leadership. Moderate elements that were closer to the party system took solace in Pat Carney's vote against the abortion bill and Kim Campbell's memoirs, as evidence that female insiders had not entirely compromised their principles. Legal changes resulting from the Charter of Rights were widely noted, and efforts to move forward on violence against women attracted attention outside the country. Although Canada had one of the most strictly disciplined legislatures in the world, women in Ottawa had apparently created a modicum of independence within that system. Perhaps the "critical mass" argument did hold some water, in that having an active and confrontational women's movement outside Parliament and enough moderate women inside it actually led to some progress. Overall, Canadian feminism looked divided after the Mulroney years but certainly not defeated.

Assessing the Divisions

As political executives, British Conservatives enjoyed the longest stretch in power of the three cases considered here, followed by the American Republicans and the Canadian Tories. During about eighteen years in office, Margaret Thatcher and John Major had ample opportunity to marginalize their critics by trivializing opposition claims and driving a wedge among groups they sought to weaken. Yet this was not easy to accomplish given the curious liquidity of British feminism. According to many activists, there really was no women's movement, just a collection of very loosely allied local groups that each went their own way. Participants often described a multitude of disparate movement fragments working on separate issue campaigns. For any government intent on stamping out such a phenomenon, the odds were daunting.

Conservatives in the United Kingdom thus faced a movement that held comparatively limited sway among the media and general public but that was building roots in a variety of other quarters. Equal rights and pro-choice lobbies made progress within the House of Commons and House of Lords, including among Conservative members. Campaigns against violence gained growing support from lawyers, younger members of the royal family, police groups, and journalists who followed the crime beat. Employment and child care issues were a core concern of many British women's groups for decades, and, over time, these claims attracted more attention from businesses and unions. In other words, the powerful presence of Margaret Thatcher was not sufficient to drive out talk of collective action. British feminism remained alive and active in its amorphous condition, stubbornly committed to the view that far more progress was needed before activists would stop campaigning.

Women's groups in the United States faced new conservatives at the helm of the executive branch for twelve years. With the aid of moral crusaders in the American media, including talk-radio hosts like Rush Limbaugh, in addition to sympathetic members of Congress and a sturdy network of foundations and political action committees, social conservative interests were ascendant through the Reagan-Bush years. Feminist organizations confronted a difficult challenge in the United States simply because the web woven by the social right was more intricate, tight, and moneyed than elsewhere. Attempts to divide American women came from many sources and could not be easily dismissed.

Yet the basis for much of this backlash—the strength of American feminism among the general public—explained the gradual demise of the divide-and-conquer campaign. Large numbers of women and men in the United States were not prepared to go over the edge against equal rights, equal pay, child care, and abortion access, even if some opinion leaders were trying to move the country in that direction. Poll data showed a firm majority of the mass public supported the core planks of the American women's movement. For example, surveys showed that even after Republican leaders had lashed out for years against the Equal Rights Amendment, about three-quarters of Americans continued to endorse the proposal.[139] New conservatives, in short, were unable to polarize opinion to the point that the feminist majority for justice and equality fell apart.

The fact that some Republican veterans broke with their own party also showed the limits of the conservative strategy. Once insider women stated publicly that they were not prepared to go this far, that they were not willing to allow their party vehicle to be taken over by unyielding social traditionalists, the spell started to break. After all, their case stood as a compelling political argument: it was no longer electorally useful for Republicans to drive out moderate activists and middle-of-the-road voters. The division could now go the other way, by moving pro-equality interests back toward the political center and leaving opponents off in the margins.

For nine years, women's groups in Canada contended with a governing party that was more influenced by Brian Mulroney's trade and constitutional agendas than by either fiscal or social conservative ideology. Contentious debates that consumed Canada through the early 1990s came out of Mulroney's responses to economic globalization and the 1982 constitutional settlement. By taking on his core positions, English Canadian women's groups gained visibility in the short term, but, over the longer haul, they risked a great deal. In campaigning against free trade and the Charlottetown Accord, organizations like NAC claimed they were representing opposition opinion that the Conservatives preferred to ignore. The outcome of the 1992 national referendum revealed the depth of this popular sentiment, and polls on free trade also showed Canadian women were considerably more opposed to Canada-U.S. and Canada-U.S.-Mexico deals than were men.

High-stakes opposition, though, carried high risks. Federal funding for the National Action Committee, the Court Challenges Program, and many other activities was dramatically reduced in 1989 and following. By joining protest coalitions against Tory policy, NAC forfeited most of the common ground that had existed between it and the governing party. Taking on trade, constitutional, and budgetary issues meant English Canadian women's groups devoted a great deal of energy to campaigning *against* Mulroney's agenda rather than *for* their own core priorities. Unlike the more positive focus of women's groups in Britain and the United States on defined movement objectives, NAC's message in Canada became a blistering critique of the federal Conservatives.

In this sense, the divide-and-conquer strategy was at least partly effective. By 1992, an array of legislative insiders who were prochoice, pro-Charter, pro-equality feminists had lined up against NAC. Some of them, however, refused to toe the line entirely for the government. A few Conservative women broke ranks by voting independently and speaking publicly about their experiences. Group consciousness, it appeared, had seeped inside the party despite the rise of Tory individualism.

One of the most challenging tasks that faced women's movements in conservative times was figuring out how to work with the leaders who would come next. This quandary is the subject of chapter 6.

CHAPTER SIX **Changing Gears**

When would the dark days be over? In 1992, some signs pointed toward a time of reckoning for conservative leaders. John Major, George Bush, and Brian Mulroney were all faltering in the polls while challengers nipped at their heels. The British Labour party led by Neil Kinnock, American Democratic presidential candidate Bill Clinton, and Canadian Liberals led by Jean Chrétien all seemed poised to win power.

The only actual change in political executives occurred in the United States after Bush lost to Clinton in the November 1992 election. In Britain, John Major stunned his critics by winning a majority victory in 1992 and clinging to power through another term. Opposition interests regrouped yet again to try to wrest power from the Tories, convinced that Labour leader Tony Blair would bring an end to Conservative rule in 1997. Canadian Tories hung on until the last possible moment and, in October 1993 under the leadership of Kim Campbell, were dealt a crushing defeat by the Liberals.

What did these developments mean for women's groups? Did it even matter whether Major, Bush, and Campbell were replaced by Blair, Clinton, and Chrétien? The argument advanced in this chapter is a nuanced one. Yes, the replacement of new conservatives by more centrist moderates *was* consequential, but primarily at the level of political rhetoric. In each case, the punitive and divisive language of Thatcher, Reagan, Mulroney, and their party successors was replaced by a less harsh and more inclusive approach. Neoliberals like Blair, Clinton, and Chrétien were less likely to lash out at the poor, for example, in the same unforgiving terms as their predecessors. They saw individuals as more than simply a cluster of ambitions and achievements, as at least in part a product of social circumstance.

Yet these shifts at the level of public discourse did not commit neo-liberals to sweeping changes in public policy. The legacy of Thatcher, Reagan, and Mulroney had bitten deep by entrenching negative perceptions of government and, in the United States and Canada, by impoverishing the federal state. The triumph of neoliberalism beginning in 1992 largely meant a tight fiscal regime fueled by less of the moralistic rhetoric that underpinned neoconservatism. New leaders entered office with a greater tolerance for the concepts of society and community than their predecessors, but they made sure to keep collectivist ideas couched in cautious, middle-of-the-road terms.

Bill Clinton, the first of this trio to assume office, had to cope with massive federal indebtedness, the continued strength of American social conservatism, and a persistent antigovernment ethos. During his first term as president, Clinton proved to be a masterful speaker but a less than effective manager of the Democratic mandate. He disappointed many supporters, including some feminist activists, with his wavering, inconsistent approach to issues. As president, Clinton was viewed as an improvement over Reagan and Bush—the question was how much of an improvement.

Jean Chrétien arrived in power carrying a wealth of political experience and a long history of pragmatism inside the Liberal party. Among the general public, Chrétien was initially viewed as more ethically principled than Mulroney. By permitting fiscal conservatives to dominate his cabinet, however, Chrétien incurred the wrath of many of the same interests that had opposed the Conservatives. Leading women's organizations portrayed the Liberals as wolves in sheep's clothing, as aggressive budget slashers who talked about caring and compassion while they dismantled the fragile Canadian welfare state.

Like his counterparts, Tony Blair tried to cultivate an image of responsible moderation. He presented the new Labour party as a respectable middle-class formation, not threatening to either British business interests or bond traders in New York. In an effort to address their doubts, Blair insisted he would retain the entrepreneurial spirit of Thatcherism along with its laws to limit trade unions. The reason that many activists in women's groups cringed with these kinds of assurances is obvious. Instead of suggesting imminent change in British public policy, Blair's approach suggested more of the same.

Women's organizations were forced to shift gears to deal with these new leaders. After 1992, movement allies were appointed to senior positions in the Clinton administration and, a year later, in the Chrétien government. Tony Blair's shadow cabinet included a number of prominent women, and many more ran successfully as Labour candidates in the 1997 elections. The fairly clear distinction between insiders and outsiders that developed during the conservative years began to break down, as more and more people who said they were committed to movement goals assumed influential roles. One crucial question loomed large: Would new leaders and the women associated with their moderate politics make much difference?

If Labour Ever Won

Of the three conservative regimes addressed in this study, the British Tories were both the first to gain power and the last to lose it. Margaret Thatcher and John Major governed for about eighteen years; together, they left a firm imprint on British society. This impact was apparent in the behavior of the Opposition leader who came closest to putting the government on the ropes. Tony Blair seemed to distance himself more from Labour's past than from the Tory imprint. His move toward the political center confirmed an age-old pattern whereby progressive parties shift toward the right in their pursuit of power. Labour's effort to outflank the Tories to win began early in the twentieth century. As British political scientist Dennis Kavanagh explains the march to the middle, "Socialism has often given way to the need to avoid financial crises, reassure business leaders and secure incomes restraint from the trade unions."[1]

The path that Labour followed back to power reveals a great deal about this move toward the political center, and the prospects of British women under a Blair government. In slow but steady steps, the transformation from old to new Labour gradually brought more women into elite positions, but it did little to entrench feminist priorities at the core of party policy. British activists worried about the implications of what one called "the huge turn to the right" in the Labour party. According to this view, innovative voices were silenced during the mid-1990s in a hasty rush to the political middle. Another activist commented, "I am a longtime Labour party member, but I'm not under any illusion that a Labour government would make many changes."[2] Doubts about the intentions of Labour in power were widely shared among activists during the Major years.

Many concerns dated back to developments during the last Labour government. James Callaghan served as prime minister during a tumultuous period from 1976 until Margaret Thatcher's victory in 1979, when Britain was rocked by high levels of industrial strife and sharp conflict between government and trade union interests. The Labour cabinet introduced measures to hold down public sector pay increases and saw its key economic policies imposed by the International Monetary Fund in 1976. A series of debilitating strikes followed involving ambulance drivers, hospital workers, and even grave diggers. Thatcher described what became known as the winter of discontent as "not just disruption but anarchy."[3] By promising to return public order to Britain and by rejecting what she viewed as "government by picket," she overcame Callaghan's lead in the polls to win power in 1979.[4]

This upset brought the first in a continuing round of reevaluations within the Labour organization. Activists on the left of the party, many of them women, pointed to reductions of more than £8 billion in public spending effected by the Labour government between 1977 and 1979. As Joel Krieger explains in his account of *Reagan, Thatcher, and the Politics of Decline,* "Alongside budgetary restrictions in a whole range of services, the [Callaghan] cuts eliminated jobs in the civil service and local councils, not insignificantly a critical area of female employment."[5] Labour also introduced a cash limits system of restraining public spending, which defined in advance a ceiling on government expenditures except in the area of social security. According to Krieger, "all was in readiness for Thatcher by the end of Callaghan's government."[6] This interpretation of Labour's last mandate thus claimed Callaghan prepared the economic ground for a thriving new conservatism.

In social terms, the Labour government also resembled elements of the Tory regime that followed. Analysts on the left maintain that James Callaghan was anxious to adopt the same moral rhetoric as Conservatives like Keith Joseph and Patrick Jenkin. In 1977, for example, the Labour prime minister contended, "Our aim is straightforward; it is to strengthen the stability and quality of family life in Britain."[7] The next year, Callaghan stated, "The overriding social concern is to preserve and enhance the influence of the family."[8] Writing as a left critic, Elizabeth Wilson rejected this approach as part of an "unthinking . . . dependence of the Labour Party on half-baked notions of 'traditional family values.'"[9]

Feminists who held a more institutional view pointed to other failings. The first head of the Equal Opportunities Commission (EOC), Betty Lockwood, was a Labour appointee. Before becoming EOC chair, Lockwood had served as the party women's officer. She adopted an insular approach to running the agency that excluded movement activists. According to Joni Lovenduski's account of the Labour period:

Administrators, lawyers, and experts pushing for more effective women's equality policy found it difficult to get jobs at the Commission. Furthermore, many feminist policy actors who were assigned to positions in the EOC departed soon after their appointments, frustrated by their inability to initiate action and by the unwillingness of the EOC to take the decisive action its founding legislation empowered it to do. Outside of the agency, feminists despaired of its caution and sought other ways to further women's rights.[10]

Levels of staff morale in the EOC were low during the Callaghan years, as was the degree of innovation and initiative coming from the agency. Clearly, doubts about the Labour legacy dating from the 1970s went beyond a circle of left critics to include moderate policy reformers also.

During the long years in opposition, party activists had plenty of time to mull over these issues. Debates between old guard trade union, hard left militant, and soft left moderate factions were heated and contentious, but their upshot was in little doubt. By the time Margaret Thatcher left 10 Downing Street, soft left or modernizer interests dominated the parliamentary wing of Labour and were trying to gain control of local and National Executive Committee levels, too.

One reason for their ascendance rested in the aftermath of Labour's 1979 defeat, when Michael Foot defeated former chancellor Denis Healey to become party leader. Foot was portrayed by Thatcher and others as an agent of the far left, as an ally of hard-liners like Arthur Scargill, Ken Livingstone, and Tony Benn—all of whom, the Tories said, would lead Britain to ruin. The rise of the Labour left meant the system of selecting party leaders was revised in a way that increased the power of unions and local constituency associations. Incumbent M.P.'s had to be renominated before every election. Each of these changes increased the clout of Labour militants in ridings and unions, while diminishing the role of moderate elements in the parliamentary party. During this same period, the Labour Women's Action Committee emerged; the group pressed for more female parliamentary candidates and greater attention to such issues as child care within the party.[11]

Centrists in the House of Commons caucus took direct aim at the leftward directions of Labour under Michael Foot. Four M.P.'s bolted in 1981 to form what became the Social Democrats. The exodus of Roy Jenkins, David Owen, William Rodgers, and Shirley Williams was important because it signaled the sentiments of key ministers from the

Callaghan years toward the orientation of Labour in opposition. Among party veterans who remained in the fold, there was little patience for further movement toward the left. In the 1981 deputy leadership contest, Denis Healey narrowly defeated Tony Benn. Healey supporters campaigned to purge the left-wing Militant Tendency from the party and won back control of the National Executive Committee.

Given these multiple fractures among opposition interests, it is not surprising that the anti-Conservative vote split in 1983 and subsequent elections. During his only campaign as Labour leader, Michael Foot endorsed nuclear disarmament, withdrawal from the European Community, renationalization of privatized industries, repeal of Conservative trade union laws, and abolition of the House of Lords.[12] Labour also promised to reverse the sale of public housing begun under Thatcher's popular Right to Buy program. As Hugo Young observes, Thatcher devoted her 1983 campaign to an "effortless dissection of a Labour Party more deeply split and chaotically disorganized than at any election it had ever fought."[13]

Foot resigned as leader after the election. His successor, Neil Kinnock, was a more centrist Labourite, neither opposed to the sale of public housing nor willing to put up with the Militant Tendency inside the party. Kinnock refused to commit Labour to renationalizing each industry the Tories privatized and insisted his government would keep Britain in the European Community. Again unlike his predecessor, Kinnock agreed to retain American Cruise missiles on British soil.[14] Like Foot, however, Kinnock was no electoral match for the Conservatives. He was tarred with the brush of extremism for failing to dissociate Labour from the tactics of the miners' union. Scandals that might have been pinned on Margaret Thatcher usually missed their target.[15] Although Kinnock was unable to bring Labour back to power in either 1987 or 1992, he did transform the organization in other ways. Veterans of the Callaghan years were replaced by a younger group of centrist front-bench M.P.'s. Hard left elements including Benn, Scargill, Livingstone, and the Militant Tendency were made to feel less and less welcome, especially after Benn lost his leadership bid in 1988. After an image makeover by Labour activist Barbara Follett, Kinnock presented himself as a polished, well-dressed, and telegenic campaigner.

The ability of British women to get their issues to the forefront was complicated by the shifting sands of political life in this period. The breakaway Labour M.P.'s who became Social Democrats in 1981 eventually merged with the Liberals. As the Alliance and later the Liberal

Democrats, they built an impressive base among educated public sector workers and gained about one-quarter of the popular vote in both the 1983 and 1987 elections.[16] The Lib-Dems pioneered a number of campaigns that won public attention, including in the areas of civil liberties and constitutional reform. The party proposed a dedicated education tax in 1992, the same year as the two major parties avoided specifics on both taxes and education. The Lib-Dems also fielded more female candidates than any other party and were the first to declare that all nomination shortlists must include at least one woman.[17]

The main problem for Liberal Democrats remained the British electoral system. Single-member plurality arrangements meant minor parties found it difficult to expand beyond a particular geographic base. Even though southwestern England provided a solid base for the Lib-Dems, many votes for party candidates in other regions seemed to be wasted because of the first-past-the-post rule. As in Canada, minor parties could obtain 25 percent of the popular vote nationwide but win less than 5 percent of the seats in Parliament.[18] In other words, the Lib-Dems raised important issues as a third party and set the standard on women candidates, but they had little chance of winning power unless the electoral system changed.

As an Opposition in turmoil, Labour seemed even less promising as a site for political action. By the mid-1980s, women recognized they were more likely to be party members than decision makers, because about 40 percent of the Labour base was female versus about one-quarter of the National Executive Committee (NEC). During the Kinnock years, pressure was brought to bear within Labour on a number of fronts. First, a women's rights post was created in the shadow cabinet, with M.P.'s Jo Richardson and later Clare Short in the position. Second, measures to increase the numbers of female candidates and NEC members were adopted. These included a 1988 annual conference resolution that every final constituency nominating slate (known as the shortlist) include at least one woman, a 1989 agreement that women be at least 40 percent of all party committee and delegation members, and a 1990 resolution that half of the Labour caucus be female by the turn of the century.[19]

How could Labour reach parity by the year 2000? Consultations conducted by the National Executive Committee in 1991 indicated that three-quarters of local riding associations rejected the idea of compulsory all-female shortlists. Because about 70 percent endorsed voluntary all-women shortlists, this option was adopted by the 1991 annual conference.[20] Labour headquarters distributed a list of women candidates to local constituencies, and, in the end, the party fielded 138, or about 21 percent, female candidates in 1992 (compared with 93, or 14 percent, in 1987). Of the Labour women who ran in 1992, a total of thirty-nine, or 28 percent, won their seats, compared with 32 (19 of 59) and 2 (3 of 144) percent of Tory and Lib-Dem women, respectively.[21]

After two tries at defeating the Conservatives, Neil Kinnock resigned in 1992 as Labour leader and was replaced by John Smith. Together with finance critic Gordon Brown, Smith moved to position Labour even more toward the center. In the summer of 1993, for example, Brown insisted Labour was "not against wealth" and instead was committed to skills training as well as joint public/private sector partnerships.[22] Sounding a great deal like neoliberals in the Clinton administration, Brown insisted Labour was not the party of high taxes and profligate government spending. Moreover, Smith and his successor put John Major on the defensive in a way that had proven impossible with Margaret Thatcher. A series of sex scandals involving Conservative M.P.'s and cabinet ministers flew directly in the face of the party's moralistic rhetoric. Internal Tory divisions over participating in the European Union contributed to a sense that Britain needed a government that could speak with one voice. Not surprisingly, Conservative fortunes took a steep turn downward.

Labour women saw enormous opportunity in these developments. Mounting evidence suggested the Opposition was fielding female candidates in marginal areas, while promising seats in Scotland, Wales, and the north of England continued to go to men. Research showed that both the Labour party and its trade union affiliates needed women's support to survive. Feminist party activists decided in 1993 to establish a separate fund for female candidates, modeled on EMILY's List in the United States. Standing for Early Money Is Like Yeast, EMILY's List U.K. was founded by Barbara Follett, who had earlier transformed Neil Kinnock's appearance. Also in 1993, Labour women won passage of a conference resolution stipulating "[t]hat all-women shortlists operate in 50 percent of all vacant Labour seats and target seats." The identification of target constituencies would be arrived at by the NEC, regional party offices, and local riding associations.[23]

Given the outcome of NEC consultations in 1991, the uproar that followed the 1993 resolution was not unexpected. All-women shortlists were fiercely debated through 1994 and 1995, as was the policy of EMILY's List U.K. to fund only pro-choice Labour women.[24] Both decisions were portrayed by party traditionalists as antidemocratic, middle-class strategies that, in the case of the shortlists, used quotas to discriminate against men.[25] After what one participant described as "a virulent backlash," the 1994 Annual Conference endorsed an NEC statement upholding mandatory short lists. EMILY's List held firm to its pro-choice filter, but the policy remained contentious for years.[26]

John Smith's sudden death in 1994 brought Tony Blair to the fore-front as party leader. In arguing for low taxes and a strong market ethos, Blair continued Labour's march to the middle.[27] As one observer commented on his years as leader:

> Labour has fashioned itself as a people's party rather than a work-ers' party. It has abandoned its hammer-and-sickle-style emblem in favor of the red rose; it relies more on the mass media and less on its own "movement" organs of propaganda; it has reduced the weight of the unions (and especially of the union leadership) in the election of its leaders and determination of policy.[28]

Blair avoided controversy at all costs, including on the testy matter of quotas.[29] Speaking in July 1995, he announced that Labour's experi-ment with all-women shortlists in safe and winnable seats would end after the next election.[30]

Blair also centralized control of the parliamentary party, placing it in the hands of loyal Blairites. In a style reminiscent of North Ameri-can politicians, he insisted that all substantive statements be cleared with the leader's office. Skillful spin doctors placed his every move in a glowing light, again a departure from the more spontaneous norms of Labour in opposition. Labour under Blair repudiated the clause 4 language in the 1918 party constitution. By backing away from public ownership in a workers' state, new Labour embraced fairness and di-versity in a market economy. The party also continued Neil Kinnock's policy of remaining within the European framework. Under Blair, La-bour made some overtures toward adopting the Social Chapter in the Maastricht Treaty and toward incorporating the 1953 European Con-vention on Human Rights into British law.[31] As was the case with quo-tas and unions, however, Blair knew where icy patches rested and made sure to steer clear of firm commitments.

Since Blair's policy statements were generally vague, he became known in some quarters as Tony Blur. Pundits accused him of Clin-tonizing the Labour party.[32] What Blair articulated through 1997 was a neoliberal vision that spoke of tempering the hard edge of Tory Brit-ain. In his words, "new Labour is the party that can unite ambition with compassion; aspiration with a desire to live in a decent society."[33]

Speaking to a business group in New York, he explained, "Today's Labour party, new Labour, is a party of the centre as well as the centre-left."[34] A caucus colleague in the House of Commons framed matters as follows:

> The defining values of the Labour party include a belief that opportunities should be opened up, that unfair privilege should be tackled and that individuals do not exist in a vacuum, but need the power of community ties to help them succeed.[35]

Labour was apparently tacking toward the broad center, anxious to assuage the lingering worries of middle-class voters about its intentions in power.

What these statements meant in concrete terms was hard to pin down. Blair said he believed in modernizing Britain by providing better public education, a reformed welfare system, and training for the unemployed.[36] He backed away from any talk of renationalizing industries that the Tories had sold off or of undoing Conservative legislation on trade unions.[37] A Blair government seemed committed to some decentralization of government power, especially in Scotland and Wales, and to the election of mayors in major cities, including London. Labour said it would consider reforms to the House of Lords, again avoiding specifics and downplaying the issue.[38]

After investing considerable energy in the fight over nominations, Labour women faced a party leadership that did not want to commit on policy substance. The new clause 4 wording spoke of gender equality in a democratic society, but the implications of this language were not obvious. Blair's government was expected to implement a national minimum wage as one way of ensuring support from unions and women's groups. But if the hourly rate began at an extremely low level, as observers predicted, it would show how business groups remained far more influential than either feminist or labor interests.

Reactions against EMILY's List in 1993 revealed another potential problem, namely, a solid antichoice element within the party. One Labour feminist who endorsed moderation on economic issues was surprised by the vigor of that campaign. Speaking in 1993 when John Smith headed the party, she declared:

> Since the 1967 Abortion Act passed, there have been twenty-two attempts to roll it back. Our [Labour] party leader has only abstained on some of these votes. People tend to push abortion away, saying it is not important, but it is a very fragile victory.

Women who held a radical outlook were even more suspicious. One argued:

> Only four of our twenty-two [Labour] cabinet jobs are reserved for women. And it was only after a bitter struggle that we got four out of twenty-two. Backlash means that "equal opportunities is a luxury we can't afford," in the words of many Labourites. . . . The socialist feminist presence in the Labour party is now very weak, nearly absent.

Efforts by Blair's closest advisers during the spring of 1996 to control statements by shadow cabinet minister Clare Short reinforced a sense that the new Labour elite was anxious to clamp down on maverick feminists.[39]

Overall, women's movement activists held a cynical view of the British party system.[40] Many believed both Labour and the Conservatives selectively borrowed the rhetoric of feminism for their own electoral purposes. In the words of one respondent, the British parties routinely engaged in "equal opportunism." Labour, for example, talked about the need for a better education system and welfare reform but would not commit to spending money on these proposals. Child care seemed to fall off the agenda during the preelection period. When Tony Blair spoke about social disintegration and weak moral values, movement activists worried that his preference that children be "brought up in a normal, stable family" was no different than the sentiments of Conservatives.[41]

Would Labour be any different in power? Tony Blair was anxious not to be pinned down on taxes or spending, and he learned from Bill Clinton's experiences in the United States to avoid an overly ambitious, unmanageable agenda. Blair could also see the difficulties of bringing a new style of political spouse onto the podium. His wife, who practiced administrative law as Cherie Booth Q. C., faced an inquisitive and often biased press corps who were uncomfortable with a different sort of political wife—much like Hillary Rodham Clinton's situation. Like Bill Clinton, Tony Blair tried to head off the critics by speaking a great deal about the need for parents to focus on the needs of their children. Once again, the omens for feminism were not altogether promising, as movement activists wondered why Britain needed a Labour prime minister to downplay women's careers and advocate traditional family values.

What women's groups could claim as an advantage in Britain was a profound turning away from elements of the Margaret Thatcher legacy. Even though personal ambition remained a positive concept through the mid-1990s, unbounded individualism had worn thin as a unifying public theme. Many Britons saw laissez-faire policies as causing society to break down, which in turn led them to lose faith in the future. Rather than blaming the welfare state for problems like violence and homelessness—as Conservatives had done—members of the general public increasingly identified too much individualism, too much personal greed, as their source. If Tony Blair spoke about revitalizing the National Health Service, for example, it was because surveys showed a wide swath of voters in the United Kingdom endorsed a more, not less, vigorous welfare state.[42]

Labour remained more than twenty percentage points ahead of the Tories in public opinion polls through 1996. Blair's mildly interventionist platform seemed to be paying off, while Conservative claims that he would tax and spend to the point of destroying the country had little effect. Possibly, just possibly, the Thatcher-Major dynasty was nearing an end with the landslide election of a Labour majority government in May 1997.

Assessing the Clinton Years

As was the case with the British Labour party, Democrats in the United States lost a series of pivotal election campaigns before returning to power. Jimmy Carter in 1980, Walter Mondale in 1984, and Michael Dukakis in 1988 ran unsuccessfully as presidential candidates and were defeated in each case by a considerable margin. Republicans seemed to hold a hammerlock on the White House until 1992, when Democrats returned after a twelve-year absence. According to exit polls from that year, more than one-quarter of Republican women crossed over to cast their ballots for Bill Clinton, giving him an edge of about five percentage points over George Bush among female voters.[43]

After a round of glittering inaugural parties in early 1993, Clinton tried to get down to the business of governing. He arrived in Washington with a somewhat indefinite mandate, produced in part by the vote split in 1992. Clinton's electoral victory was more accurately described as George Bush's defeat with the aid of independent candidate Ross Perot. By siphoning off nearly 20 percent of the popular vote, much of it from the Republicans, Perot became the Democrats' incongruous kingmaker. These electoral dynamics meant Perot cast a long shadow over Clinton in the White House. In particular, populist talk of deficit reduction dominated public debate long after 1992, when the U.S. national debt stood at about $4 trillion. This level was about $3 trillion higher than in 1980 when Ronald Reagan assumed office.[44]

During the 1992 presidential campaign, Bill Clinton advocated a "third way" between traditional big government liberals who had dominated the Democratic party, on one side, and antigovernment conservatives like Ronald Reagan and George Bush, on the other. His problem was trying to trace that path from the Oval Office. As a member of the centrist Democratic Leadership Council, Clinton stressed education, job training, and middle-class optimism as the keys to empowering his fellow Americans. As a former governor of Arkansas, he saw U.S. states as an integral part of any new approach to making government leaner, more responsive, and more innovative.

Through the mid-1990s, Bill Clinton had to lead not just in the shadow of an uncertain mandate but also under threat from an unruly Congress. Until 1994, both the House of Representatives and Senate were nominally Democratic, but the independence of elected members meant party labels held little significance. After the midterm elections, Clinton faced a Republican majority in the House under Speaker Newt Gingrich as well as in the Senate under 1996 Republican presidential candidate Bob Dole. With each bill sent up to Capitol Hill even before 1994, Clinton's aides tried to build a workable legislative coalition. Crucial votes were often won with only a slim majority, a fickle margin gained after endless cajoling on the part of the administration. This need for the White House to wheel and deal served to strengthen impressions that Bill Clinton was a president with no bottom line, a charming operator with a "Slick Willie" image and a tremendous need to be liked. The seeming lack of principle in Clinton's behavior, both publicly and in his personal life, offended many groups whose support had helped bring him to the White House.

For women's organizations, First Lady Hillary Rodham Clinton represented both the promise and the angst of a centrist Democratic presidency. Like her husband, Hillary Rodham was a graduate of Yale University Law School. She worked for the House Judiciary Committee during the Watergate period and, after moving to Arkansas, taught law and worked as an advocate on education and child welfare issues. During the 1992 campaign, Hillary Clinton became a high-profile target of Republican family values rhetoric, one part of the social conservative crusade on the American right. As political scientist Zillah Eisenstein describes:

Ms. Clinton was dangled by the Republicans as a radical feminist, an arch-critic of marriage and family, and a defender of children's rights to sue parents. Everyone, including Hillary, seemed to ignore the likelihood that if she had been a radical feminist, she would have run for the presidency herself. Instead, she had chosen to use her remarkable intelligence and skills to redefine the role of political wife.[45]

The source of anxiety for traditionalists was that Hillary Rodham Clinton was not a typical first lady, a dutiful Barbara Bush or a cagey Nancy Reagan who kept their political interventions well hidden.

Unlike others before her, Hillary Rodham Clinton took a public interest in policy issues and White House appointments. The president placed his wife front and center in 1993–94, when she oversaw a complex health care reform package from drawing board to legislation.[46] The fact that this reform tinkered with a profitable private health system led one leading Republican to accuse Hillary Clinton of sounding "a lot like Karl Marx—she hangs around a lot of Marxists."[47] On the other side of the spectrum, leading women's groups were critical of the way health care operated in the United States and endorsed White House proposals for reform. Once these proposals or any other health care package failed to win support in Congress, the political stock of Hillary Rodham Clinton fell sharply. According to observers, she retreated after the health care defeat to a more conventional role as White House hostess, decorator, and voice of the underprivileged.[48]

Related to the volatile political fortunes of Hillary Clinton were ongoing doubts about her personal qualities and those of the president. In terms of character, allegations about Bill Clinton's sex life and real estate investments the couple had made in Arkansas went on and on. Hillary Clinton protested that interest in these matters was fanned by political opponents in Little Rock and on Capitol Hill—an argument that held some validity. The point remained, however, that it was difficult to move forward any legislative program as long as doubts lingered about the president's integrity.

On a bureaucratic level, the Clintons were widely viewed as administratively inept. Some observers claimed the new Democratic administration got off to a disjointed start because of inexperience and sheer disorganization.[49] Women's movement activists who observed the White House at close range wondered how so many intelligent people could be involved in such long meetings and still come up with so little tangible direction. Appointments to the federal judiciary, for example, were very slow in coming, which worried both women's organizations and civil rights groups. When court nominations did come forward, activists wondered how centrist, moderate Supreme Court judges like Ruth Bader Ginsburg could possibly balance the fierce right-wing appointees put in place by Presidents Reagan and Bush.[50] Critics viewed the Clinton administration as insecure and indecisive, willing to raise expectations about issues like gays in the military only to back down when the opposition became heated.

Trade unions felt especially let down by the new president. Labor interests in the American Midwest had worked hard for the Democrats in 1992 but found themselves shut out in later debates over North American free trade. A North American Free Trade Agreement (NAFTA) involving the United States, Canada, and Mexico required congressional approval in the fall of 1993. Clinton insisted during the 1992 presidential campaign that without supplementary or side deals on labor and the environment, he could not endorse the agreement. Once some arrangements were added, Clinton made NAFTA passage his top priority. Leading trade unions, however, believed trilateral free trade would lead to a loss of American jobs. In their view, Clinton in power sold out to business interests and forgot his loyal allies. NAFTA easily passed in both houses of Congress despite the opposition of organized labor.[51]

In relative terms, women's groups were far more effective. Although the Clinton White House withdrew a number of controversial female appointments, including those of Zoë Baird and Lani Guinier to the Justice Department, it did go forward with the naming of Ruth Bader Ginsburg to the Supreme Court and Dr. Joycelyn Elders to the post of surgeon general.[52] Organizations including NOW and the Fund for the Feminist Majority campaigned to ensure the transition team remembered whose votes had helped Clinton win in 1992. Although the president objected at one press conference to having "bean counters" monitor his appointments, he did create more depth in senior positions than had existed in Republican administrations.[53]

Clinton acted decisively at a very early point on the question of abortion access. On his second full day in office, he signed a series of executive orders. One overturned what was known as the Reagan-Bush gag rule that prevented abortion counseling in federally funded health clinics. Another put an end to the Mexico City policy that curtailed U.S. foreign aid to agencies that endorsed contraception or abortion. A third executive order reopened the area of fetal tissue research, and a fourth restored publicly funded abortions in overseas military hospitals.[54] Following the 1993 murder of Dr. David Gunn outside a Florida abortion clinic, Attorney General Janet Reno pressed forward with the Freedom of Access to Clinic Entrances Act, known as the FACE bill.[55]

Also within weeks of his first inauguration ceremony, Clinton signed the Family and Medical Leave Act that had been blocked by presidential vetoes during the Bush years. The act required firms with more than fifty employees to provide workers up to twelve weeks per year of unpaid leave, including to care for a parent, spouse, or child. Under the terms of Family and Medical Leave, three months of unpaid time were as close as American women who worked in large and medium-sized organizations came to a federal maternity leave provision. In the area of welfare policy, the president spoke often about the need to reform the system but did not move his proposals through the Congress.[56] Instead, in 1996 he signed what many feminists saw as a punitive, mean-spirited welfare bill framed by Republican legislators on Capitol Hill.[57]

Policies in a number of other areas, however, were consistently more pro-movement than during the Reagan-Bush years. Proposals to fund violence against women programs were subsumed in a larger crime bill signed by President Clinton in 1994. This law said crimes against women deprived them of civil rights and could be pursued in the federal courts. Rape and wife battering were defined as hate crimes against women, and $26 million was authorized for violence against women programs.[58] The Head Start project for disadvantaged children was expanded in 1994, and Clinton's plans to change education policy toward a model of life-long learning also progressed.[59] Federal support for childhood immunization and infant nutrition increased after 1993, as did tax credits to assist the working poor.[60]

Feminist reactions to these changes were less decisive than they had been before 1992. Whereas it was clear during the Reagan-Bush years who was on which side, things were far less straightforward during the Clinton years. Pragmatists in the women's movement focused on what was possible in a new administration, whereas others who were more militant criticized the return to "business as usual" in Washington.[61] Clinton administration proposals on welfare reform tended to draw out their differences: militants saw Clinton's stance as essentially conservative, similar in tone to Reagan-Bush pronouncements. Coming from civil rights and grassroots feminist backgrounds, these activists argued that the imagery of black single mothers as a drain on the welfare system continued in Clinton administration statements. By way of contrast, moderates believed the president's ap-

proach was realistic and practical, although most shared the radicals'
view that changes to welfare held dangerous implications for poor
families.

Parallel tensions among feminists emerged on issues of family leave
and abortion. In the view of moderates, the passage of the Family and
Medical Leave Act was an enormous step forward. Yet militants
claimed the bill had been weakened to the point that, according to
one critic,

> [f]or 90 percent of women workers, unpaid leave is impossible,
> so the Family and Medical Leave Act is really a joke. But it does
> come out of this phony U.S. tradition of rugged individualism. I
> believe we should fight for guaranteed annual income and wel-
> fare reform and for single-payer health care. We should go for
> radical solutions and talk about welfare and education and what
> it's all doing. We need to see what *should* happen, not what we
> can settle for.

Like others who shared the same point of view, this militant argued
that race and class differences among women were ignored by moderates who framed their positions in terms of what could be won. A
similar division was clear on the abortion issue. Moderates celebrated
Clinton's executive orders overturning the gag rule and the Mexico
City policy. Militants, on the other hand, cited continued limits on
Medicaid funding for poor women's abortions as evidence that policy
success under the Clinton administration only benefited the white
middle class.[62]

What both streams shared in early 1994 was confusion over their
relationship to the Democratic administration. Clinton appointed a
number of movement activists to prominent positions, a fact that made
opposing the White House more complicated than it was during the
Reagan and Bush years. Switching from a position as policy outsiders
to insiders affected public perceptions, especially in the abortion field.
If basic rights were no longer at risk, would dollars continue to flow to
women's organizations? Through the months following Clinton's election, according to activists, the sense that earlier problems had been
solved translated into fewer donations to groups like Planned Parenthood and the National Abortion Rights Action League. Yet few worried
that a new era of movement complacency was on the horizon. According to militants as well as moderates, the presence of record numbers of elected women at all levels meant feminism was moving closer
to power in the United States.[63] In fact, 1992 was christened the "Year
of the Woman" when females took about 5 percent of seats in the U.S.

Senate, 11 percent in the House of Representatives, and 20 percent in state legislatures.[64]

It was especially hard to be complacent after the 1994 elections. The arrival of a Republican majority in both houses of Congress resulted in part from gender gap patterns that year. Among American women, turnout decreased 6 percent from 1992 levels, while it rose 7 percent among men.[65] Exit polls showed more than 60 percent of white men voted for Republican candidates in 1994.[66] As *Washington Post* columnist E. J. Dionne explained the results, "The 1994 earthquake was caused by the energy of Motivated Republicans and the indifference or outright hostility of Demoralized Democrats."[67]

Before 1994, Bill Clinton had tried to lead as a balanced voice of the American middle class. He was a concerned neoliberal who talked about education and family life, a centrist who refused to believe that only conservatives could discuss American values. Clinton insisted people needed opportunities to make their lives better. He maintained, for example, that teenagers who lived in families that worked and spent time together would not kill each other with semiautomatic weapons. Lifting a page from the Reagan book of spiritual optimism, Clinton proclaimed in 1994:

> Let's give our children a future. Let us take away their guns and give them books. Let us overcome their despair and replace it with hope. . . . Let us not reserve the better angels only for natural disasters, leaving our deepest and most profound problems to petty political fighting. Let us instead be true to our spirit, facing facts, coming together, bringing hope, and moving forward.[68]

The problem was that in 1994, less compromising voices about values were again on the ascent.

After serving as minority leader in the House of Representatives, Newt Gingrich became House Speaker in early 1995. The legislative blueprint he held in his hands at that point was covered with the fingerprints of the American social right. Gingrich's Contract with America, labeled the Contract on America by its critics, set out to overturn state and society in a manner consistent with the wishes of groups like the Christian Coalition. Among other things, it promised to reinstate the gag rule on abortion counseling, cut taxes on business and capital gains, and eliminate welfare benefits for single mothers.

Although Gingrich and his allies were not altogether successful in passing this agenda, they did make considerable headway. Early on, funds for the Congressional Caucus on Women's Issues were cut off.[69] Gingrich managed to shift the language of public debate back onto Republican turf, away from the more nuanced talk of the Clinton White House. The divisive discourse of the Reagan-Bush years was back with a vengeance, as the Republican leadership in the House of Representatives castigated single mothers, welfare entitlements, and the "sick," "pathetic" waste brought about by high-spending liberals.[70] Bill Clinton was portrayed as an unprincipled president who campaigned from the center but governed to the left. Overall, the Republican strategy was designed to topple an already shaky administration.

The impact of the midterm elections was loud and clear on two issues, abortion and affirmative action. Despite vetoing a number of Republican bills, Clinton did sign legislation containing antichoice provisions. As summarized by journalist Katha Pollitt, these laws contained

> riders that bar military hospitals from performing abortions, even if women pay for them with their own money; deny abortion coverage in health insurance for federal workers; ban research on embryos; and gut foreign aid funds for family planning.[71]

The backward motion of 1980 and following thus returned after 1994, even while a Democratic president held office.

At least as damaging as these compromises were changes that watered down affirmative action policy. After a series of employment setbacks in the Supreme Court during the Bush years, women's groups and civil rights organizations faced further erosion in 1995 and later. Attempts to end government policies that favored women as well as minorities began in California, where Republican Governor Pete Wilson raised the issue in his bid for the presidential nomination. Wilson made little progress in his campaign against Bob Dole but did add nasty invective to the fight against affirmative action. In Wilson's words, "We must not allow our country to be infected by the deadly virus of tribalism."[72]

Opposition grew from white males who claimed affirmative action was limiting their job and educational opportunities. At the same time, conservative judges continued to chip away at the same targets they had identified during the Bush years. In a crucial 1995 decision in *Adarand Constructors, Inc. v. Peña,* the Supreme Court set out strict new criteria for set-aside programs. The case involved one construction company owned by Hispanics that obtained a government contract even though its bid was higher than that of Adarand, a white-owned firm which brought forward the judicial challenge. The Court struck down the federal program giving preferential treatment to minority-owned businesses *except* in narrowly defined cases of compelling public interest. Writing for the conservative majority, Justice Sandra Day O'Connor said strict scrutiny was imposed "to smoke out illegitimate uses of race by assuring that the legislative body is pursuing a goal important enough to warrant use of a highly suspect tool."[73] Both judges appointed by the Clinton administration, Ruth Bader Ginsburg and Stephen Breyer, were in the minority on this 5–4 decision.

A firm conservative majority also held sway in other 1995 rulings by the Supreme Court. Justices imposed the same strict limits on electoral districts created to represent black or Hispanic majorities as they did on government contracting. Moreover, the high court threw out a lower court order on local school funding. Demands that inner-city schools in Kansas City be supported more generously to attract affluent suburban students were rejected on the grounds that segregated schools were not necessarily inferior ones. Civil rights supporters were upset by this string of rulings and argued that the Court was reverting to older styles of "judicial racism."[74]

The Clinton White House tried to take a more measured view. *Adarand* was presented as a decision that retained affirmative action in theory but revised it in practice. Speaking in July 1995, the president rejected quotas at the same time as he talked about empowering businesses in poor areas. His conclusion, as usual, was a saw-off that came down considerably short of where women's groups and civil rights organizations would have liked. Clinton summarized his view of affirmative action by declaring, "Mend it but don't end it."[75]

Despite an unruly Congress, the ongoing Whitewater real estate scandal, and a host of other troubles, Bill Clinton seemed over time to weather the storms better. By mid-1996, both Gingrich and Dole wallowed in the polls at the same time as Clinton seemed at last to be finding his way. Democrats described Republican proposals to reduce government spending as an angry attack on school lunch programs, Head Start, infant nutrition, and the Clinton education programs. Packaged inside Newt Gingrich's budget initiatives, major increases in defense spending were proposed, along with tax changes to assist the wealthy. Programs that assisted less fortunate Americans through Medicare, Medicaid, the Earned Income Tax Credit (for the working poor), and food stamps faced vast erosion under Republican proposals.

Although Newt Gingrich launched his term as House Speaker in triumphant style, he operated during 1996 and 1997 in a far more chastened state. President Clinton ended up vetoing about a dozen bills passed by the Republican Congress during 1995–96, while House Speaker Gingrich managed to pass only a small part of his Contract with America agenda. Among the significant pieces of legislation stopped by Clinton in his first term was one that would have prohibited late-term abortions. The president's poll ratings rose as the threat to social spending and women's rights implied by the Republican onslaught became better known. In the words of Washington commentator Elizabeth Drew, "Gingrich had provided Clinton with the means for resuscitating his Presidency."[76]

The Clinton administration, however, was unable and unwilling to return American women's groups to their pre-Reagan status. The vitality and momentum that organized feminism enjoyed before 1980 had been tested through many long, difficult years. Its articulate and well-funded critics grew more vigorous, more outspoken through the 1990s. Typified by the newly elected House Republicans, these opponents were intent on rolling back remnants of equal rights, abortion access, affirmative action, and so on, that remained in place. Attacks on targets including Hillary Rodham Clinton, pregnant teenagers, and the American counterculture were all part of a powerful brake on movement progress.

Within an environment that demanded deficit control and minimalist government, the Clinton administration tried to offer enough to its supporters to get them to the polls in 1996—but not so much that opponents could go on the offensive against the Democrats. All told, the payoffs to constituencies like women's groups were paltry in substantive terms but relatively generous at the level of rhetoric. As always, the concern of the Democratic party leadership was with the other side, the stubborn champions of the social right who treasured their core ground on values, freedom, and the American family. The scene suggested a mixed metaphor: Bill Clinton worked to keep the right-wing wolves at bay as he tried to shelter an uneasy center and center-left flock under his own tent. The fact that Clinton won a second term in 1996 demonstrated neoliberals could build a successful electoral coalition, even as they disappointed many of their supporters on policy substance.

Canadian Liberals since 1993

The 1993 Canadian elections were a watershed in many respects. Under the leadership of Kim Campbell, Brian Mulroney's successor as Conservative chief, the Tories nearly disappeared from the political map. Two new parties, one in English Canada and the other in Quebec, gained the bulk of opposition seats in the new Parliament. Canada's traditional third party at the federal level, the left-of-center New Democratic party, was vastly weakened to the point that neither it nor the Conservatives could claim official status in the House of Commons.

These shifts directly affected the behavior of the new government. Led by Jean Chrétien, a party veteran from the Trudeau years and before, the Liberals returned to power after a nine-year absence. Chrétien's cabinet could draw on members from all regions of Canada, but the strength of new parties made his majority government far less stable than in usual times. In Quebec, where Chrétien had built his political base decades earlier, a separatist party running at the federal level managed to win about half the popular vote and fifty-four of seventy-five seats. The founding of the Bloc québécois in 1990 was a direct result of constitutional fumbles during the Conservative years when Lucien Bouchard, a star Quebec minister brought to Ottawa by Brian Mulroney, left the government caucus and helped to form the Bloc. Bouchard remained a powerful thorn in the side of all federalist politicians. As de facto leader of the yes side in the 1995 Quebec referendum campaign, Bouchard came within a whisper of triumph. His ability to convey soft sovereignist arguments contrasted directly with Chrétien's creaky image in Quebec as an uncompromising federalist, "yesterday's man" in the view of many francophones.

The challenge posed by the Bloc in Quebec emerged at the same time as the right populist Reform party grew stronger in English Canada. Under the leadership of Preston Manning, Reform developed as an alternative to the Tories among fiscal conservatives and moral crusaders in western Canada and gained fifty-two federal seats in 1993. Like far right parties elsewhere, Reform drew most of its support from male voters, with women constituting less than 40 percent of the party's electorate in 1993.[77] Reform initially ran on a platform of western alienation. It argued for more regional representation in central government institutions and for a less rigidly disciplined House of Commons. Moreover, the party attracted a solid base of decentralists who wanted to reduce Ottawa's debt by downloading federal responsibilities to the provinces. Among the social right of the Reform party were devotees of REAL Women and many rank-and-file members who believed feminists wielded considerable power in Canadian politics.[78] These partisans were often antiabortion, anti–Charter of Rights, and anti–gay rights but vigorously in favor of government subsidies for mothers who stayed at home with their children.

Together, the rise of both new parties put the squeeze on women's concerns at the federal level. Bloc victories in more than fifty seats in Quebec reduced the flow of pro–social welfare M.P.'s to the Liberal caucus. Instead of being inside the government as in previous decades, these legislators sat in a separate pro-Quebec caucus that could not speak for the rest of Canada. Without their presence, the Liberals lurched farther and farther to the right. This pattern was compounded by the pressure from Reform, which threatened to eclipse Liberals (and not just Conservatives) in English Canada. In other words, the new government caucus contained only minimal progressive content from Quebec and a nervous contingent from elsewhere than kept looking over its shoulder at the Reform party.

In terms of elite-level participation, the 1993 election results were far from promising. Both major parties led by women were crushed. Kim Campbell was eased out of the Conservative leadership within months of the debacle, while Audrey McLaughlin announced her intention to quit as leader of the New Democrats. Virtually no feminist issue content made its way into election coverage, even though unprecedented numbers of women campaigned as major party candidates. Fifty-four women were elected in 1993 to the House of Commons, representing a record 18 percent of Canadian M.P.'s. Yet these women sat in an extremely fractious and polarized legislature, with thirty-six on the Liberal side, nine in the Bloc, seven in the Reform caucus, and one each in the Conservative and New Democratic rumps.[79]

If any possibilities for progress existed after 1993, they rested in the hands of Liberal women. The party's campaign cochair was Chaviva Hošek, a former president of the National Action Committee on the Status of Women who helped to write the 1993 Liberal campaign document, known as the Red Book. Hošek became a policy adviser in the Prime Minister's Office after the election. Jean Chrétien also named Sheila Copps as deputy party leader in 1993. Copps was an aggressive debater, well known in the Mulroney years for having told one Conservative cabinet minister, "I'm nobody's baby."[80]

The problems facing Hošek, Copps, and others like them, however, were enormous. The Mulroney government bequeathed a federal debt of about $500 billion, or roughly $300 billion more than the Liberals had left in 1984.[81] As a result, Chrétien named his most fiscally conservative colleagues to key economic portfolios. Liberals on the left or social side of the party found themselves marginalized by powerful business Liberals like Finance Minister Paul Martin. Copps's brash style also made things more difficult, since she promised on a number of occasions to step down if the government did not eliminate the national consumption tax (or GST) brought in by the Tories. Copps was forced to resign temporarily from cabinet and the House of Commons in 1996, which further weakened the social Liberal ranks.

Jean Chrétien pledged in opposition and during the 1993 campaign to strengthen the federal welfare state created in the 1960s and 1970s. Once in office, though, his tune changed very abruptly. Power was centralized around the prime minister and key economic ministers so that efforts to outflank the Reform party on fiscal matters and neutralize the Bloc on questions of Quebec sovereignty took precedence over all else. Within a few years of assuming power, the new Liberals under Jean Chrétien bore almost no resemblance to those of earlier times. If Chrétien and his team campaigned from the left in 1993, they clearly governed to the right after that point.

The contrast between what the Liberals promised and what they delivered was stark. Chrétien capitalized on his reputation as an earthy scrapper, the little guy from Shawinigan who, according to the title of his autobiography, spoke straight from the heart.[82] According to a critical account coauthored by feminist and anti–free trade campaigner Maude Barlow, called *Straight through the Heart,* the Liberals won office based on this phony imagery:

> The party ran on a progressive platform: opposition to NAFTA, patronage, corporate power, the GST, American dominance; support for jobs, training, little people, small business, universal social programs, Canadian culture, medicare. "I don't want a ... system for the rich and a system for the poor," said Jean Chrétien.[83]

Women's groups were particularly hopeful about one section of the Liberal platform that promised the creation of more child care spaces if economic growth reached 3 percent a year.[84]

Arguably the greatest damage the Liberals caused Canadian women came from massive spending changes. A social policy review undertaken during the fall of 1994 raised expectations in NAC and other groups that improved funding for child care might be on the way at last. These hopes proved groundless, however, once the details of the 1995 federal budget were announced. Instead of widening opportunities for working women and mothers on welfare, Paul Martin's plans undermined much of the social policy apparatus of the federal state. Ottawa proposed eliminating the foundation of shared-cost programs under the 1966 Canada Assistance Plan (CAP) and replacing it with a new Canada Health and Social Transfer (CHST). The transfer would involve smaller, U.S.-style block grants to the provinces for health, education, and social assistance. Over the first two years of the CHST, federal funding would be cut by about $7 billion.[85]

Criticism of the new CHST from women's groups was loud and clear. According to the June 1995 NAC newsletter, the federal government effectively vacated the social policy field once it decided to eliminate the Canada Assistance Plan. NAC maintained that

> [e]nding CAP will have a particularly negative effect on women. Women stand to lose the right to receive financial assistance based on need; the right to receive an amount of income adequate to meet basic requirements; the right not to be forced into workfare programs; and the right to appeal decisions of social assistance agencies.[86]

Paul Martin's restructuring of health, welfare, and higher education was thus seen as a way to cut federal spending and, at the same time, allow provinces to play off these areas against each other. In NAC's view, the losers would most likely be welfare mothers and their children.

The link between Martin's 1995 budget and earlier Mulroney initiatives was clear. NAC condemned the budget as "implementing the Charlottetown Accord through the back door," in the sense that both policies decentralized the country by offering money to provinces with few strings attached.[87] Women's ability to protest these changes was also reduced by both Conservative and Liberal governments. Under the terms of the 1995 budget, the federal Women's Program was slated to be cut 5 percent in each of the next three years. As the bulk of part-time workers, women were also likely to bear the brunt of tighter rules imposed by the Liberals on eligibility for unemployment benefits.

The imposition of the Canada Health and Social Transfer followed the broad lines of Liberal policy after 1993. Paul Martin's 1994 budget chopped $5.5 billion from Unemployment Insurance programs and $2 billion from spending on welfare and higher education.[88] Liberals closed down both the Canadian Advisory Council on the Status of Women and the Family Violence Initiative, and they backed off from earlier promises to fund fifteen thousand new child care spaces.[89] The federal government released plans in 1995 to cut forty-five thousand civil service jobs and reduce spending by about $25 billion, about one-third of it in the areas of health, education, unemployment insurance, and welfare.[90] Each of these decisions came on top of moves by the previous Conservative government to defund women's advocacy work, to limit or cap transfers under the Canada Assistance Plan, and to tighten unemployment eligibility rules while lowering benefits. In short, the money crunch begun during the Mulroney years became far more harsh under the Chrétien regime.

According to a NAC statement on the 1995 budget, "The public sector is a major source of full-time, adequately paid jobs for women."[91] As a result, the organization claimed efforts to cut forty-five thousand federal positions would have direct effects not just on unemployment rates but also on quality-of-life concerns for thousands of Canadian families. Moreover, the accompanying reductions in federal transfer payments were seen as limiting the ability of women who worked in the health, education, or welfare sectors to find jobs at provincial or local levels.

The cumulative effects of Conservative and Liberal spending reductions were clear by early 1995. NAC reported that only 27 percent of its annual budget came from federal sources, down from nearly 90 percent during the early 1980s. The organization's deficit for the fiscal year ending in March 1994 was more than $60,000—the highest since NAC was founded twenty-two years earlier.[92] Because advocacy groups focused on the impact of social policy changes, however, Liberal actions in these other areas were hardly noticed. The closing down in 1995 of the federal advisory council on the status of women, for example, was followed by what one journalist termed a "muted outcry." In the words of reporter Susan Delacourt, "the Liberals had an easy time axing the twenty-year-old institution."[93]

The Liberal government was aided in part by its conciliatory demeanor. Unlike the Mulroney Conservatives, who refused in 1989 and following to meet the NAC lobby on Parliament Hill, the Liberals insisted on appearing to be open, inclusive, and consultative. During the spring of 1994, a record thirty-nine members of the government caucus participated in the NAC lobby. According to NAC's own account of the event, the 1994 Liberal turnout was "the largest representation from any government in the history of the lobby."[94] It was also significantly different from the response of the Reform party, which refused to meet the lobby at all.

Some Canadians who had believed the substance of 1993 Liberal campaign promises felt they had been duped. Instead of a socially committed government that worked to undo the damage of the Mulroney years, the new cabinet appeared to worsen matters by handing over the social policy reins to the provinces. In the words of Maude Barlow and Bruce Campbell:

A mere fifteen months after the Canadian electorate swept the Liberals to power on a platform that flatly rejected the 'neoconservative' path, the government was embracing Tory policies on a scale their predecessors would not have dared to implement. Through changes to the fiscal structure, they were dismantling government and decentralizing the federation well beyond what was proposed in the Meech Lake Accord. . . . Canada was becoming a federation of ten sovereignties.[95]

It was little wonder that Brian Mulroney gushed with admiration when asked about the new government's policies.[96]

In terms of other costs to Canadian women, the Liberals' decision to sign NAFTA was notable. The party since 1988 had endorsed English Canadian nationalist arguments against continental integration, against the consequences of both Canada-U.S. and Canada-U.S-Mexico free trade for jobs and social standards. Like the Clinton administration, however, the Chrétien government flipped to the other side and adopted pro-business, pro-NAFTA claims once in power.

Women also suffered collateral damages in the Supreme Court of Canada. As movement activists predicted, the retirement of progressive judges appointed during the Trudeau years produced enormous effects later on. Their replacements were more conservative Mulroney appointees who put an end to the pattern of pro-movement judgments rendered before 1993. In 1994, for example, the Supreme Court ruled in *R. v. Daviault* that a drunken man who had been accused of assaulting a woman with disabilities should get a new trial.[97] In *R. v. Borden,* it upheld a lower court acquittal of a repeat sex offender who raped an elderly woman, arguing that a blood sample from the defendant had been improperly obtained. These decisions and others like them suggested an American due process approach was replacing the older social order view at the core of Canadian criminal law. Critics maintained that Mulroney's judicial appointees were turning the Charter of Rights and Freedoms into a charter of rights for criminals.[98]

In two decisions in 1995, the Court agreed to allow the use of complainants' personal records in cases of sexual assault. Summarizing the implications of *R. v. O'Connor* and *L.L.A. v. A.B.* for the Women's Legal Education and Action Fund, law professor Karen Busby maintained:

Disclosure applications will become routine in sexual violence cases and, if trial judges follow the example of the Supreme Court of Canada, equality and privacy rights will have no impact on the decisions whether to release records to the accused. Practically speaking, an accused's fair trial rights in sexual violence cases now mean use whatever means you can to secure an acquittal rather than get the truth properly and fairly.[99]

The Court's 1997 ruling in the case of Nick Carosella, a schoolteacher charged with sexual assault, reinforced this pattern. By a 5–4 margin, the justices declared Carosella was denied a fair trial because the rape crisis center where the complainant in the case sought advice had shredded the interview notes.[100] As in previous periods, women's groups pressured the federal cabinet to pass legislation that would override these decisions.

In 1995 and following, Justice Minister Allan Rock presented a series of legislative proposals designed to address critics of the Supreme Court. One bill responded to the *Daviault* decision by limiting the use of extreme drunkenness as a defense in violent crimes like sexual assault. Another was slated to limit the use of victims' counseling records and other documents in cases of sexual assault.[101] Rock also extended gun control laws enacted during the Mulroney years by imposing mandatory gun registration despite opposition from the Reform party and other pro-firearms interests.

In the family law field, women's groups were angered by the 1994 decision of the Chrétien government to appeal the *Thibaudeau* case to the Supreme Court. Suzanne Thibaudeau, a divorced social worker living in Quebec, claimed it was unfair to tax support payments received by custodial parents, usually mothers. Canada at the time made child support payments fully tax deductible for payors, usually fathers. Thibaudeau's win in the Federal Court of Appeal was overturned by the Supreme Court of Canada, despite interventions on her side by a coalition including NAC and the Women's Legal Education and Action Fund. Whereas intervenors claimed the tax system discriminated against women, Justice Minister Allan Rock maintained the appeal court ruling was confusing and costly for the federal government.[102]

In their 1996 budget, the Liberals responded to *Thibaudeau* by phasing out both tax deductibility for ex-spouses who paid and taxation for those who received child support. These revised rules affected new or renegotiated support arrangements as of May 1997 and following. The government announced that federal and provincial levels would begin a coordinated effort to get parents, mostly fathers, who failed to pay support to pay up. In addition, the Chrétien government raised annual supplements paid to the working poor from a maximum of $500 to $1,000 over a two-year period.[103] Each of these changes was viewed as inadequate by women's organizations and antipoverty groups. According to them, off-loading social programs to the provinces and refusing to help families on welfare far outweighed any positive contributions in the Liberal budget.

Additional trouble in the family law field was expected to follow from a 1996 Supreme Court ruling. In the *Goertz v. Gordon* case, a majority of justices agreed to permit a custodial parent to move herself and her daughter to Australia, but only because the child's father could afford to visit her in Australia. This judgment was viewed as a threat to maternal custody in most other cases, when monies for the father to travel and for the mother to defend her custodial decisions in court were not usually available.[104]

Overall, high court rulings after 1993 suggested the retirement of Trudeau appointees was enormously significant, because the Charter of Rights and Freedoms by itself seemed to guarantee women little in the way of substantive progress. The Chrétien government announced in 1994 that the Court Challenges Program would be reinstated, but observers questioned whether renewed funding would make much difference. After all, pro-equality judges on the Supreme Court after 1985—combined with the presence of the Charter and Court Challenges money—had put feminist litigation over the top. Without those judges, Canadian women were perhaps not much better off than they were during the pre-Charter period. Canada's constitution had changed, but this language had limited effect unless sympathetic judges breathed life into it.

Yet another area in which women's gains were under threat was in the field of public pensions. Since a proposal during the Mulroney years to deindex old age payments was shelved after it caused an uproar, the Liberals were cautious about any new ideas. They created a national consultation process to smooth the way before any major revisions were introduced but did make some changes in the 1996 budget. Paul Martin announced that beginning in 2001, a fully indexed, tax-free Seniors Benefit would replace the Old Age Security and Guaranteed Income Supplement programs. The new benefit would be targeted rather than universal, geared to low- and middle-income seniors based on the income of retired households rather than individuals.

According to the finance minister, the purpose of the changes was "to assure Canadians that the pension system will be there for them in the future, as it has been in the past."[105] As one response to an aging population, the Seniors Benefit represented a scaling back of payments to upper-income retirees to direct benefits elsewhere. The view of the National Action Committee on the Status of Women was quite different, however. NAC claimed that replacing universal programs like Old Age Security with a means-tested scheme based on household income denied many women an independent benefit in their old age. The Seniors Benefit, after all, would not be paid to women whose husbands had retirement income above a specified limit. Moreover, the ongoing review of pensions policy held out a larger threat of lower payments for all retirees.[106]

The ability of women's organizations to respond to these developments remained in question. Although Canadian feminism was far from demobilized in social movement terms by the mid-1990s, it seemed more politically distant and demoralized than during the previous decade. As one activist reluctantly concluded, "I think women are going downhill." Others argued that members of the general public were turned off by the hypocrisy, deceit, and greed of the Mulroney years and by a sense that the Liberals, too, had let them down. Attempts to rally support for a progressive position on social welfare issues were limited by this cynicism and by the spread of an individualist ethos that saw little need for the public provision of social goods. Respondents referred to "a turning away from empathy," a growing "emphasis on personal responsibility," and "the building of walls, the retrenching, the lessening of a feeling of community and openness" during the 1980s and 1990s. Among moderates, the policy agendas of NAC and other groups appeared to have grown so large and diverse as to be unmanageable in hard times.

In terms of finding an effective voice within this environment, women faced considerable odds. The most cogent defense of social spending in the House of Commons after 1993 came from the Bloc québécois, a party that hardly shared the preference of the English Canadian women's movement for a strong federal government. Yet this centralist view seemed increasingly marginal even within English Canada. Liberal plans to reduce transfer payments and shift responsibility for social policy to the provinces offered little hope for a reassertion of federal primacy. NAC and its constituent groups faced a new reality in which women's claims would have to be staked out province by province, even as government funding for advocacy continued to shrink.

Canadian feminists' ability to defend their claims was also limited by the popularity of the Chrétien government. Unlike the situation during the Mulroney years, conditions after 1993 did not permit sustained attacks on the credibility and trustworthiness of the prime minister. NAC and other vocal opponents of the Conservatives connected each object of their scorn to Brian Mulroney, who provided a useful target whether the debate concerned free trade, constitutional reform, or federal budget decisions. This convenient shorthand was gone after 1993, when a more experienced governing party held power.

Yet feminists remained doubtful about Liberal intentions, convinced that conservative times were not necessarily over in 1993. Jean Chrétien's brand of new Liberalism imposed a far tighter fiscal regime than Brian Mulroney's ostensible Conservatism ever did. Changes to the Canadian welfare state had the effect of transferring both more control and less money to the provinces, a lethal combination for any interest that desired generous benefits under firm national standards. Instead of Supreme Court decisions that pushed the limits of pro-equality thought, rulings after 1993 moved ominously in the reverse direction. The Liberals pressed forward with NAFTA, pension reform, and other changes that threatened to undercut what was left in the domain of national social policy. Overall, Canadian women's organizations found little to cheer about in the record of the Chrétien government.

Prospects for Change

Judging by the record of what the British Labour party said it would do in power and what the Clinton and Chrétien governments did once elected, women's movement activists had reason to be suspicious of these new regimes. As Labour leader in 1994 and following, Tony Blair surrounded himself with a loyal cadre of party moderates who had little patience for groups in general. The emphasis of new Labour was on the enterprising potential of aspiring individuals, not on the kinds of social obstacles and discriminatory practices that women's groups had long highlighted. Blair rejected what he described as "the old-fashioned collectivism of Labour," a group focus he associated with sclerotic trade unions and other organized interests.[107]

New Labour was in this sense close to a carbon copy of traditional Conservatism, because it talked a great deal about the need to find consensus, build toward conciliatory solutions, and allow individuals to flourish in a healthy social environment. About the only direct challenge new Labour presented to new Conservatism was its denial of social conflict as a useful device for governing. Tony Blair insisted that moral values could not develop in a vacuum, and he argued that Thatcherism had taken British society too far down the road of divisive, unbridled individualism. Blair also made some concessions to the idea that Britain had become overly centralized in the Thatcher-Major years.

Clearly, his ideas did not represent the forceful break with new Conservatism that so many women's groups desired in a post-Thatcher, post-Major Britain. There was no decisive embrace of social solutions to public problems in the Tony Blair worldview and no apparent willingness to place the concerns of organized feminism front and center in any new Labour manifesto. Like the Clinton Democrats and the Chrétien Liberals, the Blair team in the Labour party was an intensely centralized club that focused its attention on one leader and one objective: winning elections. A group of expert insiders helped to run what looked to be a permanent campaign organization within the leader's office. Party dissidents, including outspoken feminists, were wedged aside in new Labour's pursuit of top-down control and electoral respectability. For women's movement activists who had long struggled to survive the Tory dynasty, the prospects for change under Labour seemed slight but, given the absence of any viable parliamentary alternative, worth the risk in any case.

The record of President Bill Clinton since his 1993 inauguration was at least as checkered. Democrats arrived in the White House carrying tremendous expectations for change but formidable constraints on what could be accomplished. Clinton often had trouble making his way given personal scandals, differences between his views and those of many Democrats in Congress, and the legacy of the Reagan-Bush period. High government deficits plus limited support for an activist federal government meant Clinton operated with very few degrees of freedom. Part of what he delivered to pro-choice groups immediately after taking office was rolled back once Republicans won the 1994 midterm elections. Other changes including provisions for unpaid family leave were minuscule compared with the statutory paid leave in place in Britain, Canada, and elsewhere by the 1990s.

What American women's groups could claim in their favor was the decentralized federal system, in which innovation did not necessarily come from the national level as it did in the unitary British case. Also, feminism in the United States had a long history of successful lobbying, litigating, and fund-raising, activities that could continue no matter what president lived in the White House. The diffusion of power in the American system combined with the interest group strategy of women's organizations meant there was no absolute blockage of progress even in the worst of times. According to activists, the Clinton record was far from entirely negative. The problem was that good and bad were mixed together in a complicated brew. Times were obviously not as good as they had been before 1980, but neither were things as bad as they had been between 1980 and 1992.

The situation in Canada after the Liberals returned to power in 1993 and again in June 1997 was, ironically, in many ways worse than during the Mulroney years. As a more popular prime minister, Jean Chrétien was able to effect changes in federal social policy that dwarfed any revisions even contemplated by his Conservative predecessors. Brian Mulroney's appointees to the Supreme Court put a stop to the series of pro-equality judgments rendered between 1985 and 1992, when judges nominated by Pierre Trudeau dominated the high court. The Chrétien Liberals thus represented a worst-case scenario for social movements, because they arrived in power promising to right the wrongs of the Conservatives but actually went further on welfare state cuts than Tory prime ministers Brian Mulroney and Kim Campbell. Above all, Jean Chrétien oversaw an eclipse of the Canadian federal state to a degree unimaginable under earlier Liberal prime ministers.

Like the Clinton Democrats and Blairites in the Labour party, however, the Chrétien Liberals continued to talk a compassionate neoliberal line. Much of what they did to weaken federal social standards was so complicated that few Canadians grasped the significance of what was happening. Alarm bells had been ringing for so long about the previous Conservative government that few citizens wanted to believe their situation would actually deteriorate further under the new Liberal regime. Moreover, the oppositional stance of organized feminism in English Canada had become entrenched in the public mind since the period of the 1988 free trade debate. Unlike elements of the British women's movement, which moved over time toward interest group strategies and a pragmatic political orientation, and unlike the overwhelmingly moderate approach of American women's groups since the late 1960s, the Canadian movement seemed increasingly radical and confrontational during the 1990s. This pattern suggested that the formal political successes of Canadian feminism during the Mulroney years had *not* led to a shift away from social movement strategies.

Theories of group formation posit that social movement success frequently results in institutionalization and a growing reliance on standard interest group approaches.[108] Whereas the cases of the modern U.S. and British women's movements arguably fit within the broad lines of this model, developments in Canada suggested a divergent path from moderation toward radicalization—meaning rejection over time by peak organizations of conventional pressure group tactics and, concomitantly, the embrace by these interests of confrontational public protest. In short, the leadership of the Canadian women's movement became increasingly distant from mainstream politics, even as that movement appeared from a distance to be among the most effective in formal policy terms in the world.

Overall, Tony Blair, Bill Clinton, and Jean Chrétien all created new paths to the right of their partisan roots. Blair called his trail new Labour, Clinton termed his route a third way, and Chrétien named his path new Liberalism. Their main purpose in each case was to outflank opponents on the political right, but the strategy left older pro-intervention allies wondering when and if they would get any attention. Women's organizations were among those posing the question "What about us?" but neoliberals were in no rush to allay their concerns. Riding a cresting middle wave seemed to serve these leaders well. Clinton and Chrétien worked hard not to offend business interests, adopting a sudden enthusiasm for North American free trade once in office. Clinton raised millions of dollars for the 1996 presidential campaign, while the Canadian Liberals drew record contributions after returning to power.[109] In no case did these leaders want to seem too close to their old allies.

How would women's groups go forward in the shadow of neoconservative leaders and their neoliberal successors? Was it possible to reassert group values in a decidedly individualist age? Chapter 7 speculates on these larger questions.

CHAPTER SEVEN

So What?
The Impact of Conservative Times

Women's experiences in conservative times shed light on a variety of issues. One concerns how right-wing leaders shaped organized feminism and vice versa. Another involves a speculative question about strategy. What can groups do to get their claims across in a stubbornly individualist age?

Conservatives probably exerted their most sustained influence at the level of ideas, where they elevated an unrelenting anticollective ethos. The rhetoric of Margaret Thatcher, Ronald Reagan, Brian Mulroney, and their party successors effectively targeted and undermined group activism, as shown in chapter 1. By attacking the fundamental sense of shared social values that had once guided their own political parties, these leaders changed conservatism in a major way in the Conservative parties of Britain and Canada as well as in the American Republican organization. After 1979, new right-of-center leaders worked to discredit their political critics and public protest in general, while they shielded friendly groups from the same line of attack. In particular, each political executive beginning with the Tory regime in Britain was close to business interests but directed no harsh words in that direction.

Once elected, new conservatives worked to drive a wedge among their opponents. As argued in chapter 5, this tactic further eroded the legitimacy of protest groups because it suggested they did not represent cohesive or coherent interests. A number of prominent women in all three countries subscribed to a credo of unfettered individualism. Typified above all by one achieving titan, Margaret Thatcher, the efforts of these women helped to weaken movements that were critical of conservative directions. Vocal antifeminists along with a curious breed of conditional feminists, who picked away at the movement agenda while claiming to be sympathetic to it, assumed ever-greater political importance. Conservative parties flirted openly with antifeminism and conditional feminism in a manner that served both to unsettle and undermine women's movements.

Over time, right-of-center ideas that glorified the achieving individual and denigrated collective action (except by business groups) became core elements of mainstream political debate in Britain, the United States, and Canada. Government was identified more and more as part of the old-style approach, as a problem rather than a solution to the challenges facing people. The notion of a general interest embodied in civil society was effectively denied, especially in Margaret Thatcher's version of the new conservatism. These claims flew directly in the face of two waves of feminist belief in the positive potential of government action and the need for collective responses to social issues that had been seen as private troubles. The polarization of political debate grew more and more obvious. Although conservatives maintained their adversaries hardly ever found a government program they did not want to expand, it seemed these same right-of-center ideologues rarely saw one they did not want to eliminate. Public debate on many issues became more raucous, nasty, polarized and, not surprisingly, a turnoff to large numbers of citizens.

Chapters 2 through 6 reveal clearly the impact of conservative ideas. A variety of sources including court cases, legislative debates, spending decisions, and interviews with movement activists all point toward the same general conclusion. Simply put, feminist organizations and many women in the general public were often worse off because of conservative actions. Chapter 2 used a straightforward set of measures—namely, high court decisions and national legislative outcomes in key women's movement issue areas. The analysis avoided fields like pornography in which activists disagreed over what constituted a desirable outcome. Instead, it focused on five core priorities for feminists in Britain, the United States, and Canada since about 1970. They were (a) equal rights, including legislative and judicial commitment to women's equality; (b) reform of family law, including divorce policy affecting women and children following marriage dissolution; (c) choice and reproduction, most notably access for women to safe and affordable abortion services; (d) violence against women, including attention to rape and wife assault; and (e) employment rights, including equal pay and child care provisions.

To gauge the effect of conservative leaders, the formal record of pre-Thatcher, pre-Reagan, and pre-Mulroney regimes was compared with what happened *after* these elites came to power. In the British case, women's movements did better before Thatcher and Major came to power than they did following. More than three-quarters of formal outcomes in the five fields were pro-feminist before 1979, compared with 65 percent during the Thatcher years and 57 percent in the Major years. Relatively few pro-movement results from the Conservative years were actually due to British government action. Instead, many followed from pro-feminist decisions—especially in the employment field—by European institutions including the European Court of Justice.

The formal record from the United States showed a dramatic drop in movement influence after Republican presidents were elected. Before 1980, nearly 70 percent of formal outcomes in the five fields were pro-feminist. During the Reagan administration, this level declined to less than one-half; in the Bush years, it sank precipitously to less than 20 percent. Nearly 60 percent of the thirty-five U.S. Supreme Court decisions on movement priorities during the Republican years went against feminist positions. Sustained attempts by American conservatives to turn back feminist claims in the courts, the legislative branch, and the bureaucracy bore fruit in a very measurable way after 1980.

In Canada, a different formal pattern emerged. At a purely box score level of wins and losses, only 50 percent of high court and legislative decisions before 1984 were pro-feminist, versus nearly 90 percent after the Conservatives came to power. One crucial intervening factor was the coming into effect of equality provisions in the Canadian Charter of Rights and Freedoms during the first Mulroney term—a shift that had parallels in neither the United States (where the Equal Rights Amendment went down to defeat in the same period) nor Britain (where the European Court had little influence outside of employment policy). Moreover, the Mulroney Conservatives were far less ideologically driven than were their British and American counterparts.

The point about formal records is that in two of the three cases, women's movements fared demonstrably worse after conservative leaders came to power—and they fared worse over time given the slippage from Thatcher to Major and particularly from Reagan to Bush. The fact that American feminism faced so many reversals after 1980 contradicts assumptions in the comparative literature to the effect that the U.S. movement would have been relatively insulated, first by congressional (as opposed to parliamentary) arrangements and second by a strategy of political independence (as opposed to reliance on coalitions with unions or other groups). The finding that U.S. groups were far from invincible on core movement claims following 1980 casts considerable doubt on the prevailing consensus in the comparative field. In the third case, Canada, the formal record diverged because of a number of factors. Women's groups worked on the constitutional front during the Liberal years to ensure that the Charter of Rights contained strong equality language. Sympathetic judges appointed by the Liberal government before it lost power in 1984 shaped Supreme Court rulings during the Mulroney years. And because they differed from American and British conservatives, Canadian Tories devoted relatively little attention to reversing pro-movement judicial decisions.

The informal side of the record presented in chapters 3 and 4 reveals broadly similar patterns in all three countries. Women's work lives in many cases became more difficult, while public spending on social programs declined and conservatives sought to restrict protest activism. Overall, this money crunch not only impoverished elderly women and single mothers in particular, but it also made group advocacy harder to pursue, because the purse strings were tightened in all three countries. Translating specific troubles that women faced vis-à-vis work and leisure into a more broadly based sense of social problems is always difficult, as American sociologist C. Wright Mills observed decades ago.[1] Yet conservative times after 1979 were especially trying because protest activism was made to seem less valid, less politically legitimate. Official rhetoric that rejected collective mobilization meant groups had a particularly hard time communicating what the money crunch was about and organizing people to confront it.

For this study, more than a hundred women's movement activists in Britain, the United States, and Canada were interviewed about their experiences. Their reflections showed important similarities across cases, because views of Thatcher and Major, Reagan and Bush, Mulroney and Campbell tended to be bitter, negative, and often downright hostile. Women paid a huge price under these leaders, according to most activists, and feminist movements operated on a defensive posture to stop rollbacks and keep what they had previously won—let alone win new gains. The fifteen interviews presented in chapter 4 offer a capsule account of how activists assessed their efforts after 1979. Some believed women's groups had managed to wring a measure of progress out of reluctant political leaders. Many spoke about what they expected following the defeat of conservative elites.

Among the most ominous shadows cast by North American conservatives was their fiscal legacy. Both U.S. President Bill Clinton and Canadian Prime Minister Jean Chrétien faced serious debt problems when they took office in 1993. British Labour leader Tony Blair worried that he would face similar circumstances once the Major government lost power.[2] In each case, new conservatives bequeathed a state that had gradually reduced corporate taxes and personal income taxes in the upper echelons, while they relied on borrowed money and, in Britain and Canada, privatization sell-offs and consumption taxes to finance their activities. Whether defunding the state was part of a conscious plot or simply an unintended consequence of right-wing regimes hardly mattered. The point was that subsequent leaders had a less stable and less fertile revenue base on which to rely, a prospect that directly reinforced the broader goals of the new conservatism.

In addition, Thatcher, Reagan, Mulroney, and their party successors left behind weaker women's movement allies. In Britain, trade unions and local government faced a direct threat from 1979 through the mid-1990s, as a variety of restrictive laws limited labor's ability to organize and municipalities' capacity to act as they do elsewhere. Thatcher and Major centralized control in a system that was already top-down in design, heavily weighted toward traditions of conformity and uncontested power among central government elites. The fact that British Conservatives vastly reduced the clout of any competing source of domestic authority was paralleled by their sustained attack on Europe as an external threat. Elements within the European Union (EU), notably the European Court of Justice, often challenged the decisions of British Conservatives on issues involving women and work. This pattern helps to explain why Tory Euroskeptics viewed the EU as a meddlesome, interventionist body with few if any redeeming qualities.

In the United States, women's groups were on the defensive once civil rights claims came under attack. Decisions by the Reagan and Bush administrations to change sides on key court cases beginning with *Grove City College* meant the machinery of the federal state turned around in its tracks. From an earlier emphasis through the Carter years on empathy, fairness, and federal enforcement of the law, the approach to civil rights reversed with stunning rapidity. After the 1980 elections, Republican administrations elevated their distrust of regulation and their disgust with bureaucracy into a vigorous campaign against federal agencies charged with enforcing civil rights provisions. In addition, although Ronald Reagan insisted he had no animus against what he called the deserving poor, his administration went on the offensive against other recipients of government help. This dichotomy between rightful claimants and undeserving ones was mined to its fullest in a milieu where the roots of racism ran deep. Black welfare mothers were identifiable targets in what became a mean-spirited campaign against social spending.

In Canada, the attack on women's movement allies went into full swing once the Mulroney government decided to pursue continental free trade. Opponents of this policy, including leading trade union, cultural, and antipoverty groups, organized in 1987 as the Pro-Canada Network. Attempts by the network to counter pro-Conservative and pro–free trade messages from a powerful business lobby were most visible during the 1988 federal election campaign. At that point, Brian Mulroney condemned protesters and maintained he was just as Canadian, just as nationalistic, as they were. Conservatives later redoubled their efforts to isolate many of the same groups during debates over the 1992 Charlottetown Accord. Aside from other features, this constitutional proposal involved a clear retreat by the federal government from the social policy field.

As did their counterparts in Britain and the United States, conservatives in Canada cast a wide net in their strategy to marginalize the opposition. The net caught both women's movements and their closest allies, who were struggling to cope with what seemed to be a triumphant cult of individualism. The problem was that the waning power of trade unions required a new counterweight to the power of corporations and business groups. Women's organizations, environmental groups, and antipoverty activists found it difficult to fill that breach, in large part because they were fluid interests with a much less secure base of funding and cohesion than unions had traditionally enjoyed.

Yet feminist interests were more than simply reactive during these years. In all three countries, they tried to seize hold of opportunities that were available to make an impact despite tough times. British groups, for example, pursued a legal strategy that gained significant advances through the House of Lords and the European Court of Justice. Using the court of public opinion as their venue, movement activists also raised important issues of violence against women. They brought in very different allies from the royal family in addition to the police and tabloid press in this unusual campaign.

In the United States, new organizations were established to fund the election campaigns of feminist women. By the mid-1990s, EMILY's List had become one of the most effective political action committees in Washington in terms of dollars collected and candidates elected. Massive pro-choice rallies during the Bush years fueled the impression that women's groups were not about to disappear. Moreover, American women's groups after 1980 used the federal system to work for change at other levels, notably through the passage of state laws on pay equity and violence against women.

In Canada, movement groups litigated in the courts, blocked what they saw as bad legislation in Parliament, and tried to improve provincial laws during the Conservative years. In debates over free trade and constitutional change, feminists in English Canada tried to insert their issues into a larger framework. The consequences of free trade for women's jobs and for Canadian social policy became important themes on the public agenda as a result. On the constitutional front, groups challenged both the closed-door process of reaching consensus and the content of two accords that in their view threatened to decentralize the country beyond recognition.

Overall, these efforts merged social movement plus interest group strategies in a direct challenge to new conservatives. Groups worked the electoral system, the courts, the lobbying route, the mass media, and the demonstrations-in-the-streets approach to ensure their issues stayed alive. Attempts were made to find good news in bad times to keep morale from flagging. In fact, polls showed public support for core feminist priorities actually increased over time in Britain, the United States, and Canada. This pattern was arguably the strongest indicator of all that women's group claims remained viable despite hard times.

The challenge for critics of a new conservatism was turning the spotlight on the other side. Conflict between social and economic streams on the right was never far from the surface and, particularly in the United States, this clash led moral crusaders to stake out their turf in ever-harsher terms. Once in the glare of media attention, the angry talk of some conservatives actually turned off masses of moderate voters along with many moderate partisans, helping to advance a more centrist alternative. The rise of Tony Blair, Bill Clinton, and Jean Chrétien can be explained in these terms, as can the shift of their respective parties away from left and center-left positions toward a vague, mushy centrism. By 1995, British Labour, American Democratic, and Canadian Liberal leaders all denied statist solutions while they embraced the jargon of public/private partnerships and personal initiative. Each condemned the excesses of conservative individualism but, at the same time, made sure to avoid language that sounded leftist or radical.

Events like the Oklahoma City bombing in 1995 also served to turn the tide, especially in North America. As the destructive potential of the far right became more obvious, the ability of new conservatives to rail against groups that staked their claims peacefully was limited. "Extremist" and "loony left" had long been code words used by the political right, along with the epithet "liberal" in the United States. These insults were less and less believable as antiabortion and right-wing militia violence grabbed media headlines. Basic ideas that women's groups promoted about opportunities at work, for example, could no longer be dismissed in the same cavalier terms. Instead of feminists and their allies being portrayed as on the fringe, the scenario had shifted. The political right appeared to be falling off the edge once Labourites, Democrats, and Liberals began to recapture the center ground. Rather than focusing only on the conservative narrative about a crisis in government spending and too much taxation, media accounts began to consider how economic restructuring and tax changes had created both a work shortage and reduced government revenue. In short, efforts to shut down the opponents of conservatism proved ineffective in the longer term.

Yet replacing the ideas of conservative individualism with an emphasis on social belonging was no small task. In Britain, feminists faced a Labour party that remained uncomfortable with its old allies because it agreed in fundamental ways with the antigroup ethos of the Tories. In the United States, women's claims were tarred with the brush of quotas and affirmative action. These terms were pejorative ones by the 1990s, when arguments against them fit into efforts to exploit middle-class angst about work and "special privileges" for "special interests." Canadian groups became ensnared in complex constitutional issues that were difficult to explain. The three-nations vision of separate English Canadian, Quebec, and aboriginal interests was a complicated idea that offered diverse activists a common approach. The problem was that it remained incomprehensible to just about everyone else.

What can women's groups learn from life in conservative times? As a primary strategic lesson, movements were probably better off when they took the time to evaluate the other side. Conservatives continue to differ across systems and across time, and even within parties of the right. Activists need to know whether they face a predominantly economic conservatism, as in the British Conservative party since 1979. Or, by way of contrast, movements may confront a moralistic conservatism of the new right variety that became the core of the modern U.S. Republican party and held strength in the Reform party in

Canada. Feminists with an equal rights focus have maintained some momentum under economic conservative regimes. Women's movements in all their guises, however, are virtually shut out when social conservatism dominates.

A second lesson is "know thy strategy." Radicalizing when the government and the public are moving in increasingly conservative directions is a high-risk approach. The British women's movement, like much of the Labour party, adopted radical strategies during the early Thatcher years. Conservatives talked about the "loony left" to marginalize the other side, but they were less able to do so once opposition interests moved toward a more moderate approach. The Canadian case illustrates clearly how common ground gradually disappeared between government and movement, as leading women's organizations mounted a direct attack on the Mulroney Conservatives. This approach won visibility for feminist interests but also led the government to cut off public funds to defiant groups. In addition, it became harder and harder in Canada to identify any positive women's group message. In short, movements that adopt a radical strategy can find themselves isolated in the political polarization of conservative times—even when the government they face is not driven by social right ideas.

Third is the lesson "know the other side's strategy." Politicians on the right can be very adept at using divide-and-conquer tactics to their advantage. As demonstrated in earlier chapters, conservative leaders minimized public protest by turning critics against each other, by undermining the very idea of group advocacy, and, above all, by hiding what they were doing. Right-wing elites used indirect and stealthy strategies in such a way that the opposition weakened and policy consequences only appeared in the longer term. Conservative proposals were often framed in a way that the specifics of change remained unclear, while responsibility for what was occurring in terms of policy retrenchment was obscured.[3] Because so much of what new conservatives altered in terms of social benefits was complicated by the terms of program jargon and, in the United States and Canada, by the complexities of federal systems, many people simply missed what was going on. Decisions to tighten eligibility rules, for example, and reduce benefit levels were cast in the deceptive terms of making government more efficient and increasing incentives to work. The fact that these same changes stripped human beings of food, shelter, and dignity never seemed to come across as clearly.

As a fourth lesson, this study suggests language shifts are crucial to political change. When protest groups are consistently called special interests, the attempt to isolate and marginalize them takes on enormous momentum. When government programs become known as entitlements, any activist approach to social policy is probably in deep trouble. Once ideas about equal opportunity are castigated in the divisive talk of quotas and set-asides, there is little room to discuss the core issue of discrimination. When violence against women is labeled domestic violence or family violence, women's movements are likely losing control of the issue. Once the pursuit of legal equality becomes equated with radical feminism, not only is the historical record placed upside down, but, more important, core women's rights concerns are removed from the crucial middle ground in public debate. Efforts to identify and challenge this kind of discursive shift in a direct way can be useful; for example, Susan Faludi's account in *Backlash* presented a cogent delineation of the American situation to a very broad audience.[4]

Finally, this study reinforces the conclusions of previous work on the necessity for feminists to pursue both independent and partisan political paths.[5] Rather than focusing exclusively on running women candidates for public office or, at the opposite end of the spectrum, on mobilizing autonomously via the social movement route, organized feminism appears to survive hard times best when it adopts variegated strategies that keep opponents off balance. The kinds of imaginative, inventive approaches used by British groups during the 1980s and early 1990s provide an illustration: at the same time as elements of that women's movement were organizing high-profile demonstrations, pressing for more female candidates in the Labour party, and orchestrating media campaigns about violence against women, other segments were litigating in the British courts and via European Community channels. In short, a great deal can be said for fluidity, ingenuity, and versatility, because operating simultaneously along social movement, interest group, and partisan channels offered multiple sources of leverage to activists in all three countries.

One key question remains, however. What use is moderation when it abdicates responsibility for the welfare of citizens? What stands in the way of preventing North American neoliberals like Bill Clinton and Jean Chrétien from decentralizing to the point that no federal government presence exists in the social policy area? What if British activists helped to elect a Blair government that became virtually the same, except at the level of rhetoric, as a Major one? About the only lever remaining under these circumstances is the power of women's voices, which can act in the ballot booth and in polls to limit such directions. Studies of the gender gap in public attitudes show women in all three countries remain core supporters of social welfare provision.[6] Losing the approval of a constituency that has long endorsed decency and compassion in public policy would be dangerous for moderate politicians and must be made known to them. The outcome of the 1994 American midterm elections, when voter turnout declined significantly among women and blacks, offers a useful illustration of the consequences of demobilization for neoliberal parties.

Above all, progressives need to reclaim the high ground of justice, fairness, and equality. Core feminist policy claims are, at their heart, consistent with notions of individual freedom within a larger social context that form the bedrock of liberal democracy. Communities fall apart when economic decision makers are so committed to controlling inflation that they deny hope to their citizens. Obsessive talk about government spending has led parties of all stripes to focus on only one deficit and to deny the existence of other crises. Britain, the United States, and Canada all face a severe social deficit, because the absence of decent jobs has denied hope to the young and made people of all ages extremely anxious. Political parties have also ignored the revenue shortfall that was created by conservative decisions to lower corporate taxes and income taxes at the high end. These tax changes and the more general right-wing attack on government have effectively crippled efforts to discuss, let alone address, the social deficit.

Growing public cynicism about politics and politicians is also a core part of this story. Once right-of-center political leaders managed to convince large numbers of citizens that government was top-heavy, bureaucratized, and out of step with the new globalized economy, they helped to remove their own actions from the scrutiny of public debate. What political executives did with the levers of power seemed less and less important, as public expectations were dampened about the ability of government to act for the public good. In effect, the crucial notion that citizens should oversee government action and keep elites accountable through public oversight and deliberation was undermined by new conservative claims that government did not much matter.

This story offers at least one clear insight into the "Do governments make a difference?" debate. It demonstrates that through the 1980s, conservative political leaders managed to change their own parties as well as the broader climate of ideas within Britain, the United States, and Canada. In particular, the coming to power of Margaret Thatcher, Ronald Reagan, and their party successors tended to undermine the policy fortunes of organized feminism. In Canada, the damage to women's movement momentum caused by the Mulroney government was less direct and less easily measured, but the defensive posture of women's groups was obvious at the level of public rhetoric in Canada in addition to the other two cases. In short, conservative leaders did make a crucial difference in the tale of Anglo-American feminism during the late twentieth century.

On the other side, feminists and other progressives have often been unwilling to press the limits of their own approach. For example, large numbers of middle-class voters have felt overburdened and exploited by a public sector that seems unresponsive to their needs. No amount of comparative data on levels of taxation in Denmark, for example, is likely to convince British, American, and Canadian citizens that they should pay higher taxes to get better services. Progressives have also been loath to rethink their positions on unemployment and workfare programs in light of not just tax fatigue among the middle class but also the failure of traditional schemes in the view of many recipients. In some cases, trade unions have focused only on the immediate interests of their members, leaving little room for creative thinking about either work or welfare. In short, the curious situation in which activist social movements defend passive government welfare policies seems more and more inconsistent.

In the past when Thatcher, Reagan, Mulroney, and their party successors held office, women's movements tried to hold their ground and even make a few gains. Protest groups remained vigorous and engaged throughout this period; they developed a variety of inventive defenses to try to cope with hard times. Many questioned the rules of the game even as they became more adept at finding ways to obtain influence. Although activists clearly desired far more than they achieved, perhaps surviving was equivalent to political success in the dark days. What would happen under different political leaders who came later lingered above all else as an open question.

Appendix A

LEGISLATIVE AND JUDICIAL ACTION IN THREE COUNTRIES

TABLE 1

Legislative and Judicial Action before First Thatcher Government*

Equal rights
  Immigration Act, 1971 (−)
  Supplementary Benefits Act, 1976 (−)

Family law
  Divorce Reform Act, 1969 (+)
  Matrimonial Proceedings and Property Act, 1970 (+)
  Guardianship of Minors Act, 1971 (+)
  Matrimonial Causes Act, 1973 (+)
  Guardianship Act, 1973 (+)

Reproduction
  Abortion Act, 1967 (+)
  National Health Service (Family Planning) Act, 1967 (+)
  National Health Service (Reorganisation) Act, 1973 (+)
  Series of restrictive private members' bills fail (+)

Violence
  DPP v. Morgan, 1975 (−)
  Sexual Offences (Amendment) Act, 1976 (±)
  Domestic Violence and Matrimonial Proceedings Act, 1976 (+)
  Housing (Homeless Persons) Act, 1977 (+)
  Domestic Proceedings and Magistrates' Courts Act, 1978 (+)

Employment
  Income and Corporation Taxes Act, 1970 (−)
  Equal Pay Act, 1970 (+)
  Amendment to Income and Corporation Taxes Act, 1972 (+)
  Social Security Act, 1975 (+)
  Employment Protection Act, 1975 (+)
  Sex Discrimination Act, 1975 (+)
  Employment Protection (Consolidation) Act, 1978 (+)

*Plus and minus signs in this and the following tables are coded with reference to orga-
nized feminist positions. In this and other listings here, the abbreviations *EC* refer to European Community and *ECJ* to European Court of Justice.

TOTALS: Overall, twenty-three decisions are listed, of which eighteen (78.3 percent) are
coded +, four (17.4 percent) are coded −, and one (4.3 percent) is coded ±. One court decision was made, which was negative (100.0 percent); twenty-two legislative decisions
were made, of which eighteen (81.8 percent) are coded +, three (13.6 percent) are coded
−, and one (4.5 percent) is coded ±.

*SOURCES: Interviews with forty-three British women's movement activists and literature cited in
chapter 2, notes 8 through 66.*

TABLE 2

Legislative and Judicial Action during Thatcher Years

Equal rights
    British Nationality Rules, 1980 (−)
    British Nationality Act, 1981 (+)
    Drake v. Department of Health and Social Security, 1986 (ECJ, +)

Family law
    Matrimonial and Family Proceedings Act, 1984 (+)
    Family Law Act, 1986 (+)
    Children Act, 1989 (±)

Reproduction
    Series of restrictive private members' bills fail (+)
    Education Act, 1980 (−)
    Gillick v. Minister of Health and Social Security, 1985 (+)
    Education Act, 1986 (−)

Violence
    Housing Act, 1985 (+)

Employment
    Amendment to Employment Protection Act, 1980 (−)
    Amendments to Social Security Act, 1980–84 (EC pressure, +)
    Jenkins v. Kingsgate Clothing Productions Ltd., 1981 (ECJ, +)
    Equal Value (Amendment) Regulations, 1983 (ECJ pressure, +)
    Marshall v. Southampton Area Health Authority #1, 1986 (ECJ, +)
    Social Security Act, 1986 (±)
    Sex Discrimination Act, 1986 (EC pressure, ±)
    DeSouza v. the Automobile Association, 1986 (+)
    Johnston v. Chief Constable of the Royal Ulster Constabulary, 1986 (ECJ, +)
    Rainey v. Greater Glasgow Health Board, 1987 (−)
    Hayward v. Cammell Laird Shipbuilders Ltd., 1988 (+)
    Brown v. Stockton-on-Tees Borough Council, 1988 (+)
    Pickstone v. Freemans plc, 1988 (+)
    Local Government Act, 1988 (−)
    Foster v. British Gas, 1990 (ECJ, +)

TOTALS: Overall, twenty-six decisions are listed, of which seventeen (65.4 percent) are coded +, six (23.1 percent) are coded −, and three (11.5 percent) are coded ±. Eleven judicial decisions were made, of which ten (90.9 percent) are coded + and one (9.1 percent) is coded −. Fifteen legislative decisions were made, of which seven (46.7 percent) are coded +, five (33.3 percent) are coded −, and 3 (20.0 percent) are coded ±.

SOURCES: Interviews with forty-three British women's movement activists and literature cited in chapter 2, notes 8 through 66.

TABLE 3

Legislative and Judicial Action during Major Years

Equal rights
  Criminal Justice Act, 1994 (±)

Family law
  Child Support Act, 1991 (±)
  Brooks v. Brooks, 1995 (+)
  Family Law Act, 1996 (±)

Reproduction
  Human Fertilisation and Embryology Act, 1990 (±)

Violence
  R. v. Rawlinson, 1991 (+)
  Sexual Offences (Amendment) Act, 1992 (+)
  Housing Act, 1996 (−)

Employment
  Barber v. Guardian Royal Exchange Assurance Group, 1990 (ECJ, +)
  National Health Service and Community Care Act, 1990 (±)
  James v. Eastleigh Borough Council, 1990 (+)
  Scally v. Southern Board, 1991 (+)
  Trade Union Reform and Employment Rights Act, 1993 (±)
  Marshall v. Southampton Area Health Authority #2, 1993 (ECJ, +)
  Enderby v. Frenchay Health Authority, 1993 (ECJ, +)
  Webb v. EMO Air Cargo (U.K.) Ltd., 1994 (ECJ, +)
  R. v. Secretary of State for Employment, 1994 (+)
  Neath v. Hugh Steeper Ltd., 1994 (ECJ, −)
  Coloroll Pension Trustees Ltd. v. Russell, 1994 (ECJ, +)
  Smith v. Avdel Systems Ltd., 1994 (ECJ, +)
  Pensions Act, 1995 (±)
  Graham v. Department of Social Security, 1995 (ECJ, −)
  Ratcliffe v. North Yorkshire County Council, 1995 (+)

TOTALS: Overall, twenty-three decisions are listed, of which thirteen (56.5 percent) are coded +, three (13.0 percent) are coded −, and seven (30.4 percent) are coded ±. Fourteen judicial decisions were made, of which twelve (85.7 percent) are coded + and two (14.3 percent) are coded −. Nine legislative decisions were made, of which one (11.1 percent) is coded +, one (11.1 percent) is coded −, and seven (77.8 percent) are coded ±.

SOURCES: *Interviews with forty-three British women's movement activists and literature cited in chapter 2, notes 8 through 66.*

TABLE 4

Legislative and Judicial Action before First Reagan Administration

Equal rights
   Reed v. Reed, 1971 (+)
   Equal Rights Amendment (ERA) passed Congress, 1972 (+)
   Title IX of Education Amendments to Civil Rights Act, 1972 (+)
   Frontiero v. Richardson, 1973 (+)
   Geduldig v. Aiello, 1974 (−)
   Amendment to Fair Housing Act, 1974 (+)
   Equal Credit Opportunity Act, 1974 (+)
   Women's Educational Equity Act, 1974 (+)
   Weinberger v. Wiesenfeld, 1975 (+)
   Craig v. Boren, 1976 (±)
   Los Angeles Dept. of Water and Power v. Manhart, 1978 (+)

Family law*
   Gomez v. Perez, 1973 (+)
   Child Support Amendments to Social Security Act, 1975 (±)
   Stanton v. Stanton, 1975 (+)
   Orr v. Orr, 1979 (+)

Reproduction*
   Eisenstadt v. Baird, 1972 (+)
   Roe v. Wade, Doe v. Bolton, 1973 (+)
   Planned Parenthood of Central Missouri v. Danforth, 1976 (+)
   Beal v. Doe, 1977 (−)
   Maher v. Roe, 1977 (−)
   Hyde Amendments, 1976 and following (−)
   Carey v. Population Services International, 1977 (+)
   Colautti v. Franklin, 1979 (+)
   Bellotti v. Baird, 1979 (+)

Violence*
   Domestic Violence Prevention Act blocked, 1977–80 (−)

Employment*
   Phillips v. Martin Marietta Corporation, 1971 (±)
   Griggs v. Duke Power Company, 1971 (+)
   Equal Employment Opportunity Act, 1972 (+)
   Education Amendments to Equal Pay Act, 1972 (+)
   Pittsburgh Press v. Pittsburgh Commission on Human Relations, 1973 (+)
   Fair Labor Standards Amendments, 1974 (+)
   Cleveland Board of Education v. LaFleur, 1974 (+)
   General Electric Company v. Gilbert, 1976 (−)
   Dothard v. Rawlinson, 1977 (−)
   Pregnancy Discrimination Act, 1978 (+)
   Personnel Administrator of Massachusetts v. Feeney, 1979 (−)

*Aspects of divorce, abortion, criminal law, and child care policy rest within state jurisdiction in the United States.

TOTALS: Overall, thirty-six decisions are listed, of which twenty-five (69.4 percent) are coded +, eight (22.2 percent) are coded −, and three (8.3 percent) are coded ±. Twenty-four judicial decisions were made, of which sixteen (66.7 percent) are coded +, six (25.0 percent) are coded −, and two (8.3 percent) are coded ±. Twelve legislative decisions were made, of which nine (75.0 percent) are coded +, two (16.7 percent) are coded −, and one (8.3 percent) is coded ±.

SOURCES: *Interviews with thirty-nine American women's movement activists and literature cited in chapter 2, notes 67 through 163.*

TABLE 5

Legislative and Judicial Action during Reagan Years

Equal rights
  Mississippi University for Women v. Hogan, 1982 (±)
  ERA not ratified by extended deadline, 1982 (−)
  Arizona Governing Committee v. Norris, 1983 (+)
  Grove City College v. Bell, 1984 (−)
  New York State Club Association v. City of New York, 1988 (+)
  Civil Rights Restoration Act, 1988 (±)

Family law
  Child Support Enforcement Act, 1984 (+)
  Hicks v. Feiock, 1988 (+)
  Family Support Act, 1988 (±)

Reproduction
  Harris v. McRae, 1980 (−)
  H.L. v. Matheson, 1981 (−)
  Adolescent Family Life Bill, 1981 (−)
  Planned Parenthood of Kansas City, Missouri v. Ashcroft, 1983 (−)
  City of Akron v. Akron Center for Reproductive Health, 1983 (+)
  Thornburgh v. American College of Obstetricians and Gynecologists, 1986 (+)
  Bowen v. Kendrick, 1988 (−)

Violence
  Domestic Violence Prevention and Services Act blocked, 1980 (−)
  Family Violence Prevention and Services Act, 1984 (+)

Employment
  Economic Recovery Tax Act, 1981 (+)
  County of Washington v. Gunther, 1981 (+)
  Retirement Equity Act, 1984 (+)
  Hishon v. King and Spalding, 1984 (+)
  Firefighters Local Union #1784 v. Stotts, 1984 (−)
  Meritor Savings Bank v. Vinson, 1986 (±)
  Wimberly v. Labor and Industrial Relations Commission, 1987 (−)
  Johnson v. Transportation Agency of Santa Clara, 1987 (+)
  California Federal Savings and Loan v. Guerra, 1987 (±)
  Housing and Community Development Authorization Bill, 1988 (+)
  Women's Business Ownership Act, 1988 (+)

TOTALS: Overall, twenty-nine decisions are listed, of which fourteen (48.3 percent) are coded +, ten (34.5 percent) are coded −, and five (17.2 percent) are coded ±. Eighteen judicial decisions were made, of which eight (44.4 percent) are coded +, seven (38.9 percent) are coded −, and three (16.7 percent) are coded ±. Eleven legislative decisions were made, of which six (54.5 percent) are coded +, three (27.3 percent) are coded −, and two (18.2 percent) are coded ±.

SOURCES: *Interviews with thirty-nine American women's movement activists and literature cited in chapter 2, notes 67 through 163.*

TABLE 6

Legislative and Judicial Action during Bush Years

Equal rights
> *Metro Broadcasting v. Federal Communications Commission*, 1990 (+)
> *Shaw v. Reno*, 1993 (−)

Family law
> *Mississippi Choctaw Indians v. Holyfield*, 1989 (−)

Reproduction
> *Webster v. Reproductive Health Services*, 1989 (−)
> *Ohio v. Akron Center for Reproductive Health*, 1990 (−)
> *Hodgson v. Minnesota*, 1990 (−)
> *Rust v. Sullivan*, 1991 (−)
> *Planned Parenthood Federation v. Agency for International Development*, 1991 (−)
> Efforts to overturn "gag" rule on family planning blocked, 1991–92 (−)
> *Planned Parenthood of Southeastern Pennsylvania v. Casey*, 1992 (±)

Violence
> No major decisions

Employment
> *City of Richmond v. J. A. Croson Co.*, 1989 (−)
> *Price Waterhouse v. Hopkins*, 1989 (±)
> *Wards Cove Packing Co. v. Atonio*, 1989 (−)
> *Lorrance v. AT&T Technologies*, 1989 (−)
> *Martin v. Wilks*, 1989 (−)
> *Patterson v. McLean Credit Union*, 1989 (−)
> Civil Rights Act blocked, 1990 (−)
> Civil Rights Act, 1991 (±)
> Family and Medical Leave Act blocked, 1990–92 (−)
> Displaced Homemakers Job Training Act, 1990 (+)
> Child Care Act, 1990 (±)
> *United Automobile Workers v. Johnson Controls*, 1991 (+)
> Nontraditional Employment for Women Act, 1991 (+)
> *St. Mary's Honor Center v. Hicks*, 1993 (−)

TOTALS: Overall, twenty-four decisions are listed, of which four (16.7 percent) are coded +, sixteen (66.7 percent) are coded −, and 4 (16.7 percent) are coded ±. Seventeen judicial decisions were made, of which two (11.8 percent) are coded +, thirteen (76.5 percent) are coded −, and two (11.8 percent) are coded ±. Seven legislative decisions were made, of which two (28.6 percent) are coded +, three (42.8 percent) are coded −, and two (28.6 percent) are coded ±.

SOURCES: *Interviews with thirty-nine American women's movement activists and literature cited in chapter 2, notes 67 through 163.*

TABLE 7

Legislative and Judicial Action before First Mulroney Government

Equal rights*
Attorney-General of Canada v. Lavell, Isaac v. Bédard, 1974 (−)
Canadian Charter of Rights and Freedoms, 1982 (+)

Family law*
Murdoch v. Murdoch, 1973 (−)
Leatherdale v. Leatherdale, 1982 (−)

Reproduction*
Amendments to Criminal Code, 1969 (±)
Morgentaler v. The Queen, 1975 (−)
Amendments to Criminal Code, 1975 (+)

Violence
Pappajohn v. The Queen, 1980 (−)
Amendments to Criminal Code, 1983 (+)

Employment*
Amendments to Canada Labour Code, 1971 (+)
Canadian Human Rights Act, 1977 (±)
Amendments to Canada Pension Plan, 1977 (+)
Amendments to Canada Labour Code, 1978 (+)
Bliss v. Attorney-General of Canada, 1978 (−)
Amendments to Canadian Human Rights Act, 1983 (+)
Amendments to Unemployment Insurance Act, 1983 (+)

*Significant control over human rights, matrimonial property, abortion, child care, and labor law rests within provincial jurisdiction in Canada.

TOTALS: Overall, sixteen decisions are listed, of which eight (50.0 percent) are coded +, six (37.5 percent) are coded −, and two (12.5 percent) are coded ±. Six judicial decisions were made, of which six (100.0 percent) are coded −. Ten legislative decisions were made, of which eight (80.0 percent) are coded + and two (20.0 percent) are coded ±.

SOURCES: *Interviews with twenty-seven Canadian women's movement activists and literature cited in chapter 2, notes 164 through 200.*

TABLE 8

Legislative and Judicial Action during Mulroney Years

Equal rights
  Amendments to Indian Act, 1985 (+)
  Blainey v. Ontario Hockey Association, 1986 (+)
  Andrews v. Law Society of British Columbia, 1989 (+)

Family law
  Divorce Act, 1986 (+)
  Divorce Corollary Relief Act, 1986 (+)
  Family Orders Enforcement Act, 1986 (+)
  Derrickson v. Derrickson, 1986 (−)
  Moge v. Moge, 1992 (+)

Reproduction
  Morgentaler v. The Queen, 1988 (+)
  Borowski v. Attorney-General of Canada, 1989 (+)
  Tremblay v. Daigle, 1989 (+)
  Efforts to relegislate abortion fail, 1988, 1990 (+)
  Sullivan and Lemay v. The Queen, 1991 (+)

Violence
  Chase v. The Queen, 1987 (+)
  Canadian Newspapers Co. v. Attorney-General of Canada, 1988 (+)
  R. v. Lavallee, 1990 (+)
  Reddick v. The Queen, 1991 (+)
  R. v. Seaboyer, R. v. Gayme, 1991 (−)
  Amendments to Criminal Code and Customs Tariff, 1991 (±)
  Amendments to Criminal Code, 1992 (+)
  Norberg v. Wynrib, 1992 (+)
  Amendments to Criminal Code, 1993 (+)

Employment
  Amendments to Canada Labour Code, 1985 (+)
  Employment Equity Act, 1986 (±)
  Action travail des femmes v. Canadian National Railway Co., 1987 (+)
  Robichaud v. Canada (Treasury Board), 1987 (+)
  Child Care Act withdrawn, 1988 (+)
  Janzen and Govereau v. Platy Enterprises Ltd., 1989 (+)
  Brooks v. Canada Safeway Ltd., 1989 (+)
  Amendments to Unemployment Insurance Act, 1990 (+)

TOTALS: Overall, thirty decisions are listed, of which twenty-six (86.7 percent) are coded +, two (6.7 percent) are coded −, and two (6.7 percent) are coded ±. Eighteen judicial decisions were made, of which sixteen (88.9 percent) are coded + and two (11.1 percent) are coded −. Twelve legislative decisions were made, of which ten (83.3 percent) are coded + and two (16.7 percent) are coded ±.

SOURCES: *Interviews with twenty-seven Canadian women's movement activists and literature cited in chapter 2, notes 164 through 200.*

Appendix B

INTERVIEW SCHEDULES

I. BRITISH INTERVIEW SCHEDULE

1. Can you tell me about the background to your group activity? How long have you been active and in what policy fields?

2. What is the membership of your organization? Staff size? Budget per year? Main sources of funding?

3. How would you describe the Thatcher-Major years? How did having a Conservative government affect your work as a group activist?

4. What strategies did your organization use to gain policy influence during the years 1979 and following? Would you say these strategies were different than those used during previous Labour governments?

5. Would you say that any progress for British women occurred during the Thatcher-Major years? In what areas? How?

6. Can you assess changes in public consciousness during the years 1979 and following? Did the Conservative government affect public attitudes during this period?

7. Can you assess changes in national policy action during the Thatcher-Major years? Were these primarily legislative or judicial in origin?

8. Can you assess changes in policy access, meaning participation in policy making by your organization, during the years after 1979?

9. What is the relationship of your group to political parties? Does the partisan stripe of the party in power make much difference to your activities?

10. In conclusion, what would you say has been the most lasting legacy of the Thatcher-Major years?

II. UNITED STATES INTERVIEW SCHEDULE

1. Can you tell me about the background to your group activity? How long have you been active and in what policy fields?

2. What is the membership of your organization? Staff size? Budget per year? Main sources of funding?

3. How would you describe the Reagan-Bush years? How did having a Republican president affect your work as a group activist?

4. What strategies did your organization use to gain policy influence during the years 1980 and following? Would you say these strategies were different than those used during previous Democratic and current Democratic administrations?

5. Would you say that any progress for American women occurred during the Reagan-Bush years? In what areas? How?

6. Can you assess changes in public consciousness during the years 1980 and following? Did Republican presidents affect public attitudes during this period?

7. Can you assess changes in federal policy action during the Reagan-Bush years? Were these primarily legislative or judicial in origin?

8. Can you assess changes in policy access, meaning participation in policy making by your organization, during the years after 1980?

9. What is the relationship of your group to political parties? Does the partisan stripe of the president in the White House make much difference to your activities?

10. In conclusion, what would you say has been the most lasting legacy of the Reagan-Bush years?

III. CANADIAN INTERVIEW SCHEDULE

1. Can you tell me about the background to your group activity? How long have you been active and in what policy fields?

2. What is the membership of your organization? Staff size? Budget per year? Main sources of funding?

3. How would you describe the Mulroney-Campbell years? How did having a Conservative federal government affect your work as a group activist?

4. What strategies did your organization use to gain policy influence during the years 1984 and following? Would you say these strategies were different than those used during previous Liberal and current Liberal governments?

5. Would you say that any progress for Canadian women occurred during the Mulroney-Campbell years? In what areas? How?

6. Can you assess changes in public consciousness during the years 1984 and following? Did the Conservative federal government affect public attitudes during this period?

7. Can you assess changes in federal policy action during the Mulroney-Campbell years? Were these primarily legislative or judicial in origin?

8. Can you assess changes in policy access, meaning participation in policy making by your organization, during the years since 1984?

9. What is the relationship of your group to political parties? Does the partisan stripe of the party in power make much difference to your activities?

10. In conclusion, what would you say has been the most lasting legacy of the Mulroney-Campbell period?

Notes

INTRODUCTION

1. Sidney Tarrow, *Struggle, Politics, and Reform: Collective Action, Social Movements, and Cycles of Protest* (Ithaca, NY: Cornell University Center for International Studies, 1991); and Sidney Tarrow, *Power in Movement: Social Movements, Collective Action, and Politics* (Cambridge: Cambridge University Press, 1994).

2. According to Thatcher's 1987 comment, "There is no such thing as society. There are individual men and women and there are families." Margaret Thatcher as quoted in Wendy Webster, *Not a Man to Match Her: The Marketing of a Prime Minister* (London: Women's Press, 1990), 57.

3. On Thatcher's questioning of what the women's movement had done, see Donna S. Sanzone, "Women in Politics," in *Access to Power,* ed. Cynthia Fuchs Epstein and Rose Laub Coser (London: Allen and Unwin, 1981), 44.

4. Ronald Reagan, *An American Life* (New York: Simon and Schuster, 1990), 120.

5. "Colleagues Honour Thatcher," *Globe and Mail* (Toronto), 24 October 1995.

6. See Susan Faludi, *Backlash: The Undeclared War against American Women* (New York: Doubleday, 1991).

7. Margaret Thatcher as quoted in Webster, *Not a Man to Match Her,* 153.

8. See Hugo Young, *One of Us: A Biography of Margaret Thatcher* (London: Pan, 1991), ix.

9. Joel Krieger, *Reagan, Thatcher, and the Politics of Decline* (New York: Oxford University Press, 1986), 30.

10. David B. Truman, *The Governmental Process: Political Interests and Public Opinion* (New York: Knopf, 1951), 112.

11. Graeme C. Moodie and Gerald Studdert-Kennedy, *Opinions, Publics and Pressure Groups* (London: Allen and Unwin, 1970), 75. See also William Coleman, "Federalism and Interest Group Organization," in *Federalism and the Role of the State,* ed. Herman Bakvis and William M. Chandler (Toronto: University of Toronto Press, 1987).

12. R. Kent Weaver and Bert A. Rockman, "When and How Do Institutions Matter?" in *Do Institutions Matter? Government Capabilities in the United States and Abroad,* ed. R. Kent Weaver and Bert A. Rockman (Washington, DC: Brookings, 1993), 450, 457–58.

13. Joyce Gelb, *Feminism and Politics: A Comparative Perspective* (Berkeley: University of California Press, 1989), 2.

CHAPTER ONE

1. See Dinesh D'Souza, *The End of Racism: Principles for a Multicultural Society* (New York: Free Press, 1995).

2. Brian Mulroney, December 1984 speech to the Economic Club of New York, as quoted in Lawrence Martin, *Pledge of Allegiance: The Americanization of Canada in the Mulroney Years* (Toronto: McClelland and Stewart, 1993), 69.

3. Frances Dana Gage, "A Hundred Years Hence," reprinted in *Up from the Pedestal,* ed. Aileen S. Kraditor (Chicago: Quadrangle, 1968), 285.

4. Sheila Rowbotham, *Hidden from History: 300 Years of Women's Oppression and the Fight against It* (London: Pluto, 1977).

5. J. Stanley Lemons, *The Woman Citizen* (Urbana: University of Illinois Press, 1973), 159.

6. McClung as quoted in Candace Savage, *Our Nell: A Scrapbook Biography of Nellie L. McClung* (Saskatoon: Western Producer Prairie Books, 1979), 171.

7. See Lemons, *The Woman Citizen.*

8. See Olive Banks, *Faces of Feminism: A Study of Feminism as a Social Movement* (Oxford: Blackwell, 1986), chaps. 9, 10.

9. See Elsie Gregory MacGill, *My Mother the Judge,* with an introduction by Naomi Black (Toronto: Peter Martin, 1981).

10. Mary Fainsod Katzenstein, "Feminism within American Institutions: Unobtrusive Mobilization in the 1980s," *Signs: Journal of Women in Culture and Society* 16, no. 1 (1990): 27–54.

11. See Joan Sangster, *Dreams of Equality: Women on the Canadian Left, 1920–1950* (Toronto: McClelland and Stewart, 1989), 111–14; and John Manley, "Women and the Left in the 1930s: The Case of the Toronto CCF Women's Joint Committee," *Atlantis* 5, no. 2 (spring 1980): 111–13.

12. On the evolution and eventual decay of these programs, see Paul Pierson, *Dismantling the Welfare State? Reagan, Thatcher, and the Politics of Retrenchment* (Cambridge: Cambridge University Press, 1994).

13. Betty Friedan, *The Feminine Mystique* (New York: Dell, 1963).

14. Simone de Beauvoir, *The Second Sex,* trans. H. M. Parshley (New York: Vintage, 1952).

15. See Sara M. Evans, *Personal Politics: The Roots of Women's Liberation in the Civil Rights Movement and the New Left* (New York: Vintage, 1979); and Jo Freeman, *The Politics of Women's Liberation* (New York: Longman, 1974).

16. Margaret Thatcher, *The Downing Street Years* (New York: HarperCollins, 1993), 15.

17. Thatcher's best-known comment on this subject was made in 1987, when she stated in an interview, "There is no such thing as society. There are individual men and women and there are families." Margaret Thatcher as quoted in Wendy Webster, *Not a Man to Match Her: The Marketing of a Prime Minister* (London: Women's Press, 1990), 57.

18. For her views of moderate "wets" in the Conservative party, see Thatcher, *The Downing Street Years,* 50–51, 124.

19. Webster, *Not a Man to Match Her,* 150.

20. Thatcher, *The Downing Street Years,* 7.

21. Ibid., 6, 8.

22. Ibid., 159.

23. Ibid., 149.

24. Ibid., 146–47.

25. See Hugo Young, *One of Us: A Biography of Margaret Thatcher* (London: Pan, 1991), 597.

26. John Major as quoted in Joan Isaac, "The Politics of Morality in the UK," *Parliamentary Affairs* 47, no. 2 (April 1994): 184.

27. For a skeptical view of the Citizens' Charter, see Hilary Land, "Whatever Happened to the Social Wage?" in *Women and Poverty in Britain: The 1990s,* ed. Caroline Glendinning and Jane Millar (London: Harvester Wheatsheaf, 1992), 51–52.

28. See Thatcher, *The Downing Street Years,* 562; and Joni Lovenduski and Vicky Randall, *Contemporary Feminist Politics: Women and Power in Britain* (Oxford: Oxford University Press, 1993), 45, 365.

29. Thatcher, *The Downing Street Years,* 307.

30. Ibid., 296.

31. Sheila Rowbotham, *The Past Is before Us: Feminism in Action since the 1960s* (Harmondsworth, England: Penguin, 1989).

32. Juliet Mitchell, *Woman's Estate* (Harmondsworth, England: Penguin, 1971), and *Psychoanalysis and Feminism* (Harmondsworth, England: Penguin, 1974).

33. Anna Coote and Beatrix Campbell, *Sweet Freedom: The Struggle for Women's Liberation* (Oxford: Blackwell, 1987), 16.

34. See Juliet Mitchell, "Women: The Longest Revolution," *New Left Review* 40 (1966): 11–37.

35. According to Susan Bassnett, *Feminist Experiences: The Women's Movement in Four Cultures* (London: Allen and Unwin, 1984), 157, the Greenham Common protests of 1982 attracted thirty thousand women. According to Elizabeth Wilson with Angela Weir, "The British Women's Movement," in Wilson with Weir, *Hidden Agendas: Theory, Politics, and Experience in the Women's Movement* (London: Tavistock, 1986), 131, the march by Women against Pit Closures in August 1984 drew ten thousand women.

36. See Sylvia Walby, *Theorising Patriarchy* (Oxford: Blackwell, 1990); and Elizabeth Wilson, *Women and the Welfare State* (London: Tavistock, 1977).

37. See Rowbotham, *The Past Is before Us*, 70.

38. Coote and Campbell, *Sweet Freedom*, 14–15.

39. Compare, for example, Hugo Young's account in *One of Us*, 234, 239, on Thatcher's views with Rowbotham's perspective in *The Past Is before Us*, 145, on women's movement positions.

40. On the Greater London Council (GLC) support for women's groups, see Lovenduski and Randall, *Contemporary Feminist Politics*, 12, 104; Wilson with Weir, "The British Women's Movement," 129–30; and Coote and Campbell, *Sweet Freedom*, 105–8.

41. After the dismantling of the GLC, reduced funding for women's groups was channeled through central government departments as well as a system of quasi-autonomous nongovernmental organizations, known as QUANGOs, supported by local councils. Departments and QUANGOs usually supported well-defined, short-term project work rather than offering the kind of open-ended, longer-term core funding of the type provided by the GLC.

42. Lovenduski and Randall, *Contemporary Feminist Politics*, 160. See also Clare Short, "Women and the Labour Party," *Parliamentary Affairs* 49, no. 1 (January 1996): 17, 24.

43. Barbara Follett, "Closing the Gender Gap," *Fabian Society* (May–June 1993): 13.

44. Beatrix Campbell, *The Iron Ladies: Why Do Women Vote Tory?* (London: Virago, 1987), 2, 3.

45. See Clare Short, "Women and the Labour Party," 17–25; and Sarah Perrigo, "Women and Change in the Labour Party, 1979–1995," *Parliamentary Affairs* 49, no. 1 (January 1996): 116–29.

46. See Lovenduski and Randall, *Contemporary Feminist Politics*, 159–60.

47. Michael A. Genovese, "Margaret Thatcher and the Politics of Conviction Leadership," in *Women as National Leaders*, ed. Michael A. Genovese (Newbury Park, CA: Sage, 1993), 191.

48. Lou Cannon, *President Reagan: The Role of a Lifetime* (New York: Simon and Schuster, 1991), 56, 73.

49. Beth Fischer, seminar presentation, Department of Political Science, University of Toronto, 14 January 1994.

50. See Charles Tiefer, *The Semi-Sovereign Presidency: The Bush Administration's Strategy for Governing without Congress* (Boulder, CO: Westview, 1994).

51. Steven A. Shull, *A Kinder, Gentler Racism? The Reagan-Bush Civil Rights Legacy* (Armonk, NY: Sharpe, 1993), 83.

52. Reagan, *An American Life*, 219.

53. Ibid., 67.

54. For portions of Reagan's 1964 speech, see ibid., 141–43. On the change in his party registration, see Cannon, *President Reagan*, 74.

55. See Reagan, *An American Life*, 189.

56. See Cannon, *President Reagan,* 48, 75, 518–19.

57. Reagan, *An American Life,* 189.

58. Cannon, *President Reagan,* 56.

59. See Reagan, *An American Life,* 337.

60. See ibid.; and Cannon, *President Reagan,* 153.

61. Reagan speech dated June 1981, as quoted in Shull, *A Kinder, Gentler Racism?* 52.

62. See Cannon, *President Reagan,* 235, on the breadth of this coalition on the political right.

63. On the evolution of the American right in this period, see Gary Dorrien, *The Neoconservative Mind: Politics, Culture, and the War of Ideology* (Philadelphia: Temple University Press, 1993); and Jerome L. Himmelstein, *To the Right: The Transformation of American Conservatism* (Berkeley: University of California Press, 1990).

64. NOW Statement of Purpose, adopted at organizing conference in Washington, DC, 29 October 1966, 1.

65. The NAACP was founded in 1909. On NOW's early evolution, see Toni Carabillo, Judith Mueli, and June Bundy Csida, *Feminist Chronicles, 1953–1993* (Los Angeles: Women's Graphics, 1993), 31.

66. "NOW Origins," 1972 brochure, 2.

67. For the full text of the amendment, see Jane J. Mansbridge, *Why We Lost the ERA* (Chicago: University of Chicago Press, 1986), 1.

68. See Myra Marx Ferree and Beth B. Hess, *Controversy and Coalition: The New Feminist Movement* (Boston: Twayne, 1985); and Sara M. Evans and Barbara J. Nelson, *Wage Justice: Comparable Worth and the Paradox of Technocratic Reform* (Chicago: University of Chicago Press, 1989).

69. See Irene Tinker, ed., *Women in Washington: Advocates for Public Policy* (Beverly Hills, CA: Sage, 1983).

70. Friedan, *The Feminine Mystique.*

71. Kate Millett, *Sexual Politics* (New York: Doubleday, 1970); Shulamith Firestone, *The Dialectic of Sex* (New York: Morrow, 1970); and Susan Brownmiller, *Against Our Will* (New York: Simon and Schuster, 1975).

72. See Flora Davis, *Moving the Mountain: The Women's Movement in America since 1960* (New York: Simon and Schuster, 1991).

73. See Carabillo et al., *Feminist Chronicles,* 96; and Tanya Melich, *The Republican War against Women* (New York: Bantam, 1996), 161.

74. See Carabillo et al., *Feminist Chronicles,* 108.

75. Joyce Gelb, *Feminism and Politics: A Comparative Perspective* (Berkeley: University of California Press, 1989), 66.

76. Melich, *The Republican War,* 179–80.

77. See Carabillo et al., *Feminist Chronicles,* 120.

78. Melich, *The Republican War,* 207.

79. Carabillo et al., *Feminist Chronicles,* 128; and Melich, *The Republican War,* 231.

80. Stevie Cameron, *On the Take: Crime, Corruption and Greed in the Mulroney Years* (Toronto: Macfarlane Walter and Ross, 1994).

81. Senior federal officials as quoted in Donald J. Savoie, *Thatcher, Reagan, Mulroney: In Search of a New Bureaucracy* (Toronto: University of Toronto Press, 1994), 268, 271, 272.

82. Brian Mulroney, *Where I Stand* (Toronto: McClelland and Stewart, 1983), 90.

83. Mulroney as quoted in Savoie, *Thatcher, Reagan, Mulroney*, 4.

84. Mulroney as quoted in Andrew B. Gollner and Daniel Salée, "A Turn to the Right? Canada in the Post-Trudeau Era," in *Canada under Mulroney*, ed. Andrew B. Gollner and Daniel Salée (Montreal: Véhicule, 1988), 14–15.

85. Brian Mulroney, December 1984 speech to the Economic Club of New York, as quoted in Martin, *Pledge of Allegiance*, 69.

86. Mulroney as quoted in John Sawatsky, *Mulroney: The Politics of Ambition* (Toronto: Macfarlane Walter and Ross, 1991), 543; and Savoie, *Thatcher, Reagan, Mulroney*, 91.

87. Brooke Jeffrey, *Breaking Faith: The Mulroney Legacy of Deceit, Destruction and Disunity* (Toronto: Key Porter, 1992), 18, 175, 180.

88. See Richard Simeon, "National Reconciliation: The Mulroney Government and Federalism," in *Canada under Mulroney*, ed. Gollner and Salée, 25.

89. Mulroney as quoted in Sawatsky, *Mulroney*, 470. See also Sawatsky, *Mulroney*, 545–46.

90. The classic statement of the red tory thesis is presented in Gad Horowitz, *Canadian Labour in Politics* (Toronto: University of Toronto Press, 1968), 22–23.

91. For detailed breakdowns on NAC membership and budgets, see Jill Vickers, "Bending the Iron Law of Oligarchy: Debates on the Feminization of Organizations and Political Process in the English Canadian Women's Movement, 1970–1988," in *Women and Social Change*, ed. Jeri Dawn Wine and Janice L. Ristock (Toronto: Lorimer, 1991), 89.

92. According to the March 1995 issue of NAC's *ACTION NOW!* newsletter, "In the early 1980s, almost 90 per cent of NAC's funding came from the Federal Government" (2). For detailed figures on grants from the federal Women's Program, see Leslie A. Pal, *Interests of State* (Montreal: McGill-Queen's University Press, 1993), 221–25.

93. See Jill Vickers, Pauline Rankin, and Christine Appelle, *Politics as If Women Mattered: A Political Analysis of the National Action Committee on the Status of Women* (Toronto: University of Toronto Press, 1993).

94. See Chaviva Hošek, "Women and the Constitutional Process," in *And No One Cheered*, ed. Keith Banting and Richard Simeon (Toronto: Methuen, 1983), 280–300.

95. See Vickers et al., *Politics as If Women Mattered*, 5–6, 41, 148–52.

96. See Sylvia B. Bashevkin, *True Patriot Love: The Politics of Canadian Nationalism* (Toronto: Oxford University Press, 1991), chap. 6.

97. See Sylvia B. Bashevkin, *Toeing the Lines: Women and Party Politics in English Canada*, 2d ed. (Toronto: Oxford University Press, 1993), chap. 2.

98. Lisa Young, "Can Feminists Transform Party Politics? Women's Movements and Political Parties in Canada and the United States, 1970–1993" (Ph.D. diss., University of Toronto, 1996), chap. 5.

99. See Bashevkin, *Toeing the Lines,* 59–60.

100. See Ethel Klein, *Gender Politics: From Consciousness to Mass Politics* (Cambridge, MA: Harvard University Press, 1984).

101. Cannon, *President Reagan,* 812.

102. See Faludi, *Backlash,* 273; and Zillah R. Eisenstein, *The Color of Gender: Reimaging Democracy* (Berkeley: University of California Press, 1994), 121. According to American activists, Bush had been a donor to Planned Parenthood during his career on Capitol Hill.

103. Himmelstein, *To the Right,* 105.

104. See Mary Frances Berry, *The Politics of Parenthood* (New York: Viking, 1993), 142.

105. Republicans had consistently endorsed the Equal Rights Amendment since 1940. See Ferree and Hess, *Controversy and Coalition,* 119.

106. Melich, *The Republican War,* 296.

107. On the growth of organized antifeminism on the American political right, see Pamela Johnston Conover and Virginia Gray, *Feminism and the New Right* (New York: Praeger, 1983); and Rebecca Klatch, *Women of the New Right* (Philadelphia: Temple University Press, 1987).

108. According to an account of his previous decisions prepared by the Senate Judiciary Committee, Bork had consistently opposed the ERA, abortion, and "virtually every major civil rights advance on which he has taken a position." See Senate Judiciary Committee account, as quoted in Melich, *The Republican War,* 191.

109. Midge Decter, "Liberating Women: Who Benefits?" *Commentary* 77, no. 3 (March 1984): 36.

110. Himmelstein, *To the Right,* 105.

111. See Paul M. Sniderman and Thomas Piazza, *The Scar of Race* (Cambridge, MA: Harvard University Press, 1993).

112. See Martin Durham, *Moral Crusades: Family and Morality in the Thatcher Years* (New York: New York University Press, 1991).

113. See Vickers et al., *Politics as If Women Mattered,* 146–48; and Pal, *Interests of State,* 147.

CHAPTER TWO

1. This strategy therefore excludes action other than at the federal level in the United States and Canada. Moreover, it does not consider national-level initiatives that fall outside formal legislative and judicial parameters. The latter would include policy directives, commissions of inquiry, ministerial guidelines, bureaucratic reorganizations, administrative regulations, and budgets. Although each of these dimensions is relevant to research on feminism and neoconservatism, the

formal realm of legislative and judicial decisions is sufficiently rich as to provide a useful baseline for comparative work in the field.

The specific laws and court cases listed in appendix A were cited by women's movement activists in interviews and by academic studies of women and public policy. Because feminists in all three countries remained divided over the question of pornography, that particular policy area is not considered in this study.

2. These institutional and political opportunities structures arguments are presented in R. Kent Weaver and Bert A. Rockman, "When and How Do Institutions Matter?" in *Do Institutions Matter? Government Capabilities in the United States and Abroad,* ed. R. Kent Weaver and Bert A. Rockman (Washington, DC: Brookings, 1993); and Joyce Gelb, *Feminism and Politics: A Comparative Perspective* (Berkeley: University of California Press, 1989).

3. For a succinct review of this pattern, see Susan Gluck Mezey, *In Pursuit of Equality: Women, Public Policy, and the Federal Courts* (New York: St. Martin's, 1992), chap. 11.

4. See Steven A. Shull, *A Kinder, Gentler Racism? The Reagan-Bush Civil Rights Legacy* (Armonk, NY: Sharpe, 1993).

5. See Weaver and Rockman, "When and How Do Institutions Matter?" 450, 457–58; and Gelb, *Feminism and Politics,* 2.

6. Paul Byrne, "The Politics of the Women's Movement," *Parliamentary Affairs* 49, no. 1 (January 1996): 62, claims forty thousand women participated in the 1983 mass action and thirty thousand in the 1982 one.

7. Thomas R. Rochon, "The West European Peace Movement and the Theory of New Social Movements," in *Challenging the Political Order,* ed. Russell J. Dalton and Manfred Kuechler (New York: Oxford University Press, 1990), 107.

8. Elizabeth Wilson with Angela Weir, "The British Women's Movement," in *Hidden Agendas: Theory, Politics, and Experience in the Women's Movement,* ed. Elizabeth Wilson with Angela Weir (London: Tavistock, 1986), 131.

9. Women, Immigration, and Nationality Group (WING), *Worlds Apart: Women under Immigration and Nationality Law* (London: Pluto, 1985), 26.

10. David Bouchier, *The Feminist Challenge* (London: Macmillan, 1983), 189; and Jennifer Dale and Peggy Foster, *Feminists and State Welfare* (London: Routledge and Kegan Paul, 1986), 107–8.

11. Susan Atkins and Brenda Hoggett, *Women and the Law* (Oxford: Blackwell, 1984), 154; Roger Bird and Stephen Cretney, *Divorce: The New Law* (Bristol, England: Jordan, 1996), 1–2; April Carter, *The Politics of Women's Rights* (London: Longman, 1988), 63; and Susan Williscroft, "Women and the Law," in *The Invisible Decade,* ed. Georgina Ashworth and Lucy Bonnerjea (Brookfield, VT: Gower, 1985), 100–1.

12. Margaret Thatcher, *The Path to Power* (New York: HarperCollins, 1995), 151.

13. See Vicky Randall, "Great Britain and Dilemmas for Feminist Strategy in the 1980s: The Case of Abortion and Reproductive Rights," in *Women Transforming Politics,* ed. Jill M. Bystydzienski (Bloomington: Indiana University

Press, 1992), 88. See also Joan Isaac, "The Politics of Morality in the UK," *Parliamentary Affairs* 47, no. 2 (April 1994): 175–76.

14. Martin Durham, *Moral Crusades: Family and Morality in the Thatcher Years* (New York: New York University Press, 1991), 39.

15. See ibid., chap. 2.

16. Joni Lovenduski and Vicky Randall, *Contemporary Feminist Politics: Women and Power in Britain* (Oxford: Oxford University Press, 1993), 223.

17. Zsuzsanna Adler, *Rape on Trial* (London: Routledge and Kegan Paul, 1987), 26–29.

18. Ibid., 19; Bouchier, *The Feminist Challenge*, 142; Jalna Hamner, "Violence to Women: From Private Sorrow to Public Issue," in *The Invisible Decade*, ed. Ashworth and Bonnerjea, 147; and Joni Lovenduski, *Women and European Politics* (Amherst: University of Massachusetts Press, 1986), 79, 261.

19. See Stefania Abrar, "Feminist Intervention and Local Domestic Violence Policy," *Parliamentary Affairs* 49, no. 1 (January 1996): 192.

20. On the 1976 Domestic Violence Act, see Carter, *The Politics of Women's Rights*, 72; and Lovenduski, *Women and European Politics*, 78–79. On the 1978 Domestic Proceedings and Magistrates' Courts Act, see Roger Bird, *Domestic Violence: The New Law* (Bristol, England: Jordan, 1996), 2–6; and Susan Edwards, "Male Violence against Women: Excusatory and Explanatory Ideologies in Law and Society," in *Gender, Sex, and Law*, ed. Susan Edwards (London: Croom Helm, 1985), 196.

21. Anna Coote and Beatrix Campbell, *Sweet Freedom: The Struggle for Women's Liberation* (Oxford: Blackwell, 1987), 57–58; and Frances Bennett, "Social Security and Taxation," in *The Invisible Decade*, ed. Ashworth and Bonnerjea, 67–68.

22. Carter, *The Politics of Women's Rights*, 57–58, 116, 123–24; and Lovenduski, *Women and European Politics*, 74, 256, 259.

23. Bouchier, *The Feminist Challenge*, 10; Carter, *The Politics of Women's Rights*, 61–62, 92–93, 104; and Coote and Campbell, *Sweet Freedom*, 90–91.

24. Carter, *The Politics of Women's Rights*, 61–62, 103; Coote and Campbell, *Sweet Freedom*, 93; Anne E. Morris and Susan M. Nott, *Working Women and the Law: Equality and Discrimination in Theory and Practice* (London: Routledge, 1991), 70, 95–102; and Vicky Randall, *Women and Politics* (London: Macmillan, 1987), 296.

25. Carter, *The Politics of Women's Rights*, 59–60; Lovenduski, *Women and European Politics*, 77, 256–57; Morris and Nott, *Working Women and the Law*, 43–47; and Jeanne Gregory, "Equal Value/Comparable Worth: National Statute and Case Law in Britain and the USA," in *Equal Value/Comparable Worth in the UK and the USA*, ed. Peggy Kahn and Elizabeth Meehan (London: Macmillan, 1992), 46–47.

26. European Community levers were particularly helpful to British women's groups because EC standards exceeded domestic ones; a reverse situation confronted Scandinavian feminists who suspected European levers would drag down

the standards set by their existing national provisions. See Elizabeth Meehan, *Citizenship and the European Community* (London: Sage, 1993), chap. 6, especially 119 n. 2.

27. One provision of the 1986 Social Security Act, responding to the *Drake* decision by the European Court, recognized married women as carers who might forego paid employment and thus be eligible for the Invalid Care Allowance. See Caroline Glendinning, "'Community Care': The Financial Consequences for Women," in *Women and Poverty in Britain: The 1990s,* ed. Caroline Glendinning and Jane Millar (London: Harvester Wheatsheaf, 1992), 172.

28. Carter, *The Politics of Women's Rights,* 64; WING, *Worlds Apart,* 44–47, 66, 74–76, 164–68; and Williscroft, "Women and the Law," 103–5.

29. Coote and Campbell, *Sweet Freedom,* 92; Glendinning, "Community Care," 172; and Jane Pillinger, *Feminising the Market: Women's Pay and Employment in the European Community* (London: Macmillan, 1992), 89.

30. Coote and Campbell, *Sweet Freedom,* 89–90; and Lovenduski and Randall, *Contemporary Feminist Politics,* 267.

31. Lovenduski and Randall, *Contemporary Feminist Politics,* 267–68.

32. Durham, *Moral Crusades,* 19–31; and Isaac, "The Politics of Morality in the UK," 176–77.

33. Durham, *Moral Crusades,* 100–2.

34. Ibid., 46.

35. Abrar, "Feminist Intervention," 194.

36. Morris and Nott, *Working Women and the Law,* 149, 151; Glendinning, "Community Care," 172; Lovenduski and Randall, *Contemporary Feminist Politics,* 49; and Dulcie Groves, "Women and Financial Provision for Old Age," in *Women's Issues in Social Policy,* ed. Mavis Maclean and Dulcie Groves (London: Routledge, 1991), 43.

37. Lovenduski and Randall, *Contemporary Feminist Politics,* 188–89; and Katherine O'Donovan and Erika Szyszczak, *Equality and Sex Discrimination Law* (Oxford: Blackwell, 1988), 136–39.

38. Pillinger, *Feminising the Market,* 88; Morris and Nott, *Working Women and the Law,* 157, 190; and O'Donovan and Szyszczak, *Equality and Sex Discrimination Law,* 50 n. 74.

39. On the *Jenkins* ruling, see Morris and Nott, *Working Women and the Law,* 131; and O'Donovan and Szyszczak, *Equality and Sex Discrimination Law,* 130, 206. On the *Johnston* decision, see Morris and Nott, *Working Women and the Law,* 38; and O'Donovan and Szyszczak, *Equality and Sex Discrimination Law,* 199.

40. Carter, *The Politics of Women's Rights,* 61–62, 103; Coote and Campbell, *Sweet Freedom,* 93; and Randall, *Women and Politics,* 296.

41. Paul Pierson, *Dismantling the Welfare State? Reagan, Thatcher, and the Politics of Retrenchment* (Cambridge: Cambridge University Press, 1994), 59, 62; Claire Callender, "Redundancy, Unemployment and Poverty," in *Women and Poverty in Britain,* ed. Glendinning and Millar, 135–37; Dulcie Groves, "Occupational Pension Provision and Women's Poverty in Old Age," in *Women and Poverty in Britain,* ed. Glendinning and Millar, 204–5; and Alan Walker, "The Poor

Relation: Poverty among Older Women," in *Women and Poverty in Britain,* ed. Glendinning and Millar, 188–89.

42. Evan Davis et al., *1985 Benefit Reviews: The Effects of the Proposals* (London: Institute for Fiscal Studies, 1985), 25–27.

43. Durham, *Moral Crusades,* 116–18; and Lovenduski and Randall, *Contemporary Feminist Politics,* 38, 40, 196.

44. Lovenduski and Randall, *Contemporary Feminist Politics,* 336; and Morris and Nott, *Working Women and the Law,* 91.

45. Morris and Nott, *Working Women and the Law,* 98–99, 124, 132; and Michael Rubenstein, *Discrimination: A Guide to the Relevant Case Law on Race and Sex Discrimination and Equal Pay,* 8th ed. (London: Eclipse Group, 1995), 73, 76.

46. Editorial, "The Criminal Injustice Bill," *Everywoman,* October 1994, 5; Lorna Russell, "Shattering the Peace," *Everywoman,* October 1994, 16–17; and Alix Sharkey, "Saturday Night: Blue-Rinse Grannies Join Hardcore Ravers," *Independent* (London), 30 July 1994.

47. See Isaac, "The Politics of Morality in the UK," 81; Lovenduski and Randall, *Contemporary Feminist Politics,* 267; and Mavis Maclean and John Eekelaar, "Child Support: The British Solution," *International Journal of Law and the Family* 7 (1993): 205–29.

48. Lovenduski and Randall, *Contemporary Feminist Politics,* 267; Susan Millns, "Legislative Constructions of Motherhood," *Parliamentary Affairs* 49, no. 1 (January 1996): 167–68, 173–74; Robert Crampton, "Cops or Robbers? Child Support Agency," *Times* (London), 13 August 1994; Pat Eddery, "Poor Mum, Cheapskate Dad," *Today* (London), 1 August 1994; "Child Support, April Alert No. 1: Do Not Sign the Form Unless . . . ," *Welfare Rights Bulletin* 113 (April 1993): 12; Julia Bard, "Confusion on Child Support," *Everywoman,* March 1993, 12; and Sue Ward, "Harder Times for Single Mothers?" *Everywoman,* March 1993, 40.

49. Watson Wyatt, *Pensions News* 3 (July/August 1995): 4; "Court Can Vary Pension Fund Scheme as a Marriage Settlement," *Times* (London), 3 July 1995, 35–36; "Wife Wins Part of Husband's Pension in Divorce Victory," *Occupational Pensions Law Reports* (August 1995): 8–10.

50. Bird and Cretney, *Divorce,* 8.

51. On antiabortion protest, see Isaac, "The Politics of Morality in the UK," 178. On the 1990 act, see Lovenduski and Randall, *Contemporary Feminist Politics,* 232–33, 251–57; and Millns, "Legislative Constructions of Motherhood," 163–64.

52. Millns, "Legislative Constructions of Motherhood," 161; and Linda Tyler, "Towards a Redefinition of Rape," *New Law Journal,* 24 June 1994, 860–61.

53. "Newspaper Pays Rape Victim £10,000," *Everywoman,* October 1994, 10.

54. Bird, *Domestic Violence.*

55. Rubenstein, *Discrimination,* 57–58.

56. Ibid., 57, 72, 74, 76; and Emma Seymour, "How Far Have We Come?" *Everywoman,* March 1994 supplement, 5.

57. Seymour, "How Far Have We Come?" 4–5; Elizabeth Meehan and Evelyn

Collins, "Women, the European Union, and Britain," *Parliamentary Affairs* 49, no. 1 (January 1996): 228; and "ECJ Rules That UK's Compensation Limit Is Too Low," news release from the Equal Opportunities Commission, London, 2 August 1993.

58. Clare Dyer, "Bosses Who Sack Mothers-to-Be Risk Huge Claims," *Guardian* (Manchester) 15 July 1994; and Aine McCarthy, "Courts Help Fight for Equal Rights," *Everywoman,* December 1994–January 1995.

59. Margaret Dibben, "Women Lose Out in Benefit Ruling," *Observer* (London), 13 August 1995; and Clare Dyer, "European Court Rules against Disabled Women," *Guardian* (Manchester), 12 August 1995.

60. *Maternity Rights: A Guide to the New Law* (London: Labour Research Department, 1994), 2.

61. Ibid., 9; Meehan and Collins, "Women, the European Union, and Britain," 228; and Vivien Hart, "Redesigning the Polity: Women, Workers, and European Constitutional Politics in Britain," in *Redesigning the State: The Politics of Constitutional Change,* ed. Brian Galligan and Peter H. Russell (forthcoming). One of the EOC's arguments in this case was that the differential treatment of part-timers under British law contravened a European Court ruling on indirect discrimination.

62. Rubenstein, *Discrimination,* 77; and "Dinner Ladies Win Victory on Equal Pay," *Guardian* (Manchester), 7 July 1995, 10.

63. Hilary Land, "Whatever Happened to the Social Wage?" in *Women and Poverty in Britain,* ed. Glendinning and Millar, 52.

64. "Maternity Rights and Dismissal," *Labour Research* 83, no. 7 (July 1994): 21; and Seymour, "How Far Have We Come?" 6.

65. Susan Lonsdale, "Patterns of Paid Work," in *Women and Poverty in Britain,* ed. Glendinning and Millar, 100.

66. See *The Pensions Bill: Implications for Sex Equality* (Manchester: Equal Opportunities Commission, n.d.); and Sue Ward, "Retirement Ages: All over Bar the Shouting?" *Everywoman,* March 1994, 38.

67. See, for example, the argument advanced in Ethel Klein, *Gender Politics: From Consciousness to Mass Politics* (Cambridge, MA: Harvard University Press, 1984).

68. Gelb, *Feminism and Politics,* 206.

69. See Jane J. Mansbridge, *Why We Lost the ERA* (Chicago: University of Chicago Press, 1986); Mary Frances Berry, *Why ERA Failed: Politics, Women's Rights, and the Amending Process of the Constitution* (Bloomington: Indiana University Press, 1986); Joan Hoff-Wilson, ed., *Rights of Passage: The Past and Future of the ERA* (Bloomington: Indiana University Press, 1986); and Janet K. Boles, *The Politics of the Equal Rights Amendment* (New York: Longman, 1979).

70. Mezey, *In Pursuit of Equality,* 148–49.

71. Flora Davis, *Moving the Mountain: The Women's Movement in America since 1960* (New York: Simon and Schuster, 1991), 147–52.

72. Ibid., 211–14.

73. Mezey, *In Pursuit of Equality*, 17–18; Davis, *Moving the Mountain*, 403–4; Judith A. Baer, *Women in American Law* (New York: Holmes and Meier, 1991), 32–33; and Joan Hoff, *Law, Gender, and Justice* (New York: New York University Press, 1991), 247–48.

74. Baer, *Women in American Law*, 33; Davis, *Moving the Mountain*, 404–5; Hoff, *Law, Gender, and Injustice*, 248; and Mezey, *In Pursuit of Equality*, 18–19.

75. Mezey, *In Pursuit of Equality*, 21; and M. Margaret Conway, David W. Ahern, and Gertrude A. Steuernagel, *Women and Public Policy: A Revolution in Progress* (Washington, DC: Congressional Quarterly Press, 1995), 146.

76. Mezey, *In Pursuit of Equality*, 120–21.

77. Baer, *Women in American Law*, 108–9; Hoff, *Law, Gender, and Injustice*, 295; and Mezey, *In Pursuit of Equality*, 115–18.

78. Hoff, *Law, Gender, and Injustice*, 249. See also Baer, *Women in American Law*, 34–35.

79. Eva R. Rubin, *The Supreme Court and the American Family: Ideology and Issues* (New York: Greenwood, 1986), 33–37.

80. Baer, *Women in American Law*, 126–27; Conway et al., *Women and Public Policy*, 191; and Mezey, *In Pursuit of Equality*, 21–23.

81. Baer, *Women in American Law*, 140.

82. Mezey, *In Pursuit of Equality*, 215.

83. Ibid.; Baer, *Women in American Law*, 188; and Leslie Friedman Goldstein, *Contemporary Cases in Women's Rights* (Madison: University of Wisconsin Press, 1994), 13–15.

84. Baer, *Women in American Law*, 188–95; Mezey, *In Pursuit of Equality*, chap. 10; Marian Faux, *Roe v. Wade* (New York: Penguin, 1993); Sarah Weddington, *A Question of Choice* (New York: Grosset Putnam, 1992); and Norma McCorvey with Andy Meisler, *I Am Roe* (New York: HarperCollins, 1994).

85. Goldstein, *Contemporary Cases in Women's Rights*, 16–19; and Mezey, *In Pursuit of Equality*, 218.

86. Baer, *Women in American Law*, 202–4; Hoff, *Law, Gender, and Injustice*, 303–5; and Mezey, *In Pursuit of Equality*, 244–48.

87. Baer, *Women in American Law*, 195–98; Hoff, *Law, Gender, and Injustice*, 306; and Mezey, *In Pursuit of Equality*, 220–23, 236–38.

88. Gelb, *Feminism and Politics*, 47; and Joyce Gelb, "The Politics of Wife Abuse," in *Families, Politics, and Public Policy*, ed. Irene Diamond (New York: Longman, 1983), 253–55.

89. Gelb, *Feminism and Politics*, 123–25; and Gelb, "The Politics of Wife Abuse," 255–57.

90. Baer, *Women in American Law*, 82; and Mezey, *In Pursuit of Equality*, 48.

91. Text of Supreme Court decision, as quoted in Mezey, *In Pursuit of Equality*, 59.

92. Baer, *Women in American Law*, 89; Hoff, *Law, Gender, and Injustice*, 396; and Mezey, *In Pursuit of Equality*, 58–61.

93. O'Donovan and Szyszczak, *Equality and Sex Discrimination Law*, 98.

94. Mezey, *In Pursuit of Equality,* 50–51.

95. Ibid., 114–15; Baer, *Women in American Law,* 106; and Hoff, *Law, Gender, and Injustice,* 397.

96. Mezey, *In Pursuit of Equality,* 39–40; and Toni Carabillo, Judith Meuli, and June Bundy Csida, *Feminist Chronicles, 1953–1993* (Los Angeles: Women's Graphics, 1993), 61.

97. Conway et al., *Women and Public Policy,* 66; and Davis, *Moving the Mountain,* 336.

98. Hoff, *Law, Gender, and Injustice,* 234; and Mezey, *In Pursuit of Equality,* 92–93.

99. Baer, *Women in American Law,* 109; and Mezey, *In Pursuit of Equality,* 118–21.

100. Pregnancy Discrimination Act as quoted in Mezey, *In Pursuit of Equality,* 121. See also Baer, *Women in American Law,* 109–10.

101. Baer, *Women in American Law,* 90; and Mezey, *In Pursuit of Equality,* 48–49.

102. Baer, *Women in American Law,* 44–47; and Davis, *Moving the Mountain,* 407.

103. See Hoff, *Law, Gender, and Injustice,* 323–24.

104. See Rebecca Klatch, *Women of the New Right* (Philadelphia: Temple University Press, 1987), 166.

105. See ibid., 136, 148–49, 171.

106. Mansbridge, *Why We Lost the ERA.*

107. Mezey, *In Pursuit of Equality,* 156.

108. Baer, *Women in American Law,* 224–27; Hoff, *Law, Gender, and Injustice,* 256–57; and Mezey, *In Pursuit of Equality,* 158–59.

109. Baer, *Women in American Law,* 227–29; and Mezey, *In Pursuit of Equality,* 160–61.

110. Leslie Friedman Goldstein, *The Constitutional Rights of Women* (Madison: University of Wisconsin Press, 1989), 523–36.

111. Hoff, *Law, Gender, and Injustice,* 255–56; and Mezey, *In Pursuit of Equality,* 203–4.

112. Baer, *Women in American Law,* 140; Conway et al., *Women and Public Policy,* 141; Mary Frances Berry, *The Politics of Parenthood: Child Care, Women's Rights, and the Myth of the Good Mother* (New York: Viking, 1993), 153; and Katherine Teghtsoonian, "Neo-Conservative Ideology and Opposition to Federal Regulation of Child Care Services in the United States and Canada," *Canadian Journal of Political Science* 25 (1993): 115–16.

113. Berry, *The Politics of Parenthood,* 167–70; and Catherine S. Chilman, "Welfare Reform or Revision? The Family Support Act of 1988," *Social Science Review* 66 (September 1992): 349–77; Nancy A. Naples, "A Socialist Feminist Analysis of the Family Support Act of 1988," *Affilia* 6, no. 4 (winter 1991): 23–38; and Wendy Sarvasy, "Reagan and Low-Income Mothers: A Feminist Recasting of the Debate," in *Remaking the Welfare State,* ed. Michael K. Brown (Philadelphia: Temple University Press, 1988), 253–76.

114. Baer, *Women in American Law*, 203–4; Hoff, *Law, Gender, and Injustice*, 304–24; and Mezey, *In Pursuit of Equality*, 248–49.

115. Baer, *Women in American Law*, 197; and Mezey, *In Pursuit of Equality*, 239–40.

116. Baer, *Women in American Law*, 198; and Mezey, *In Pursuit of Equality*, 211, 227.

117. Anne L. Harper, "Teenage Sexuality and Public Policy: An Agenda for Gender Education," in *Families, Politics, and Public Policy*, ed. Diamond, 226–28.

118. Barbara Hinkson Craig and David M. O'Brien, *Abortion and American Politics* (Chatham, NJ: Chatham House, 1993), 188.

119. Hoff, *Law, Gender, and Injustice*, 257; and Mezey, *In Pursuit of Equality*, 160.

120. Baer, *Women in American Law*, 196, 199; and Mezey, *In Pursuit of Equality*, 223–24.

121. Baer, *Women in American Law*, 199; and Hoff, *Law, Gender, and Injustice*, 306.

122. Gelb, "The Politics of Wife Abuse," 256–58.

123. Davis, *Moving the Mountain*, 322–23.

124. The same provisions also made child benefits taxable and offered assistance to many two-earner families. See Berry, *The Politics of Parenthood*, 11, 155–56; and Shelah Gilbert Leader, "Fiscal Policy and Family Structure," in *Families, Politics, and Public Policy*, ed. Diamond, 144.

125. Berry, *The Politics of Parenthood*, 153; Conway et al., *Women and Public Policy*, 95–96; Davis, *Moving the Mountain*, 345; and Hoff, *Law, Gender, and Injustice*, 273, 402.

126. Carabillo et al., *Feminist Chronicles*, 128; and Sara E. Rix, *The American Woman: 1990–91* (New York: Norton, 1990), 49.

127. Rix, *The American Woman: 1990–91*, 35.

128. Baer, *Women in American Law*, 71; Hoff, *Law, Gender, and Injustice*, 253; and Mezey, *In Pursuit of Equality*, 103–6. On the broader legal development of comparable worth strategies, see Michael W. McCann, *Rights at Work: Pay Equity Reform and the Politics of Legal Mobilization* (Chicago: University of Chicago Press, 1994).

129. Hoff, *Law, Gender, and Injustice*, 402; and Mezey, *In Pursuit of Equality*, 194–96.

130. Baer, *Women in American Law*, 99–104; Hoff, *Law, Gender, and Injustice*, 404; and Mezey, *In Pursuit of Equality*, 81–86.

131. Hoff, *Law, Gender, and Injustice*, 263; and Mezey, *In Pursuit of Equality*, 78–80.

132. Hoff, *Law, Gender, and Injustice*, 298; and Mezey, *In Pursuit of Equality*, 126–27.

133. Hoff, *Law, Gender, and Injustice*, 358–59; and Mezey, *In Pursuit of Equality*, 176–78. Reaction to the *Meritor Savings Bank v. Vinson* decision included the publication by NOW and other groups of do-it-yourself guides to sexual harassment law.

134. See Berry, *The Politics of Parenthood,* 159–60; Conway et al., *Women and Public Policy,* 163–64; and Mezey, *In Pursuit of Equality,* 124–25.

135. Hoff, *Law, Gender, and Injustice,* 407; Mezey, *In Pursuit of Equality,* 88 n. 38; and Zillah R. Eisenstein, *The Color of Gender: Reimaging Democracy* (Berkeley: University of California Press, 1994), 58.

136. Carabillo et al., *Feminist Chronicles,* 152.

137. Goldstein, *Contemporary Cases in Women's Rights,* 167, 193–203.

138. Eisenstein, *The Color of Gender,* chap. 4; Mezey, *In Pursuit of Equality,* 253–62; Craig and O'Brien, *Abortion and American Politics,* chap. 6; and Goldstein, *The Constitutional Rights of Women,* 633–36.

139. See Carabillo et al., *Feminist Chronicles,* 130, 144.

140. Carabillo et al., *Feminist Chronicles,* 135; and Hoff, *Law, Gender, and Injustice,* 314–15.

141. Carabillo et al., *Feminist Chronicles,* 135; and Hoff, *Law, Gender, and Injustice,* 314.

142. Eisenstein, *The Color of Gender,* 116–18; and Goldstein, *Contemporary Cases in Women's Rights,* 75–94.

143. Carabillo et al., *Feminist Chronicles,* 141; and Goldstein, *Contemporary Cases in Women's Rights,* 95–96.

144. Carabillo et al., *Feminist Chronicles,* 139.

145. Eisenstein, *The Color of Gender,* 113–16; Goldstein, *Contemporary Cases in Women's Rights,* 96–151; and Leon Friedman, ed., *The Supreme Court Confronts Abortion: The Briefs, Argument, and Decision in* Planned Parenthood v. Casey (New York: Farrar, Straus, and Giroux, 1993).

146. Hoff, *Law, Gender, and Injustice,* 264–70.

147. Baer, *Women in American Law,* 104; and Hoff, *Law, Gender, and Injustice,* 270–71.

148. Eisenstein, *The Color of Gender,* 61–62; and Hoff, *Law, Gender, and Injustice,* 271.

149. Baer, *Women in American Law,* 104; and Eisenstein, *The Color of Gender,* 56–57.

150. Eisenstein, *The Color of Gender,* 55–56; and Hoff, *Law, Gender, and Injustice,* 271–72.

151. Schroeder as quoted in Berry, *The Politics of Parenthood,* 215.

152. Carabillo et al., *Feminist Chronicles,* 136; Eisenstein, *The Color of Gender,* 72; Shull, *A Kinder, Gentler Racism?* 185–86; and Paula Ries and Anne J. Stone, eds., *The American Woman, 1992–93: A Status Report* (New York: Norton, 1992), 69.

153. Cynthia Costello and Anne J. Stone, eds., *The American Woman, 1994–95: Where We Stand* (New York: Norton, 1994), 54.

154. Conway et al., *Women and Public Policy,* 72; and Eisenstein, *The Color of Gender,* 74–75.

155. Carabillo et al., *Feminist Chronicles,* 152.

156. Comment quoted in Mezey, *In Pursuit of Equality,* 198.

157. Eisenstein, *The Color of Gender,* 59–61; and Mezey, *In Pursuit of Equality,* 56–57, 198–200.

158. Berry, *The Politics of Parenthood,* 176–85; and Carabillo et al., *Feminist Chronicles,* 125, 128.

159. On Public Law 101–508, part of the Omnibus Budget Reconciliation Act of 1990, see Berry, *The Politics of Parenthood,* 192–93.

160. Shull, *A Kinder, Gentler Racism?* 60; and *Congressional Quarterly Almanac* (Washington, DC: Congressional Quarterly, 1990), 366.

161. Carabillo et al., *Feminist Chronicles,* 138; and Sally J. Kenney, *For Whose Protection? Reproductive Hazards and Exclusionary Policies in the United States and Britain* (Ann Arbor: University of Michigan Press, 1992).

162. Ries and Stone, eds., *The American Woman, 1992–93,* 60, 63.

163. The bill was initially introduced in 1985 as H. R. 2020, the Parental and Disability Leave Act, by Representative Patricia Schroeder, a Democrat from Colorado. Over time, it was altered significantly in response to opposition by business groups. See Berry, *The Politics of Parenthood,* 161–62.

164. Sylvia B. Bashevkin, *True Patriot Love: The Politics of Canadian Nationalism* (Toronto: Oxford University Press, 1991), 116.

165. See Sean Fine, "Mulroney and Wilson Criticized for Avoiding Budget Protesters," *Globe and Mail* (Toronto), 13 June 1989, A13.

166. See Virginia Galt, "Tens of Thousands Are Primed to Rail against Mulroney," *Globe and Mail* (Toronto), 14 May 1993.

167. Decision as quoted in Beverley Baines, "Law, Gender, Equality," in *Changing Patterns: Women in Canada,* ed. Sandra Burt, Lorraine Code, and Lindsay Dorney, 2d ed. (Toronto: McClelland and Stewart, 1993), 261. See also Douglas Sanders, "The Renewal of Indian Special Status," in *Equality Rights and the Canadian Charter of Rights and Freedoms,* ed. Anne F. Bayefsky and Mary Eberts (Toronto: Carswell, 1985), 540–47; and Sally M. Weaver, "The Status of Indian Women," in *Two Nations, Many Cultures,* ed. Jean Leonard Elliott (Scarborough, Ontario: Prentice Hall Canada, 1983), 56–79.

168. Canadian Charter of Rights and Freedoms, pt. 1 of the Constitution Act, 1982, being Schedule B of the Canada Act, 1982 (U.K.), 1982. Because of a three-year waiting period designed to permit governments to bring their laws into conformity, section 15 did not come into effect until 17 April 1985. See Chaviva Hošek, "Women and the Constitutional Process," in *And No One Cheered,* ed. Keith Banting and Richard Simeon (Toronto: Methuen, 1983), 280–300.

169. Irene Murdoch as quoted in Linda Silver Dranoff, *Women in Canadian Life: Law* (Toronto: Fitzhenry and Whiteside, 1977), 52. See also Alison Prentice, Paula Bourne, Gail Cuthbert Brandt, Beth Light, Wendy Mitchinson, and Naomi Black, *Canadian Women: A History,* 2d ed. (Toronto: Harcourt Brace, 1996), 439–40.

170. See Angus McLaren and Arlene Tigar McLaren, *The Bedroom and the State: The Changing Practices and Politics of Contraception and Abortion in Canada, 1880–1980* (Toronto: McClelland and Stewart, 1986).

171. Stan Persky, introduction to *The Supreme Court of Canada Decision on Abortion,* ed. Shelagh Day and Stan Persky (Vancouver: New Star Books, 1988), 3–9.

172. On Morgentaler's campaign, including in the courts, see Catherine Dunphy, *Morgentaler: A Difficult Hero* (Toronto: Random House, 1996); F. L. Morton, *Morgentaler v. Borowski: Abortion, the Charter and the Courts* (Toronto: McClelland and Stewart, 1992); and Janine Brodie, Shelley A. M. Gavigan, and Jane Jenson, *The Politics of Abortion* (Toronto: Oxford University Press, 1992).

173. Toni Pickard, "Culpable Mistakes and Rape: Harsh Words on *Pappajohn,*" *University of Toronto Law Journal* 30 (1980): 415–20.

174. Prentice et al., *Canadian Women,* 440; and Maria Los, "The Struggle to Redefine Rape in the Early 1980s," in *Confronting Sexual Assault: A Decade of Legal and Social Change,* ed. Julian V. Roberts and Renate M. Mohr (Toronto: University of Toronto Press, 1994), 26–30.

175. Maureen Baker, *Canadian Family Policies: Cross-National Comparisons* (Toronto: University of Toronto Press, 1995), 161–63; and Sandra Burt, "The Changing Patterns of Public Policy," in *Changing Patterns,* ed. Burt et al., 222.

176. Baker, *Canadian Family Policies,* 294; and Prentice et al., *Canadian Women,* 365.

177. Baker, *Canadian Family Policies,* 138; and Ken Battle, "The Politics of Stealth: Child Benefits under the Tories," in *How Ottawa Spends, 1993–1994,* ed. Susan D. Phillips (Ottawa: Carleton University Press, 1993), 419.

178. Burt, "The Changing Patterns of Public Policy," 224; Lorna R. Marsden, "The Role of the National Action Committee on the Status of Women in Facilitating Equal Pay Policy in Canada," in *Equal Employment Policy for Women,* ed. Ronnie Steinberg Ratner (Philadelphia: Temple University Press, 1980), 242–60; and Marjorie Griffin Cohen, "Paid Work," in *Canadian Women's Voices. Vol. 2: Bold Visions,* ed. Ruth Roach Pierson and Marjorie Griffin Cohen (Toronto: Lorimer, 1995), 99–100.

179. Prentice et al., *Canadian Women,* 365–66; W. A. Bogart, *Courts and Country: The Limits of Litigation and the Social and Political Life of Canada* (Toronto: Oxford University Press, 1994), 143–44; and Leslie A. Pal and F. L. Morton, *"Bliss v. Attorney General of Canada:* From Legal Defeat to Political Victory," *Osgoode Hall Law Journal* 24 (spring 1986): 141–60.

180. Bogart, *Courts and Country,* 147, 279.

181. Sally Weaver, "First Nations Women and Government Policy, 1970–92: Discrimination and Conflict," in *Changing Patterns,* ed. Burt et al., 115–30.

182. Baines, "Law, Gender, Equality," 267.

183. Ibid., 269–70; and Women's Legal Education and Action Fund, *Equality and the Charter: Ten Years of Feminist Advocacy before the Supreme Court of Canada* (Toronto: Emond Montgomery, 1996), 5–25.

184. Baker, *Canadian Family Policies,* 294, 296; and Bogart, *Courts and Country,* 139–40.

185. Bogart, *Courts and Country,* 140–41; and Women's Legal Education and Action Fund, *Equality and the Charter,* 323–43.

186. Bogart, *Courts and Country,* 147–51; Women's Legal Education and Action Fund, *Equality and the Charter,* 49–65; and Michael Mandel, *The Charter of Rights and the Legalization of Politics in Canada* (Toronto: Thompson Educational Publishing, 1994), 405–28.

187. Mandel, *The Charter of Rights,* 429; and Women's Legal Education and Action Fund, *Equality and the Charter,* 101–16.

188. Bill C-43 made abortion punishable by as much as two years in prison unless a doctor determined that continuing the pregnancy would threaten a woman's physical, mental, or psychological health. See Leslie A. Pal, "How Ottawa Dithers: The Conservatives and Abortion Policy," in *How Ottawa Spends: 1991– 92,* ed. Frances Abele (Ottawa: Carleton University Press, 1991), 269–306.

189. Bogart, *Courts and Country,* 145–46; Women's Legal Education and Action Fund, *Equality and the Charter,* 27–47, 223–44; and Sheila Noonan, "Strategies of Survival: Moving beyond the Battered Woman Syndrome," in *In Conflict with the Law: Women and the Canadian Justice System,* ed. Ellen Adelberg and Claudia Currie (Vancouver: Press Gang, 1993), 247–70.

190. Mandel, *The Charter of Rights,* 383–86; and Women's Legal Education and Action Fund, *Equality and the Charter,* 173–99.

191. Canada Labour Code, section 247.1–247.4, amended in 1985, in *Consolidated Federal Employment and Labour Statutes and Regulations, 1995* (Toronto: Carswell, 1994), 103–4.

192. Burt, "The Changing Patterns of Public Policy," 223.

193. Teghtsoonian, "Neo-Conservative Ideology and Opposition"; Derek P. J. Hum, "Compromise and Delay: The Federal Strategy on Child Care," in *Canada: The State of the Federation 1989,* ed. Ronald L. Watts and Douglas M. Brown (Kingston, Ontario: Queen's University Institute of Intergovernmental Relations, 1989), 151–65; and Susan D. Phillips, "Rock-a-Bye, Brian: The National Strategy on Child Care," in *How Ottawa Spends, 1989–90,* ed. Katherine A. Graham (Ottawa: Carleton University Press, 1989), 165–208.

194. Baker, *Canadian Family Policies,* 162.

195. Prentice et al., *Canadian Women,* 358.

196. Cohen, "Paid Work," 154–55; Bogart, *Courts and Country,* 145; and Women's Legal Education and Action Fund, *Equality and the Charter,* 87–99.

197. Chief Justice Brian Dickson as quoted in "Can't Discriminate against Pregnant Staff, Court Rules," *Toronto Star,* 5 May 1989, A1. See also Baines, "Law, Gender, Equality," 271; Bogart, *Courts and Country,* 144–45; and Women's Legal Education and Action Fund, *Equality and the Charter,* 67–85.

198. Margaret Atwood, ". . . The Only Position They've Ever Adopted toward Us, Country to Country, Has Been the Missionary Position," in *If You Love This Country: Facts and Feelings on Free Trade,* ed. Laurier LaPierre (Toronto: McClelland and Stewart, 1987), 20.

199. See Bashevkin, *True Patriot Love,* chap. 6.

200. Judy Rebick, "The Charlottetown Accord: A Faulty Framework and a Wrong-Headed Compromise," in *The Charlottetown Accord, the Referendum,*

and the Future of Canada, ed. Kenneth McRoberts and Patrick Monahan (Toronto: University of Toronto Press, 1993), 102–6.

201. Similar conclusions are reached in Meehan and Collins, "Women, the European Union, and Britain," 221–32; and Ian Forbes, "The Privatisation of Sex Equality Policy," *Parliamentary Affairs* 49, no. 1 (January 1996): 148.

202. See Kenneth J. Meier and Deborah R. McFarlane, "Abortion Politics and Abortion Funding Policy," in *Understanding the New Politics of Abortion,* ed. Malcolm L. Goggin (Newbury Park, CA: Sage, 1993), 251.

CHAPTER THREE

1. Flora Davis, *Moving the Mountain: The Women's Movement in America since 1960* (New York: Simon and Schuster, 1991), 332.

2. See Caroline Glendinning and Jane Millar, eds., *Women and Poverty in Britain* (London: Harvester Wheatsheaf, 1987), and *Women and Poverty in Britain: The 1990s* (London: Harvester Wheatsheaf, 1992).

3. Janine Brodie, *Politics on the Margins: Restructuring and the Canadian Women's Movement* (Halifax: Fernwood, 1995), 19.

4. For an overview of these patterns in all three countries, see Maureen Baker, *Canadian Family Policies: Cross-National Comparisons* (Toronto: University of Toronto Press, 1995).

5. See Kate Figes, *Because of Her Sex: The Myth of Equality for Women in Britain* (London: Macmillan, 1994), 155.

6. See Paul Pierson, *Dismantling the Welfare State? Reagan, Thatcher, and the Politics of Retrenchment* (Cambridge: Cambridge University Press, 1994), 63.

7. Sara E. Rix, "The Reagan Years: Budgetary Backlash," in *Women, Power, and Policy,* ed. Ellen Boneparth and Emily Stoper, 2d ed. (New York: Pergamon, 1988), 75–76.

8. Cynthia Costello and Anne J. Stone, eds., *The American Woman, 1994–95: Where We Stand* (New York: Norton, 1994), 265.

9. *Women in Canada: A Statistical Report* (Ottawa: Minister of Industry, 1995), 54; and Joyce Gelb, *Feminism and Politics: A Comparative Perspective* (Berkeley: University of California Press, 1989), 218.

10. Comparative rates of unionization are drawn from Organization for Economic Cooperation and Development data in *The Integration of Women into the Economy* (Paris: OECD Publications, 1985) and from Hilary Land, "Whatever Happened to the Social Wage?" in *Women and Poverty in Britain: The 1990s,* ed. Glendinning and Millar, 51; Costello and Stone, eds., *The American Woman, 1994–95,* 294; and Paula Ries and Anne J. Stone, eds., *The American Woman, 1992–93* (New York: Norton, 1992), 351.

11. The percentage of paid employed females belonging to a union increased slightly over time in Canada, whereas the percentage of working men holding union membership declined slightly. See *Women in Canada,* 68.

12. For comparative data on mothers at work and child care provisions, see Baker, *Canadian Family Policies,* chaps. 2–6.

13. Data are drawn from E. F. Jones, J. D. Forrest, N. Goldman, S. Henshaw, R. Lincoln, J. I. Rosoff, C. F. Wesloff, and D. Wulf, *Teenage Pregnancy in Industrialized Countries* (New Haven, CT: Yale University Press, 1986).

14. Ibid.

15. See Baker, *Canadian Family Policies,* 61–62; and Nancy E. Adler and Jeanne M. Tschann, "The Abortion Debate: Psychological Issues for Adult Women and Adolescents," in *American Women in the Nineties,* ed. Sherri Matteo (Boston: Northeastern University Press, 1993), 208.

16. See Martin Durham, *Moral Crusades: Family and Morality in the Thatcher Years* (New York: New York University Press, 1991), chap. 3.

17. Anne L. Harper, "Teenage Sexuality and Public Policy: An Agenda for Gender Education," in *Families, Politics, and Public Policy,* ed. Irene Diamond (New York: Longman, 1983), 220–35.

18. Lesley Abdela, *What Women Want: A Guide to Creating a Better and Fairer Life for Women in the UK* (London: Body Shop, 1994), 39–40.

19. Maureen Baker, *Canadian Family Policies,* 76–77; *Women in Canada,* 86.

20. Costello and Stone, eds., *The American Woman, 1994–95,* 291, 309; Ries and Stone, eds., *The American Woman 1992–93,* 351.

21. See Costello and Stone, eds., *The American Woman, 1994–95,* 307; Ries and Stone, eds., *The American Woman 1992–93,* 350; *Women in Canada,* 86; and Susan Lonsdale, "Patterns of Paid Work," in *Women and Poverty in Britain : The 1990s,* ed. Glendinning and Millar, 99.

22. Costello and Stone, eds., *The American Woman, 1994–95,* 295–99; and *Women in Canada,* 70.

23. Lonsdale, "Patterns of Paid Work," 97.

24. Figes, *Because of Her Sex,* 29; also 155, 195.

25. Baker, *Canadian Family Policies,* 49, 57–61.

26. Ibid., 43.

27. Costello and Stone, eds., *The American Woman, 1994–95,* 258.

28. Ibid., 261.

29. Baker, *Canadian Family Policies,* 43.

30. Ibid., 212–13.

31. Abdela, *What Women Want,* 21; Alan Walker, "The Poor Relation: Poverty among Older Women," in *Women and Poverty in Britain: The 1990s,* ed. Glendinning and Millar, 176–92; Dulcie Groves, "Occupational Pension Provision and Women's Poverty in Old Age," in *Women and Poverty in Britain: The 1990s,* ed. Glendinning and Millar, 193–206; Costello and Stone, eds., *The American Woman, 1994–95,* 143–44, 318–19, 339; *Women in Canada,* 85, 89–90; and Huguette Léger and Judy Rebick, *The NAC Voters' Guide* (Hull, Quebec: Voyageur, 1993), 44, 70.

32. Costello and Stone, eds., *The American Woman, 1994–95,* 143.

33. Juliet Cook and Shantu Watt, "Racism, Women and Poverty," in *Women*

and Poverty in Britain: The 1990s, ed. Glendinning and Millar, 18; and Jane Millar, "Lone Mothers and Poverty," in *Women and Poverty in Britain: The 1990s,* ed. Glendinning and Millar, 153.

34. Léger and Rebick, *The NAC Voters' Guide,* 25–26; and *Women in Canada,* 122–23.

35. Ries and Stone, eds., *The American Woman 1992–93,* 407.

36. Thatcher as quoted in Hugo Young, *One of Us: A Biography of Margaret Thatcher* (London: Pan, 1991), 373.

37. See Joni Lovenduski and Vicky Randall, *Contemporary Feminist Politics: Women and Power in Britain* (Oxford: Oxford University Press, 1993), 156; and Beatrix Campbell, *The Iron Ladies: Why Do Women Vote Tory?* (London: Virago, 1987), 73.

38. See Vivien Hart, *Bound by Our Constitution: Women, Workers, and the Minimum Wage* (Princeton, NJ: Princeton University Press, 1994).

39. See Vivien Hart, "Redesigning the Polity: Women, Workers and European Constitutional Politics in Britain," in *Redesigning the State: The Politics of Constitutional Change,* ed. Brian Galligan and Peter H. Russell (forthcoming); and Lovenduski and Randall, *Contemporary Feminist Politics,* 183–85.

40. Lovenduski and Randall, *Contemporary Feminist Politics,* 27–29; and Abdela, *What Women Want,* 39.

41. Abdela, *What Women Want,* 43; and Lonsdale, "Patterns of Paid Work," 100–2.

42. See Abdela, *What Women Want,* 47–49; Lonsdale, "Patterns of Paid Work," 104–5; and "Part-Timers' Rights—Europe Drags UK," *Labour Research* (October 1990): 14–15.

43. Lovenduski and Randall, *Contemporary Feminist Politics,* 47–49; and Figes, *Because of Her Sex,* 156–57.

44. Lonsdale, "Patterns of Paid Work," 102–3.

45. Ibid., 102; and Heather Joshi, "The Cost of Caring," in *Women and Poverty in Britain: The 1990s,* ed. Glendinning and Millar, 110–25.

46. Abdela, *What Women Want,* 29.

47. Ibid.; and Equal Opportunities Commission, *The Key to Real Choice: An Action Plan for Childcare* (Manchester: EOC, 1990).

48. See Vicky Randall, "The Irresponsible State? The Politics of Child Daycare Provision in Britain," *British Journal of Political Science* 25 (1995): 327–48; Vicky Randall, "Feminism and Child Daycare," *Journal of Social Policy* 25, no. 4 (1996): 485–505; and Vicky Randall, "The Politics of Childcare Policy," *Parliamentary Affairs* 49, no. 1 (January 1996): 176–90.

49. Randall, "The Politics of Childcare Policy," 185–86.

50. Christine Crawley and Jane Slowey, *Women and Europe, 1985 to 1995,* booklet produced for the Birmingham East European Constituency Labour Party (n.d.), 13–14.

51. Randall, "The Politics of Childcare Policy," 187–88.

52. Abdela, *What Women Want,* 33.

53. See Hart, "Redesigning the Polity;" and Suzanne Bosworth, "Workwise, Snakes and Ladders," *Everywoman*, July 1994.

54. The minimum period of paid maternity leave under British statute was fourteen weeks, and the maximum was forty weeks for mothers with twenty-four months of continuous employment. Statutory maternity pay in 1996 was calculated at 90 percent of regular pay for the first six weeks of leave and about £56 per week for the rest of the leave period. See Linda Clarke, *Discrimination*, 2d ed. (London: Institute of Personnel and Development, 1995), 58–59; Debbie Hill and Naomi Caine, "The Birth of the Blues," *Sunday Times* (London), 28 April 1996; Abdela, *What Women Want*, 37–38; and Figes, *Because of Her Sex*, 80, 82.

55. Abdela, *What Women Want*, 37.

56. Young, *One of Us*, 129–30; and Dennis Kavanagh, *Thatcherism and British Politics: The End of Consensus?* 2d ed. (Oxford: Oxford University Press, 1990), 247, 251.

57. Young, *One of Us*, 148; and Kavanagh, *Thatcherism and British Politics*, 230.

58. Kavanagh, *Thatcherism and British Politics*, 218–24; and Pierson, *Dismantling the Welfare State*, 151.

59. Kavanagh, *Thatcherism and British Politics*, 230; and Pierson, *Dismantling the Welfare State*, 151.

60. Pierson, *Dismantling the Welfare State*, 63, 79.

61. Joel Krieger, *Reagan, Thatcher, and the Politics of Decline* (New York: Oxford University Press, 1986), 79–101.

62. See Dennis Kavanagh and Anthony Seldon, eds., *The Thatcher Effect* (Oxford: Oxford University Press, 1989), 265; Chris Mihill, "Women's Lot Is Still Less Pay, More Work," *Guardian* (Manchester), 9 August 1995, 4; Campbell, *The Iron Ladies*, 228; and Abdela, *What Women Want*, 50. According to one account, full-time employed women spent forty-six hours per week on household tasks in 1992 compared with twenty-six hours per week for full-time employed men. See Joni Lovenduski, "Sex, Gender, and British Politics," *Parliamentary Affairs* 49, no. 1 (January 1996): 10.

63. Pierson, *Dismantling the Welfare State*, 58–64; and Alan Walker, "The Poor Relation," 187–89.

64. Walker, "The Poor Relation," 189.

65. Ibid., 176–78; and Abdela, *What Women Want*, 21.

66. Pierson, *Dismantling the Welfare State*, 76, 79.

67. Ibid., 81.

68. Hilary Land, "Whatever Happened to the Social Wage?" in *Women and Poverty in Britain: The 1990s*, ed. Glendinning and Millar, 55.

69. Pierson, *Dismantling the Welfare State*, 86–87; and Land, "Whatever Happened to the Social Wage?" 56.

70. Thatcher as quoted in Land, "Whatever Happened to the Social Wage?" 56.

71. Ibid., 57–58; and Pierson, *Dismantling the Welfare State*, 82–83.

72. Pierson, *Dismantling the Welfare State*, 105–7.

73. Ibid., 107–09.

74. Ibid., 112.

75. Ibid., 113–15.

76. Ibid., 115.

77. Land, "Whatever Happened to the Social Wage?" 51.

78. Ian Forbes, "The Privatisation of Sex Equality Policy," *Parliamentary Affairs* 49, no. 1 (January 1996): 152.

79. Ibid.

80. Abdela, *What Women Want,* 15; and Millar, "Lone Mothers and Poverty," 149–51.

81. Joyce Gelb, "Movement Strategies: Inside or Outside the 'System,' in *The New Women's Movement,* ed. Drude Dahlerup (London: Sage, 1986), 115; and Gelb, *Feminism and Politics,* 97.

82. Margaret Thatcher, as quoted in Wendy Webster, *Not a Man to Match Her: The Marketing of a Prime Minister* (London: Women's Press, 1990), 159.

83. Kavanagh and Seldon, *The Thatcher Effect,* 130.

84. Lovenduski and Randall, *Contemporary Feminist Politics,* 73–74; and Joan Isaac, "The Politics of Morality in the UK," *Parliamentary Affairs* 47, no. 2 (April 1994): 185.

85. Isaac, "The Politics of Morality in the UK," 183–85.

86. See Lovenduski and Randall, *Contemporary Feminist Politics,* 104, 151; and Gelb, *Feminism and Politics,* 86.

87. Lovenduski and Randall, *Contemporary Feminist Politics,* 193–98, 289.

88. Ibid., 151.

89. Young, *One of Us,* 499; and Kavanagh, *Thatcherism and British Politics,* 286–87.

90. Land, "Whatever Happened to the Social Wage?" 50.

91. Lovenduski and Randall, *Contemporary Feminist Politics,* 289–90.

92. Lorna Russell, "Shattering the Peace," *Everywoman,* October 1994, 16–17.

93. In June 1993, the Conservative government appointed Kamlesh Bahl, a corporate lawyer in her midthirties, as part-time head of the EOC. Bahl's limited experience in the area of equality law combined with her part-time status reinforced older concerns about the clout of the EOC. See Polly Toynbee, "Why the EOC Is Utterly Useless," *Cosmopolitan,* September 1993, 12–15; Melissa Benn, "Measured Equality: Interview with Kamlesh Bahl," *Everywoman,* December 1994–January 1995, 24–26; Yasmin Alibhai-Brown, "Would You Buy an Equal Opportunities Policy from This Woman?" *Guardian* (Manchester), 11 January 1995; and Sally Weale, "Opportunity Knocks," *Guardian* (Manchester), 26 April 1995.

94. Costello and Stone, *The American Woman, 1994–95,* 265; and Gelb, *Feminism and Politics,* 218.

95. Davis, *Moving the Mountain,* 340–42; and Sara M. Evans and Barbara J. Nelson, *Wage Justice: Comparable Worth and the Paradox of Technocratic Reform* (Chicago: University of Chicago Press, 1989), 3–4.

96. Pierson, *Dismantling the Welfare State,* 106, 158–61.

97. Krieger, *Reagan, Thatcher, and the Politics of Decline,* 161, 169.

98. Steven A. Shull, *A Kinder, Gentler Racism? The Reagan-Bush Civil Rights Legacy* (Armonk, NY: Sharpe, 1993), 12, 94, 112; and Gelb, *Feminism and Politics,* 102–3.

99. Judith A. Baer, *Women in American Law: The Struggle toward Equality from the New Deal to the Present* (New York: Holmes and Meier, 1991), 224–27.

100. Shull, *A Kinder, Gentler Racism?* 186–88; Virginia Sapiro, "The Women's Movement, Politics, and Policy in the Reagan Era," in *The New Women's Movement,* ed. Dahlerup, 130–31; and M. Margaret Conway, David W. Ahern, and Gertrude A. Steuernagel, *Women and Public Policy: A Revolution in Progress* (Washington, DC: Congressional Quarterly Press, 1995), 77, 197–99.

101. Mary Frances Berry, *The Politics of Parenthood: Child Care, Women's Rights, and the Myth of the Good Mother* (New York: Viking, 1993), 161–62, 184, 193.

102. Ibid., 156.

103. Ibid., 155, 178.

104. Ibid., 180.

105. Ibid., 188–89.

106. Hatch as quoted in ibid., 187.

107. Pierson, *Dismantling the Welfare State,* 67, 153, 177.

108. Kathleen B. Jones, "Toward a Woman-Friendly New World Order," in *American Women in the Nineties,* ed. Matteo, 22–23.

109. Data from a 1985 study by the Boston University School of Social Work showed a leisure gap of 19 hours per week between married mothers and fathers in the United States, whereas those from a 1977 Quality of Employment survey by researchers at the University of Michigan showed a daily leisure gap of 2.2 hours. See Judith Finlayson, "Leisure Gap between the Sexes," *Globe and Mail* (Toronto), 30 December 1995.

110. Pierson, *Dismantling the Welfare State,* chaps. 3–5, passim.

111. Senator Jesse Helms as quoted in ibid., 116.

112. Ronald Reagan, *An American Life* (New York: Simon and Schuster, 1990), 189; and Lou Cannon, *President Reagan: The Role of a Lifetime* (New York: Simon and Schuster, 1991), 48, 75, 518–19.

113. Pierson, *Dismantling the Welfare State,* 118; Baker, *Canadian Family Policies,* 112–13; and Davis, *Moving the Mountain,* 439.

114. Rix, "The Reagan Years," 71, 74–75; Joan Hoff, *Law, Gender, and Injustice: A Legal History of U.S. Women* (New York: New York University Press, 1991), 290; and Steven P. Erie, Martin Rein, and Barbara Wiget, "Women and the Reagan Revolution: Thermidor for the Social Welfare Economy," in *Families, Politics, and Public Policy,* ed. Irene Diamond (New York: Longman, 1983), 95.

115. Baker, *Canadian Family Policies,* 111–13.

116. Erie et al., "Women and the Reagan Revolution," table 5.1, 97.

117. Ibid., 110–12; Pierson, *Dismantling the Welfare State,* 115–18; and Diana

B. Dutton, "Poorer and Sicker: Legacies of the 1980s, Lessons for the 1990s," in *American Women in the Nineties,* ed. Matteo, 114.

118. Rix, "The Reagan Years," 77.

119. Pierson, *Dismantling the Welfare State,* 87–89; and Rix, "The Reagan Years," 72.

120. Pierson, *Dismantling the Welfare State,* 119–20.

121. See David R. Beam, "New Federalism, Old Realities: The Reagan Administration and Intergovernmental Reform," in *The Reagan Presidency and the Governing of America,* ed. Lester M. Salamon and Michael S. Lund (Washington, DC: Arbor Institute Press, 1985), 415–42.

122. Pierson, *Dismantling the Welfare State,* 118.

123. Ibid., 125.

124. For commentary on the 1988 act, see Catherine S. Chilman, "Welfare Reform or Revision? The Family Support Act of 1988," *Social Science Review* 66 (September 1992): 349–77; Nancy A. Naples, "A Socialist Feminist Analysis of the Family Support Act of 1988," *Affilia* 6, no. 4 (winter 1991): 23–38; and Wendy Sarvasy, "Reagan and Low-Income Mothers: A Feminist Recasting of the Debate," in *Remaking the Welfare State: Retrenchment and Social Policy in America and Europe,* ed. Michael K. Brown (Philadelphia: Temple University Press, 1988), 253–76.

125. Erie et al., "Women and the Reagan Revolution," 95.

126. Ibid., 103, 104, 106–7; Davis, *Moving the Mountain,* 420; and Costello and Stone, eds., *The American Woman, 1994–95,* 298–99.

127. Erie et al., "Women and the Reagan Revolution," 102.

128. Teresa L. Amott, "Black Women and AFDC: Making Entitlement Out of Necessity," in *Women, the State, and Welfare,* ed. Linda Gordon (Madison: University of Wisconsin Press, 1990), 291.

129. Ibid., 292.

130. Costello and Stone, eds., *The American Woman, 1994–95,* 145.

131. Pierson, *Dismantling the Welfare State,* 91–92.

132. Erie et al., "Women and the Reagan Revolution," 112.

133. Sapiro, "The Women's Movement," 130.

134. Cheryl Hyde, "Feminist Social Movement Organizations Survive the New Right," in *Feminist Organizations: Harvest of the New Women's Movement,* ed. Myra Marx Ferree and Patricia Yancey Martin (Philadelphia: Temple University Press, 1995), 313.

135. On the dynamics of shifts in language, see Susan Faludi, *Backlash: The Undeclared War against American Women* (New York: Doubleday, 1991), 238, 276, 405. Chapter 9 of Faludi's book addresses the tactics of Paul Weyrich and the Heritage Foundation.

136. See ibid., 259–63; and Davis, *Moving the Mountain,* 360, 443.

137. Article by anonymous author in *Conservative Digest,* as quoted in Faludi, *Backlash,* 261.

138. Gelb, *Feminism and Politics,* 124.

139. Joyce Gelb and Ethel Klein, *Women's Movements: Organizing for Change* (Washington, DC: American Political Science Association, 1988), 28 n. 5.

140. Toni Carabillo, Judith Mueli, and June Bundy Csida, *Feminist Chronicles, 1953–1993* (Los Angeles: Women's Graphics, 1993), 116, 124; and Tanya Melich, *The Republican War against Women* (New York: Bantam, 1996), 185.

141. Davis, *Moving the Mountain*, 466.

142. See Clyde Wilcox, "Why Was 1992 the 'Year of the Woman'? Explaining Women's Gains in 1992," in *The Year of the Woman,* ed. Elizabeth Adell Cook, Sue Thomas, and Clyde Wilcox (Boulder, CO: Westview, 1994), 10.

143. Margaret Thatcher, *The Downing Street Years* (New York: HarperCollins, 1993), 321.

144. See Judy Fudge and Patricia McDermott, eds., *Just Wages: A Feminist Assessment of Pay Equity* (Toronto: University of Toronto Press, 1991).

145. In 1990, the Canadian Conservative government amended parental leave benefits so that both birth and adoptive parents could claim paid leave. The challenge to Unemployment Insurance rules governing leave in *Schachter v. Canada* (reported in a 1992 Supreme Court of Canada ruling) had been initiated by a Toronto labor lawyer, Shalom Schachter, who argued that birth fathers were disadvantaged relative to adoptive ones under an older UI amendment.

146. Maude Barlow, "Global Pillage," *This Magazine,* March–April 1996, 10, argues that 344,000 Canadian manufacturing jobs were lost to low-wage U.S. states between 1989 and 1994. Advocates of free trade, however, maintained that Canadian job losses resulted from an unfavorable currency situation, global recession, and high interest rates—in short, from factors other than free trade. For an assessment of the debate over free trade, see Sylvia B. Bashevkin, *True Patriot Love: The Politics of Canadian Nationalism* (Toronto: Oxford University Press, 1991), chap. 6.

147. Statistics Canada data are presented in Baker, *Canadian Family Policies,* 75, 79; and Marjorie Griffin Cohen, "Paid Work," in *Canadian Women's Issues. Vol. 2: Bold Visions,* ed. Ruth Roach Pierson and Marjorie Griffin Cohen (Toronto: Lorimer, 1995), 107.

148. On patterns of involuntary part-time work, see *Women in Canada,* 66.

149. Harold D. Clarke, Jane Jenson, Lawrence LeDuc, and Jon Pammett, *Absent Mandate,* 3d ed. (Toronto: Gage, 1996), table 2.3, 43.

150. Susan D. Phillips, "Rock-a-Bye, Brian: The National Strategy on Child Care," in *How Ottawa Spends, 1989–90,* ed. Katherine A. Graham (Ottawa: Carleton University Press, 1989), 165–208; Katherine Teghtsoonian, "Neo-Conservative Ideology and Opposition to Federal Regulation of Child Care Services in the United States and Canada," *Canadian Journal of Political Science* 26 (1993): 97–121; and Derek P. J. Hum, "Compromise and Delay: The Federal Strategy on Child Care," in *Canada: The State of the Federation, 1989,* ed. Ronald L. Watts and Douglas M. Brown (Kingston, Ontario: Queen's University Institute of Intergovernmental Relations, 1989), 151–65.

151. Baker, *Canadian Family Policies,* 202–3.

152. Ibid., 203.

153. See Canadian Centre for Policy Alternatives, *Canada under the Tory Government* (Ottawa: CCPA, 1988), 34–37; Harold Chorney and Andrew Molloy, "The Myth of Tax Reform: The Mulroney Government's Tax Changes," in *Canada under Mulroney,* ed. Andrew B. Gollner and Daniel Salée (Montreal: Véhicule, 1988), 206–27; and Ken Battle, "The Politics of Stealth: Child Benefits under the Tories," in *How Ottawa Spends, 1993–94,* ed. Susan D. Phillips (Ottawa: Carleton University Press, 1993), 417–48.

154. See Susan A. McDaniel, "The Changing Canadian Family," in *Changing Patterns: Women in Canada,* ed. Sandra Burt, Lorraine Code, and Lindsay Dorney, 2d ed. (Toronto: McClelland and Stewart, 1993), 431. A 1996 report by Statistics Canada found the percentage of Canadian women stating they were "highly stressed" was highest among those who were married with children; compared with 16 percent of unmarried women, 33 percent of married ones with children said they were highly stressed. See Alanna Mitchell, "Family-Friendly Job Plans Doing More for Men: Study," *Globe and Mail* (Toronto), 8 January 1997, A1.

155. Bashevkin, *True Patriot Love,* 105–9, chap. 6.

156. Baker, *Canadian Family Policies,* chap. 4; Battle, "The Politics of Stealth;" and James J. Rice and Michael J. Prince, "Lowering the Safety Net and Weakening the Bonds of Nationhood: Social Policy in the Mulroney Years," in *How Ottawa Spends, 1993–94,* ed. Phillips, 381–416.

157. Battle, "The Politics of Stealth," 435–38.

158. Rice and Prince, "Lowering the Safety Net," 392–94.

159. Rebick and Léger, *The NAC Voters' Guide,* 18, 37–38, 72–73.

160. Baker, *Canadian Family Policies,* 72–73; and Rice and Prince, "Lowering the Safety Net."

161. Rice and Prince, "Lowering the Safety Net," 381.

162. See Bashevkin, *True Patriot Love,* chap. 6.

163. Proportions of elite-level women in Canada during the Mulroney years were considerably higher than in Britain or the United States during the same period; this pattern was the same whether comparing percentages of female cabinet ministers, high court judges, national legislators, or senior bureaucratic appointees. See Sylvia Bashevkin, "Confronting Neo-Conservatism: Anglo-American Women's Movements under Thatcher, Reagan, and Mulroney," *International Political Science Review* 15, no. 3 (July 1994): 290; and Sylvia Bashevkin, "Losing Common Ground: Feminists, Conservatives, and Public Policy in Canada during the Mulroney Years," *Canadian Journal of Political Science* 29, no. 2 (June 1996): 240–41.

164. Bashevkin, *True Patriot Love,* 140–42.

165. Marjorie Cohen, "Election Priorities," *Feminist Action* (September 1988): 12.

166. Bashevkin, *True Patriot Love,* 143.

167. Jill Vickers, Pauline Rankin, and Christine Appelle, *Politics as if Women Mattered: A Political Analysis of the National Action Committee on the Status of*

Women (Toronto: University of Toronto Press, 1993), 21–22; Susan D. Phillips, "How Ottawa Blends: Shifting Government Relationships with Interest Groups," in *How Ottawa Spends, 1991–92,* ed. Frances Abele (Ottawa: Carleton University Press, 1991), 200–1; and Leslie A. Pal, *Interests of State: The Politics of Language, Multiculturalism, and Feminism in Canada* (Montreal: McGill-Queen's University Press, 1993), 147–48, 228, 232.

168. See Pal, *Interests of State,* 147; and Doris Anderson, "Ottawa Puts Squeeze on Feminists," *Toronto Star,* 25 February 1989.

169. The literature covering feminist interventions on Meech Lake is enormous; see Bashevkin, "Losing Common Ground," 234.

170. See ibid.

171. Brian Mulroney as quoted in Robert M. Campbell and Leslie A. Pal, *The Real Worlds of Canadian Politics,* 3d ed. (Peterborough, Ontario: Broadview, 1994), 175.

172. Rebick and Léger, *The NAC Voters' Guide,* 111.

173. David Vienneau, "Many Women Just Saying No to No," *Toronto Star,* 10 October 1992, A9.

174. Confidential interviews with Canadian activists.

175. See Young, *One of Us,* 390–91, 616; and Martin, *Pledge of Allegiance,* 157–59.

CHAPTER FOUR

1. A simple method was used to locate activists who were willing to discuss their experiences. Three experts on women's movements in Britain, the United States, and Canada were asked to list significant groups and individuals in each of the policy areas. Letters requesting meetings went out to the various respondents, after which one assistant in London and one in Washington, DC, helped to set up appointments for the author. Canadian interviews were arranged directly by the author. Each interview lasted about one hour, on the average, and the questions posed are listed in appendix B.

2. Each interviewee had participated in women's groups in England, but some had experience in Scotland, Wales, and Northern Ireland in addition to Canada and the United States. A few were from Asian and black backgrounds. The author questioned a total of forty-two British activists across the five policy fields about their experiences, and an assistant interviewed one activist using the same set of questions.

3. The author questioned a total of thirty-seven respondents, and a research assistant met two more. The American activists had a wide range of experience pressuring federal, state, and local governments in various regions of the United States. About one-quarter came from African American, Asian, and Hispanic backgrounds.

4. Although most were active in organizations that had offices in Ottawa or Toronto, their backgrounds were quite diverse. Of the twenty-seven activists in-

terviewed by the author, more than one-quarter had worked in ethnic, aboriginal, or disabled women's groups. Their backgrounds covered all of Canada, including Quebec and the Atlantic region. A few had lived for long periods in the United States and Britain.

CHAPTER FIVE

1. See Ethel Klein, *Gender Politics: From Consciousness to Mass Politics* (Cambridge, MA: Harvard University Press, 1984).

2. On the dynamics of partisanship versus independence for political women, see Sylvia B. Bashevkin, *Toeing the Lines: Women and Party Politics in English Canada,* 2d ed. (Toronto: Oxford University Press, 1993), chap. 1.

3. On the relative strength of the British movement, see Joyce Gelb, *Feminism and Politics: A Comparative Perspective* (Berkeley: University of California Press, 1989), 188, 190.

4. Klein, *Gender Politics.*

5. Roberta Spalter-Roth and Ronnee Schreiber, "Outsider Issues and Insider Tactics: Strategic Tensions in the Women's Policy Network During the 1980s," in *Feminist Organizations,* ed. Myra Marx Ferree and Patricia Yancey Martin (Philadelphia: Temple University Press, 1995), 105–27.

6. See Tanya Melich, *The Republican War against Women* (New York: Bantam, 1996).

7. Tanya Melich, for example, left the Republican fold by 1992. See Melich, *The Republican War,* 275.

8. See Clyde Wilcox, "Why Was 1992 the 'Year of the Woman'? Explaining Women's Gains in 1992," in *The Year of the Woman,* ed. Elizabeth Adell Cook, Sue Thomas, and Clyde Wilcox (Boulder, CO: Westview, 1994), 10; and Sarah Weddington, *A Question of Choice* (New York: Grosset/Putnam, 1992), 264.

9. See Karen Dubinsky, *Lament for a Patriarchy Lost: Anti-Feminism, Anti-Abortion, and R.E.A.L. Women in Canada* (Ottawa: Canadian Research Institute for the Advancement of Women, 1985); and Didi Herman, "The Christian Right and the Politics of Morality in Canada," *Parliamentary Affairs* 47 (1994): 268–79.

10. Kim Campbell, *Time and Chance: The Political Memoirs of Canada's First Woman Prime Minister* (Toronto: Doubleday Canada, 1996), 352–414.

11. A number of critical North American writers, including Camille Paglia, Christina Hoff Sommers, Elizabeth Fox-Genovese, Danielle Crittendon, and Donna Laframboise, are discussed later in this chapter. On the growth of what she terms "an increasingly organized but still diffuse collection of critical scholar/ writers," see Catharine R. Stimpson, "Women's Studies and Its Discontents," *Dissent* (winter 1996), 71 ff.

12. Hugo Young, *One of Us: A Biography of Margaret Thatcher* (London: Pan, 1991), 3.

13. Ibid., 30.

14. Margaret Thatcher, *The Path to Power* (New York: HarperCollins, 1995), 77.

15. April Carter, *The Politics of Women's Rights* (London: Longman, 1988), 30–39.

16. Thatcher as quoted in Donna S. Sanzone, "Women in Politics," in *Access to Power,* ed. Cynthia Fuchs Epstein and Rose Laub Coser (London: Allen and Unwin, 1981), 44.

17. Gelb, *Feminism and Politics,* 190ff; and Joyce Gelb, "Feminism in Britain: Politics without Power?" in *The New Women's Movement,* ed. Drude Dahlerup (London: Sage, 1986), 104.

18. Lesley Abdela, *What Women Want* (London: Body Shop International, 1994), 91–99.

19. Levels were about 0.003 in the U.S. female population versus roughly 0.001 in the U.K. population. See Gelb, *Feminism and Politics,* 188, 190.

20. On the limited national political presence of British feminism, see Paul Byrne, "The Politics of the Women's Movement," *Parliamentary Affairs* 49, no. 1 (January 1996): 58–60.

21. Beatrix Campbell, *The Iron Ladies: Why Do Women Vote Tory?* (London: Virago, 1987).

22. See Joan Isaac, "The Politics of Morality in the UK," *Parliamentary Affairs* 47, no. 2 (April 1994): 175–89.

23. Wendy Webster, *Not a Man to Match Her: The Marketing of a Prime Minister* (London: Women's Press, 1990), 66–67.

24. Margaret Thatcher speaking at the first Dame Margery Corbett-Ashby Memorial Lecture, July 1982, as quoted in Elizabeth Wilson, "Thatcherism and Women: After Seven Years," in Ralph Miliband et al., *Socialist Register 1987* (London: Merlin, 1987), 205.

25. Maureen Baker, *Canadian Family Policies: Cross-National Comparisons* (Toronto: University of Toronto Press, 1995), 109–10, 123–24.

26. Kate Figes, *Because of Her Sex: The Myth of Equality for Women in Britain* (London: Macmillan, 1994).

27. Abdela, *What Women Want,* 65.

28. Ibid., 49.

29. Joni Lovenduski and Vicky Randall, *Contemporary Feminist Politics: Women and Power in Britain* (Oxford: Oxford University Press, 1993), 55.

30. Abdela, *What Women Want,* 17, 31, 44; and Ian Forbes, "The Privatisation of Sex Equality Policy," *Parliamentary Affairs* 49, no. 1 (January 1996): 153–56.

31. Thatcher, *The Path to Power,* 94.

32. Ibid., 81; and Young, *One of Us,* 36–37.

33. Thatcher, *The Path to Power,* 459.

34. Thatcher as quoted in Young, *One of Us,* 306.

35. Thatcher as quoted in Webster, *Not a Man to Match Her,* 57.

36. See Young, *One of Us,* 307; and Webster, *Not a Man to Match Her,* 76.

37. Margaret Thatcher, inaugural lecture to the George Thomas Society, January 1990, as quoted in Isaac, "The Politics of Morality in the UK," 184.

38. Sir Keith Joseph's comments were published in *Times* (London) on 21 Oc-

tober 1974 and are reprinted in many sources, including Campbell, *The Iron Ladies,* 159–60; Isaac, "The Politics of Morality in the UK," 184; and Wilson, "Thatcherism and Women," 224.

39. Joseph as quoted in Campbell, *The Iron Ladies,* 160, 162.

40. Jenkin as quoted in ibid., 161.

41. Tebbit as quoted in Martin Durham, *Moral Crusades: Family and Morality in the Thatcher Years* (New York: New York University Press, 1991), 133, 134. See also Campbell, *The Iron Ladies,* 174.

42. See Durham, *Moral Crusades;* and Isaac, "The Politics of Morality in the UK."

43. See Durham, *Moral Crusades;* Isaac, "The Politics of Morality in the UK," 181; and Wilson, "Thatcherism and Women," 201, 215.

44. Currie as quoted in Campbell, *The Iron Ladies,* 212, 275.

45. See ibid., 214, 229; and Eben Black, "Major Got Us by the Goolies but We'll Take Our Revenge," *Today* (London), 24 July 1993.

46. Angela Rumbold interview with the Family Policies Studies Centre in *Family Policy Bulletin* (March 1991), as quoted in Isaac, "The Politics of Morality in the UK," 183.

47. Webster, *Not a Man to Match Her,* 84, 157.

48. Thatcher as quoted in ibid., 43.

49. See Wilson, "Thatcherism and Women," 206–7, 210–11.

50. Figes, *Because of Her Sex,* 47.

51. Abdela, *What Women Want,* 39; and Figes, *Because of Her Sex,* 52.

52. Figes, *Because of Her Sex,* chap. 3; Heather Joshi, "The Cost of Caring," in *Women and Poverty in Britain: The 1990s,* ed. Caroline Glendinning and Jane Millar (London: Harvester Wheatsheaf, 1992), 110–25; and Sue Innes, *Making It Work: Women, Change, and Challenge in the 90s* (London: Chatto and Windus, 1995).

53. Figes, *Because of Her Sex,* 194.

54. Carter, *The Politics of Women's Rights,* 30–39.

55. Baker, *Canadian Family Policies,* 47, 59.

56. For an overview of the public consciousness dimension, see Thomas R. Rochon and Daniel A. Mazmanian, "Social Movements and the Policy Process," in *Citizens, Protest, and Democracy,* ed. Russell J. Dalton, *Annals of the American Academy of Political and Social Science,* vol. 528 (Newbury Park, CA: Sage, 1993), 75–87. On the British case, see Lovenduski and Randall, *Contemporary Feminist Politics,* 12; Anna Coote and Polly Pattullo, *Power and Prejudice: Women and Politics* (London: Weidenfeld and Nicolson, 1990), 65; Elizabeth Wilson with Angela Weir, "The British Women's Movement," in *Hidden Agendas: Theory, Politics, and Experience in the Women's Movement,* ed. Elizabeth Wilson with Angela Weir (London: Tavistock, 1986), 131–32; Carter, *The Politics of Women's Rights,* 99–102; and Paul Byrne, "The Politics of the Women's Movement," *Parliamentary Affairs* 49, no. 1 (January 1996): 63–65.

57. This and other quotes from movement participants cited in this chapter are from confidential interviews with the author.

58. Chairs of the Equal Opportunities Commission included Baroness Platt, Joanna Foster, and Kamlesh Bahl. On the evolution of the organization, see Lovenduski and Randall, *Contemporary Feminist Politics,* 185–91.

59. Teresa Gorman as quoted in "Parliament and Politics: Review of Female Judges Is Urged," *Financial Times,* 16 March 1993, 13. See also Isaac, "The Politics of Morality in the UK," 179–80, 186.

60. See Wilson, "Thatcherism and Women," 223.

61. See "More Tories May Quit under Major," *Globe and Mail* (Toronto), 1 January 1996. On the background to her decision, see Emma Nicholson, "The Strange Death of Conservatism," *Brown Journal of World Affairs* 3, no. 1 (winter/spring 1996): 191–98; and Emma Nicholson, *Secret Society: Inside—and Outside—the Conservative Party* (London: Indigo, 1996).

62. For example, on 22 March 1993, the Princess of Wales cut the ribbon at a London-area shelter service known as Refuge. Previously known as Chiswick Family Rescue, the service operated four shelters as well as a twenty-four-hour national crisis line. This ribbon cutting by Princess Diana generated a file of press clippings that was approximately one inch thick.

63. Lovenduski and Randall, *Contemporary Feminist Politics,* 1; and Figes, *Because of Her Sex,* 217–18.

64. Schlafly as quoted in Rebecca Klatch, *Women of the New Right* (Philadelphia: Temple University Press, 1987), 50.

65. Ibid., 50.

66. See Melich, *The Republican War,* 27.

67. Schlafly as quoted in ibid., 46.

68. Ibid., 87.

69. Ibid., 76.

70. Ibid., 129.

71. See Jeane J. Kirkpatrick, *Political Woman* (New York: Basic Books, 1974); *The New Presidential Elite* (New York: Russell Sage Foundation, 1976); "Dictatorships and Double Standards," *Commentary* 68, no. 5 (November 1979).

72. Melich, *The Republican War,* 152.

73. See Martin Fletcher, "Sister Frigidaire v. Steel Magnolia," *Times* (London), 11 April 1996, 17.

74. Melich, *The Republican War,* 162–63.

75. Senator Bob Dole as quoted in Fletcher, "Sister Frigidaire."

76. Anne N. Costain, "Representing Women: The Transition from Social Movement to Interest Group," in *Women, Power, and Policy,* ed. Ellen Boneparth and Emily Stoper, 2d ed. (New York: Pergamon, 1988), 35.

77. Ferraro as quoted in Joan Hulse Thompson, "The Congressional Caucus for Women's Issues," paper presented at meetings of the American Political Science Association, Washington, D.C, September 1993, 16.

78. Melich, *The Republican War,* 163.

79. Thompson, "The Congressional Caucus," 10.

80. Melich, *The Republican War,* 224.

81. On Martin's efforts, see M. Margaret Conway, David W. Ahern, and Ger-

trude A. Steuernagel, *Women and Public Policy: A Revolution in Progress* (Washington, DC: Congressional Quarterly Press, 1995), 73.

82. See Steven A. Shull, *A Kinder, Gentler Racism? The Reagan-Bush Civil Rights Legacy* (Armonk, NY: Sharpe, 1993), 165; Zillah Eisenstein, *The Color of Gender: Reimaging Democracy* (Berkeley: University of California Press, 1994), 52, 112–14; Rosalind Pollack Petchesky, *Abortion and Woman's Choice*, 2d ed. (Boston: Northeastern University Press, 1990), 314; and Ian Shapiro, introduction to *Abortion: The Supreme Court Decisions*, ed. Ian Shapiro (Indianapolis: Hackett, 1995), 2, 8–10.

83. Klatch, *Women of the New Right*, 202.

84. See Melich, *The Republican War*, 247.

85. Patrick Buchanan as quoted in ibid., 272.

86. Marilyn Quayle as quoted in ibid., 273.

87. Ibid., 275.

88. Lisa Young, *Can Feminists Transform Party Politics? Women's Movements and Political Parties in Canada and the United States, 1970–1993* (Ph.D. diss., University of Toronto, 1996).

89. On the demographic backgrounds of feminists and antifeminists, see Klein, *Gender Politics*, on the former and Klatch, *Women of the New Right*, on the latter.

90. Cynthia Costello and Anne J. Stone, eds., *The American Woman, 1994–95: Where We Stand* (New York: Norton, 1994), 271. Note that among men, the increase in numbers in postsecondary education was far less significant, from 5.0 million in 1970 to 6.2 million in 1990.

91. Costello and Stone, eds., *The American Woman, 1994–95*, 291.

92. These data are drawn from American National Election Study surveys from 1972 to 1992 in Elizabeth Adell Cook, "The Generations of Feminism," in *Women in Politics*, ed. Lois Lovelace Duke, 2d ed. (Upper Saddle River, NJ: Prentice Hall, 1996), table 1, 48.

93. Warm feelings were defined as 60 degrees or more on a thermometer scale from 0 to 100 degrees. See Cal Clark and Janet Clark, "Whither the Gender Gap? Converging and Conflicting Attitudes among Women," in *Women in Politics*, ed. Duke, 83.

94. Toni Carabillo, Judith Meuli, and June Bundy Csida, *Feminist Chronicles, 1953–1993* (Los Angeles: Women's Graphics, 1993), 124.

95. Ibid., 48, 50, 55, 61, 67, 77, 85, 103.

96. Flora Davis, *Moving the Mountain: The Women's Movement in America since 1960* (New York: Simon and Schuster, 1991), 472.

97. Carabillo et al., *Feminist Chronicles*, 130, 147.

98. Camille Paglia, *Sexual Personae: Art and Decadence from Nefertiti to Emily Dickinson* (New York: Vintage, 1990); *Sex, Art, and American Culture: Essays* (New York: Vintage, 1992); and *Vamps and Tramps: New Essays* (New York: Vintage, 1994).

99. Paglia, *Vamps and Tramps*, 107.

100. Ibid., 111.

101. Ibid., 24.

102. Christina Hoff Sommers, *Who Stole Feminism? How Women Have Betrayed Women* (New York: Simon and Schuster, 1994). See also Daphne Patai and Noretta Koertge, *Professing Feminism: Cautionary Tales from the Strange World of Women's Studies* (New York: Basic Books, 1994).

103. Sommers, *Who Stole Feminism?* 25.

104. Ibid., 275.

105. Elizabeth Fox-Genovese, *"Feminism Is Not the Story of My Life"* (New York: Doubleday, 1996), 28.

106. Some of the most colorful rhetoric during the free trade debate came from a Conservative cabinet minister in Mulroney's government, John Crosbie. See Sylvia B. Bashevkin, *True Patriot Love: The Politics of Canadian Nationalism* (Toronto: Oxford University Press, 1991), 112.

107. Jennifer Lynch, president of the Progressive Conservative Party of Canada Women's Federation, as quoted in Robert Fife, *Kim Campbell: The Making of a Politician* (Toronto: HarperCollins, 1993), 105.

108. On the events of May 1988, see Ann Rauhala, "Largest Feminist Association Faces Crisis," *Globe and Mail* (Toronto), 16 May 1988. Alison Edgar of the Ottawa Progressive Conservative Women's Caucus, appearing on CBC Radio's *Morningside* program on 19 May 1988, stated that free trade and the Meech Lake Accord did not belong on the NAC policy agenda. Edgar argued NAC was too conflictual in its relations with the federal government.

109. Poll data cited in Naomi Black, "The Canadian Women's Movement: The Second Wave," in *Changing Patterns: Women in Canada,* ed. Sandra Burt, Lorraine Code, and Lindsay Dorney, 2d ed. (Toronto: McClelland and Stewart, 1993), 151–52.

110. See Brian Milner, "Poll Finds Men Preferred as Boss," *Globe and Mail* (Toronto), 27 March 1996.

111. The percentage of women in Mulroney's 1984 federal cabinet was 21 percent. See Sydney Sharpe, *The Gilded Ghetto: Women and Political Power in Canada* (Toronto: HarperCollins, 1994), 114–15.

112. Dubinsky, *Lament for a Patriarchy Lost,* 30–31.

113. R.E.A.L. Women publication dated 1984 as quoted in ibid., 31–32.

114. Ruth Roach Pierson, "The Politics of the Domestic Sphere," in Ruth Roach Pierson and Marjorie Griffin Cohen, *Canadian Women's Issues. Vol. 2: Bold Visions* (Toronto: Lorimer, 1995), 27.

115. Danielle Crittenden, "The Mother of All Problems," *Saturday Night,* April 1996, 44–54.

116. Donna Laframboise, *The Princess at the Window: A New Gender Morality* (Toronto: Penguin, 1996), 314.

117. See Fife, *Kim Campbell,* 137–38; and Sharpe, *The Gilded Ghetto,* 41.

118. It is not surprising that opposition parties decided to boycott the committee. See Murray Dobbin, *The Politics of Kim Campbell* (Toronto: Lorimer, 1993), 158; and Roger Gibbins, *Conflict and Unity: An Introduction to Canadian Political Life,* 3d ed. (Toronto: Nelson, 1994), 217.

119. Dobbin, *The Politics of Kim Campbell,* 168.

120. Kim Campbell as quoted in Fife, *Kim Campbell,* 91.

121. Ibid., 92.

122. Kim Campbell as quoted in ibid., 101.

123. Margaret Purcell, vice president of Campaign Life, as quoted in ibid., 120.

124. Ibid., 133.

125. Ibid., 104.

126. Kim Campbell's 1992 speech, as quoted in ibid., 149.

127. Kim Campbell as quoted in ibid., 115. The opponents of Bill C-43 included retired Supreme Court justice Bertha Wilson, the Canadian Medical Association, and the Society of Obstetricians and Gynecologists of Canada.

128. See Fife, *Kim Campbell,* 129.

129. NAC eventually opposed both the Canadian Panel on Violence against Women and the Royal Commission on New Reproductive Technologies. See Alison Prentice, Paula Bourne, Gail Cuthbert Brandt, Beth Light, Wendy Mitchinson, and Naomi Black, *Canadian Women: A History,* 2d ed. (Toronto: Harcourt Brace, 1996), 386, 456.

130. Judy Rebick, "The Charlottetown Accord: A Faulty Framework and a Wrong-Headed Compromise," in *The Charlottetown Accord, the Referendum, and the Future of Canada,* ed. Kenneth McRoberts and Patrick Monahan (Toronto: University of Toronto Press, 1993), 104, 106. Other prominent opponents of the Charlottetown Accord included Reform party leader Preston Manning, who did not then have a seat in the House of Commons, and former prime minister Pierre Elliott Trudeau.

131. Brian Mulroney, as quoted in Jill Vickers, "The Canadian Women's Movement and a Changing Constitutional Order," *International Journal of Canadian Studies* 7–8 (1993): 277; and in Robert M. Campbell and Leslie A. Pal, *The Real Worlds of Canadian Politics,* 3d ed. (Peterborough, Ontario: Broadview, 1994), 175. According to activists in NAC, some of this smear campaign during the Charlottetown period also emanated from the parliamentary opposition, including the New Democratic party.

132. Kim Campbell speech delivered at Harvard University, as quoted in Dobbin, *The Politics of Kim Campbell,* 164.

133. Kim Campbell, speaking at the 1993 Progressive Conservative party leadership debate, as quoted in Fife, *Kim Campbell,* 193.

134. Barbara McDougall as quoted in David Vienneau, "Many Women Are Just Saying No to No," *Toronto Star,* 10 October 1992, A9.

135. See Vienneau, "Many Women Are Just Saying No to No," and Ontario NDP premier Bob Rae quoted in Paul Maloney, "'No' Targets Bad Accord," *Toronto Star,* 27 October 1992, B7.

136. Brian Mulroney as quoted in Sharpe, *The Gilded Ghetto,* 29.

137. Campbell, *Time and Chance,* 408.

138. On change over time in education and employment, see *Women in Canada: A Statistical Report,* 3d ed. (Ottawa: Statistics Canada, 1995), 54–64.

139. Carabillo et al., *Feminist Chronicles,* 124.

CHAPTER SIX

1. Dennis Kavanagh, *Thatcherism and British Politics: The End of Consensus?* 2d ed. (Oxford: Oxford University Press, 1990), 152.

2. This and other quotes from movement participants cited in this chapter are from confidential interviews with the author.

3. Margaret Thatcher as quoted in Hugo Young, *One of Us: A Biography of Margaret Thatcher* (London: Pan, 1991), 128.

4. Margaret Thatcher as quoted in ibid., 130.

5. Joel Krieger, *Reagan, Thatcher, and the Politics of Decline* (New York: Oxford University Press, 1986), 93.

6. Ibid., 94.

7. James Callaghan as quoted in Elizabeth Wilson, "Thatcherism and Women: After Seven Years," in Ralph Miliband et al., *Socialist Register 1987* (London: Merlin, 1987), 203.

8. James Callaghan as quoted in Joni Lovenduski and Vicky Randall, *Contemporary Feminist Politics: Women and Power in Britain* (Oxford: Oxford University Press, 1993), 37–38.

9. Wilson, "Thatcherism and Women," 230.

10. Joni Lovenduski, "An Emerging Advocate: The Equal Opportunities Commission in Britain," in *Comparative State Feminism,* ed. Dorothy McBride Stetson and Amy G. Mazur (Thousand Oaks, CA: Sage, 1995), 116.

11. According to Sarah Perrigo, the committee's demands were generally not met. See Sarah Perrigo, "Women and Change in the Labour Party, 1979–1995," *Parliamentary Affairs* 49, no. 1 (January 1996): 121–22.

12. Dennis Kavanagh, "The Changing Political Opposition," in *The Thatcher Effect: A Decade of Change,* ed. Dennis Kavanagh and Anthony Seldon (Oxford: Oxford University Press, 1989), 92.

13. Young, *One of Us,* 323.

14. Kavanagh, "The Changing Political Opposition," 92.

15. Hugo Young's account of the Westland affair is illustrative. See Young, *One of Us,* 453–55.

16. Dennis Kavanagh, "Britain: Stirrings of Change," *Journal of Democracy* 6, no. 3 (July 1995): 21.

17. On numbers of female candidates over time, see Barbara Follett, "Barriers to Women's Involvement in Politics," unpublished manuscript, September 1994. On mandatory shortlisting of female candidates, see Lovenduski and Randall, *Contemporary Feminist Politics,* 159.

18. Kavanagh, "Britain: Stirrings of Change," 24.

19. Follett, "Barriers to Women's Involvement in Politics," 3; and Clare Short, "Women and the Labour Party," *Parliamentary Affairs* 49, no. 1 (January 1996): 19.

20. Follett, "Barriers to Women's Involvement in Politics," 3.

21. Ibid., 1.

22. Gordon Smith as quoted in Patricia Wynn-Davies, "Labour's Pre-election Tax Policy Rejected," *Independent* (London), 18 August 1993.

23. Follett, "Barriers to Women's Involvement in Politics," 4.

24. EMILY's List in the United States targeted its funds toward politically viable, pro-choice Democratic women candidates.

25. See Short, "Women and the Labour Party," 21.

26. In addition, it is notable that until 1996, EMILY's List funds were not taken up by Labour women in Scotland. See Alice Brown, "Women and Politics in Scotland," *Parliamentary Affairs* 49, no. 1 (January 1996): 30.

27. Survey data indicated Labour had indeed become the party of middle-class Britain, more so than the Conservatives. See David Smith and Rajeev Syal, "Official: Labour Is Middle Class," *Sunday Times* (London), 7 April 1996, 1.

28. Peter Mandler, "Letter from London: The Americanization of Britain?" *Dissent* (Summer 1995): 304.

29. The quota policy was contested in a legal action by one party member, Peter Jepson, and was criticized by Labour veterans including Neil Kinnock. See Short, "Women and the Labour Party," 21; and Perrigo, "Women and Change in the Labour Party," 128.

30. Judith Squires, "Quotas for Women: Fair Representation?" *Parliamentary Affairs* 49, no. 1 (January 1996): 71.

31. See Mandler, "Letter from London," 305; and Kavanagh, "Britain: Stirrings of Change," 26.

32. Mandler, "Letter from London," 303.

33. Tony Blair as quoted in Andrew Grice, "Two Tory MPs Poised to Defect," *Sunday Times* (London), 14 April 1996, 1.

34. Tony Blair as quoted in Michael Prescott, Andrew Grice, and Rajeev Syal, "Major Stares at Defeat in Battle for Middle England," *Sunday Times* (London), 14 April 1996, section 1, 12.

35. Kim Howells M. P., "Labour Must Defuse the Tax Bombshell," *Sunday Times* (London), 28 April 1996, section 3, 2.

36. See Michael Jones, "Wary Major Looks East as Blair's Star Rises in West," *Sunday Times* (London), 7 April 1996, section 3, 2. See also Tony Blair, *New Britain: My Vision of a Young Country* (London: Fourth Estate, 1996); Andy Mc-Smith, *Faces of Labour: The Inside Story* (London: Verso, 1996); Mark Perryman, ed., *The Blair Agenda* (London: Lawrence and Wishart, 1996); and Giles Radice, ed., *What Needs to Change: New Visions for Britain* (London: HarperCollins, 1996).

37. Mandler, "Letter from London," 304.

38. Kavanagh, "Britain: Stirrings of Change," 25.

39. Short's comments were initially published in Steve Richards, "Interview: Clare Short," *New Statesman* (9 August 1996): 24–26. On press and party reactions, see David Wastell, "New Labour, New Anger," *Sunday Telegraph* (London), 11 August 1996, 17.

40. On women in the major British political parties, see Lovenduski and Randall, *Contemporary Feminist Politics,* chap. 5.

41. Tony Blair as quoted in Hamish McRae, "Breaking Up Is Expensive to Do: Every Time a Family Divorced, It Cost the Taxpayer £10,500," *Independent* (London), 28 July 1994. See also Tony Blair on "the breakdown of family life" in Peter Mandelson and Roger Liddle, *The Blair Revolution: Can New Labour Deliver?* (London: Faber and Faber, 1996), 48.

42. Mandler, "Letter from London," 305.

43. Tanya Melich, *The Republican War against Women* (New York: Bantam, 1996), 275, 276.

44. See Elizabeth Drew, *On the Edge: The Clinton Presidency* (New York: Simon and Schuster, 1994), 60.

45. Zillah Eisenstein, *The Color of Gender: Reimaging Democracy* (Berkeley: University of California Press, 1994), 95–96.

46. For thorough accounts of the health care reform debate, see Haynes Johnson and David S. Broder, *The System: The American Way of Politics at the Breaking Point* (Boston: Little, Brown, 1996); and Theda Skocpol, *Boomerang: Health Care Reform and the Turn against Government* (New York: Norton, 1997).

47. Richard Armey, who became Republican majority leader in the U.S. House of Representatives after the 1994 midterm elections, as quoted in Elizabeth Drew, *Showdown: The Struggle between the Gingrich Congress and the Clinton White House* (New York: Simon and Schuster, 1996), 329. Armey's comment was made in 1993.

48. See ibid., 69.

49. See Drew, *On the Edge;* and E. J. Dionne, Jr., *They Only Look Dead: Why Progressives Will Dominate the Next Political Era* (New York: Simon and Schuster, 1996).

50. One early account of Judge Ginsburg's record since her appointment to the Supreme Court supported these claims. It showed she sided with conservative appointees on criminal justice cases and, even in the area of equal rights litigation, proved unwilling to press the kinds of arguments she had made earlier in her career. See Joyce Ann Baugh, Thomas R. Hensley, Scott Patrick Johnson, and Christopher E. Smith, "Justice Ruth Bader Ginsburg: A Preliminary Assessment," paper presented at the American Political Science Association meeting, New York, September 1994.

51. Drew, *On the Edge,* 338–55.

52. On the details of these appointments and that of Kimba Wood, see ibid.; and Richard Davis, "The Ginsburg Nomination: The Role of the Press, Interest Groups, and the Public in the Selection of a Supreme Court Nominee," paper presented at the American Political Science Association meeting, New York, September 1994.

53. Bill Clinton as quoted in Drew, *On the Edge,* 25.

54. See ibid., 42; and Toni Carabillo, Judith Mueli, and June Bundy Csida, *Feminist Chronicles, 1953–1993* (Los Angeles: Women's Graphics, 1993), 153.

55. See Cynthia Costello and Anne J. Stone, eds., *The American Woman, 1994–95* (New York: Norton, 1994), 80, 85.

56. Drew, *On the Edge,* 438.

57. See R. Kent Weaver, "Ending Welfare as We Know It: Policymaking for Low-Income Families in the Clinton/Gingrich Era," in *Social Policy in the Clinton Years,* ed. Margaret Weir (Washington, DC: Brookings Institution, forthcoming).

58. See "New US Office Aims to Protect Women," *Globe and Mail* (Toronto), 25 March 1995.

59. See Drew, *On the Edge,* 374.

60. Ibid., 79.

61. These strategic tensions were reflected in a number of other areas not cited in the text. For example, feminists divided over their endorsement of the established party system versus support for a new, third party to the left of the Democrats. See Susan Faludi, *Backlash: The Undeclared War against American Women* (New York: Doubleday, 1991), 271, 277. They also split over how to get more women elected; moderates in such groups as EMILY's List tended to target and fund only viable feminist candidates, whereas others in organizations like the Fund for the Feminist Majority were willing to "flood the ticket" with lots of women in the belief that most would be pro-feminist.

62. On this failure to overturn Hyde Amendment limits on abortion funding, see Carabillo et al., *Feminist Chronicles,* 153.

63. On changes in public office holding, see Elizabeth Adell Cook, Sue Thomas, and Clyde Wilcox, eds., *The Year of the Woman* (Boulder, CO: Westview, 1994). It should be noted that record numbers of U.S. women elected in 1992 hardly constituted a breakthrough in comparative terms. See Barbara J. Nelson and Najma Chowdhury, eds., *Women and Politics Worldwide* (New Haven, CT: Yale University Press, 1994).

64. See Clyde Wilcox, "Why Was 1992 the 'Year of the Woman'? Explaining Women's Gains in 1992," in *The Year of the Woman,* ed. Cook et al., 1.

65. Melich, *The Republican War,* 283.

66. Drew, *On the Edge,* 440.

67. Dionne, *They Only Look Dead,* 85.

68. Bill Clinton as quoted in Drew, *On the Edge,* 418.

69. Drew, *Showdown,* 37.

70. See ibid., 32, 45, 91. According to Drew (45), Speaker Gingrich used the terms *sick* and *pathetic* frequently.

71. Katha Pollitt, "Take Back the Right," *The Nation,* 18 March 1996, 11.

72. Governor Pete Wilson as quoted in Timothy Appleby, "California Vote Could Trigger Rollback of Affirmative Action," *Globe and Mail* (Toronto), 20 July 1995.

73. Justice Sandra Day O'Connor as quoted in Aaron Epstein, "Conservative Justices Reverse the Race Issue," *Detroit Free Press,* 1 July 1995, 4A. On the background and responses to the *Adarand* decision, see *The Affirmative Action Debate,* ed. George E. Curry (Reading, MA: Addison-Wesley, 1996).

74. Roger Wilkins, professor of history at George Mason University, as quoted in Graham Fraser, "US Supreme Court Drops Role of Minority Advocate," *Globe and Mail* (Toronto), 14 June 1995.

75. Bill Clinton as quoted in Drew, *Showdown,* 296.

76. Ibid., 375.

77. Neil Nevitte, Richard Johnston, André Blais, Henry Brady, and Elisabeth Gidengil, "Electoral Discontinuity: The 1993 Canadian Federal Election," *International Social Science Journal* 146 (December 1995), table 3.

78. See Keith Archer and Faron Ellis, "Opinion Structure of Party Activists: The Reform Party of Canada," *Canadian Journal of Political Science* 27, no. 2 (June 1994): 292.

79. Roger Gibbins, *Conflict and Unity: An Introduction to Canadian Political Life,* 3d ed. (Toronto: Nelson, 1994), 394.

80. Sheila Copps, *Nobody's Baby: A Survival Guide to Politics* (Toronto: Deneau, 1986).

81. On debt levels, see D'Arcy Jenish, *Money to Burn: Trudeau, Mulroney, and the Bankruptcy of Canada* (Toronto: Stoddart, 1996).

82. See Jean Chrétien, *Straight from the Heart* (Toronto: Key Porter, 1985, 1994); and Lawrence Martin, *Chrétien. Vol. 1: The Will to Win* (Toronto: Lester, 1995).

83. Maude Barlow and Bruce Campbell, *Straight through the Heart: How the Liberals Abandoned the Just Society* (Toronto: HarperCollins, 1995), 96.

84. The Liberal Red Book promised 50,000 new child care spaces per year to a total of 150,000 spaces if growth reached 3 percent a year. See *Creating Opportunity: The Liberal Plan for Canada* (Ottawa: Liberal Party of Canada, 1993).

85. See Edward Greenspon, "Provincial Cash Transfers Cut by $700 Million for Two Years," *Globe and Mail* (Toronto), 7 March 1996; and Barlow and Campbell, *Straight through the Heart,* 151.

86. "Bill C-76: Redefining Our Rights," *ACTION NOW!* June 1995, 2. *ACTION NOW!* was the monthly newsletter of the National Action Committee on the Status of Women.

87. National Action Committee on the Status of Women, "Stop, There Is Another Way," statement on the 1995 federal budget, 2.

88. Barlow and Campbell, *Straight through the Heart,* 171.

89. Ibid., 218–19.

90. Ibid., 127, 161.

91. "Stop, There Is Another Way," 1.

92. See *ACTION NOW!,* March 1995, 2; and Ron Eade, "Women's Group Racks Up Deficit," *Calgary Herald,* 13 June 1994, A2.

93. Susan Delacourt, "Losing Interest," *Globe and Mail* (Toronto), 1 April 1995, section D, 1.

94. "Lobby a Success," *ACTION NOW!,* June/July 1994, 1.

95. Barlow and Campbell, *Straight through the Heart,* 126.

96. See Brian Mulroney quotation in ibid., 91. For an assessment of how the Liberals went farther with Conservative policies than the Tories ever did, see Jeffrey Simpson, "Liberals Sail Easily over Shoals That Wrecked the Conservatives," *Globe and Mail* (Toronto), 17 April 1996.

97. Alison Prentice, Paula Bourne, Gail Cuthbert Brandt, Beth Light, Wendy Mitchinson, and Naomi Black, *Canadian Women: A History,* 2d ed. (Toronto: Harcourt Brace, 1996), 441.

98. See Sean Fine, "Has the Highest Court Lost Touch with Reality?" *Globe and Mail* (Toronto), 8 October 1994.

99. Karen Busby, "Supreme Court Decisions on the Use of Personal Records in Sexual Assault Cases," *LEAF Lines* (spring 1996): 5.

100. Kirk Makin, "Top Court Tosses Out Sex Case," *Globe and Mail* (Toronto), 7 February 1997, A1; and Margaret Wente, "Therapy or Evidence?" *Globe and Mail* (Toronto), 8 February 1997, D9.

101. See Anne McIlroy, "Rock Plans Law to Define Access to Victims' Records," *Globe and Mail* (Toronto), 11 May 1996.

102. See David Vienneau, "Ottawa Appealing Child Support Ruling," *Toronto Star,* 19 May 1994, A11.

103. See Canadian Institute of Chartered Accountants, "1996 Federal Budget Commentary," 6 March 1996, 3.

104. Kirk Makin, "Supreme Court Puts Child First," *Globe and Mail* (Toronto), 3 May 1996, A1.

105. Paul Martin as quoted in Scott Feschuk, "Ottawa Backs Off Immediate Cuts for Seniors," *Globe and Mail* (Toronto), 7 March 1996, A12.

106. Canadian Labour Congress and National Action Committee on the Status of Women, *Women's March against Poverty: For Jobs and Justice! For Bread and Roses!* May 1996, 5.

107. Tony Blair as quoted in Mandelson and Liddle, *The Blair Revolution,* 34.

108. For a critical discussion of this view, see Myra Marx Ferree and Patricia Yancey Martin, "Doing the Work of the Movement: Feminist Organizations," in *Feminist Organizations,* ed. Myra Marx Ferree and Patricia Yancey Martin (Philadelphia: Temple University Press, 1995), 6–11; and Sandra Burt, "Canadian Women's Groups in the 1980s: Organizational Development and Policy Influence," *Canadian Public Policy* 16 (1990): 17–28.

109. In fact, the fund-raising success of the Clinton-Gore campaign team in 1996 formed the basis for yet another presidential scandal, this one concerning the sources of financial contributions and the quid pro quo attached to them. On the Canadian case, see Barlow and Campbell, *Straight through the Heart,* 123.

CHAPTER SEVEN

1. C. Wright Mills, *The Sociological Imagination* (New York: Oxford University Press, 1959).

2. See Peter Mandelson and Roger Liddle, *The Blair Revolution: Can New Labour Deliver?* (London: Faber and Faber, 1996), 78.

3. See Paul Pierson, *Dismantling the Welfare State? Reagan, Thatcher, and the Politics of Retrenchment* (Cambridge: Cambridge University Press, 1994).

4. Susan Faludi, *Backlash: The Undeclared War against American Women* (New York: Doubleday, 1991).

5. See Sylvia Bashevkin, *Toeing the Lines: Women and Party Politics in English Canada,* 2d ed. (Toronto: Oxford University Press, 1993).

6. See Joanna Everitt, "Changing Attitudes in Changing Times: The Gender Gap in Canada, 1965–1990" (Ph.D. diss., University of Toronto, 1996).

Index